S0-AYB-858

PENGUIN BOOKS

THE TRIARCHIC MIND

Robert J. Sternberg is IBM Professor of Psychology and Education in the Department of Psychology at Yale University. The author of many books and articles, he was named one of the top one hundred "Young Scientists in the U.S." by *Science Digest* and was listed in the 1986 *Esquire* magazine register of "Outstanding Men and Women Under 40." His most recent book, *Beyond IQ*, received the Outstanding Book Award from the American Educational Research Association in 1987. He is the recipient of numerous grants and awards, including a John Simon Guggenheim Fellowship, and is a Fellow of the American Psychological Association. He lives in Mt. Carmel, Connecticut.

THE
TRIARCHIC
MIND

A
*New Theory of
Human Intelligence*

ROBERT J. STERNBERG

PENGUIN BOOKS

PENGUIN BOOKS
Published by the Penguin Group
Viking Penguin, a division of Penguin Books USA Inc.,
40 West 23rd Street, New York, New York 10010, U.S.A.
Penguin Books Ltd, 27 Wrights Lane,
London W8 5TZ, England
Penguin Books Australia Ltd, Ringwood,
Victoria, Australia
Penguin Books Canada Ltd, 2801 John Street,
Markham, Ontario, Canada L3R 1B4
Penguin Books (N.Z.) Ltd, 182–190 Wairau Road,
Auckland 10, New Zealand

Penguin Books Ltd, Registered Offices:
Harmondsworth, Middlesex, England

First published in the United States of America by Viking Penguin, a division of
Penguin Books USA Inc. 1988
Published in Penguin Books 1989

3   5   7   9   10   8   6   4   2

Grateful acknowledgment is made for permission to reprint material from *Intelligence Applied: Understanding and Increasing Your Intellectual Skills*, by Robert J. Sternberg. Copyright © 1986 by Harcourt Brace Jovanovich, Inc. Reprinted by permission of the publisher.

LIBRARY OF CONGRESS CATALOGING IN PUBLICATION DATA
Sternberg, Robert J.
The triarchic mind: a new theory of human intelligence/
Robert J. Sternberg.
p.   cm.
Bibliography: p.
Includes index.
ISBN 0 14 00.9210 2
1. Intellect.   2. Mental discipline.   3. Success.   I. Title.
[BF431.S7383   1989]
153.9—dc19   89–30030

Printed in the United States of America
Set in Century Expanded

To my children, Seth and Sara

Acknowledgments

A number of people have contributed to making this book possible. Joyce Gastel assisted in the construction of many of the exercises and in copyediting. Numerous other people have contributed to the ideas behind the exercises, including Barbara Conway, Janet Davidson, Louis Forster, Michael Gardner, Ann Kirkland, Robin Lampert, Diana Marr, Elizabeth Neuse, Susan Nolen-Hoeksema, Janet Powell, Margarita Rodriguez-Lansberg, Craig Smith, Larry Soriano, Rebecca Treiman, and Richard Wagner. Sandra Wright typed all of the versions of the manuscript, patiently putting up with the many revisions that writing the book entailed. Mindy Werner, my editor at Viking Penguin, contributed many suggestions to making the book more readable and lively, and my literary agent, John Brockman, was responsible for the book being placed with Viking Penguin in the first place. My research on intelligence over the past few years has been funded by the Office of Naval Research, the Army Research Institute, and El Dividendo Voluntario Para la Comunidad. I am grateful to these agencies for making possible the research on the nature and development of intelligence upon which this book is based.

Contents

Preface

I knew exactly what our school psychologist looked like. Whenever she entered the classroom, I would panic: her grand entry meant that we were about to take an IQ test, and the mere thought of it left me petrified. She was cold, impersonal, and as scary to me as the Wicked Witch of the West must have been to Dorothy.

As she distributed the test booklets I could feel my insides chill. "Don't open them until I say so," we were told. "Go," she said, but I could scarcely begin—I was too scared. I saw my classmates turning pages while I was still on the second or third item, with nine or ten to go until I could turn the page. Usually I never got that far before time was called.

I knew I had bombed, and with every disaster my fear grew. There are those who think they fail but really succeed, and there are those who really fail. Unfortunately, I was among the latter.

In sixth grade I was sent back to a fifth-grade classroom to retake the fifth-grade intelligence test. If I hadn't known before what it meant to be embarrassed, I did then. I was being told to take a test with a bunch of babies. In later life a difference of a year doesn't mean much; in grade school it means a great deal. But there was a silver lining in it all. Whereas I had been afraid to compete with children of my own age, I certainly wasn't going to be scared off by kids a year younger. They might as well have been infants, for all I cared. I breezed through the test, not the least bit worried. I was never test-anxious again.

In the meantime, though, my curiosity had been piqued. What exactly was this intelligence that the tests were supposed to measure? I began studying intelligence in earnest, pursuing my interest by doing a seventh-grade science project on the development of the mental test. There were three major parts to the project. First, I did a review of the literature on mental testing. No problem. Next, I created my own test—the Sternberg Test of Mental Abilities (STOMA). Again no problem—especially since no one ever took the test. Finally, for practice, I started giving my classmates the Stanford-Binet Intelligence Test, which I had conveniently found in the adult books section of the town library. Oops. Trouble. My girlfriend at the time (or, to be more accurate, the girl whom I wanted to be my girlfriend) didn't seem to mind, but the mother of one of my classmates apparently did, and she reported me to the school psychologists.

One day during my morning social-studies class, I was mysteriously summoned to the guidance counselor's office. Waiting for me were the guidance counselor and the head school psychologist—the boss of the woman who for years had caused me such fright. The boss was plain and direct: If I ever brought the Stanford-Binet book into the school again, he would personally see to it that the book was burned. (And that was a book from the town library.) Of course, I hadn't brought the book into school—I'd tested my friends in the comfort of my own home. But the upshot of it all was that I wouldn't be testing any more classmates. Fortunately, my seventh-grade science teacher stood up for me. When the psychologist suggested that I study rats, my teacher—called down to a second meeting later in the day—suggested that I stay with humans, just skip the testing.

Thus began my lifelong interest in intelligence. Call it the lure of the forbidden; or perhaps it was the experience of flunking those earlier tests. Whatever the impetus, my interest had been sparked, and it would continue throughout my life.

What exactly does it mean to be intelligent or unintelligent? Can intelligence be increased? If so, how? These are a few of the questions this book addresses. The basis of my book is that intelligence is not just some dry and dusty quality of mind that is brought to bear when we take IQ tests or try to solve complicated algebra or physics problems. Rather, it is a quality that we use continually in our everyday lives—on the job, in our interpersonal relationships, in decision making. In this context, intelligence can be understood as *mental self-management*—the manner in which we order and make sense of events that take place around and within us. Traditional intelligence tests measure only a narrow spectrum of our mental self-management skills. As a result, in order to fully understand intelligence, we need to look beyond these tests and beyond the conventional conceptions of intelligence to see how it operates in our everyday lives.

Traditional conceptions of intelligence have been inextricably linked with notions of how well people perform in school. And it's little wonder. At the turn of the century Alfred Binet, inventor of the first significant intelligence test, was commissioned by the city government of Paris to devise a test that would distinguish between those who could potentially do well in school and those who could not. Largely as a result of this historical accident, intelligence has come to be associated with academic achievement. But there is obviously much more to this quality of mind than simply doing well in school. Some people who perform superbly within an academic setting don't quite follow through outside in the "real" world, and vice versa. Many intelligent people have come to think of themselves as "slow" or "stupid" because their forte did not happen to be getting good grades in school. At the same time, many people with just such a forte have come to be quite smug about their intelligence even in the face of repeated failure outside the classroom. My claim is not that intelligence is unrelated to schoolwork but rather that it is related to a great deal more.

Part I of the book opens with a review and critique of some of our most cherished ideas about the nature of intelligence (chapter 1). It then goes on to explore some of the myths that have developed around conventional intelligence tests (chapter 2). Next, some traditional notions of intelligence are considered, along with a growing body of evidence that these notions are limited by the underlying models, or metaphors, that have always been used to define and measure intelligence (chapter 3). By asking only a limited set of questions about intelligence, we have limited our understanding of just what intelligence is.

Part II presents my "triarchic theory" of human intelligence. According to this theory, intelligence must be examined in terms of three manifestations (chapter 4):

• 1. What is its relationship to the internal world of the individual? In other words, what goes on inside a person's head when that person thinks intelligently? What kinds of mental processes and strategies result in more, or less, intelligent thinking?

• 2. What is the relationship of intelligence to the external world of the individual? How does the environment in which we live affect our intelligence, and even our conception of what intelligence is? Moreover, how does our intelligence affect the kinds of environments that are available to us and that we create for ourselves?

• 3. What is the relationship of intelligence to experience? In other words, how do the experiences we have from the time we are born help shape our intelligence, and how does experience mediate between the internal and the external world of the individual?

The next three chapters discuss how we apply our intelligence to the internal and the external world as well as to personal experience. They are organized around three kinds of mental processes that have been found to be an essential part of intellectual functioning: metacomponents (chapter 5), performance components (chapter 6), and knowledge-acquisition components (chapter 7).

Part III of the book opens with a chapter on "executive intelligence"— the question of how intelligence is applied by managers both inside and outside of the business setting. There is a general belief that business acumen and managerial skills demonstrate a particular mental aptitude that is separate and distinct from intelligence. But according to the theory of intelligence as mental self-management, skill in business is a prime example of what is meant by intelligence as it applies to our everyday lives. Chapter 9 examines the popular, everyday conceptions of intelligence—What do people believe intelligence to be? In the end it was found that these everyday conceptions of intelligence came a lot closer to providing a useful basis for defining a construct than did the narrow conceptions that permeate traditional intelligence testing.

Chapter 10 shows how intelligence is "socialized"—how our experiences at home and in school result in our abilities being channeled in certain directions rather than others. A basic premise of this chapter is that before we can understand intelligence, we must go beyond genetics and heredity to see what role experience plays in shaping and perhaps modifying certain kinds and levels of intelligence that cannot be accounted for by genetic makeup alone.

Part IV begins with examination of issues foreshadowed throughout the book—how we utilize our intelligence and, in particular, how intelligence combines with personality to form "intellectual styles" (chapter 11). It is argued that people direct their intelligence in a variety of ways and that how we direct our intelligence affects our success in life at least as much as the raw intelligence we apply to everyday problem solving.

Finally, chapter 12 deals with how personality and motivational variables can obstruct the free flow of intelligence and prevent us from making the most of ourselves. Along with the preceding chapter, it stresses the point that intelligence, like any other personal trait, is influenced by the total person. In other words, personality can enhance intelligence or detract from it, and being sensitive to the difference is the key to being our best intelligent selves.

The book is more than another description of what intelligence is.

Included are numerous exercises that will challenge you and help you to develop your intellectual potential. These exercises are scattered throughout the book but are concentrated in the three chapters on the metacomponents, performance components, and knowledge-acquisition components of intelligence. Of course, no single book can be expected to effect dramatic gains in your intelligence. But the exercises will help you hone your intellectual skills and provide the basis for further development of these skills as you apply what you've learned to situations beyond the book. Indeed, a major premise of this book is that the principles you learn about the nature of intelligence can immediately be applied to everyday situations. The intelligent person is not someone who merely does well on a test or in the classroom but one who can use his or her mind to fullest advantage in all the various transactions of everyday life.

This book is intended for anyone interested in the nature of intelligence and how it can be developed. It provides an opportunity for the serious layperson to learn what intelligence is all about and to work on improving the intelligence he or she already has. The book will also be of interest to students who want to understand how they can best apply their intelligence to enhance their academic performance.

New Haven, Connecticut
September 1987

PART
I

Traditional Views of Human Intelligence

C H A P T E R

1

Stalking an Elusive Quarry: The Search for Intelligence

When I was an undergraduate at Yale in the early seventies, Henry Chauncey, then president of the Educational Testing Service, came to speak. I'd taken the Scholastic Aptitude Test (SAT) and the achievement tests that go along with it, and was already preparing for the Graduate Record Examination and Psychology Advanced Test, all of which are products of the Educational Testing Service; so I was eager to hear what Chauncey had to say. I no longer remember most of it, but one offhand comment stuck in my mind: Chauncey said he was proud that the SAT his company was administering was virtually the same test Carl Brigham had invented early in the century. I remember wondering whether Ford would be proud if his company were still manufacturing the Model T. Would IBM be proud today if, instead of manufacturing PCs, it were still manufacturing clunky, room-size computers?

If I had had any doubts about where things stood with the field of intelligence, they were dispelled in college and graduate school. During my college days there was only one professor in the Yale psychology department who worked on the topic of human intelligence, and he seemed to be spending most of his time predicting grade-point averages of Yale freshmen based on their high school averages and test scores. There were two big problems with his approach. First, the grade-point-average prediction system had recently been computerized by someone else, so that he was actually just checking each of the computer computations by hand. Second, Yale had recently switched from a percentage-point grading system to an Honors–High Pass–Pass–Fail grading system. The new system had wreaked havoc with the professor's predictions, which were no longer applicable. But old ideas die hard, and he wasn't about to let this one go.

In my graduate human abilities course at Stanford, Lee Cronbach, a famous test psychologist, said that for all intents and purposes intelligence research was dead. I knew he was right.

Among scientific disciplines the field of intelligence has not been notable for rapid progress, either in theory or in practical application. Tests, for the most part, look pretty much the way they did when Alfred Binet and his junior collaborator, Theophile Simon, invented the first one at the turn of the century. By contrast, other sciences have made stunning progress. Physics today would be almost unrecognizable by turn-of-the-century scientists. Similarly, few turn-of-the-century biologists could have imagined modern techniques of genetic engineering, and even within psychology, such fields as vision and the psychology of decision making have taken enormous strides. Why, then, have investigators in the field of intelligence continued to move at such a snail's pace? Perhaps it is because, like Dorothy Sayers's sleuth Lord Peter Wimsey, they have had to confront five red herrings.

Five Red Herrings

THE PURLOINED CONCEPT

Consider for a moment another mystery, Edgar Allan Poe's short story "The Purloined Letter," which revolves around a difficult search for a stolen letter. Detective C. Auguste Dupin finds the letter after numerous painstaking but unsuccessful attempts by the police; he has realized that the thief, an ingenious government minister, could have eluded the police search only by hiding the letter in the most obvious place. The letter, in fact, has always been in plain sight, but the police, blinded by their conviction that it must have been concealed in a secret place, are unable to see it. As Dupin says to the prefect of the Parisian police, "Perhaps it is the simplicity of the thing which puts you at fault."

Investigators of intelligence have behaved in much the same way as the prefect: they have looked for intelligence in the most unlikely places. Psychometricians—psychologists who design and analyze tests—have constructed myriad ingenious intelligence test items that have little if anything to do with the kinds of thinking people do in their everyday lives. We know more about reasoning with artificial concepts than about reasoning with real ones. Time and again, investigators of human reasoning have found that people do not reason with artificial concepts (for example, the concept of *grue*—green until the year 2000 and blue thereafter) in the same way they reason with the concepts encountered in their everyday lives.[1] Here is an example of a standard syllogism: "All robins are birds. Some birds are chickens." Can you conclude from this that some robins are chickens? Now consider how much more difficult this syllogism would be if it were presented as "All gerbits are devins. Some devins are clancies." Can you then conclude that some gerbits are clancies? Yet psychologists have persisted in measuring intelligence through just such artificial and unnatural constructs instead of investigating reasoning within a more natural framework. Reasoning with artificial concepts such as "gerbits" or unnatural concepts such as "grue" should indeed be of interest, but only in addition to—not instead of—reasoning with natural concepts.

In contrast, cognitive psychologists, who study the mental processes of thought, have sought to foment a "revolution" by examining intelligence through experimental tasks rather than through test items. These tasks, however, are often even more artificial and unnatural than the items that appear on intelligence tests. For example, how often do you have to say, as quickly as possible, whether "A" and "a" represent the same letter? How often do you have to memorize a series of digits, such as "2, 8, 6, 1, 5," and then say, as quickly as you can, whether a given digit, such as 6, was in the series? Such tasks may measure important cognitive processes, such as speed in perceiving symbols and memory, but they certainly do not measure intelligence as we use it in our everyday lives, or what I call "practical intelligence."

One of the greatest intelligence theorists of all time, Jean Piaget, was often equally obscure. For example, he might show a child a set of ten blue marbles and five red marbles and then ask, "Are there more marbles or more blue marbles?" Young children will often answer that there are more blue marbles than there are marbles. At least some of them are actually answering the question they thought the examiner meant to ask: "Are there more red marbles or blue marbles?" They are thus correctly answering what seems to be the sensible question. But if there ever was a trick question, this is it. In fact, recent research shows that children looked much worse in Piaget's tasks than they actually were,[2] because they often did not understand the questions they were asked. Some of the tasks they were given have proved difficult even for adults. When children understand the tasks and task instructions, they actually prove to be quite a bit smarter than Piaget thought they were.[3]

The emphasis on the unusual and the bizarre persists even in modern-day theories of intelligence. For example, Howard Gardner,[4] who argues for the existence of seven different kinds of intelligence, supports his theory with case studies of famous poets, artists, musicians, and other geniuses, as well as cases of idiots savants (people who are mentally retarded but have some unusual skill, such as being able to quickly calculate the day of the week upon which any past or future date will fall), brain-damaged patients, and other severely impaired individuals. Finding examples of average people in Gardner's system of intelligence is much harder. Extreme cases are interesting, to be sure, but how much do they really tell us about how typical people function intelligently in their everyday lives?

In seeking to understand intelligence, we should inhibit our desire to look in obscure nooks and crannies, and dampen our fascination with the unusual and the bizarre. Instead, we should first look in the most obvious of places—ordinary people living their everyday lives—to gain some insight into what intelligence is, how it should be measured, and how it might be improved. Most important, we need to understand that intelligence comprises those abilities that order and make the most of our daily environment, not just environments artificially created in psychologists' tests or laboratories.

MIXING OIL AND WATER: THE POLITICIZATION OF A SCIENCE

Politics and science, like oil and water, do not mix well. Each is important but is best left to its own domain. Politicians do not always understand science very well, and the same can be said of scientists about politics. The unfortunate result of mixing science and politics in the field of intelligence has been a tendency to focus on peripheral or subsidiary issues before the basic ones have been resolved. As a result, there has been a great deal of debate on such issues as the relative effects of heredity and environment on intelligence, race-related differences in intelligence, and social-class differences in intelligence—all in the absence of any good underlying theory of just what intelligence is. Such issues may be worthy of study and debate, but preferably after the basic research on the nature of intelligence is well under way. And it is only recently that this research has gained any appreciable footing.

The debates on such issues as heritability and race and ethnic differences have a troubled history—troubles that derive at least as much from the people who have studied these topics as from the topics themselves. One of the greatest scandals in the history of psychology resulted from the work of Sir Cyril Burt, during the first three decades of the twentieth century, on the heritability of intelligence. Burt claimed to have collected data demonstrating conclusively that the lion's share of an individual's intellectual ability is inherited. For years his data went unchallenged. Then, in the mid-seventies, Leon Kamin noticed certain irregularities that did not make sense. He discovered that at least some of Burt's data were wildly implausible. On further examination it became clear that Burt had to have faked some of his data. Moreover, some of the assistants who reportedly helped him collect the data appear not to have existed. It goes without saying that not all researchers in the field followed Burt's example, but his dishonesty nevertheless gave the area a bad reputation for many years.

The literature on race differences has fared somewhat better, but not much. In 1969 Arthur Jensen published an article in the *Harvard Educational Review* in which it was suggested that black people have lower IQs, on the average, than white people and, moreover, that this difference is inherited. Since the publication of this article, Jensen has become, if anything, more entrenched in this belief. In his 1969 article, he even went so far as to suggest that because of their differing patterns of ability, blacks and whites might profit from different forms of education—with the emphasis on rote learning for the former and on reasoning for the latter. A furor naturally resulted from the publication of the article, the uproar stemming as much from Jensen's educational prescription as from his claims of inherited racial differences. Many psychologists, myself included, believe that existing analyses tend to underestimate the effects of environmental variables. In the aftermath of the Jensen article there has been at least as much smoke as fire in the controversy on racial differences, and the arguments have at times obfuscated rather than clarified the issues. But one thing has emerged with relative certainty: the sources of racial differences in test performance are complex, as will be discussed in the chapter on the socialization of intelligence. Oversimplified explanations of racial differences do justice to hardly anyone, including the investigators, who sometimes make claims that go beyond their data.

One of the saddest chapters in the history of the testing of intelligence occurred when the members of many different ethnic groups arrived at Ellis Island after immigrating from overseas. Fresh off the boat, tired, and often ill after a long journey, these immigrants were given tests that were completely foreign to them and whose instructions they often did not understand. Not surprisingly, they usually performed worse than did most Americans, giving rise to unjustified fears that the immigrants were diluting the intellectual level of the country. Ironically, IQ test scores have gone up in the years since these new arrivals disembarked. And scores tended to increase with the length of an immigrant's residency in the United States.

The politicization of issues surrounding intelligence not only has diverted attention from more fundamental issues but often has colored the research as well as the choice of research topics. Extreme positions have been common, but they have rarely been supported by data.

WHEN TECHNOLOGY DRIVES SCIENCE

In most fields science drives technology. Most of the great technological innovations of the twentieth century—the telephone, the television, the computer—have resulted from a solid foundation of basic research. The same cannot be said of intelligence tests, however, for they were in use before the groundwork had been laid. Intelligence testing was a multi-million dollar business even when research on intelligence was just getting under way, and such research as there was focused primarily on intelligence tests rather than intelligence. Researchers simply assumed that the tests measured intelligence and proceeded to study test scores as though they were accurate indicators of people's intelligence. Today many investigators of intelligence question this simplistic assumption. But for many years people have been dissected, classified, analyzed, and categorized on the basis of test scores that provided only the most marginal measurement of the phenomenon—intelligence—that they proposed to measure.

THE UNITARIAN PERSPECTIVE

Unitarianism may work as a religion, but it hardly provides a sound basis for a science of intelligence. For decades intelligence testers have been selling the public on the notion that a single test score—the IQ—reveals the single basic fact about people's intelligence. Yet there is little evidence that any scientist studying intelligence—past or present—actually has believed it is just a single thing. All the same, the idea has a long history. But even Charles Spearman,[5] who originated the idea of a general "factor" (called "g") underlying human intelligence, argued against "monarchist" views of intelligence as a single thing. Of course, a tester can always average over multiple scores. But are such averages revealing, or do they camouflage more than they reveal? If one person is a wonderful visualizer but can barely compose a sentence, and another person can write glowing prose but cannot begin to visualize the simplest spatial images, what do you really learn about these two people if they are reported to have the same IQ? Similarly, if one student is a math whiz but is unable to learn foreign languages, and another student has easily absorbed three foreign languages but can't get through elementary algebra, does it mean anything to say that they have the same "average" level of intelligence? The point being made is simple: in averaging, we often lose more than we gain.

The "Fixed" Entity That Won't "Fix"

Conventional testers of intelligence obviously have something to gain by selling the notion of intelligence as a fixed entity. After all, what good would the tests be if scores were unstable, varying from one time or place to another? Test manuals praise the high "reliability" of their tests, meaning that the test scores do not tend to change much with time or place. But is intelligence really a fixed entity? The bulk of the evidence suggests that it is not.[6] Intelligence can be increased, and there now exists a variety of programs designed to do just that.[7] These programs can result not only in better test scores but in better problem solving, both within school and without. These programs are not likely to transform the mentally retarded into geniuses, but they can substantially raise an individual's level of intellectual functioning. Programs for increasing intelligence operate under the assumption that through guided instruction and practice, anyone can improve his or her intellectual functioning. Different programs go about this in different ways. Reuven Feuerstein's Instrumental Enrichment program, for example, relies heavily on individuals solving problems similar to those found in IQ tests, but a major aspect of the program is that the skills required for good performance on these tests can be extended to everyday tasks and situations such as buying a car or deciding whether to have surgery. Feuerstein's program is used mostly for young adolescents. My own program, *Intelligence Applied: Understanding and Increasing Your Intellectual Skills* (used in high-school and college courses), contains a variety of instruction and exercises, a substantial cross section of which has been included in this book.

Intelligence Applied arose out of a challenge: in the early 1980s the government of Venezuela decided to embark on a massive campaign to raise the intelligence of the Venezuelan population. To achieve this goal the government—and, in particular, the newly formed Ministry for the Development of Intelligence—called in experts from around the world. I was one of those experts, and my task was to prepare a program that would increase the intellectual skills of high-school- and college-age young people. The result was Intelligence Applied, which has now been used in high schools and colleges throughout the United States as well as Venezuela. The course has been shown to result in significant gains in cognitive performance.

Intelligence Applied is a course, requiring a teacher and a classroom.

Unfortunately, many people who are interested in learning about and improving their intelligence do not have access to such a course. Others may simply prefer the convenience of a book with a solid focus on the everyday world. *The Triarchic Mind* was written largely with this latter group in mind.

Can courses on thinking and intelligence actually result in improved intellectual skills? The evidence suggests that they can. Janet Davidson (formerly a graduate student at Yale) and I obtained significant and substantial increases in children's insight skills after only five weeks of instruction.[8] And when we tested our subjects again a year later, it was obvious that these gains had been retained. In another study,[9] whose results were perhaps even more dramatic, we obtained significant and substantial gains in adults' ability to figure out the meaning of words from a written context after just three hours of instruction.

If the five red herrings have diverted us from understanding intelligence, we need a path that will lead us beyond the five red herrings.

BEYOND THE FIVE RED HERRINGS

The theory of intelligence presented in this book, though certainly not the final word on the subject (either from myself or from anyone else), does not succumb to the five red herrings.

First, it deals with intelligence not only as the term is used in artificial and strictly academic settings but also as we use it in our daily lives. The theory is equally applicable to business executives choosing what products to market and homemakers selecting a washer or dryer as to the test taker who must solve a problem in abstract reasoning.

Second, the theory has been developed and applied independent of political issues. It is a scientific theory, and its application is a direct extension of the basic science of that theory. You will find little about politics in the pages that follow. The theory and its application are intended to serve scientific and educational purposes, not political ones.

Third, it is the science behind the theory that has driven the technological application, not the other way around. Although some technological innovations have resulted from the theory—including a test of and program for measuring intelligence—these did not precede the theory but followed it.

Fourth, the triarchic theory is pluralistic rather than unitarian in its perspective on intelligence. It recognizes three distinct but interrelated aspects of intelligence and makes further distinctions within each of these. Multiplicity is therefore one of the main characteristics of intelligence as it is presented in this book. The result is that a given individual can be strong in some aspects of intelligence but weak in others.

Finally, intelligence here is regarded as a dynamic rather than a static entity. As such, it can be increased and it can be taught. The primary goal of this book is to help the reader increase his own intelligence.

Intelligence as Mental Self-management

The basic position taken in this book is that intelligence can be defined as a kind of *mental self-management*—the mental management of one's life in a constructive, purposeful way. From this point of view it is not surprising that in the past few years some of the hottest-selling new books have concerned intelligent business management or intelligent self-management. In my opinion these books have said more about intelligence than many books written specifically on the subject.

Mental self-management, too, can be said to have three basic elements: adapting to environments, selecting new environments, and shaping environments. Let us consider how each of these elements functions in our everyday lives.

ENVIRONMENTAL ADAPTATION

Intelligence involves the ability to adapt to one's environment. Indeed, traditional definitions of intelligence have generally acknowledged this attribute. As a rule, however, intelligence tests neither measure nor attempt to account for adaptive skills. The following examples illustrate this point.

Most of us take for granted that certain life settings require more intelligence than others: for example, that learning algebra or history demands intelligence whereas walking on the street does not. Yet this assumption may be one of the unfortunate legacies of our test-oriented culture, which has always emphasized the academic rather than the everyday aspects of intelligence. In her fieldwork the ethnographer Shirley Heath found that a community of a particular lower socioeconomic class tended to emphasize nonverbal communication and acute awareness of the surrounding environment in training its children to be intelligent.[10] By contrast, a community of an upper socioeconomic class stressed verbal communication and sensitivity to oral and written messages in teaching its children. A few years ago I had an experience that made me painfully aware of just how important it is to be aware of the surrounding environment and its nonverbal signals. I had driven my mother to a graduation ceremony. Finding a parking space near the ceremony was difficult, and over my mother's protest I left the car in a rough section of town. As we walked through the streets we found ourselves consciously monitoring the area. And it was a good thing we did: Within a few minutes an empty beer bottle came flying down from a tenement window above us. I saw it coming and blocked my mother's next step; the bottle landed right in front of her. Another step or two and it would have crashed on her head. If the acid test of adaptation is survival, we passed that one. But we might easily have had another story to tell if we hadn't used our intelligence to monitor our surroundings. Similarly, urban police departments routinely broadcast tips on ways to avoid getting mugged by staying alert and shaping our behavior appropriately. If, through using these strategies, you are able to stave off an attacker, can there be any doubt that walking on the street does indeed involve intelligence?

Just as we often assume that certain activities, such as walking on the street, require only minimal intelligence, we also generally think that some jobs make greater demands on our intelligence than others. A case in point is working in a milk-packing plant, where workers pack crates according to the amount of milk indicated on packing slips. Sylvia Scribner and her colleagues have studied the routine of workers in such a milk-processing plant as well as in other ostensibly mundane occupations.[11] Her findings would surprise those who subscribe exclusively to an academic conception of intelligence. The milk packers, she discovered, used highly sophisticated strategies to expedite their work. They looked at what appeared to be identical orders in a variety of ways depending on the availability of empty or partially filled milk cases on hand. They then engaged in mental calculations in a variety of number bases (other than 10) and alternated among them as necessary. The solutions they developed enabled them to fill the cases using a minimum of moves, which resulted in substantial savings of time. On closer examination, a seemingly "unintelligent" job actually involved a considerable amount of intelligence.

Intelligence pops up in curious ways in play as well as work. Stephen Ceci and Jeffrey Liker studied handicappers in an effort to discover the secret of their success at the race track.[12] They found that most of these people were unremarkable in terms of conventional IQs, and many of them were well below average. Yet successful handicappers routinely used an astonishingly complex statistical model for predicting winners. Furthermore, their ability to generate and implement these complex models was unrelated to their IQs. This left little doubt that successful handicappers were using adaptive strategies: They were winning money in a way that to all intents and purposes required considerable intelligence—intelligence that simply isn't predicted by conventional measures.

In his book *The Cloak of Competence* Robert Edgerton describes the lives of mentally retarded individuals released from an institutional setting.[13] He gives special attention to some of the adaptive strategies these people use to make their lives a bit easier. For example, someone who couldn't tell time wore a watch that didn't work. When he wanted to know the time, he would look at the watch, "notice" that it didn't tell the correct time, and then say to a passing stranger, "Excuse me, but I notice my watch isn't working. Could you tell me the correct time?" Certainly this person lacks an important aspect of intelligence: he cannot tell time. But the use of an adaptive and even ingenious strategy enabled him to find out the time without being able to tell it himself, and without embarrassment. Small wonder that investigators today often refer to many of the mentally retarded as "academically retarded," because the retardation has almost no effect on their everyday lives.[14]

Of course, what is adaptive can vary not only from one setting to another but also from one culture to another. Consider, for example, an obvious difference between the culture of the United States and that of Venezuela. In the United States time is of the essence. Meetings, classes, and appointments all start on time. Although lateness is tolerated in some settings (parties, for one), people are usually expected to be prompt. It would be considered very bad form to show up late for a job interview or for a meeting with a supervisor. But Venezuelans (and members of many other cultures—including most South Americans and Africans) don't place the same value on time. This was dramatically illustrated to me when I attended a meeting on the nature of intelligence held in Venezuela. The meeting was scheduled to begin at 8:00 a.m. I was miffed because I was tired and didn't like the idea of having to get up so early. But I was on time, as were the other four North Americans in the group. We were the only ones there; none of the one hundred or so South Americans arrived on time. Indeed, we alone seemed to have assumed that the meeting would start on time. It did not, in fact, start until around 9:30—a full hour and a half after it had been scheduled to begin.

I discovered that this was standard behavior in Venezuela. To North Americans, perhaps, this perpetual lateness seems counterproductive, even unintelligent. In Venezuela, however, it is the only sensible way to behave. After all, why spend time waiting for meetings to begin when there are so many other things to be done—or so they reason. One Venezuelan I spoke with readily admitted that Venezuelans tend to be late. But she also pointed out that although they start late, once they begin, Venezuelans waste no time getting into full swing. They are also less likely to take time out for coffee breaks and idle conversation, which is a common practice in this country.

While adaptation is an important part of mental self-management, there is more to it than that. Indeed, there may be times when it is maladaptive to adapt. In such cases, another strategy for coping with the environment may be needed.

ENVIRONMENTAL SELECTION

When an environment is unsatisfactory for any number of reasons, it may well be maladaptive to adapt.

The problem may be one of *values*. For example, suppose you start working for an up-and-coming computer company hoping to make a difference in the hot technology of software development. Instead, you find yourself involved in industrial espionage, spying on other computer companies to see what they're doing. Your best course of action may not necessarily be to adapt—that is, to become an adept spy. It might be better to either insist on a transfer to another part of the company or leave the company altogether. It may be more intelligent to change your environment rather than your values.

Similarly, one hesitates to argue that in Nazi Germany the intelligent course of action for Germans was to adapt. Many Germans found the values of the Nazis offensive and sought either to leave or to find some means of coping that did not involve adoption of or adaptation to Nazi values.

Alternatively, the problem may be one not of values but of *interests*. You may have had your heart and ambition set on becoming a lawyer, then found that the only thing duller than law school itself is sitting in the basement of a legal firm looking up precedents. Or perhaps you went on a fishing trip expecting to enjoy an idyllic day in the country only to find that all you do is sit in a boat and wait—and wait—for a fish to bite the line. In both of these cases environmental selection may be called for. In other words, you may need to find a new occupation or a new leisure pastime.

Another problem with the environment might be posed by a lack of *ability*. It didn't take me long to discover that I would never be a professional cellist, no matter how hard I tried. If I wanted an environment in which I would make a difference, it certainly wasn't an orchestra. I often meet graduate students who think that being a scientist is merely a continuation of undergraduate school—getting good grades in courses and making the right impression on their teachers—but soon discover that they do not have the creative ability to become truly excellent scientists. In these and other cases an individual would be wise to choose another environment that provides a better match for his abilities.

Finally, the problem with the environment may be one of overall fit, or *compatibility*. Any number of people enter into marriages in which they do not function well as a couple, even though they may function perfectly well as individuals. Similarly, anyone who has been on a committee knows that people who function well individually cannot always work together as a group. The best course of action in these instances may be to find another environment—a different marriage, a different committee, or, in general, a different and more compatible situation.

Knowing when to quit is every bit as important as knowing when to persist. The field of scientific research offers a case in point. The scientist inevitably encounters any number of ideas that prove unfruitful for further research and lead to years of wasted effort. Indeed, I recently went to a scientific conference at which a well-known scientist described ten years of frustration spent trying to solve a problem. I expected her to say that the problem was intractable or that it was not yet ready to be studied or even that perhaps she was just the wrong person to do it. Instead, she discussed her plans to spend what sounded like another ten years on the same dead-end issue.

By the same measure, a successful manufacturer has to know when to drop a product as well as when to introduce it. You can attempt to remarket a product once or twice, trying a new image, for example, or a reformulation of ingredients. But when successive attempts to move the product fail, the company has to face the possibility that it's time to quit. A "try, try again" philosophy has its merits up to a point, but you must also know when to stop banging your head against the wall.

Consider how environmental selection can operate in the career choices of individuals, especially gifted individuals. A poignant set of real-world examples is provided by Ruth Feldman in her *Whatever Happened to the Quiz Kids?*[15] The quiz kids were selected, first for the radio show and later for the television show of the same name, on the basis of a variety of intellectual and personality traits. Records suggest that all or most of them had exceptionally high IQs, typically well over 140 and in some cases in excess of 200. Yet their later lives have been noticeably much less distinguished than might be expected, even, in many cases, by their own standards. There are undoubtedly a number of reasons for this, including so-called regression effects, according to which extreme performance in the early years tends to be followed by less extreme performance later on. But what is most striking in biography after biography of these quiz kids is that those who were most successful in later life were the ones who found what most interested them and then pursued it relentlessly. The less successful among the group had difficulty focusing on any single interest and in a number of cases floundered in the process of carving out a niche for themselves.

In sum, there are times when adapting to a given environment is maladaptive and it would simply be more productive to select another one. But sometimes neither adaptation nor selection is the preferred course of action. For example, if your first major argument with your spouse takes place on your honeymoon, the recommended course of action is not necessarily an immediate divorce. (There are those who would question this, however. A major news magazine recently ran an article on yuppies that described a woman who, in the interest of efficiency, combined her honeymoon with a business trip. On the business part of the trip she met another man whom she decided she liked better than the one she had just married. Her solution was to get a divorce! This is an extreme case of the implementation of environmental selection.) In some cases, you may wish to consider environmental shaping rather than selection.

ENVIRONMENTAL SHAPING

Intelligence involves the shaping of, adaptation to, and selection of your environment. Environmental shaping becomes operative when your attempts to adapt to a given environment have failed or when it is impractical or undesirable to select a new environment. For example, if you are committed by religious belief to the permanence of marriage, you may not consider divorce an acceptable alternative to an unhappy situation. You might, however, attempt to reshape your environment in order to create a better "fit" between yourself and that environment. Thus, whereas adaptation involves fitting oneself to the environment, shaping involves fitting the environment to oneself. In keeping with this premise, the marital partner may attempt to restructure the marriage; the employee may try to convince his employer that industrial espionage is not the royal road to increased sales; and the citizen may take an active role in government in an attempt to change it.

What this means is that there may be no single set of behaviors that is intelligent for everyone; it is understood that people can react to their environment in different ways. While the components of intelligent behavior are in all likelihood universal, their use in shaping environmentally appropriate behavior probably varies not only across groups but across individuals as well. What does appear to be common among successful people is the ability to capitalize on their strengths and compensate for their weaknesses. Successful people are not only able to adapt well to their environment but also to modify this environment in order to increase the fit between the environment and their adaptive skills.

Consider, for example, the "stars" in any given field. What is it that distinguishes them from their peers? Now think about the "stars" in your own profession. The chances are that these people have no single ability in common but tend to have some set of talents that they make the most of in their work. At the same time, they underplay the skills they lack, either by delegating tasks requiring those skills to others or by structuring their work in such a way that those skills never come into play. My own list of "stars" includes one person with extraordinary spatial visualization skills, someone with a talent for always coming up with unexpected research findings, and another person who has an extraordinary way of predicting the outcome of a particular event. It would be difficult to capture the full range or richness of such talents in any simple scheme for understanding the abilities that characterize and define intelligence. All of these "stars," however, are excellent mental self-managers: they know how to make the most of what they have and how to expand the range of what they are able to do. I will discuss these issues further in Chapter 8, "Executive Intelligence."

There are some very accomplished people who do not have stellar IQs, but this has never impeded their success. The handicapper can laugh his way to the bank as he contemplates his relatively low score on intelligence tests. The successful business executive who manages thousands of employees hardly need worry that his intelligence test scores were merely average. The scientist whose creativity never showed through on intelligence tests need feel no guilt about his test scores as he collects his Nobel Prize.

Clearly, intelligence is more than conventional tests measure—a lot more. To make matters worse, these tests can sometimes test for unintelligence. How they manage to do this is explored in the next chapter.

CHAPTER

2

IQ Tests: Measuring IQ, Not Intelligence

"Lies" We Live By

Simplicity has its virtues. Sometimes we need to say things simply even though we know that our simplification is inaccurate. We say that the world is round, knowing full well that it is not truly round. We say that Columbus discovered America, knowing that America was inhabited well before Columbus ever set foot on these shores. We speak of the free world, knowing that not all of the countries in the free world are truly free. These simplicities are useful fictions because they enable us to say things concisely, although we know that what we are saying is not quite true.

The potential danger that lurks behind simplifications such as these is that we may come to believe our fictions merely from saying and hearing them said over and over again. Some simplicities are not likely to be misconstrued. Airplane pilots would be in sad shape indeed if they operated under the illusion that the world is truly round, a two-dimensional circle! Other simplicities are more likely to be misconstrued. Appeals to our notions about the "free world" have been used to support dictatorships and to hide the inequities that exist even in the more democratic societies.

Truly, it would be disastrous for airplane pilots to navigate as though the world were round, or for economists to believe that people always spend their money in a rational way. In fact, though, economists once believed spending behavior to be rational and formulated theories on this basis. Today they know better. An equally profound social disaster could result from believing that IQ tests fully measure intelligence. I would argue that we have often come close to this disastrous state, because many psychologists and lay people alike still believe this fiction and act as though it were true.

To this day, countless students are excluded from institutions of higher education—colleges, graduate schools, law schools, medical schools, and the like—because they score low on admissions tests due to anxiety and unfamiliarity with the rules of the testing game, despite the fact that they may possess valuable skills not measured by these tests. If the IQ and similar tests (Scholastic Aptitude Test, Law School Admission Test, and Graduate Record Examination) actually measured intelligence, and if that intelligence as it is conventionally interpreted were all we needed to ensure success, then these exclusions might be fair. But IQ tests cannot even be said to measure most of what we need to know about intelligence—and success of practically any kind depends on much more than raw intelligence. That's why we may be in serious trouble—and all because of a fiction that so many people have come to believe.

Tests of intelligence, which assume a variety of names and guises, are widely administered in the United States and many other parts of the world. They are given in many elementary and secondary schools, sometimes for placement and counseling purposes but often for no apparent reason. They are used for college admissions in the form of the Scholastic Aptitude Test (SAT) and the American College Test (ACT) and for admission to graduate programs in the form of the Graduate Record Examination (GRE) and the Miller Analogies Test (MAT). Most professional schools also require such tests, for example, the Medical College Admissions Test (MCAT) for admission to medical schools, the Law School Admissions Test (LSAT) for admission to law schools, and the Graduate Management Admissions Test (GMAT) for admission to business schools. If you think that intelligence tests have infested many of the nooks and crannies of our lives, you're right! And to what avail? As you will see throughout this book, they measure only a very limited set of abilities. And if we take a serious look around us, the entire fiction that IQ tests fully measure intelligence rapidly disintegrates.

WHEN SMART IS STUPID AND STUPID IS SMART: THE CURIOUS CASE OF THE KPELLE

In an effort to assess the intelligence of people outside maintream North American or European cultures, psychologists often take our tests to those cultures. One of these is the so-called sorting test, in which the examiner presents a set of either pictures or words and asks participants to sort them into categories. For example, an individual might be instructed to sort the words *animal, bird, fish, robin, fly, halibut, fruit, eat, blue jay, orange, trout,* and *apple* into piles containing words that somehow belong together. The typical finding is that more intelligent people sort hierarchically. Thus, the word *animal* would be sorted as a category that also includes *bird* and *fish*, and *robin* and *blue jay* would be sorted as members of *bird; trout* and *halibut,* however, would be sorted as members of *fish.* Less intelligent people sort functionally. According to their reasoning, *fish* might be sorted with *eat,* because people eat fish, or *bird* with *fly,* because birds fly.

Western theories of intelligence value the sorting behavior of the typical Western adult. According to Piaget's theory, as well as other theories of child development, as children get older their sorting should change from functional to hierarchical, reflecting the shift from lesser to greater intelligence. Standard intelligence tests are scored with the same value in mind. On the vocabulary sections of major tests, such as the Stanford-Binet and the Wechsler intelligence scales, children and adults are asked to define words. Suppose one such word is *apple.* If the individual defines an apple as a kind of fruit, she will receive more credit than she would by defining it as something we eat. Or if asked to define *automobile,* the respondent will receive more credit for saying it is a vehicle of conveyance than for saying it is something that uses gas, or something we drive.

When adult members of the Kpelle, an African tribe, were asked to sort, they did so functionally rather than hierarchically. Thus *fish* might be sorted with *eat.* Even when urged to reconsider their sorting procedure, the Kpelle continued to sort in this seemingly intellectually primitive way. Typically, cross-cultural psychologists might cite this sorting pattern as yet another example of how the people of another culture, in this case, the Kpelle, are less intelligent than their North American counterparts. But the psychologists who conducted this study were persistent in their examination.[1] In desperation, they finally asked the Kpelle to sort the way they thought a stupid person would. The Kpelle then had no trouble sorting hierarchically. It became obvious that they lacked not the intelligence to sort hierarchically but the Western notion of intelligence that would have led them to sort this way. They initially sorted in what they believed to be the intelligent way. And, indeed, if you think about apples, for example, you're just as likely to think of eating them as of their being a kind of fruit.

It could, of course, be argued that IQ tests were never meant to be applied to people in strange and exotic cultures, and that the tendency of the Kpelle to sort functionally should not discredit the use of IQ tests in our own culture. Consider, though, a second disquieting example.

How Retarded Are the "Mentally Retarded"?

Seymour Sarason, now a psychologist at Yale, eagerly reported for his first job, administering IQ tests at a school for the mentally retarded. When he arrived, however, he found that he was instantly out of business: the students at the school had just escaped. Eventually they were rounded up and brought back to the school, where Sarason diligently gave them the Porteus Maze Test—a test of intelligence. To his chagrin, Sarason found that most of the students could not successfully complete even the first problem on the test. The very students who had successfully (if temporarily) outwitted the school administrators were unable to make it to square one on a standard IQ test. They may well have been lacking in some or even many academic skills, but certainly they had other skills that this standard test simply didn't take into account.

All right. The mentally retarded are an atypical group anyway, you say, and it's hardly fair to draw strong conclusions from a small group of students who, by many standards, are at the bottom of the barrel intellectually. Let's have a look higher up in the barrel, then.

The Case of the Curious Curve

Some years ago Lita Hollingworth, an expert on the study of gifted children and adults, conducted seminal studies on the performance of intellectually gifted children. One of her many interesting findings had to do with the nature of the relationship between IQ and other kinds of performance, such as your grades, the job you eventually take, and the salary you eventually earn. Basically Hollingworth discovered a curvilinear relationship. Up to a certain point, it seems, performance improved with increases in IQ, after which it actually got worse. Pinpointing exactly where this takes place has been difficult, and it probably varies with different kinds of performance; but there is strong evidence that some decline occurs. High IQ seems to be an impediment in some situations. But why?

Interpreting this finding hasn't been easy, but there are a number of explanations that attempt to account for it. One of these places blame on society: society doesn't know how to handle its most intelligent members, this theory maintains. Perhaps there is a general tendency to hold a grudge against very intelligent individuals. Another interpretation suggests that people with very high IQs have some correlated trait or traits that are in some way maladaptive. For example, they may be socially inept. Yet another interpretation of the finding is that people with very high IQs attempt to overcapitalize on their IQ-based abilities, using them even when they are not particularly appropriate. A case in point is some-one who tries to apply the same methods used to recall factual information to some creative task at hand. Such a person might then look at things in old, well-worn ways instead of in new, untried ways. Regardless of the interpretation of this finding, the message it conveys is that if we are to understand intelligence as it is applied to performance, we must go beyond IQ. We need to remember, of course, that Hollingworth's curve applies on the average, not to each particular case. Moreover, the point at which the decline starts to take place usually corresponds with a *very* high IQ.

This list of examples could go on, but the message would not change: conventional intelligence tests are missing something. They do not mea-sure the full range of intellectual functioning. For example, they do not test insight or practical abilities. To compound the issue, in some instances the behavior valued by intelligence-testing situations is actually unintel-ligent. Let us consider why.

Looking for Smarts in All the Wrong Places

Many IQ tests, and tests like them, operate on assumptions that do not correspond with what we know about intelligence. In some cases behavior that would be smart in a testing situation would not be considered smart outside that situation. Look at the following assumptions and why they are wrong.

FALLACY 1: TO BE "QUICK" IS TO BE "SMART"

The assumption that to be "quick" is to be "smart" permeates our society. When we refer to someone as "quick," we are endowing that person with one of the primary attributes of what we believe intelligence to be. In-terestingly, this assumption is by no means universal. For example, it is not prevalent in most parts of South America or Africa. The pervasiveness of this assumption in the United States became clear in a study we did of people's conceptions of intelligence, described in detail in chapter 9.[2] We asked lay people (nonpsychologists) to list behaviors characteristic of an intelligent person. Behaviors such as "learns quickly," "talks quickly," and "makes judgments quickly" were commonly listed.

The average person is not alone in believing that quickness is an es-sential attribute of intelligence. The same assumption underlies the over-whelming majority of intelligence tests. It is rare to find a group test that is not timed, or a timed test that virtually every participant can finish by working at a comfortable rate. But the assumption that to be quick is to be smart is a gross overgeneralization, true only for some people and for some mental processes. What is critical is not speed per se but, rather, *speed selection*—knowing when and when not to perform tasks rapidly. Several sources of evidence support this alternative point of view.

The importance of reflectivity.   We have all made hasty decisions that we later regretted. The decisions might have been as important as deciding whom to marry, which house to buy, or which career to pursue, or as unimportant as choosing a store from which to buy a particular product. Almost all of us have had the experience of buying an item at a store "for a good price" only to find it being sold more cheaply somewhere else.

Psychologists have found that a *reflective* cognitive style is generally associated with greater intelligence than is an *impulsive* cognitive style.[3] Jumping to conclusions without adequate reflection can often lead to false starts and erroneous conclusions. In making purchases we can often save a tidy sum by shopping around first. Of course there are some people, such as air traffic controllers, who must make important split-second decisions as part of their jobs. But most of us encounter few significant problems in our work or personal lives that do not warrant some time for reflection.

The importance of reflection has not gone unnoticed by psychologists, even those concerned with ability testing. In a classic but little-known book published in 1924 on the nature of intelligence, Louis Thurstone,[4] one of the foremost psychological testers of his day, proposed that a critical element of intelligence is the ability to withhold rapid, instinctive responses and to substitute more rational, better-thought-out responses. Thurstone believed that the instinctive response to problems is often not the best means of solving them. More recently, David Stenhouse[5] has arrived at the same conclusion by comparing intelligence across different animal species. Interestingly, Stenhouse appears to have been unaware of Thurstone's work; his analysis was arrived at independently.

Instinctive responses can be costly. The proverbial yelling of "Fire!" in a crowded movie house is a case in point. Similarly, in a building that really is on fire, our instinct is often to open the door and run out. But if the fire has reached the hallway, opening the door is one of the worst things we can do. The solution: to first feel the door to find out whether it is hot, and if not, to open it very gradually in case it has to be closed again quickly.

As a child, I sometimes had to pay for my own impulsiveness in unpleasant ways. My primary-school teachers often gave us strictly timed addition and subtraction tests. I thought the teachers would be impressed if I was the first one done, but I paid for my speed with reduced accuracy and ended up making a worse impression than I would have if I had been slower but more accurate. Unfortunately, because timed tests are administered in many elementary schools, students at an early age learn to equate accuracy with speed, which clearly is wrong.

Some studies of human reasoning. My colleagues and I have conducted a number of studies on human reasoning in which we discovered just how important it is to know when to be fast but also when to be slow in solving reasoning problems. Some of these studies involved reasoning by analogy, two of which are especially relevant to the issue of speed in problem solving.

In one study[6] we asked adult participants to solve analogies like those below. Consider a few of the examples we have used, answering them for yourself.

1. CANDLE is to TALLOW as TIRE is to (a. AUTOMOBILE, b. ROUND, c. RUBBER, d. HOLLOW)
2. SPOUSE is to HUSBAND as SIBLING is to (a. FATHER, b. UNCLE, c. BROTHER, d. SON)
3. MISDEMEANOR is to CRIME as PECCADILLO is to (a. STUTTER, b. PRETENSE, c. AMNESIA, d. SIN)
4. STUBBORN is to MULE as FICKLE is to (a. CHAMELEON, b. SALAMANDER, c. TADPOLE, d. FROG)
5. TRAP is to PART as RAT is to (a. GOOD-BYE, b. WHOLE, c. BAIT, d. TAR)

Make sure you have your answers before reading on. The correct answers appear in the Appendix.

We "decomposed" our participants' reasoning into the elementary mental processes used in solving the analogies. In other words, we were able to pinpoint the step-by-step processes people used to solve these reasoning problems. More will be said later in the book about the exact techniques used to solve analogies, but roughly speaking there are three kinds of processes: (a) *identifying* the meaning of each of the terms of the analogy; (b) *comparing* the meanings of the words; and (c) *responding* to the analogy. For example, in the first analogy an identification process would involve thinking about what you know about a candle: that it can burn, that it can produce light, that it has a wick, that it was often used in olden times, and so on. Similar processing would be done for each word of the analogy. The comparison process would involve matching what you know about a candle with what you know about tallow. In this case, you might conclude that a candle is made of tallow. A response process would then be used to write down the correct answer on a piece of paper or perhaps to push a button on a computer.

We found that, on the whole, better reasoners were faster in solving these analogies. But this speed did not extend to all the processes of analogical reasoning. The better reasoners were quick in comparing the meanings of words and in responding, but they were actually slower than the poor reasoners in identifying these meanings.

Consider the following example. When I first arrived as an assistant professor at Yale, I hurriedly stacked my books on the bookshelf with no regard for order. After all, I had countless other things to do. But whenever I wanted a book I had to search the entire collection before I could find it. When I realized that sacrificing order to speed was taking its toll, I took the time to arrange the books in alphabetical order. Initially, I did what the poorer reasoners have been found to do: I tried to save time at the beginning but ended up losing even more time later on. Cataloguing (identifying) the books more carefully resulted in my being able to find them (by comparison) more rapidly. Libraries, of course, work on the same principle. Better reasoners spend more time identifying the attributes of each word in the analogy so that they can use these attributes to reason more rapidly. The poorer reasoners, by contrast, do not initially think about these attributes and must then rethink the problem entirely.

There is another reason why slower identification time may pay off. Look at the last analogy of the sample. This is an example of what is sometimes called a "set breaker." Whereas the first four analogies require you to process the meanings of the words, this one requires you to process the order of the letters of the words. Most people initially respond by trying to solve such problems semantically and will not succeed. The better reasoners, however, will go back and look for aspects of the words they may have missed. Eventually they realize that the key to the solution of the analogy is recognizing letter order. The poorer reasoners, on the other hand, persist in making comparisons on the basis of their initial assumptions. As a result, they fail to solve the analogy correctly. Again, the better reasoners profit from their willingness to devote more time to identification, which facilitates later comparison and response.

Set breakers like the last analogy were used in early editions of the Miller Analogies Test, a high-level test of reasoning and knowledge often used for admissions to graduate schools and even in job selection. Although these items were found to be among the most useful for discriminating between better and poorer reasoners, they were eventually eliminated from later editions of the test because they involved an unexpected risk: some people were finding out that set breakers were included before they took the test, giving them an unfair advantage over those who had to figure it out for themselves.

The difference we found between better and poorer reasoners actually reappeared in a different study in which analogical reasoning was examined developmentally from childhood to adulthood.[7] We gave picture analogies to children in the second, fourth, and sixth grades and to college students. We found that as children grew older, their comparison and response processes speeded up, as was expected. After all, older children are generally faster reasoners. But the identification processes did not show this continually increasing speed over the age range. The youngest children were slow encoders, or perceivers of information—they had difficulty figuring out the attributes of the pictures. The fourth-graders were faster, because they had an easier time identifying these attributes. But after fourth grade, children became slower, not faster, encoders of analogy attributes. They had learned that spending more time at this stage would allow them to save time in the long run.

Clearly, intelligence is not defined by speed alone but, more important, by knowing when to be quick and when to take time to deliberate. Strictly timed tests often force an individual to behave impulsively—unintelligently, in a sense. Some psychologists would argue that the strict timing of tests merely reflects the dictates of our pressured modern-day society. But consider how many times we must solve a problem or make a decision that requires split-second judgment of the kind required by IQ tests: the number is not a large one. In fact, few important decisions can or should be made impulsively. The tests do not truly reflect the time constraints on most of us, and they reward a kind of behavior that may actually turn out to be detrimental. If you have an important paper or memorandum to write, an important personal decision to make, or an important car repair to take care of, the last thing you'd want to do is rush through without giving some thought to the quality of your work.

FALLACY 2: THE "HIGH VERBAL" READS EVERYTHING WITH GREAT CARE AND COMPREHENSION

In typical reading comprehension tests like those found in many scholastic and other aptitude tests, the test taker is presented with a series of readings followed by a set of reading comprehension questions. The "high verbal" is the person who can read the passages with care and comprehension, absorbing all of the material in some depth. As an adolescent taking various scholastic aptitude tests, I wondered what it must be like to be able to "soak in" everything you read. What I didn't realize is that truly high-verbal people do nothing of the kind.

Almost everyone who is literate, from school age onward, has much more to read than time permits. The freshman in college who plans to turn over a new leaf and read all of her assignments carefully may suffer a rude awakening when she learns that she is expected to read *War and Peace* in a week, or when she discovers that after reading her entire course load—literature, history, biology, and sociology—she has no time for anything else. Business executives find themselves in a similar position, with stacks of reports and memoranda to digest within a few hours. Teachers, too, must read far more than they assign their students, in addition to students' papers, professional journals, and other material. For all of us, regardless of occupation, reading newspapers, magazines, and books in general could take up every minute of our time, leaving us no time to live. Given this grim prospect, could it really be smart to read everything with the greatest care?

After observing high-verbal people in action, Richard Wagner and I[8] came to the conclusion that contrary to the myth, and to the way the tests operate, high verbals read everything neither with great care nor with high comprehension. However, they do have the ability to do so when they choose to. They also have the intelligence to know what to read and how to read it. The good reader, like the good reasoner, is a master of time allocation and wastes no time responding inappropriately.

We decided to test some of our ideas in an experiment. Our experimental subjects, college students, were given some reading tests. This material bore no resemblance to the standard reading comprehension test. Read the following passage, which we actually used, taken from a newspaper article. Read it the way you would read a newspaper article:

The United Nations Human Rights Commission today condemned Israel's policies concerning the occupied Arab territories, including alleged "war crimes that are an affront to humanity."

The vote was 31 to 3, with 8 abstentions. The United States, Canada, and Australia voted against the resolution and most Western European countries abstained.

The resolution said that Israel had failed to acknowledge that one of the Red Cross conventions, or treaties, on the protection of war victims, applied to the territories occupied by Israel.

Although Israel questions on legal grounds the applicability of the pact to the territories, in practice it allows the International Red Cross to visit them, meet privately with prisoners, and otherwise carry out the protective functions provided by the conventions, Red Cross sources say.

The coalition of countries that submitted the resolution also obtained the commission's recognition of the right of the Palestinian people to a "fully independent and sovereign state in Palestine."

In our study the subjects were presented with sets of four passages like the one above. Each passage was roughly 150 words in length and was taken equally from novels, newspapers, introductory liberal arts textbooks, and introductory science textbooks. But we did not merely ask the subjects to read the passages as carefully as possible, as would be done in a standard reading comprehension test. Instead, we instructed them to read each passage with one of four different purposes in mind: gist, main idea, detail, or analysis. At the end of each passage we then asked questions that were appropriate to the level of detail at which it was read.

Questions on gist asked about the basic theme of a passage and were designed to be the easiest to answer—selecting the best title or identifying the theme of the passage, for example. Here are two gist questions on the above passage (answers to all questions appear in the Appendix):

1. Which of the following titles best fits this passage?
   a. Human Rights Dispute with Israel
   b. Red Cross Conventions Updated
   c. Policies of the United Nations
   d. The Palestinian Question

2. The theme of the passage is
   a. how the Red Cross functions abroad
   b. a UN Human Rights Commission against Israel
   c. the right of the Palestinian people to self-determination
   d. the problem of the legal rights of prisoners of war

Main-idea questions, which were more difficult, asked about the main ideas of a passage and were similar to questions commonly used to measure reading comprehension. Test your own skill in answering these questions:

3. The United Nations Human Rights Commission's resolution condemned Israel for failing to
   a. acknowledge a Red Cross convention
   b. recognize the right of the Palestinian people to a sovereign state in Palestine

    c. permit the Red Cross to visit prisoners
    d. relinquish occupied territories

4. Which of the following best characterizes Israel's position?
    a. It questions the authority of the Human Rights Commission.
    b. It questions the applicability of the Red Cross conventions.
    c. It refuses the Red Cross visits for national security reasons.
    d. It refuses to acknowledge the existence of the resolution.

Detail questions, which were even more difficult, required subjects to recall specific details in a passage. Try a couple:

5. Israel questions the applicability of the Red Cross pact on
    a. moral grounds
    b. legal grounds
    c. religious grounds
    d. political grounds

6. Which of the following countries voted against the resolution?
    a. United States, France, and West Germany
    b. United States, Egypt, and Saudi Arabia
    c. United States, Great Britain, and Mexico
    d. United States, Canada, and Australia

Finally, analysis questions, which were the most difficult, required subjects to analyze the ideas presented in a passage or to extend the ideas to a new domain. Consider two such questions:

7. From the information presented in the passage it can be inferred that Israel and France have a poorer relationship than do Israel and
    a. West Germany
    b. Australia
    c. Great Britain
    d. Egypt

8. The nature of the second issue on which the coalition obtained the Commission's recognition suggests that the coalition countries are
    a. more pro-Israel than the original resolution would suggest
    b. largely anti-Israel

    c. divided into anti- and pro-Israel camps
    d. moderating their position

Although examples of each question type appear above, subjects in the experiment saw only one question type for each passage. For each set of four passages, however, they were asked to read one passage for a specific purpose. Our goal in the experiment was to determine not merely how carefully subjects read but how *flexibly* they did so given specific objectives. We were particularly interested in how subjects allocated their time across the four reading passages as a function of the purpose specified. Because passages were presented by computer, we were actually able to monitor the time allocated for each, and hence for each reading purpose.

We divided subjects into high verbals and low verbals. The results for the two groups were clearly different. Low verbals allocated time equally across the reading purposes. In other words, they read passages in the same way, regardless of purpose. They spent no more time reading a passage for detail, for example, than for gist. High verbals, by contrast, allocated their time differentially as a function of reading purpose. The more complex the reading purpose, the more time they allocated to a given passage. This led us to conclude that high-verbal people are *not* always more careful readers. Instead, they adjust the way in which they read a passage to the purpose for which it is being read. Low verbals, on the other hand, use the same technique in reading everything, regardless of purpose.

Did our reading-purpose test actually measure something more than conventional reading tests measure, or was it just a fancier version of essentially the same thing? In order to find out, we attempted to predict comprehension (number of questions answered correctly) from our measure of time allocation, which was essentially a measure of how much more time subjects spent on complex reading purposes than on simple reading purposes. We found a high correlation. Moreover, this correlation held true even when we corrected for scores on a standardized test of reading comprehension. In other words, our test measured something more than the standard reading tests measure.

The point being made here, as in the above illustrations on reasoning, is simple: More intelligent people are not merely faster or slower, more careful or less careful. Instead, they are more flexible in allocating their mental resources to the task at hand, tailoring their approach to a particular set of demands. By contrast, intelligence tests often require a brute-force approach to solving problems, which does not reflect what we actually need to do in our everyday lives.

FALLACY 3: YOU CAN TELL HOW SMART A PERSON IS BY THE SIZE OF HIS VOCABULARY

The overwhelming majority of intelligence and scholastic aptitude tests contain vocabulary items that require the test taker to recognize synonyms or antonyms for generally difficult words. Sometimes the words are so rare, even esoteric, that one might wonder whether they would have any place except in a vocabulary test. Here are two typical items that might be found in the vocabulary section of an intelligence test (answers appear in the Appendix):

1. A *jingoist* is always
   a. lucky
   b. chauvinistic
   c. impetuous
   d. obstinate

2. A *whippet* is a kind of
   a. dog
   b. cat
   c. fox
   d. rat

Test makers have good reason for including vocabulary in their battery of tests: It offers a high level of prediction for overall score and further establishes the correlations that make these tests so cohesive. The implication here, of course, is that all of the test items measure the same or nearly the same thing. This in turn makes the tests more attractive to those who buy them. Moreover, the test items correlate highly with achievement in various school subjects. But there are two fairly obvious, related problems with including these items in intelligence tests.

First, vocabulary items measure achievement rather than the ability to achieve. If scores on these items correlate with achievement, it is hardly surprising, because they are themselves measures of one kind of achievement. Achievement tests no doubt have their place, but to the extent that one wishes to distinguish between achievement and the ability to achieve, it would appear to be "cheating" to include vocabulary items in an ability test.

Second, vocabulary items are patently unfair to those who have not been exposed to them. For the middle-class or upper-middle-class test taker, these items may serve their purpose reasonably well. But for the individual who has not grown up in a highly verbal environment and has had neither the best schooling nor the advantage of books in the house, vocabulary may measure only what has been learned while taking no account of the ability to learn. The prominence of vocabulary items on so many aptitude tests has had a pernicious effect not only on the testing of intelligence but on the methods used to prepare people for these tests. Very often test-preparation courses, as well as courses designed to improve intelligence, concentrate on enlarging the test taker's vocabulary. There is nothing wrong with improving your vocabulary, but it's not the same as improving your intelligence. Moreover, memorizing words is probably not even the best way to prepare for the tests.

The rote-memorization strategy poses two problems. The first, as anyone who has crammed for an exam knows, is that within a few days it is very difficult to remember much, if any, of what was memorized. By the time you take a vocabulary test, you're likely to have forgotten the meanings of many of the words you've studied. Memorizing the words is no guarantee of retention.

The other problem posed by rote memorization is that the chance of any single memorized word's appearing on a test is fairly small. There are hundreds of thousands of words in the English language, and the odds of your memorizing the right words are not particularly good. In addition, if your goal is to improve your vocabulary for general use, this strategy has very limited value.

My own strategy for measuring verbal learning skills has been very different from the approach used by conventional test makers.[9] As with reasoning and reading, I was interested in knowing just what it is that distinguishes the learning behavior of highly intelligent people. The conclusion I arrived at is that more intelligent people, on the average, have better vocabularies because they are better able to learn the meaning of words in their natural contexts as they encounter them in their daily lives. During the lifetime course of our reading and listening, we come across innumerable words, many of which are unfamiliar to us. The more intelligent person can more easily determine the meaning of these words from their context. As more words are learned, these in turn facilitate learning still more words, and eventually the more intelligent person is at a distinct advantage in terms of having a better vocabulary. Note, however, that there can still be good word-learners who do not necessarily have large vocabularies, simply because of a lack of exposure.

For an example of the kind of test items we use to measure word-learning skills, read the following passage and try to figure out the meaning of the words in italics. (Answers appear in the Appendix.)

Although the others were having a marvelous time at the party, the couple on the blind date was not enjoying the merrymaking in the least. A *pococurante*, he was dismayed by her earnestness. Meanwhile, she, who delighted in men with full heads of hair, eyed his substantial *phalacrosis* with disdain. When he failed to suppress an *eructation*, her disdain turned to disgust. He, in turn, was equally appalled by her noticeable *podobromhidrosis*. Although they both love to dance, the disco beat of the music did not lessen either their ennui or their mutual discomfort. Both silently vowed that they would never again accept a blind date.

In our research on problems of this kind, we found that there is, as would be expected, a moderate correlation of the ability to learn the meaning of words from context with an individual's existing vocabulary. However, the correlation is moderate, not high. In other words, there is a large number of people whose ability to acquire words is greater than would be expected on the basis of their vocabulary alone. Similarly, there may be people whose vocabularies, for one reason or another, exceed what would be expected on the basis of their ability to learn. But the results showed that to the extent to which one wishes to measure intelligence, it is the ability to learn, rather than the learning itself, that provides the most direct measure.

FALLACY 4: INTELLIGENT PEOPLE SOLVE PROBLEMS IN THE SAME WAY AS LESS INTELLIGENT PEOPLE, BUT BETTER

Intelligence testers have traditionally assumed that everyone taking a given test item solves it in the same way. Indeed, the statistical methods used to analyze test performance *assume* that this is the case, resulting in considerable loss of validity when individual differences are taken into account. The general assumption among testers is that what distinguishes more from less intelligent people is the skill with which they implement fixed strategies for solving test problems. Nothing could be further from the truth.

Early in my career as a psychologist I made it a priority to understand the mental processes people use in solving intelligence-test items. To this end I devised some processing models (representing strategies for problem solving) to characterize various approaches people might use in solving those items. I then compared these models to determine which one best described the data collected. For example, in studying patterns of errors or response times, I might administer a test of analogies and record for each test item how long the participants took to solve it and whether they made any errors. I quickly found that the data were almost always the same in one crucial respect: Although one strategy might best characterize the averaged data, there was never any great correspondence between the models and the data. I soon discovered why. Using the model to explain and describe the group data was essentially the same as mixing apples and oranges. In other words, people were using different strategies. The best model was the one used by the most people, but there was almost always a substantial number of people whose behavior could be described only by using other models. To examine this further, look at the following examples of linear syllogisms:

Jean is faster than Pete. Pete is faster than Sam. Who is slowest?

John is not as tall as Mary. Beth is not as short as Mary. Who is tallest?

Problems like these can be solved using a primarily verbal strategy, which involves the interrelation of the terms through linguistic propositions; a primarily spatial strategy, involving the interrelation of the terms through a visual image depicting the relations among the three persons; or through a mixture of both verbal and spatial strategies. In a study of how people solve these problems, we found that most people use a mixed strategy, but a substantial number use either a pure verbal or pure spatial strategy.[10] Moreover, instructing people to use a strategy that did not suit their pattern of abilities often resulted in their either ignoring the instruction or actually performing worse than they did when they spontaneously used the strategy that best suited them. So much for the assumption that everyone solves problems in the same way!

I noticed a long time ago that despite my lack of spatial skill, I could often get respectable scores on supposedly "spatial" ability tests. I was especially good with those requiring the test taker mentally to rotate abstract figures. The key to my success was my ability to solve the problems verbally.

What does all of this say about existing intelligence tests? No test or single index can measure all or even most of the diverse intellectual skills that underlie intelligence, such as reasoning, insight, and practical know-how. Indeed, because intelligence can involve different skills for different people, there is no single wholly appropriate test of it.

Given the fallibility of present tests, must we stop using them altogether in order to achieve a viable solution to the problem of interpretation? I do not believe so. Used judiciously, test scores have generally been found to be informative. Moreover, there simply are no strong alternatives. But what is important is that the tests be used judiciously and prudently. If they are not used in this way, their use becomes worse than their nonuse. There is an allure to exact-sounding numbers. An IQ of 119, an SAT score of 580, a mental-abilities score in the 74th percentile—all sound very precise. Social psychologists have actually found that people tend to weigh accurate-sounding information highly, almost without regard to its validity. But the appearance of precision is no substitute for the fact of validity. Indeed, a test may be precise in its measurements, but there is no guarantee that what it actually measures is intelligence.

Few people are willing to admit that they are entranced by test scores. When they hear the results of experiments showing that people overvalue precise-sounding information of low validity, they assume that these results apply to others. Because of this tendency to discount the experimental evidence, I would like to offer some anecdotal evidence to back up my claim.

When I worked at The Psychological Corporation one summer with the Miller Analogies Test, I heard what I considered then, and still consider, to be an amazing story. A teachers college in Mississippi required a score of 25 on the Miller for admissions. The use of this cutoff was questionable, to say the least, in that 25 represents a chance score on this test. A promising student was admitted to the college despite a sub-25 Miller score, completing the program with distinction. When it was time for the student to receive her diploma, she was informed that it would be withheld until she could take the test and get a score of at least 25. The test had become an end rather than a means.

I related this pathetic story to a well-attended meeting of teachers of the gifted, using it as an example of how bad things could be at an isolated teachers college. Afterward a teacher came up to me and told me an essentially identical story (except for a higher cutoff score) as it pertained to her own quite reputable university.

I've personally encountered, and heard numerous stories of similar experiences at major universities. Consider, for example, the cases of applicants to graduate (and often undergraduate) programs who have stellar credentials except for marginal test scores. In my experience these applicants have earned the right to a "full and open discussion," only to be rejected. These negative decisions are particularly frustrating when applicants have demonstrated excellent competence at the criterion task (in my profession, psychological research) and yet are rejected on the basis of test scores that are, at best, highly imperfect predictors of general performance. Again, the means becomes the end, and educators forget which is the criterion and which the predictor. In the absence of criterion information, test scores can serve a useful function; people who might otherwise be denied admission to programs on the basis of inadequate evidence may be admitted because their test scores show them capable of high-level performance. But when criterion information is available, the tests may be superfluous, even counterproductive. The criterion information in these cases should receive the lion's share of attention in serving as the basis for decisions on future performance.

Intelligence tests as they now exist work for some people some of the time, but they do not work for a great many people much of the time. Moreover, the people for whom they do not work are often the same ones, again and again. For these individuals behavioral checklists of the kind described in chapter 9 may be a better way of assessing intelligence. Applied conservatively and with full respect for all of the available information, tests can be useful. Misapplied or overused, they are worse than nothing.

Of course, not all psychologists are slaves to intelligence test scores. Although the intelligence-testing approach to studying intelligence is the best known, there are other approaches. Some of these are discussed in the next chapter.

CHAPTER 3

Human Intelligence: The Model Is the Message

On her deathbed (wishing to know whether the doctors had decided to operate on her), Gertrude Stein is reputed to have inquired, "What is the answer?" Getting no answer, she said, "In that case, what is the question?" In the study of human intelligence, perhaps no response is more apt, because the questions scientists have asked about intelligence have largely determined their answers. But in the study of intelligence one must go back yet one step further and wonder "Why that question?" Why ask, for example, what the mental processes underlying intelligence are, or how society affects the development of intelligence?

There are good reasons for asking why. Consider the question of mental processes. I discovered long ago that I just wasn't very good at solving spatial problems that require me to manipulate pictures mentally in my mind. But many IQ tests require just that. For example, you might be shown a picture of a geometric form and asked to figure out what the form would look like if it were rotated to another position. In high school I discovered that many so-called spatial problems could be solved verbally: I could talk out the solutions to myself. When I discovered this, my scores on the spatial tests shot up. But clearly, my score did not mean the same thing as the equivalent score gotten by someone who solved the problems the way they are supposed to be solved—spatially. Process analysis enables the psychologist to ascertain not only *how well* the test taker solved the problems but also *how* the problems were solved.

Now give some thought to the question of how society affects intelligence. If each society affects intelligence in a different way, then the tests that work in one culture will be different from those that work in another culture; there can be no universal intelligence test.

So let's see how psychologists have dealt with the question of what intelligence is and how it relates to the individual, to society, and to the experience of the individual in society.

What Is the Relationship of Intelligence to the Internal World of the Individual?

The majority of people studying intelligence have attempted to "look inside the head" in order to understand its natural underpinnings. This has led to a concomitant view of intelligence as *something to be discovered*. Although those who regard intelligence as an internal property of the human organism generally agree that it is an entity in search of a discoverer, they have not agreed on the form this "something inside the head" should take. During the twentieth century two major models have competed for the allegiance of the explorers in search of intelligence.

THE GEOGRAPHIC MODEL: INTELLIGENCE AS A MAP OF THE MIND

The view of intelligence as a map of the mind extends back at least to Franz Gall, perhaps the most famous of phrenologists.[1] Gall implemented the model of a map in a literal way: he investigated the bumps on an individual's head, looking (and feeling!) for the hills and valleys in each specific region of the head that he believed would reveal the nature of that person's abilities. For him, the measure of intelligence resided in the pattern of cranial bumps found on a person's head.

During the first half of the twentieth century the model of intelligence as something to be mapped dominated theory and research. However, the model of the map became more abstract than it had been for Gall. The psychologist studying intelligence was both an explorer and a cartographer, seeking to chart the innermost regions of the mind. Visual inspection and touching just would not do. But like any explorer, the psychologist studying intelligence needed tools; and in the case of research on intelligence, the indispensable tool appeared to be a statistical method and model called factor analysis—a means of separating intelligence into a number of hypothetical factors or abilities that are believed to form the basis of individual differences in test performance. The major debate among these theorists of intelligence centered on the issue of the "true" factorial structure, or map, of intelligence. Although there were many competing theories, the main ones were perhaps those of Spearman, Thurstone, Guilford, Cattell, and Vernon.

Charles Spearman, who is usually credited with inventing factor analysis, believed that intelligence could be understood in terms of a single general factor that pervaded performance on all tests of mental ability, as well as a set of specific factors, each of which was involved in performance on only a single type of mental-ability test.[2] Because of their specificity, the specific factors were of only casual interest. The general factor, however, provided the key to understanding intelligence. Spearman labeled the general factor "g," and believed it was derived from individual differences in mental energy.

Louis Thurstone, in contrast, believed that the core of intelligence resided not in one single factor but in seven such factors, which he referred to as *primary mental abilities*.[3] According to him, the primary mental abilities are verbal comprehension (measured by vocabulary tests); verbal fluency (measured by tests requiring the test taker to think of as many words as possible that begin with a given letter, in a limited amount of time); inductive reasoning (measured by tests such as analogies and number series); spatial visualization (measured by tests requiring mental rotation of pictures of objects); number (measured by computation and simple mathematical problem-solving tests); memory (measured by picture and word-recall tests); and perceptual speed (measured by tests that require the test taker to recognize small differences in pictures, or to cross out the *a*'s in strings of varied letters).

J. P. Guilford proposed as many as 120 factors in his *structure-of-intellect* model.[4] According to him, intelligence could be understood in terms of a cube that represented the crossing of various operations, contents, and products. Operations, in Guilford's theory, are simply mental processes, such as cognition (understanding, in Guilford's theory), convergent production (reaching a "correct" answer to a problem that requires a unique response, such as a word problem in algebra), and divergent production (generating multiple answers to a problem that has many possible answers, such as "Think of as many words as you can that have *c* as a third letter"). Contents are the kinds of terms that appear in a problem, such as verbal (words), symbolic (e.g., numbers), and figural (pictures). Products are the kinds of responses required, such as units (single words, numbers, or pictures) or relations (John is *taller than* Mary). For example, one of Guilford's factors of the mind would be cognition (operation) of figural (content) relations (product), all of which would be involved in perceiving figural terms in an analogies test. Another factor would be divergent production (operation) of verbal (content) units (product), which would be involved in producing as many words as possible beginning with a certain letter in a fixed amount of time. In his most recent version of the theory, Guilford proposed as many as 150 factors![5]

Some believed that with the structure-of-intellect model, things were getting out of hand. The number of factors made the model complex and unwieldy,[6] and there were serious questions about the methodology used to extract the various factors. J. L. Horn and J. R. Knapp, for example, found that with Guilford's statistical methodology, Guilford's data could be made to support random theories as well as they supported his own theory.[7] A more parsimonious way of handling a number of factors of the mind appeared to be through a hierarchical model. One such model, developed by Raymond Cattell, proposed that general intelligence could be understood as comprising two major subfactors, fluid ability and crystallized ability.[8] Fluid ability requires understanding of abstract and often novel relations, as is required in inductive reasoning tests such as analogies and series completions. Crystallized ability represents the accumulation of declarative knowledge (facts and ideas) and procedural knowledge (strategies) and is measured, for example, by vocabulary tests and general-information tests. Nested under these general factors are other, more specific factors. A similar view was proposed by Philip Vernon, who made a general division between practical-mechanical and verbal-educational abilities.[9]

The model of mental maps, and the factor-analytic methods used to create the maps, became decreasingly popular in some circles by the second half of the twentieth century. There were several reasons for this growing skepticism.

First, the model of maps and the factor-analytic methods used to create it said little, if anything, about mental processes. Two individuals could receive the same score on a mental-ability test through very different processes, and indeed, by getting completely different items correct.[10] By the 1960s psychologists in all aspects of cognitive study were becoming especially concerned with information processing; and research on intelligence, like so much other research in the field, got caught up in this new wave of interest.

Second, it was difficult to test factor-analytic models against each other and so compare their respective merits. In factor analysis, the user of the technique has many options as to how to proceed. In fact, he has so many options that it is possible to use the factor analysis of a given set of data to support alternative theories. This is not to say that the analysis will support *any* theory, but it might, for example, support either Spearman's or Thurstone's, depending on how the analysis is done. Clearly, then, the factor-analytic method could not be used as a single measure to distinguish among theories.

Third, the entire notion of trying to understand intelligence primarily on the basis of data showing differences in scores among people came under attack. Quinn McNemar questioned whether a pair of identical twins, stranded on a desert island and growing up together, would ever come up with the notion of intelligence if they never encountered individual differences in their mental abilities.[11] Psychologists had begun to think that they would, and to believe in placing less reliance on the existence of substantial individual differences for isolating abilities. But isolation of a factor requires that there be individual differences in scores. For example, almost all adults are able to speak a language. The ability to speak a language would seem to be a part of intelligence. Yet according to factor analysis, this would not be counted among the components of intelligence, because it is something virtually everyone (except mutes) can do.

Psychologists had to find a new model, a new method, or both. Most of them opted for both, and during the 1970s psychologists in intelligence research employed neither the map model nor factor analysis. But before moving on to the theory and research of these psychologists, it may be worthwhile to describe the most recent attempt to keep the model of the map alive. According to Howard Gardner's theory of multiple intelligences, we have at least seven distinct "intelligences": linguistic, musical, logical-mathematical, spatial, bodily-kinesthetic, interpersonal, and intrapersonal.[12] So far, Gardner's theory sounds pretty much like the conventional factor theories. But it differs in two major respects. First, the intelligences were derived not through factor analysis but through a series of converging operations. Gardner used multiple criteria, such as potential isolation by brain damage, evidence from exceptional individuals (at both ends of the spectrum), and evolutionary history, to identify his intelligences. Second, the range of mental abilities designated as intelligences is considerably broader than that in conventional factorial theories. For example, none of the conventional theories would identify musical ability as an intelligence.

The theory of multiple intelligences, like all theories, is not without its shortcomings and limitations. If factorial evidence has shown anything unequivocally, it is that various abilities are not independent, as Gardner claims, but interrelated. For example, logical-mathematical and spatial abilities are remarkably difficult to test for separately because they tend to occur together. People who are good problem solvers in the areas of logic and mathematics tend, on the average, to be good spatial problem solvers as well. This correlation is understandable, especially since some people solve mathematical problems spatially, as by creating a diagram that shows the relations among parts.

In addition, naming intelligences is not tantamount to explaining these intelligences. Neither is it clear exactly what each intelligence consists of, because Gardner's theory, like other map-based theories, does not specify processes. In other words, it is one thing to identify a linguistic intelligence but quite another to specify the underlying processes. How do we read, learn vocabulary, write prose or poetry, produce oral speech, summarize, and so on? Gardner's theory names the so-called intelligences without pinning down just what they are (and aren't).

Finally, what Gardner refers to as multiple intelligences might be better referred to as multiple *talents*. For example, some might argue that the tone-deaf person who scores low in one important aspect of musical intelligence is not thereby mentally retarded in the same way as an adult lacking verbal skills. Rather, the tone-deaf individual lacks an aspect of musical talent. Being tone-deaf is not in the same class as being unable to plan ahead. Look at it this way: an individual who is totally unable to plan or reason could not adapt to the normal world. Such a person might have to be institutionalized and might not even be able to survive in an institution. At least some minimal planning or reasoning ability is necessary for normal functioning. But someone with no musical ability can fare quite well in the world; most people would never even know that he was unmusical. Clearly, the difference between intelligence and talent is qualitative. Intelligence is general: without it we cannot function independently. Talents, however, are specialized. Although we may be excluded from participation in some activity because we lack a talent for it, there are nevertheless many other things we can do, and do well. An ability is a component of intelligence when we cannot get along without it and a talent when we are not noticeably handicapped by its absence.

The theory of multiple intelligences represents a new and interesting attempt to keep the model of the map alive, and so provides grist for the mill of future research. But it is a theory of talents, not one of intelligence.

THE COMPUTATIONAL MODEL: INTELLIGENCE AS A COMPUTER PROGRAM

During the last decade the predominant model among researchers on intelligence has been the computer program. Using this model, researchers have attempted to understand intelligence in terms of the information processing people do when they think intelligently. The modus operandi has been to draw an analogy between the way people think and the computations a computer program does when it solves a problem.

Information-processing investigators have varied primarily in the complexity of the processes they have studied. Some of the main proponents of this approach have been Arthur Jensen, Earl Hunt, Robert Sternberg, and Herbert Simon.

Arthur Jensen proposed that intelligence can be understood in terms of speed of neural conduction: in other words, the smart person is someone whose neural circuits transmit information rapidly.[13] But because we have no means of measuring speed of neural transmission, Jensen has proposed choice reaction time (the time it takes to select an answer) as an appropriate means for indirectly (*very* indirectly) measuring this speed. The problem with this procedure is that there is no evidence that choice reaction time, or any other reaction time, has anything to do with speed of neural conduction. In tests of Jensen's model, one of a set of lights flashes on a board and the subject must extinguish it by pressing a button as rapidly as possible. The experimenter then measures the subject's speed in performing this task.

Earl Hunt suggested that intelligence, particularly verbal intelligence, be measured not by mental speed in general but by a specific kind of mental speed—namely, speed of access to lexical information (e.g., letter names) stored in long-term memory.[14] In measuring this speed Hunt has used a task proposed in 1967 by Michael Posner in which subjects, shown pairs of letters such as "A A," "A a," and "A b," must indicate whether they constitute a match in name (e.g., "A a" matches in name of letter of the alphabet but "A b" does not).[15] In a simpler task, subjects are required to indicate whether the letters match physically (e.g., "A A" is physically identical while "A a" is not). Hunt has taken as the measure of speed of lexical access the difference between name match and physical match time. Thus, he subtracts from his equation the elementary reaction time that is so important to Jensen's theory. For Hunt, the response time in indicating that "A A" is a physical match is unimportant. What interests him is a more complex reaction time—that for recognizing names of letters.

More recently, Hunt and Marcy Lansman have been studying the relationship between people's intelligence and their ability to divide their attention.[16] Suppose you are asked to perform two tasks at once—for example, to solve mathematical problems and simultaneously to listen for a tone and press a button when you hear it. According to Hunt and Lansman, more intelligent people are better able to time-share between the tasks and to perform both effectively. A simple example would be reading or writing while listening to the radio. According to Hunt and Lansman, the more intelligent person would be better able to read or write and at the same time understand what is being said on the radio.

In 1983 I set out to understand information processing in more complex tasks, such as analogies, series problems, and syllogisms.[17] My goal was to find out just what it was that made some people more intelligent processors of information than others. The idea was to take the kinds of tasks used on conventional intelligence tests and isolate the mental processes and strategies used in performing these tasks. Through a technique I invented, called componential analysis, I decomposed reaction times and error rates on these tasks into underlying processes such as inferring relations between stimuli, mapping higher-order relations between relations, and applying previously inferred relations to new situations.

Consider *why* it is important to do this kind of analysis. Suppose a student takes a difficult verbal analogies test. It might include the following items—MERCURY is to HERMES as NEPTUNE is to (a. ZEUS, b. VULCAN, *c. POSEIDON, d. HADES) (the correct answer is starred). Similar analogies appear on high-level verbal reasoning tests, such as the Miller Analogies Test. To get this question right, though, you not only have to be able to recognize the relationship underlying the analogy—the Greek equivalents for ancient Roman names of gods—but you also need to be familiar with Greek mythology. And solution of the analogy 2^{-2} is to $4^{1/2}$ as 5^0 is to (a. 2^0, b. 2^1, c. 2^2, *d. 2^3) requires recognition not only of the 1–8 ratio but also of the meaning of the terms (i.e., that $2^{-2} = \frac{1}{4}$, $4^{1/2} = 2$, $5^0 = 1$, and $2^3 = 8$).

Similarly, componential analysis provides a way of separating various mental processes. For example, it would be desirable, from the tester's standpoint, to be able to separate the time it takes to infer the relationship between the first two analogy terms from the time it takes to press the response button. Componential analysis permits such separation in analyzing data.

Herbert Simon, in his information-processing work conducted in the 1960s and 1970s, attempted to understand intelligence by studying the information processing subjects did when solving very complex problems, such as chess problems and logical derivations.[18] In his work with Allen Newell and others, computer simulations were created that could solve these complex problems.[19] More recently, Simon and others (Micheline Chi, Robert Glaser, Jill Larkin, Allan Lesgold) have been studying intelligent performance on tasks requiring a substantial degree of expertise—such as medical diagnoses and the solution of physics problems.[20] In a typical study the performance of experts is compared with that of novices on a particular task, such as solving physics problems or playing chess. A typical finding in these experiments is that experts and novices differ not so much in the mental processes they use to perform the task but in the amount and organization of knowledge they apply to it. Expert chess players, for example, may have stored as many as fifty thousand chessboard patterns in memory, whereas novices may have stored only a relatively small number.

The problems encountered with the computational model and the information-processing methods used to test it center on the fact that it is not clear just how like computer programs human intelligence really is.[21] There are those who would argue that we should focus attention not on the programs but on the programmers themselves in our search for the meaning of intelligence. People differ from computer programs in a number of ways, not the least of which is their considerably greater complexity and range of mental functioning. In using the computational model, these differences may be given short shrift. People, for example, have emotions; computers do not. People are motivated to perform some tasks but not others; computers are not motivated at all. People do things because *they* want to; computers do things because *others* want them to. People can do some things without instructions from others; computers always require at least some instruction, if only to get started. There are enough differences between people and computers to provide ample evidence that computers are not just mirrors of the human mind, or vice versa.

Suppose you met someone who could carry on a reasonably intelligent conversation until he was asked a few challenging questions, at which point it became obvious that he was simply unable to respond in an intelligent way. This might lead you to conclude that he had been "preprogrammed" for the conversation. Unexpected questions invariably elicited the same response: none. We sometimes encounter this phenomenon in job interviews. As long as people are asked questions for which they have been primed, they are able to answer in an intelligent way. But throw them a "curve ball" and it becomes obvious that they are unable to think for themselves. Of course, nervousness could be an alternative explanation. But computers do not get nervous, nor do they think for themselves. Computer programs are much like these job candidates. As long as they are restricted to areas in which they have been programmed, they may perform quite well. Extend this area too far beyond the one for which they have been preprogrammed, however, and the grave limitations of their own independent performance become clear.

Another problem with the computational model is that, in common with most map-based theories, it is not clear whether the tasks computers are given to perform truly measure what is relevant to the outside world. For example, even the most sophisticated computer programs have some difficulty with language comprehension and production. And when they play chess, they usually do so by brute force, considering tens or even hundreds of thousands of possible board positions. Obviously, chess masters do not function this way. Everyone knows people who perform well on tests but fall abysmally short of expectations in their everyday lives, and neither the computational nor the map model seems to account for just what, if anything, is wrong or missing when these people use their intelligence in their everyday lives.

The computational model also does not seem to take sufficient account of, or specify the differences in, what is meant by intelligence in various parts of the world. The assumption of the computational model has been that we need to discover programs of operation that are intelligent for a given set of tasks. But life tasks differ from one place and time to another, and so, it can be argued, does the nature of intelligence. These arguments lead us to the next important question underlying theory and research on intelligence.

What Is the Relationship of Intelligence to the External World of the Individual?

Not all psychologists have looked at human intelligence exclusively as an internal property of the organism. Some have turned to the external world, and particularly to culture, in an attempt to understand what intelligence is. These psychologists have viewed intelligence not as something to be discovered but as a cultural invention: it is something that a culture creates to define what is good performance in that culture, and to account for why some people perform better than others on the tasks that culture happens to value.

Many psychologists subscribing to this point of view have specialized in cross-cultural studies on the nature of intelligence. Others have stayed within one culture but have sought to understand intelligence as a *prototype*, or cultural ideal, of the intelligent person. For example, Ulric Neisser has suggested that the concept of intelligence is much like the concept of a chair: just as there are chairs that conform in varying degrees to our ideal of a chair, so too there are people who conform in varying degrees to our ideal of an intelligent person.[22] Barbara Conway, Jerry Ketron, Morty Bernstein and I actually assessed these prototypes statistically and showed that people both have them and use them in their judgments of their own and others' intelligence.[23] John Berry has compared such prototypes in a variety of cultures, showing that they differ with culture.[24] According to such views, then, to understand intelligence, one should look not inside the head, metaphorically, but at the culture in which an individual resides.

THE ANTHROPOLOGICAL METAPHOR: INTELLIGENCE AS A CULTURAL INVENTION

Psychologists who believe that the nature of intelligence is wholly or partly determined by what a culture values are often called *contextualists*. Within this metaphor at least four positions of varying degrees of extremity can be designated:

A radical cultural relativist view. John Berry has argued that indigenous notions of cognitive competence should be the sole basis for any valid description and assessment of intelligence.[25] Accordingly, the Western concept of intelligence has no universal merit, for intelligence is a different thing in each culture, and the goal of the psychologist should be to understand what constitutes intelligence in the culture at hand.

A conditional comparative view. Michael Cole and his colleagues in the Laboratory of Comparative Human Cognition[26] have accepted the view of John Berry, Franz Boas,[27] and others that there is no single notion of intelligence that is appropriate for all members of all cultures. But Cole and his colleagues assert that the radical cultural-relativist position does not take into account the fact that cultures interact. In their view, it is possible to do a kind of "conditional comparison" in which the investigator sees how different cultures have organized experience to deal with a single activity, such as writing, reading, or computing. This comparison is possible, however, only if the investigator is in a position to assert that performance of the task or tasks under investigation is an achievement that is attained in every culture, and if he has a developmental theory of performance in the task domain—that is, a theory of how and why performance in that domain improves over time.

Intellectual dualism. Still less radical is the position of William Charlesworth, whose ethological approach to studying intelligence has focused on what he refers to as the "other part" of intelligence—intelligent behavior as it occurs in everyday life rather than in test situations—and how these situations may be related to developmental changes.[28] Thus, Charlesworth is content to leave the conventionally tested aspect of intelligence to psychometricians and cognitive psychologists and to concentrate on its other, contextually determined aspect.

Integrated viewpoints. Least radical is the position taken by such contextualists as Daniel Keating,[29] James Jenkins,[30] and Paul Baltes, Freya Dittman-Kohli, and Peter Dixon,[31] who have combined this approach with more or less standard psychological research and experimentation. Baltes has conducted fairly standard psychometric research, but he has viewed it contextually. He and his colleagues have proposed some theories regarding the nature of intelligence over the individual's life span that take into account the context in which intelligence occurs at different points in people's lives. They note that with aging an individual's life goals and cognitive tasks change. For example, a typical task for a high-school student would be to solve plane geometry problems, with the goal of obtaining a good grade in the course. This student is unlikely to flinch when he sees similar problems on an ability test, because the problems are familiar to him. A sixty-year-old, in contrast, may not have solved any plane geometry problems in more than forty years or have had any reason to. As a result, he probably would be alarmed at seeing plane geometry problems on an abilities test, because the problems have become unfamiliar and irrelevant to his life (except for the test!). Older individuals are less oriented toward cognitive efficiency as measured by traditional intelligence tests. The evidence suggests that they are probably slower than younger people in performing tasks. But the quality of their work may be unimpaired, or even, in some cases, better than that of younger people. Moreover, most of the tasks older people encounter on a daily basis are unlikely to require great speed.

The contextualist approach has the appeal of accounting for the fact that not all cultures view intelligence in the same way or consider the same behaviors to be intelligent. At the same time, it is not without its limitations from a scientific point of view. First, cognitive functioning is all but ignored, with the result that even if you accept the contextual point of view, you still have little idea of the cognitive processes underlying intelligence even within a particular culture. Second, parsimony is strained to the extreme: if intelligence differs across cultures, and even subcultures, you might conceivably have to dissect levels of subcultures before the level of the individual is reached. Each individual does, in fact, live in at least a slightly different subculture or intermeshing of subcultures. But if intelligence is seen as being completely particular to each individual, it is not clear that science can say much about it. The goal of science is to achieve some sort of reduction, and this can be done only if there is at least some generality to a scientific finding. If a separate theory of intelligence were required for each person, then no reduction would be achieved, no generality would obtain, and science would no longer have a role. Third, the contextual view often tends to be vague, making it difficult to identify exactly which theory of intelligence is associated with it. In contrast, the theory of Jean Piaget, considered below, is probably the most fully specified theory of intelligence ever proposed.

What Is the Relationship of Intelligence to the Experience of the Individual?

Because experience plays such an indispensable role in mediating the relationship between the internal and external worlds of the individual, any theory of intelligence would be incomplete without emphasizing the interaction between experience on the one hand and intelligence on the other. Experiential theories tend to be developmental in character, focusing on how the nature of intelligence changes over part or all of the life span of the individual. Among these theories the two most influential have been those of Piaget and Vygotsky.

A BIOLOGICAL MODEL: INTELLIGENCE AS AN EVOLVING SYSTEM

Jean Piaget's theory of intelligence is so rich and variegated that it is almost impossible to do justice to it in one paragraph.[32] There are perhaps two particularly crucial aspects of this theory. The first is the notion of *equilibration*—that an individual acquires cognitive capacity through a delicate balance of two mechanisms, *assimilation* and *accommodation*. In assimilation, the individual fits new environmental inputs into his existing cognitive structures. In accommodation, he transforms his cognitive structures in order to accept environmental inputs. Thus, accommodation, but not assimilation, requires restructuring of one's cognitive system.

Consider this example. Suppose you work for Widgets Unlimited as a manager in charge of quality control. If you move to Gidgets Unlimited, a similar company, as their quality-control manager, you are likely to require assimilation to learn how to cope with your new job. But if you move to Gidgets with a completely new responsibility, say, as a manager in charge of product development, you will probably require accommodation to learn your new job. In the first instance you can apply your old knowledge and strategies to the new job with only minimal changes. In the second, however, you will need to develop new knowledge and strategies in order to make a go of your new job.

The second critical aspect of Piaget's theory is his concept of incremental periods of intellectual development that build upon one another. In the sensorimotor period (lasting from birth to approximately two years of age), the infant's interaction with the environment is achieved through relatively simple, overt sensory and motor schemas. In the preoperational period (lasting roughly from age two to age seven), the child acquires advanced symbolic capacity—the ability to let one object represent another object which is not present. In the concrete-operational period (lasting roughly from age seven to twelve), he learns to apply mental operations to concrete objects. An example of this is the realization that if you pour water from a tall, thin vessel into a short, fat one, the amount remains the same. In the formal-operational period (lasting roughly from age twelve upward), the child is able to apply mental operations to abstract or formal objects. An example would be realizing for the first time not only relations between objects but higher-order relations between relations (as in thinking by analogy). Thus, the intellectual growth of the child is characterized by the development of increasingly broad and complex cognitive functions.

A Sociological Model: Intelligence as the Internalization of Social Processes

In one respect, the developmental theory of Lev Vygotsky is in direct opposition to that of Piaget.[33] Whereas Piaget argues that intelligence moves from the inside outward, Vygotsky maintains that it moves from the outside inward. According to Vygotsky, intelligence has its origins in social processes—in the individual's interaction with other persons—and is internalized only after it is manifested socially. Thus, whereas Piaget emphasizes the role of internal maturation, Vygotsky stresses that of external interactions with one's peers and, especially, with one's parents. The child becomes able to do later what he is initially able to do only with the guidance of an adult mentor, such as a parent or tester.

An important concept in Vygotsky's theory is the *zone of proximal development*, or the distance between an individual's realized and latent potential. According to Vygotsky, this zone can best be measured by examining a child's response to guided instruction. By watching the child learn under the guidance of an adult mentor, you can infer the extent to which his realized potential departs from his latent potential. For example, a low performer who profits well from instruction may actually have a great deal of potential locked away and waiting for realization through social processes.

The experiential theories of Piaget, Vygotsky, and others have strongly influenced the field of intelligence, and have forced theorists to consider the roles of maturation and experience in intelligence and its development. Today many criticisms have been leveled at these theories, especially Piaget's.[34] It is now widely acknowledged that Piaget overestimated the age at which children are able to accomplish many intellectual tasks, largely because many of the children did not understand the instructions. In addition, Piaget's conception of intelligence was probably both too formalistic and too logical. Neither children nor adults appear to resemble logicians to the extent required by his theory. Finally, the entire notion of a period or stage is now being seriously questioned,[35] and many developmental psychologists have abandoned it altogether. People just do not seem to progress through discrete and separable stages in their intellectual development.

This chapter has posed three questions about intelligence: What is its relationship to the internal world? What is its relationship to the external world? What is its relationship to the experience of the individual? It can be argued—rightfully, I believe—that a complete theory of intelligence should address not just one of these questions but all three. My own "triarchic" theory of human intelligence, described in the next chapter, attempts to do exactly that.

The Triarchic View of Human Intelligence

CHAPTER 4

Understanding Mental Self-management: The Triarchic Theory of Human Intelligence

Consider three types of graduate students with whom I have been associated. If you understand the similarities and differences among these students—we'll call them Alice, Barbara, and Celia—and their strengths and weaknesses, you will have a better basis for understanding the triarchic theory of human intelligence that provided the motivation for this book.

Three Profiles of Intelligence

Alice was the admissions officer's dream. She was easily admitted to our graduate program at Yale. She came with stellar test scores, outstanding college grades, excellent letters of recommendation, and, overall, close to a perfect record. Alice proved to be more or less what her record promised. She had excellent critical and analytical abilities, which earned her outstanding grades during her first two years at Yale. When it came to taking tests and writing papers, she had no peer among her classmates. But after the first two years, Alice no longer looked quite so outstanding. In our graduate program, as in most, emphasis shifts after the first couple of years. It is not enough just to criticize other people's ideas or to study concepts that other people have proposed. You must start coming up with your own ideas and figuring out ways of implementing them. Alice's synthetic abilities were far inferior to her analytic ones. But there was no way of knowing this from the evidence available in the admissions folder, for although conventional measures can give us a good reading on analytic abilities, they give virtually no assessment of synthetic abilities. Thus, Alice was "IQ test" smart but not equally distinguished in the synthetic, or practical, areas of intelligence.

In sharp contrast to Alice, Barbara was the admissions officer's nightmare. When she applied to Yale, she had good grades but abysmal aptitude test scores, at least by Yale standards. Still, she had superlative letters of recommendation, which described her as an exceptionally creative young woman who had designed and implemented creative research with only minimal guidance. Moreover, her résumé showed her to have been actively involved in important research. Unfortunately, people like Barbara are rejected from many graduate programs. As a result, they either have to enter a program that is much less competitive or change their field altogether.

This pattern of events is not limited to graduate schools: thousands of people like Barbara are rejected similarly from law schools, medical schools, business schools. Some never even reach this point, having been rejected earlier from competitive colleges. But there are occasional exceptions, and in these instances people like Barbara often show themselves to be fine students with excellent research abilities. They may not excel in course performance (although they may do much better than test scores predict), but when the demands of the graduate program shift, for example, to an emphasis on synthetic abilities, people like Barbara are in their element. Lacking Alice's analytic abilities, they may greatly surpass her in their synthetic abilities.

Celia, on paper, appeared to be somewhere between Alice and Barbara in terms of suitability for admission to the graduate program. She was good on almost every measure of success but not truly outstanding on any. We admitted her, expecting her to come out near the middle of the class. This did not happen. Celia proved to be outstanding, though in a way that is quite different from Alice's or Barbara's. Celia's expertise lies in figuring out and adapting to the demands of the environment. Placed in a totally new setting, she loses no time identifying what is required of her and behaving accordingly. She knows exactly what to do to get ahead. In conventional parlance, Celia is "street smart." She excels in practical intelligence.

Just how would you characterize the similarities and differences among Alice, Barbara, and Celia? Clearly, all are exceedingly intelligent, though in very different ways. People like Alice excel in conventional academic, or analytic, intelligence. To the extent that intelligence is measured by conventional factors or information-processing components, by its relationship to the internal world, Alice and individuals like her would be considered very, very smart. Individuals like Barbara, on the other hand, do not appear nearly so intelligent by conventional standards. Where they excel is in their synthetic ability, the ability to deal with novelty— to view new things in old ways or old things in new ways. Hence Barbara's intelligence, and that of others like her, becomes truly apparent only if it is viewed in terms of the relationship of intelligence to experience, particularly novel experience. People like Celia have neither Alice's nor Barbara's pattern of strength. Instead, they excel in terms of the relationship between intelligence and the external world of the individual. Their excellence lies in practical intelligence—the ability to apply their mental abilities to everyday situations. Their street smarts are not measured by conventional tests but quickly show up in their performance in real-world settings.

Conventional Theories of Intelligence: How Do They Interrelate?

The actual ideas for my theory of intelligence were inspired by contact with people I have known. In developing a rationale for a theory of intelligence, however, it is necessary to have both a scientific and an observational basis for making theoretical claims. I therefore decided to look back at the major theories of intelligence that have been proposed during the twentieth century. As I noted in the preceding chapter, all of these seemed to be doing one, or in rare cases two, of three things. The first kind of theory attempted to relate intelligence to the internal world of the individual: What goes on inside a person's head when he thinks intelligently? In the second kind of theory, psychologists sought to relate intelligence to the experience of the individual: How does experience affect a person's intelligence, and how does his intelligence affect the kinds of experiences he has? The third kind of theory is concerned with the relationship of intelligence to the external world of the individual. How does his interaction with the world at large affect his intelligence, and how does his intelligence affect the world in which he lives? Furthermore, how does the world in which we live shape our very notions of what intelligence is?

After conducting this extensive review of the literature on intelligence, I was impressed with the fact that my review led me to exactly the same place that my observations of Alice, Barbara, and Celia had taken me. To understand intelligence completely, it seems that one needs to understand the relationship of intelligence to three things: the internal world of the individual, the external world of the individual, and the experience with the world that mediates between the internal and the external worlds.

Formulation of the Triarchic Theory

The convergence of my analysis of the research literature and my personal experience convinced me that what was needed was a "triarchic" theory of human intelligence—one that did justice to each of these three aspects of intelligence. It is important to mention that my goal in constructing the triarchic theory was quite different from that of most psychologists who have developed theories of intelligence. The field has been notoriously contentious, with every theorist setting out to prove that his theory is right and everyone else's is wrong. For example, Arthur Jensen argues for the predominance of a single, general factor in human intelligence,[1] while Howard Gardner maintains that there are at least seven or eight multiple intelligences.[2] For me, the most disturbing element of these and other opposing theorists has been that while they have done reasonably well in amassing evidence to support their own point of view, they have generally failed to disprove the views of others. How could this be? After reviewing earlier theories, I came to the conclusion that the reason for this was that virtually all of them have been incomplete. Though proposed as full theories of intelligence, each has dealt with only some limited aspect. Often, too, these theories have proved to be complementary rather than contradictory, as might be expected. It is not difficult to show that a theory of general intelligence and the theory of multiple intelligences can be integrated in a hierarchical framework, with general intelligence at the top of the hierarchy and multiple intelligences lower down. More specific abilities would then be viewed as sub-abilities. The point to be made, then, is that often the competition among theorists has been spurious. Their theories are really theories of different aspects of intelligence.

The goal of the triarchic theory is not to compete with other theories but to subsume them in a sense; that is, to view them as subdivisions of a more general theory. The triarchic theory is so named because it attempts to deal with each of the three aspects of intelligence described earlier. It is not the only possible theory that might successfully account for the interplay of intelligence with the internal world of the individual, with experience, and with the external world of the individual. Indeed, I hope other theories will be proposed. But for the present, it does seem to be somewhat more complete than existing theories.

Let's have a look at each of the three aspects of the triarchic theory.

The Relationship of Intelligence to the Internal World of the Individual: Components of Intelligence

The triarchic theory of human intelligence proposes to describe the relationship of intelligence to the internal world of the individual through the components, or mental processes, involved in thinking. As mentioned in the preface, these processes are of three kinds: metacomponents, performance components, and knowledge-acquisition components. Metacomponents are the executive processes used to plan, monitor, and evaluate problem solving. Performance components are the lower-order processes used to implement the commands of the metacomponents. And knowledge-acquisition components are the processes used to learn how to solve the problems in the first place. Each of these kinds of components is described in some detail in chapters 5, 6, and 7, respectively. It soon becomes obvious that components are highly interdependent. For example, it would not be feasible to have a business that consists only of managers or workers or student trainees; nor could any of these three classes of individuals function properly in isolation from each other. In effective mental self-management (and, analogously, in business management), the metacomponents control or activate the performance and knowledge-acquisition components at the same time that the performance and knowledge-acquisition components provide feedback to the metacomponents. Those interrelationships are shown in figure 1.

Consider the example of a typical academic requirement—writing a term paper. Metacomponents are used to decide on a topic, plan the paper, monitor the writing, and to evaluate how well the finished product succeeds in accomplishing its goals. Knowledge-acquisition components are used for research. Performance components are used for the actual writing. But the three could never function in isolation. Before actually writing the paper, you would first have to decide on a topic and then do some research. Similarly, your plans for writing the paper might change as you gather new information. It may turn out that there just isn't enough information on certain aspects of the chosen topic, and you are forced to shift your emphasis. Your plans may also change if certain aspects of the writing go more smoothly than others.

Now have a look at a very practical kind of problem solving—namely, deciding whether to buy a particular new house. From the outset you must decide what criteria are important in making this purchase (metacomponents). This in turn requires you to learn what kinds of things you should look for (knowledge-acquisition components). Finally, you actually

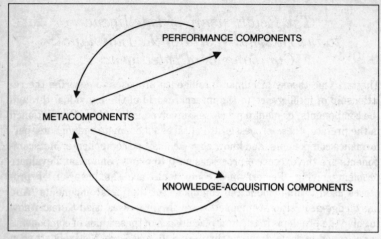

Figure 1. The relationships among metacomponents, performance components, and knowledge-acquisition components. Metacomponents activate the other two kinds of components, which in turn provide feedback to the metacomponents.

have to perform "tests" on the new house to see whether it meets your specifications (performance components). Again, these steps in problem solving are interactive. As you examine the house, you may come up with new criteria for making a decision, or discard old ones. As you learn more and more about houses, similarly, you may add to or delete from your developing list. Good problem solving always requires interaction among metacomponents, performance components, and knowledge-acquisition components.

The Relationship of Intelligence to the Experience of the Individual: Facets of Human Intelligence

All three kinds of information-processing components are applied to tasks and situations at varying levels of experience. The first time you encounter a new task, it probably seems quite novel, but after a few encounters it usually becomes familiar. Figure 2 represents the relationship between an individual's experience with a given task and its degree of novelty. According to the triarchic theory, two aspects of an individual's experience with tasks are particularly relevant to understanding intelligence: performing a task when it is relatively novel and rendering that performance automatic. Consider each of these in turn.

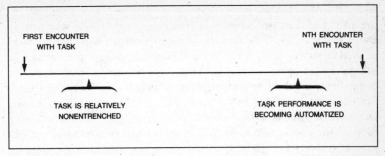

Figure 2. The relationship between nonentrenchment and automatization. When a task is first encountered, it may be nonentrenched. Through successive encounters, performance on the task may become automatized.

COPING WITH NOVELTY

The idea that intelligence involves the ability to cope with novelty is itself far from novel, having been proposed earlier by a number of investigators. I have suggested that intelligence involves not merely the ability to learn and reason with new concepts but the ability to learn and reason with new *kinds* of concepts, which can then be brought to bear on existing knowledge.[3] It is important to note, however, that the usefulness of a test for measuring intelligence is not a straightforward, linear function of how novel the task is. A task that measures intelligence should be novel, but not totally outside an individual's experience. If the task is too novel, it remains outside the individual's range of comprehension because she has no relevant past experience to draw upon as a frame of reference. Calculus, for example, would present such a novelty to most five-year-olds: because it is so removed from their range of experience, it would be useless in assessing their intelligence.

Novelty can be a function of the situation in which tasks are presented as well as a function of the tasks themselves. The idea is that a person's intelligence is best shown not in the run-of-the-mill situations of everyday life but in those extraordinary situations that challenge the individual's ability to cope with her environment. Almost everyone knows someone who performs well when confronted with tasks presented in a familiar setting but who falls apart in the face of similar or even identical tasks in an unfamiliar setting. Someone who performs well in her everyday environment might find it difficult to function in a foreign country, even when it is in many respects similar to the home environment. In general, some people can perform well but only under circumstances that are highly favorable to their work. When the environment is less supportive, the quality of their performance is greatly reduced. This is why performance in one stage of life does not necessarily predict what performance in another stage will be. For example, students who get good grades in college do not necessarily go on to become successful in their chosen occupations. In school, an individual is in a fairly supportive environment. But once she graduates and takes a job, she often confronts a harsh, unfamiliar environment that offers much less support. As a result, only some of the people who succeeded in school will be successful in their jobs. The ability to cope with novel tasks and situations is therefore an important aspect of intelligence.

AUTOMATIZING INFORMATION PROCESSING

Many tasks requiring complex information processing seem so intricate that it is a wonder we can perform them at all. Consider reading, for example. The number and complexity of mental operations involved in reading are staggering, and even more staggering is the rate at which these operations are performed. The only plausible explanation is that a substantial proportion of the mental operations required are automatized and thus require minimal effort. In fact, deficiencies in reading are believed to result in large part from the brain's failure to automatize operations that have become automatic in normal readers. Other activities, such as speaking, also rely on automatization for successful performance. It would be very difficult to speak intelligently if we had to consciously struggle to come up with every word. Driving is another example of an automatized task: When you first learn it, you need to concentrate on every aspect, but eventually it becomes so automatic as to be reflexive.

If complex tasks can be executed only because many of the mental operations involved in their performance have been automatized, failure to automatize these operations, fully or in part, results in a breakdown of information processing and therefore in less intelligent task performance. Intellectual operations that can be performed smoothly and automatically by more intelligent individuals are performed only haltingly and with more conscious effort by those who are less intelligent. The result is that individuals who are intellectually more able can better automatize information processing.

RELATIONSHIP BETWEEN COPING WITH NOVELTY AND AUTOMATIZATION OF INFORMATION PROCESSING

For many (but probably not all) kinds of tasks, the ability to cope with novelty and the corresponding ability to automatize information processing may occur along what might be viewed as an experiential continuum. When an individual first encounters a task or situation, the ability to cope with novelty immediately comes into play. The more intelligent person will respond with ease in coping with the novel demands being made on her. For example, the first day in a foreign country involves adjusting to the many demands of an unfamiliar culture, and your intelligence must rise to the demands of the situation. Moreover, the less attention needed for processing the novelty (i.e., dealing with the strangeness) of a given task or situation, the more there is left over to automatize performance. By the same measure, more efficient automatization of performance leaves additional attention for dealing with novel tasks and situations. Going back to the individual in a foreign country, the less attention she devotes to getting used to the strange currency, the more attention she will have for enjoying the pleasures of shopping.

There is an obvious trade-off between novelty and automatization: the more efficient the individual is at the one, the more resources will be left over for the other. As experience with a new kind of task or situation increases, novelty decreases and the task or situation becomes a less appropriate measure of intelligence. With practice, however, the task becomes an increasingly appropriate measure of automatization skill.

This view carries with it certain implications for the selection of tasks to measure intelligence. First, it is important to select tasks that involve some blend of automatized and controlled behaviors in response to novelty. This might be achieved by presenting subjects with a novel task, then giving them enough practice to ensure that their performance becomes automatized. More intelligent people will tend to be more adept at responding to the initial novelty and will also automatize the task more efficiently. Such a task would measure both response to novelty and degree of automatization, although at different times during the course of testing. For example, if subjects are taught a new mathematical procedure, they will at first find it novel but eventually use it automatically.

The experiential view suggests one of the reasons why it is so difficult to compare levels of intelligence fairly across different sociocultural groups. Even if a given task requires the same mental processes for members of various groups, it is unlikely to be equivalent for the groups either in its novelty or in the degree of automatization prior to the test. For example, everyone may solve time-rate-distance problems in algebra in roughly the same way, but the problems will be differentially novel for different people. An individual who is familiar with them may solve them automatically, whereas someone who is unfamiliar with them may have difficulty finding the right solutions.

Consider, for example, nonverbal reasoning tests, requiring skills such as analogy solution and matrix solution. In such tests, one might have to reason with relations such as those of size, shape, or shading of geometric figures. These tests indicate even greater differences in performance of various sociocultural groups than do the verbal tests that they were designed to replace. But the nonverbal tests, contrary to the claims often made for them, are *not* culture fair, and they are certainly not culture free! Individuals who have been brought up in a test-taking culture are likely to have had much more experience with these kinds of items than are individuals not brought up in such a culture. Thus, the items are less novel and performance on them more automatized for members of the standard American culture than for its nonmembers, so the tests do not measure the same thing across populations. As useful as the tests may be for within-group comparisons, between-group comparisons may be deceptive and unfair. A fair comparison between groups would require comparable degrees of novelty and automatization of test items as well as comparable mental processes and strategies.

I have proposed that behavior draws upon intelligence particularly when it requires coping with novelty and automatization of performance. It is not enough merely to specify a set of processing components or steps involved in intelligence. Consider ordering a lunch from a menu at a restaurant. This action involves a wide variety of metacomponents, performance components, and knowledge-acquisition components. For example, you need to decide what kind of meal to eat, what to drink with it, whether or not to have dessert, and so on. Yet, even though the task of deciding upon a meal may be chock full of components of cognition, it is not a particularly good index of individual differences in intelligence for most people, because it involves neither coping with novelty nor the development of automatization. It tests an aspect of experience that is just not very interesting from the standpoint of individual differences in intelligence. We do not learn much about a person's intelligence from her preferences in food. What we need is to consider the *context* of intelligent behavior, not just any routine behavior at all.

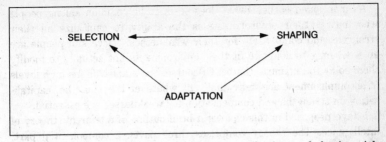

Figure 3. The relationships among adaptation, selection, and shaping. Adaptation is usually tried first, and if it fails or is deemed unsatisfactory, selection or shaping is tried.

The Context of Intelligence: Functions of Mental Self-management

In the triarchic theory, intelligence in everyday life is defined as the *purposive adaptation to, selection of, and shaping of real-world environments relevant to one's life and abilities.*

Consider just what this definition means. The intelligence of an African pygmy could not legitimately be assessed by placing the pygmy in a North American culture and using North American tests, unless it was relevant to test the pygmy for survival in a North American culture (as, for example, if the pygmy moved to America and had to adapt to it). Similarly, a North American's intelligence could not legitimately be assessed in terms of his adaptation to pygmy society unless adaptation to that society was relevant to the person's life. Moreover, intelligence is purposive—directed toward goals, however vague or subconscious they may be.

Intelligence serves three distinguishable functions when it is applied to the everyday world. These functions, as mentioned in chapter 1, are adaptation to existing environments, selection of new environments, and shaping of existing environments into new environments, as shown in figure 3.

Clearly, there is no one set of behaviors that is "intelligent" for everyone, and people adjust to their environments in different ways. Whereas the components of intelligent mental self-management are very likely to be universal, and the need to use these components in novel settings and to automatize them may also be universal, the goals to which they are applied are likely to vary not only across various groups but among individuals as well. Is there, then, any practical strategy that does seem to be common among intelligent individuals?

As mentioned earlier, what does seem to be common among people who master their environments is the ability to capitalize on their strengths and compensate for their weaknesses. Successful people are able not only to adapt to fit their environments but actually to modify them so as to maximize the fit. Of course, the standards for high levels of accomplishment are individual, but whatever they may be, capitalization on strengths and compensation for weaknesses are essential.

I have proposed in this chapter a brief outline of a triarchic theory of intelligence. The theory comprises three parts: a componential part, which relates intelligence to the internal world of the individual; an experiential part, which relates intelligence to both the external and the internal world of the individual; and a contextual part, which relates intelligence to the external world of the individual.

An important thing to realize about the triarchic theory is that the parts of it, although distinguishable, work together in an integrated fashion. Figure 4 shows how this integration takes place. The figure shows that in the triarchic theory, we need to look at intelligence in three ways. First, we need to look at the components of intelligence and the interrelations among them. Second, we need to look at the relation of these components to experience, taking into account that a given component can be applied to a task with which a person is more or less familiar. Finally, we need to take into account how the first two aspects of intelligence impact on the external world—the context in which we live.

The components of intelligence are interactive, with the metacomponents directing the performance and knowledge-acquisition components and these latter kinds of components providing feedback to the metacomponents. For example, when you make a budget, metacomponents are used to decide how much you are willing to spend on what. Performance components are used to do the computations—to balance the ledger. Knowledge-acquisition components are used to learn how to budget in the first place.

The components are applied to experience—to dealing with tasks of varying degrees of novelty. In familiar tasks, the execution of the components becomes automatized. Thus, for example, when one is first learning to walk, the task is relatively novel and consumes one's full attention. Eventually, walking becomes relatively automatic, and some of the attention that was formerly directed to walking can now be directed to other things such as listening to a radio or carrying on a conversation, or both.

Finally, the components are applied to experience in order to serve three contextual functions—adaptation, selection, and shaping. One uses one's mental abilities to achieve the best possible response to the demands of the environment.

An important issue concerns combining the abilities specified by the three parts of the theory. How does the intelligence of a person average in all three kinds of abilities compare with that of a person gifted in some abilities but poor in others? Or what can we say of the intelligence of a person whose environmental opportunities are so restricted that he is unable to adapt to, select, or shape the environment? I am very reluctant to specify any combination rule at all, in that I do not believe that a single index of intelligence is likely to be very useful. Different individuals may be more or less intelligent due to different patterns of abilities. Consider as an example the comparison between (a) a person who is very adept at applying analytic mental processes to abstract problems, and thus likely to score well on standard IQ tests, but who lacks insight, or, more generally, the ability to cope well with novel tasks or situations, and (b) a person who is very insightful (see chapter 7) but not particularly adept at testlike analytic functioning. The first individual might come across as "smart" but not terribly "creative" (see chapter 9); the second might appear creative but not terribly smart. Although it might well be possible to obtain some average score on componential abilities and abilities to deal with novel tasks and situations, such a composite would obscure the critical differences between the functioning of the two individuals. Or consider a person who is both componentially adept and insightful but who makes little effort to fit into the environment in which he lives. Certainly one would not want to take some overall average that hides the person's academic intelligence in a combined index that is reduced because of reduced adaptive skills. Clearly, intelligence is not a single thing: it comprises a very wide array of skills.

Where does this theory leave us with regard to existing intelligence tests? No existing test measures all or even most of the skills that have been discussed in this chapter. Indeed, to the extent that intelligence comprises somewhat different skills for different people, there is no one wholly appropriate test of it. Whereas it might be possible to construct tests of componential skills that would apply to a broad range of individuals, tests of skills involved in attaining contextual fit would almost certainly apply to only a narrow range of individuals. The ideal instrument for assessing intelligence would probably be one that combines measurements of different kinds that together take into account the considerations above. No one measurement, and no combination, would yield a definitive IQ, because any one instrument can work only for some people some of the time. Moreover, it is unclear that any single index can do justice to

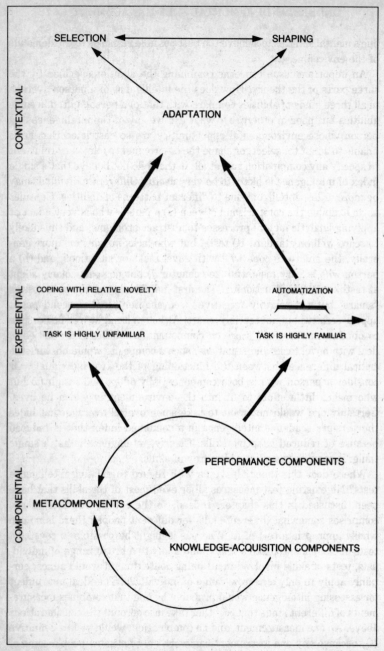

Figure 4. Relationships among the various aspects of the triarchic theory of human intelligence.

the variety of skills that constitute the basis for the triarchic theory of intelligence. A single index would be more likely to obscure than to elucidate a person's levels and patterns of abilities. Which instruments work for which people will vary among people within and between sociocultural groups. The best one can hope for is a battery of assessments that would enable an individual to learn more about intelligence than any one kind of assessment could tell.

General Implications for the Study of Intelligence

THEORIES OF INTELLIGENCE

A theory of intelligence should specify the nature of intelligence in terms of the external world, the internal world, and the interrelation between the two. Contextual theories have been limited to the first of these, most other theories to the second. For example, factorial theories and cognitive theories have generally concentrated on internal mechanisms without regard to the environmental consequences of the behaviors studied. Oddly enough, the early theorists often had the broadest theories of intelligence; but their disciples have often chosen to dwell only on limited aspects of their theories. Thus, for example, Binet, Spearman, and Wechsler all dealt in some detail with both the internal mechanisms of intelligence and the role of intelligence in the world, yet it often is not easy to recognize the breadth of these seminal theorists from the work of their followers.

One implication of the triarchic theory is that many existing theories of intelligence are incomplete rather than incorrect. Indeed, as noted earlier, many of them say essentially the same thing in different languages. Competitive theorists seem to have devoted too much attention to highlighting the differences among their theories, which often are not great, and not enough attention to highlighting the ways in which their theories are similar or identical. Factor theories and certain cognitive theories, for example, say pretty much the same things, but in terms of different units of analysis.[4] The processes of cognitive theories map into the factors of psychometric theories, and vice versa. For example, one of the factors in Thurstone's theory of primary mental abilities is inductive reasoning. This factor is supposed to underlie individual differences in tasks such as analogical reasoning and number-series completions. But what does labeling such tasks "inductive reasoning" really tell us about the nature of what a person does when he reasons analogically or completes a number series? Not much. Cognitive theories help us further understand the mental skills underlying performance on various kinds of cognitive tasks. For example, it will tell us what mental processes are involved in solving analogies or completing number series, how long these processes take to perform, how susceptible they are to error, and so on. These processes are not inconsistent with the psychometric account of "inductive reasoning" as an ability. Rather, they help us understand what inductive reasoning is in terms of process. There is an unfortunate tendency on the part of many psychologists to view intelligence in an overly restrictive way, although progress is now being made toward broader conceptualizations of intelligence. Intelligence is not quite like cognitive processes such as perception, learning, and problem solving, but neither is it totally different from them. A wholly cognitive theory that tries to equate intelligence to some aspect or aspects of cognition fails to recognize the "stipulative" nature of the concept: "intelligence" is a concept we invented in order to provide a useful way of evaluating and, occasionally, ordering people in terms of their performance on tasks and in situations that are valued by the culture; but this performance is based upon cognitive (as well as motivational and affective) functioning—a point that seems not to be dealt with explicitly by many existing contextual accounts of intelligence.

MEASURES OF INTELLIGENCE

Even the most highly regarded of the currently available measures of intelligence, such as the Wechsler and Stanford-Binet tests, fail to do justice to their creators' conceptions of intelligence. They measure well memory and analytic skills but not synthetic and practical ones. They certainly fail to do justice to the conception of intelligence proposed in this book. According to my view, an adequate test would have to measure, at least, the aspects of intelligence dealt with by each of the three parts of the triarchic theory of intelligence. The aspects of the theory that are dealt with most inadequately by present tests are, I believe, (a) adaptation to, selection of, and shaping of real-world environments; (b) dealing with novel kinds of tasks and situations; and (c) metacomponential planning and decision making. The present tests measure best (a) the outcomes of knowledge-acquisition components (via tests such as vocabulary and reading) and (b) the current functioning of performance components.

My own efforts toward new kinds of tests are taking the form of development of a triarchic test of intelligence—the Sternberg Multidimensional Abilities Test, to be published in 1991 by the Psychological Corporation. It will be appropriate for people as young as five years of age and as old as senior citizens. The test will employ three kinds of item contents: verbal (word-based problems), quantitative (number-based problems), and figural (form-based problems). Separate scores will be obtainable for each of these three types. Separate scores will also be obtainable for each of the three main parts of the triarchic theory: components of intelligence, coping with novelty and automatization (two separate subscores), and practical intelligence. The test will be in paper-and-pencil, multiple-choice format and will be suitable for group administration.

An important feature of the test will be the availability of two parallel forms, making it possible to test and retest a given individual without giving that individual the same test items twice. The importance of the two alternative forms lies in the possibility of an intervention, in between tests, for developing intellectual skills. Ideally, then, the first form would be used to get a preliminary reading on strengths and weaknesses. Then the individual would work on improving intellectual skills and eventually would be retested.

Note that a fundamental assumption underlying my test is that intelligence is malleable rather than fixed. Many intelligence testers feel it incumbent on themselves to assume that scores will remain stable, that people's intelligence is fixed and unchangeable. I disagree. To me, the whole point of testing is not to obtain an immutable score but rather to suggest strengths upon which the individual can capitalize and weaknesses that he can remediate.

The triarchic theory of human intelligence can be used as a basis for answering a number of questions about the nature of human intelligence. The next section addresses some of them.

Questions and Answers about Intelligence: A Triarchic Perspective

IS THERE REALLY SUCH A THING AS INTELLIGENCE?

Yes, but not in the way we often conceive of it. Intelligence is essentially a cultural invention to account for the fact that some people are able to succeed in their environment better than others. We define as "intelligence" those mental self-management skills that enable these people to do so. Even if we dispense with "intelligence," we dispense only with the term, not with the concept. As soon as people attempt to get rid of the term, they invent another in its place. Several years ago, the president of the Educational Testing Service wrote me indicating, to my amazement, that the Educational Testing Service does not construct intelligence tests. Nevertheless, they do construct "scholastic aptitude tests" and similar instruments, which correlate about as highly with intelligence tests as the intelligence tests correlate with each other. By avoiding the term, he somehow thought he was eliminating the construct. This view may serve social or commercial purposes but not a scientific one.

What, Then, Is Intelligence?

It is purposive adaptation to and selection and shaping of real-world environments relevant to one's life. Stated simply, it is mental self-management. Because people will always have to manage themselves mentally, there will always be intelligence, no matter what term we use to represent it.

Is Intelligence the Same for Everyone?

In a sense, yes; and in a sense, no. The components of human cognition are the same from one culture to another and one time to another, and among individuals. Everyone has to recognize the existence of problems, define problems, make inferences, selectively encode new information, and the like. Moreover, as long as there is novelty in their environment, people will have to adjust their lives to it. But the contextual uses of the components of intelligence in experience can differ radically across cultures, and even among individuals within a single culture. What is adaptive for one culture or person is not necessarily so for another. What constitutes an optimal selection or shaping of environments for one individual does not necessarily do so for another. For example, given the same set of external circumstances, the right thing for one person to do may be to find another job; for another person, it may be to stay where he is. The two individuals may have different standards or want different things out of life. There is no one set of criteria for fitting into environments that can suit everyone. We all need to adapt, select, and shape environments at various times, but we do so in different ways. What all of us need to do is to capitalize on our strengths and to compensate for our weaknesses.

Is Intelligence One Thing or Many?

Clearly, it is many. By using various sorts of statistical techniques such as factor analysis, one can identify a "general factor" in human intelligence, which results from the interplay of the various aspects of intelligent mental self-management. The various parts of the system work together, but the interaction of these aspects of human intelligence should not obscure its fundamental diversity.

WHAT ABOUT GARDNER'S THEORY OF MULTIPLE INTELLIGENCES?

Gardner is correct in noting that there are multiple aspects of intelligent mental self-management. The notion that these different aspects are independent, however, is simply wrong. There is overwhelming statistical evidence against this view, and not citing it does not eliminate it. This evidence takes the form of positive correlations among most ability tests: people who do better on one tend to do better on others too. An intelligent system has to work cohesively. Consider an analogy to government. Many governments, such as that of the United States, start off as a series of fairly independent units, such as states or provinces. These different units may be very jealous of their autonomy and guard their prerogatives. But inevitably, some kind of federated system, no matter how loose, emerges. This is because no government can work effectively as a set of independent parts, nor can any business. Similarly, mental self-management would break down if there were truly independent intelligences. In solving a mathematical word problem, for example, verbal and quantitative abilities need to work together. Gardner's point of view just doesn't seem to be right, either statistically or psychologically.

DO THINGS LIKE MUSICAL TALENTS AND KINESTHETIC TALENTS CONSTITUTE INTELLIGENCES?

Conceivably there are cultures in which musical or kinesthetic talents are needed in order to adjust to the environment. Indeed, there are mini-environments in which these talents are needed to survive—a symphony orchestra, for example, or an athletic team. But there are reasons why we refer to these skills as "talents" rather than intelligences, not only within our culture but in virtually all cultures around the world. There is a qualitative difference between kinesthetic ability and intelligence. Consider someone who has a serious case of cerebral palsy and hence is spastic. You would not say that this person is mentally retarded because she lacks kinesthetic intelligence. But now consider someone who is totally unable to define problems or totally unable to make inferences about her environment. In the total absence of these skills, she could not survive in our culture or in any other.

WHY DO PEOPLE BECOME MORE "INTELLIGENT" AS THEY GROW OLDER—BETTER ABLE TO MANAGE THEMSELVES MENTALLY?

In the triarchic theory, a number of mechanisms account for intellectual development. First, metacomponents receive feedback from performance and knowledge-acquisition components, which increases the effectiveness of their functioning. Second, knowledge-acquisition components in and of themselves increase one's ability to adapt to or select or shape environments. Third, as one applies the components of intelligence to experiences, fewer and fewer tasks and situations remain novel; more and more of them become automatic, rendering us more effective mental self-managers.

WHAT DOES IT MEAN TO BE "INTELLECTUALLY GIFTED"?

As noted in the examples of Alice, Barbara, and Celia, being intellectually gifted does not mean any one thing, for there are many kinds of intellectual gifts. A valuable function of multiaptitude theories of intelligence, such as Thurstone's, Guilford's, or Gardner's, is that they remind us of the many ways in which people can be intellectually gifted. Regrettably, current tests and screening procedures for admission to special programs for the intellectually gifted do not do justice to the diversity and complexity of human intelligence. Those gifted individuals who make the greatest long-range contributions to society are probably those whose gifts involve coping with novelty—specifically, in the area of insight. Creative and insightful individuals are those who make discoveries and devise the inventions that ultimately change society. This does not mean that insight is a better form of giftedness than others, merely that it is likely to have the greatest long-range consequences for society.

WHAT DOES IT MEAN TO BE "MENTALLY RETARDED"?

Mental retardation, like intellectual giftedness, is multifaceted, but our society has been slow to recognize this fact. There are some individuals who score low on IQ tests because of relatively poor componential skills, such as reasoning, but who nevertheless are able to adapt to their environments by making the most of what they have in applying their intelligence to context. Research suggests that the most common locus of mental retardation is in metacomponential deficits.[5] But again, mental retardation can take multiple forms.

WHY DO SOME GROUPS SCORE LOWER THAN OTHERS ON CONVENTIONAL INTELLIGENCE TESTS?

There are many reasons, including heredity, environment, and the interactions between the two. My own explanation would emphasize different socialization processes, as discussed later, in chapter 10. Different groups have different conceptions of intelligence, and parents socialize their children to be intelligent accordingly. This conception may be valid for one environment but not for another. As a result, when a child enters a school controlled by the mainstream majority, he may look unintelligent, despite the intelligence he shows in his own environment. Conventional intelligence tests are not culturally or subculturally fair. Even if individuals in different groups use the same components or strategies to solve test problems, it is doubtful that the problems are equally novel or automatized for all groups, and equally relevant for contextual adaptation, selection, and shaping across groups. Hence, all existing tests tend to favor certain groups over others, and the favored groups are virtually always the societal "in groups."

IS INTELLIGENCE INHERITED?

There is overwhelming evidence that suggests that intelligence is *in part* genetically determined. But there are two important things to remember. First, genetics only sets an upper limit on the level of intelligence someone can achieve. As far as we know, no one has ever reached his upper limit, and hence, everyone can be more intelligent than he is at present. This does not mean that mentally retarded people are likely to become geniuses, but only that everyone can improve the intelligence he has to some extent. The standard 50 percent figure for heritability of intelligence does not imply anything at all about how much intelligence can be increased. Consider height as an analogy. Height is 90 percent genetically determined. Yet people in general have grown considerably over the last several generations, in the United States and especially in Japan. Better nutrition and a healthier overall environment have resulted in this increase. Similarly, improved intellectual stimulation and training could very likely increase everyone's level of intelligence. Second, heritability figures are not fixed constants but rather are susceptible to change as a function of time, place, environmental circumstances, the diversity of the particular group from which the heritability coefficient was computed, and so on. In other words, the 50-percent figure is not etched in stone. It could vary greatly. Hence, it is a mistake to take it too seriously.

How Can We Go About Improving Intelligence?

The best thing to do is to learn and keep learning throughout your life, never believing that there's a time when learning stops. We should constantly try to absorb and grow from new kinds of experiences that broaden our horizons. Evidence suggests that just using your intellect helps improve it, so you should never give up on intellectual challenges or allow yourself to become stale. There exist a variety of programs for improving intellectual skills.[6] My own training program, *Intelligence Applied: Understanding and Increasing Your Intellectual Skills*, is aimed at individuals of high-school level and beyond.[7] I have purposely included in this book training exercises; by doing them, you will be taking a first step toward improving your intellectual skills.

Why Are Intelligence Tests Such Imperfect Predictors of Both Academic Success and Success in Later Life?

They are imperfect predictors because they are so narrow in their view of intelligence, and because so much more enters into any kind of success than just intelligence. Issues of personality, motivation, values, and people's own expectations determine what eventually becomes of them. These issues are discussed in the final chapter. It is important to remember that some people may be successful by their own standards, even if they are not by societal standards, and vice versa.

Why Are People Occasionally Quite Good at One Aspect of Intellectual Functioning but Quite Poor at Another?

Everyone knows of people who exhibit unusual and sometimes bizarre discrepancies in intellectual functioning. A person who is mathematically gifted may have trouble writing a sentence, or an accomplished novelist may have trouble adding simple columns of numbers. In the triarchic framework, the discrepancy can be accounted for in either of two ways. First, an individual may never have learned how to apply certain mental processes in particular domains. For example, someone might have a good memory but have difficulty remembering words in a foreign language because the words have no meaning to her. Or someone might reason well but have difficulty on verbal analogies because she does not know what the words mean. Second, the discrepancy can be accounted for by difficulty in operating upon a particular form of mental representation. Different kinds of information are probably represented in different ways, at least at some level of information processing. For example, there is good reason to believe that linguistic and spatial representations differ in at least some respects from each other.[8] A given component may operate successfully on one form of representation but not on another. A person may reason well with verbal material, for example, but not with figural material.

JUST HOW IMPORTANT IS INTELLIGENCE, ANYWAY?

In the broad sense in which intelligence is defined here, it is quite important to everyday living. Conventional academic intelligence begins to lose its importance after school ends. But intelligence in a broader sense of mental self-management continues to be important throughout one's life. Hence, it pays off to understand intelligence and to do what you can to improve it. But I would hasten to add that there is more to life than intelligence, and people who forget that are likely to be doomed to limited and unhappy lives. So, unfortunately, are their children. Everything in life must be kept in perspective, and intelligence is no exception.

In the next three chapters, you will learn more about how the components of intelligence are applied to experience in order to serve the contextual functions of adaptation, selection, and shaping. In order to present as unified an account as possible, I have combined the experiential and contextual aspects of intelligence with the componential aspect and have divided these three chapters according to the three kinds of components: metacomponents, performance components, and knowledge-acquisition components.

CHAPTER
5

Metacomponents: The "White Collar" Processes of Human Intelligence

Metacomponents are used to plan, monitor, and evaluate your problem solving. In this chapter, you will be introduced to various metacomponents and perform exercises to help you improve your facility with each one.

Consider Gordon, Carol, and Jack.

Gordon is a biologist supported by government grants. He is in great demand as a speaker and hence travels a great deal. Unfortunately, he wastes a small fortune because of his poor *planning* skills. He seeks to maintain maximum flexibility in his travel schedule by booking his flight reservations at the last minute. Unfortunately, a result is that he almost never is able to obtain the inexpensive fares that are available for air travel booked well in advance. And, ironically, his failure to plan ahead does not gain him the flexibility he seeks: his first-choice flights are sometimes filled to capacity and he has to fly on less desirable flights. Despite its disadvantages he persists in this pattern of behavior.

Carol is in business for herself and does a substantial amount of entertaining which entitles her to substantial tax deductions. But although she carefully peels away her credit-card receipts, she almost invariably loses them. Her failure to *monitor* her business expenses results in a substantial overpayment at tax time. Carol knows this, but she has been unable to change her behavior.

Jack works in the marketing division of a middle-sized corporation. His major task is to come up with marketing plans for new cosmetic products.

His colleagues and superiors agree that he has some great ideas. Yet Jack has consistently been passed over for promotion and has reached a dead end in terms of job prospects. His problem is that he is unable to *evaluate* his creative work accurately. Although he has some genuinely brilliant ideas, many of them are not practical, and when it comes time to select which ones to implement, he often makes a wrong choice. His supervisors have taken over much of the evaluation function for him, but his inability to separate the wheat from the chaff in his own work is an obstacle to future advancement.

Each of these stories illustrates a failure in the metacomponents—the higher-order executive processes—of human intelligence. Metacomponents are at the core of mental self-management, so that no matter how able one is in other aspects of intelligence, deficits in executive processing can often result in truly unintelligent behavior.

This chapter will focus on seven executive processes critical to intelligent problem solving. They are not the only metacomponents, but my own research and that of others[1] suggests that they are among the most important, because they must be used in the solution of almost every real-world problem. The processes are: recognizing the existence of a problem, defining the nature of the problem, generating the set of steps needed to solve the problem, combining these steps into a workable strategy for problem solution, deciding how to represent information about the problem, allocating mental and physical resources to solving the problem, and monitoring the solution to the problem. Each of these executive processes will be discussed in turn.

Recognizing the Existence of a Problem

Let's consider an example. For years, IBM had been the undisputed leader in the computer marketplace. Their mainframe computers were by far the most popular, and their strategy of keeping many of the specifications a secret had resulted in their garnering a substantial business in peripherals and software as well as in the selling of mainframes. Just as had happened with automobiles, however, the "small is beautiful" philosophy reached the computer industry. More and more computer users became taken with minicomputers, and the Digital Equipment Corporation (DEC), recognizing a gap in the availability of quality minicomputers, stole the show. Their sales of the smaller minicomputers dominated those of all the other manufacturers. But they, too, were caught unawares when the microcomputer revolution burst upon the scene. The Apple Computer Company, consisting of two enterprising young men and a small staff, helped to create a new market with the introduction of the Apple microcomputer. In a short time both IBM and DEC had lost tremendous ground in this potentially enormous market. Both companies eventually recognized their error and stepped in to get a share of the market. IBM's recognition of the problem, of course, resulted in the production of the IBM Personal Computer (PC), and IBM quickly regained its lost foothold, establishing itself as the leader in sales of microcomputers to businesses.

This case illustrates, in a business setting, the critical importance of recognizing the existence of a problem. The manufacturers eventually recognized that a problem existed but lost a great deal of time and profit by letting an "upstart" get the better of them.

Of course, the importance of recognizing the existence of a problem is not limited to the business sector. Consider the case of Bill and Judy, whose beautiful son, Tim, in their opinion, could do no wrong. They were very proud of him and bent over backward to please him. Some people thought they were spoiling Tim, but Bill and Judy did not see it that way at all. In elementary school, Tim had a series of conflicts with his teachers, but the parents always blamed it on the rigid authoritarianism of the teachers. By junior high, Tim had been in a few minor scrapes with the law, but Bill and Judy wrote these off as part of growing up. They talked to him, and when it seemed to do no good, they decided that "boys will be boys" and patiently waited for him to sow his wild oats and grow up. In his senior year of high school, Tim got involved in a serious confrontation with the law when he was identified as a drug pusher. He was convicted of selling drugs and sent to prison. From early on, Bill and Judy had been faced with a problem child, but they had simply refused to recognize this. By ignoring the problem, they had never seriously confronted the issue of how to correct Tim's behavior, and they lived to see their pride and joy a convicted felon.

Problems arise in virtually every domain of living, both for individuals and for organizations. How can you spot these problems before they become serious, or at least while they are still remediable? Unfortunately, there is no surefire way of ensuring that you will notice problems when they crop up, but steps can be taken to facilitate problem recognition.

Be receptive rather than resistant to adverse feedback. In almost every case in which a problem goes unrecognized, adverse feedback is staring you in the face, waiting to be noticed. In some cases, the "staring" may be literal, as when someone ignores an odd-looking blemish or freckle that might actually be malignant.

For many years a pharmaceutical company made an intrauterine device (IUD) that later was found to have serious consequences for a large number of users, many of whom ultimately were left sterile. When the word got out that the device was dangerous, lawsuits resulted and the company eventually went bankrupt. Though evidence of adverse effects from the device had been filtering in for quite a long time, the company had chosen to ignore the reports.

Both people and institutions stick their heads in the sand in order to avoid facing up to potentially unpleasant problems. People may not like to visit doctors or to find out that they have a potentially serious disease. Institutions may not like to admit that a corporate strategy that has been successful for many years is no longer working. But the longer we wait to face a problem, the higher the price we are likely to have to pay.

Seek out criticism as well as praise. It is not enough to accept criticism: we should seek it out. Most people like to be praised, few like to be criticized; yet it is from criticism that we are most likely to recognize the existence of a problem. There are any number of reasons why people avoid criticism—defensiveness, low self-esteem, unwavering belief in the rightness of their own ways, an unwillingness to make the effort to change. Whatever the reason, the outcome is the same—an inability to make the most of their experience.

When Jonathan started as an associate in a prestigious Chicago law firm, he was highly praised by the firm's partners. He came from a first-class law school, and his abilities and training showed him to be superior to his peers. Jonathan soaked up the praise like a sponge. When he had been on the job for six months, the partners began a serious effort to shape the briefs of their associates to fit the style and needs of the firm. Some of the associates eagerly sought the partners' criticism, hoping to improve their work. Jonathan not only did not seek such criticism; he actively avoided it. As the work of the other associates improved while Jonathan's did not, the partners became more and more critical of him. Jonathan's avoidance of criticism and failure to seek out advice for constructive change eventually resulted in his dismissal.

Defensiveness almost never pays off, and much of the time it can result in failure to recognize correctable problems, or in those problems becoming so severe that it is too late to surmount them.

Be on the lookout for strategies that no longer work. One of the most difficult things we have to face in life is the passing success of most strategies. A given strategy works for a while and then simply stops working. Often we are reluctant to give up on a strategy that has served us so well in the past.

We often see people who succeed at one stage of life, only to fail at the next. The phenomenally successful high-school student becomes an average college student; the highly successful college student becomes a mediocre graduate student; the star of the graduate program becomes an unknown college professor. Some attribute this phenomenon to the funnellike nature of success in life: that is, there is steadily decreasing room for success as one moves up the ladder, whether in a corporation, in a profession, or in a trade. The believers in the funnel metaphor would argue that yesterday's star was simply good, but not good enough to make it at the next level of advancement. No doubt this argument is correct in some cases. But the argument fails to recognize the qualitatively different requirements for success at different stages of life's endeavors and, in particular, fails to recognize that the fading of many stars is due to their inability to recognize the new problems that come to face them.

Keith was a rising star in his company. His boss did not mind the fact that Keith was inconsiderate of his subordinates and seemed uncaring of their needs. Keith's boss cared about profits, and the profits in Keith's division were excellent. Keith's boss was eventually transferred and a new boss brought in. Keith had hoped to get the promotion himself but was passed over. As a result, he worked his staff even harder and became even less popular. Keith's new boss, unlike his old one, cared about human relations and warned Keith to ease up. But Keith was concerned that if his profits did not stay high or go higher, he would lose all hope of a promotion. Meanwhile, his dictatorial practices were taking their toll, and profits in his division were declining. Eventually, Keith himself was transferred—to a position of lesser responsibility.

Keith, like so many of us, refused to recognize the need to change and persisted in strategies that had long since ceased to lead to success. He was simply unable to recognize the need to adapt to the changing requirements of his job.

Changing requirements for success are not limited to occupational or academic settings. They apply every bit as much in the personal domain. Indeed, the high divorce rate in American society is probably partly due to the fact that the requirements for success later in a relationship are not the same as the requirements earlier on, and many people cannot adjust to these changing priorities.

Joe and Mary had, by anyone's standards, a wonderful courtship. They spent a great deal of time together, exchanged intimate secrets about their lives, enjoyed similar interests, shared many of the same values, and felt remarkably close to each other and happy together. When they got married, they felt they had every reason to believe that theirs was a marriage made in heaven. Seven years later, they were in divorce court.

What had happened? Although they had a variety of problems, one was that they had simply never been able to adjust to the passing of the courtship phase of their relationship. They could not make a go of living together and found that they were remarkably ill prepared to face the practicalities of life. Neither one knew how to manage finances, and they found themselves further and further in debt. Money arguments ensued. Both were involved full-time in professional careers, and neither wanted to spend time cleaning the house. But because of their financial misman-agement, they were unable to afford help. They both became disgusted with their living conditions. One problem after another cropped up, and eventually they were unable to face them all. Oddly enough, the problems in the relationship had begun to appear almost immediately after their marriage, but it was not until well into their fifth year that they actually recognized them; they had been too busy concentrating on other aspects of their lives. By then, it was too late. The styles of interrelating that had worked so well in their courtship had simply ceased to work in their marriage, but they were unwilling or unable to face this fact, with the result that eventually their marriage dissolved. If they had been able to recognize their problems sooner, they might have been able to salvage their marriage.

People and institutions must be open to recognizing the existence of problems, so that they can actively try to solve them. Probably more problems remain unsolved because they are never recognized than be-cause they are solved inappropriately. Good mental self-management re-quires us to seek to recognize our problems and face them squarely.

Defining the Nature of a Problem

It is important not only to recognize the existence of problems but to define them properly. Consider some examples.

During the late 1970s, a break-in at the Democratic Party headquarters in the Watergate Hotel in Washington, D.C., caused a major political scandal for the administration of President Richard M. Nixon. To this day, it is not known exactly why the break-in took place. What is well known, however, is how the members of the Nixon administration defined the problem they faced. When they started receiving details regarding the break-in, they immediately set about covering up as many of them as possible. As more and more of the details leaked out to the press, it became obvious to practically everyone that the efforts at cover-up were becoming increasingly futile. Eventually, the cover-up became more of a problem than the break-in itself. By defining the problem as covering up the break-in rather than as providing full or nearly full disclosure in a minimally harmful way, the Nixon administration seriously reduced its own credibility, and especially the credibility of President Nixon. Eventually, Nixon found himself obliged to resign.

Defining problems applies in family as well as political situations. Many families find themselves getting increasingly into debt, partially as a result of impulsive and ill-considered credit-card spending. It is exceedingly easy today to sign up to buy now and pay later, but eventually the bills come home, and the funds to pay them are not always there. Families who approach or reach bankruptcy show a surprisingly common pattern of credit-card use: they define their problem as one of insufficient income rather than as one of overspending. Rather than cutting down on their spending or literally cutting their credit cards in two, they seek ways to meet their expenses. Often, this means borrowing money, which itself must be paid back with interest later on. Eventually, these families get in over their heads. To a large extent, the financial disaster that confronts them can be traced to their misdefinition of their problem in terms of having sufficient funds to meet expenses rather than gearing expenses to available funds.

Defining problems applies to individuals, too. When Jackie received an anonymous phone call informing her that her husband was having an affair, she was crushed. She had always believed their relationship was a sound one, based on trust and deep religious values. But the caller provided evidence that could not be ignored. When Jackie confronted her husband, he readily admitted to the affair but insisted that it had been a brief fling that he had since recognized as a mistake. Jackie could not see things this way and felt that she could never trust him again. The couple split up, and she filed for a divorce. Several years later, Jackie deeply regretted her decision. She realized that she had defined the problem of the affair in a way that was vastly different from her husband's definition of the problem and, moreover, that her definition did not correspond to what had actually happened. Her misdefinition of the problem resulted in the destruction of a marriage that in general had been mutually rewarding and that could have continued to be happy and satisfying for both of them.

The effects of misdefinition of problems can also be seen strikingly in some psychological investigations. For example, Bathsheva Rifkin and I asked children in grades two, four, and six, as well as college students, to solve picture analogies.[2] The pictures were schematic illustrations of people, and the subjects in the experiment had to recognize analogies between them. In these analogies, items were presented in the form A is to B as C is to (D_1, D_2), where D_1 and D_2 are alternative answer options.

We were interested in how many analogies children at the different grade levels could solve correctly.

We encountered an unwelcome surprise when we attempted to score the test booklets of some of the second-graders. Rather than circling either the first or the second of the two answer options, as the instructions had indicated they should, they had circled either the first term or the second term (A or B) of the analogy. At first this strategy seemed to make no sense at all; we had no idea why these children had circled one of the first two terms rather than one of the answer options. We soon realized what had happened. The children in the experiment were elementary-school students at a Jewish day school. At this school, instruction was typically in English in the morning and in Hebrew in the afternoon. As a result, the children were accustomed to reading in a left-to-right fashion in the morning and in a right-to-left fashion in the afternoon. What some of these children had done was inappropriately to transfer their right-to-left reading behavior to the analogy problem, which in fact had been administered in the afternoon. In other words, they had defined the problem in a way that was appropriate to their usual afternoon activity—reading Hebrew—but in a way that was inappropriate to the activity of solving analogies.

This illustration is important not only for its implications for defining problems per se but for its implications for defining problems in intelligence tests for children. There are many cases in which children may look much less intelligent than they are because they fail to define the problem the way that the test constructor had intended. Looking at a test score, one might come to the conclusion that the children were unable to solve problems when in fact they never even understood the directions.

This problem was particularly salient in the research of Piaget. During the 1960s and early 1970s, when Piaget's point of view regarding children was very much in fashion, psychologists, teachers, and parents believed that there were many fairly simple cognitive tasks that young children simply could not do because of a lack of reasoning skill or problem-solving ability. Later in the 1970s it became clear that Piaget had rather grossly underestimated children's reasoning abilities. For example, Peter Bryant and Tom Trabasso found that children's failure to perform well on transitive-inference tasks was due primarily to memory limitations rather than to limitations in their reasoning ability.[3] Consider, for example, the problem:

John is taller than Mary. Mary is taller than Pete. Pete is taller than Sam. Is John taller than Sam?

Young children of about four years of age generally have great difficulty solving this kind of problem. But what Bryant and Trabasso found was that the difficulty was due to their inability to remember the terms of the problem rather than their inability to reason. Rochel Gelman and Renee Baillargeon have reviewed a wide range of literature suggesting that when children understand the instructions and remember the terms of the problems with which they are presented, their performance is much better than previously had been thought.[4]

There are several things you can do to improve the ways in which you define problems. Consider three of these.

Ask yourself whether the problem you are addressing is really the one you want to solve. We frequently find ourselves attempting to solve problems that aren't the ones we should be attempting to solve in the first place. Often, we set out to solve the right problem but end up solving a different one. It is therefore important to ask yourself from time to time whether the problem that you are trying to solve is truly the one that ought to be solved.

For example, several years ago, Israel invaded Lebanon. Repeated border attacks had driven the Israelis to consider various ways of securing their borders, and the government decided that a presence on the Lebanese side of the border would prevent, or at least deter, guerrilla attacks. The move was widely supported within Israel and received at least some support from the outside. But what started off as an attempt to secure borders became a full-scale invasion of the country, culminating in the invasion of Beirut. The invasion was in many respects disastrous. There were huge military losses as well as the loss of innocent lives, and the government became less and less clear as to just what purpose the invasion was supposed to serve. Eventually, support for the invasion dwindled greatly both within Israel and around the world. Ultimately, Israel withdrew from Lebanon, leaving a situation that was not recognizably better than the situation before the invasion. Somewhere along the line, the original definition of the problem—to secure Israel's borders—got lost, and what might have been a satisfactory solution to that problem was replaced by an unsatisfactory solution to a problem that was never clearly defined.

This kind of situation is not, of course, limited to Israel. It happened to the United States in Vietnam and to the Soviet Union in Afghanistan. Indeed, it appears to be a frequent occurrence in military intervention: military problems have a way of resisting containment. The exact nature of the problem often becomes fuzzier and fuzzier, and hence the intervention no longer seems to be directed toward any clear aims.

Flexibility in the definition of a problem can reap tremendous rewards. Consider another example. By the mid-1980s it had become clear that the Coca-Cola Company was losing ground steadily to the Pepsi-Cola Company in sales of its mainstay product, Coca-Cola. Top management felt that something had to be done. In the course of testing formulas for their recently introduced Diet Coke, the company had come upon a non-diet cola formula that consumers seemingly preferred to the existing formula. Management decided to change the formula for Coca-Cola as a response to the slippage in sales. The result, which received a great deal of national attention, was hardly what the Coca-Cola Company expected: massive outrage on the part of Coke drinkers, who were fiercely loyal to the old blend. The company was in danger of losing many of its most loyal customers because it had misdefined its problem. Too much concerned with gaining new Coke drinkers and winning back people who had switched to Pepsi, management realized in the nick of time that it also had to hang on to the customers it already had. Redefining the problem, management reintroduced the old Coke under a new label name—Coca-Cola Classic. Coke loyalists got their old formula back, and those who preferred a sweeter taste had the new Coca-Cola to compete with Pepsi. The Coca-Cola Company turned a potential disaster into a great success.

Redefine an insoluble problem to make it soluble. More often than we would like, we simply set unreachable goals for ourselves. We define problems in ways that they cannot be solved. People can struggle a long time trying to solve a problem that no amount of effort will ever solve. In such cases, it is often best to redefine the problem to make it soluble.

Mary was fed up with the almost incessant travels of her husband, Tom, a salesman for a major manufacturer of sports equipment. Tom's job carried him to all parts of the country and occasionally abroad, and Mary felt that she never got to see him. She asked Tom to find another job, but he was reluctant to do so because he enjoyed it and saw good opportunities for advancement within his firm. They started growing apart and, eventually, seriously considered splitting up. Finally, they sought marital counseling in a last-ditch effort to save the marriage. Redefining their problem, the counselor made a very simple suggestion: that Mary accompany Tom on at least some of his trips. Because they had no children and Mary did not work, this solution was a feasible one. Tom was able to arrange for Mary to travel with him on occasion. Mary found that she loved travel and appreciated the opportunities she had to be with Tom. What had seemed like a disaster ended up enriching the marriage. Originally, Mary had defined Tom's travels as the problem. Now, she realized that their problem was being apart, and that it could be solved by her traveling with Tom. A rather simple redefinition not only saved the marriage but made it better.

Sometimes we redefine problems so that they are different from the original ones, without realizing that the problem we are solving is no longer the one we intended to solve.

Ever since the early 1900s, psychologists have been eager to measure the intelligence of both school children and adults. The first psychologist to work on testing in a serious and somewhat successful way was Alfred Binet. He recognized that the intelligence test he created did not do justice to his much broader conception of intelligence in terms of a person's adaptation to her everyday life circumstances—the kind of adaptation illustrated in this and other chapters. But it is very difficult to measure intelligence in everyday life, so Binet came up with what he viewed as a workable compromise—the intelligence test as we now know it. A serious problem arose when later investigators forgot what Binet had known: that there is more to intelligence than what the tests test. Many investigators came to view intelligence as synonymous with what intelligence tests measure, and some of them even suggested that the two be equated.[5] Binet had sought to measure the whole of intelligence but recognized that he had to be satisfied with just a part. Later psychologists often came to believe that Binet's redefinition of the problem—to measure that part of intelligence which readily can be measured—was the whole problem. As a result, they came to believe that intelligence tests measure more than they really do.

Redefining a problem in order to make it soluble can be useful, but you must ask whether the redefined problem is truly worthy of solution and whether the losses in redefining the problem outweigh the gains. Most importantly, you must realize that the problem has indeed been redefined.

Consider whether the goal toward which you are striving is really the one you want to reach. Sometimes, you come to realize that the goal you're (unsuccessfully) trying to reach is not realistic. The solution is not to create a more modest goal but to create one that is realistic and responsive to your needs.

Consider the case of Sara, who was about to enter her fifth "serious" relationship within a year. The pattern in each relationship had been the same. She had started off being very taken with a man and idealizing him. As she got to know him better, she began to see more and more faults and to realize that he did not come anywhere close to her ideal. Finally, she terminated the relationship, preparing to move on to a different relationship which she hoped would be better. When her long string of unsuccessful relationships, which actually extended back almost five

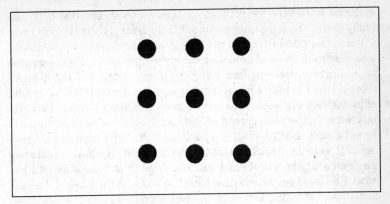

Figure 5. The nine-dot problem.

years, showed no sign of abating, she entered psychotherapy. She came to realize that she had defined her problem in relationships as one of finding the ideal man and that in all likelihood no such man existed. Her goal had been unrealistic from the start. She stopped setting impossibly high ideals for men and instead started to focus on the positive aspects of her relationships. Within six months she had entered into a satisfying relationship, which lasted for two years, longer than any of her previous relationships. When the new relationship finally ended, it was not because of failed expectations but rather because the man moved away and she chose not to follow him.

The importance of correctly defining a problem is highlighted by some of the classic problems in the psychological literature, which are difficult to solve precisely because people tend to misdefine their nature. Let's consider two of them.

The nine-dot problem. Figure 5 shows nine dots arrayed in a three-by-three matrix. The task sounds simple: Connect all nine dots with a set of line segments so that you never lift your pencil off the page and so that you use no more than four distinct line segments. Try the problem before reading on.

Now look at the solution in figure 15 in the Appendix. Although the problem may seem easy at first, people find it extremely difficult to arrive at the correct solution, and most people never do, no matter how hard they try. Once you have examined the solution, you can see why. Most people assume that the line segments must be confined to the interior of the boundaries formed by the nine dots. But there is nothing in the directions to the problem that suggests this constraint. Put simply, almost everyone misdefines the problem by adding a constraint that is not actually there. The same thing tends to happen frequently in our own lives.

For years, I defined myself as a "cognitive psychologist," a psychologist who studies the mental processes and structures underlying things such as intelligence, thinking, reasoning, problem solving, and the like. Although I did not realize it, my defining myself in this way limited the set of problems I was willing to tackle. Somewhere along the line, I became interested in the phenomenon of love. At first, I was hesitant to study love, because it didn't seem to be a topic fitting for a cognitive psychologist. Eventually, I realized that the way I defined myself was preventing me from studying a problem I was interested in and about which I had what I believed were some good ideas. To hell with the labels, I decided, and started studying love. I have never regretted it. In the meantime, other psychologists started to question me, asking me whether I still saw myself as a cognitive psychologist. I realized that they were doing exactly what I had done for several years: by defining themselves in terms of a fairly meaningless label, they were restricting what was possible for themselves in their lives. Similarly, many women raised to become "good housewives" had neglected potentially rewarding careers, while others, career-oriented, define themselves strictly in terms of their jobs.

Generating the Set of Steps Needed to Solve the Problem

Once a problem is recognized and defined, it still needs to be solved. A critical metacomponent for achieving solution requires the generation of a set of steps toward solution.

It repeatedly has been reported that many thousands of unnecessary medical procedures are performed each year. In most cases, these operations are neither beneficial nor detrimental, although there are cases in which the operation can have negative or even life-threatening results. Some of these unnecessary operations could be prevented if people thought about them carefully and in advance. An important step that many people neglect is to get a second opinion from another surgeon; in some cases, even a third opinion may be desirable.

Many salesmen employ high-pressure techniques to try to close a sale rapidly, promising that the full benefits being offered can be obtained only if the potential customer buys the product then and there. I once came close to investing in what I later found out was worthless real estate because of such a sucker ploy. Since then, I have decided that I always would think overnight before making a major purchase. In some cases this policy has resulted in lost opportunities; however, I have never regretted my decision to think things over. Adding that step to my decision-making process has saved me from a number of worthless investments.

Once you define the nature of a problem, you have to generate a set of steps to solve it. The steps you choose can make the difference between success and failure, and certainly between better and worse solutions. It is therefore important that you spend the time and effort to decide on these steps before rushing into the problem solving. Haste can make waste.

What, then, can be done to improve your deciding upon steps for problem solving?

Budget the time necessary to decide upon a sequence of steps. Very often we are eager to jump into solving a problem without taking the time properly to formulate it and to generate the steps needed for its solution. This is poor mental self-management. Some years ago, Benjamin Bloom studied the problem-solving processes of more and less able college students.[6] He found that the more able students consistently spent more time in deciding on a set of steps for solving problems than did the less able students. This extra time spent more than paid off in their ability to solve problems more efficiently.

Consider how a failure in budgeting time resulted in a major fiasco in the computer world. After the introduction of the Apple II computer, the Apple Computer Company decided rather quickly that the time had come for a bigger and better machine. It rapidly put together the Apple III. The Apple III was, quite simply, a bust. It didn't work right, and there were many complaints. After a short period of time, Apple discontinued the original Apple III. Its haste to introduce the new machine without going through the planning necessary to perfect it resulted in a machine that was a lemon. Apple is not the only computer company that has been guilty of such practices. After Apple introduced its original microcomputer, a number of other companies jumped in with alternative machines. Many of these machines were ill conceived and were either taken off the market or forced off it through lack of sales. Had the companies spent the additional time needed to come up with better products, they ultimately would have been better off. This was the strategy followed by IBM in its introduction of its Personal Computer, with considerable success.

Make the first step an easy one. The greatest difficulty in accomplishing a task or solving a problem is often taking the very first step. People wait until the last minute to file their tax returns because they dread even getting started. Students put off Ph.D. dissertations because they cannot conceive of beginning such a major project. Couples put off buying a house because it seems such an enormous undertaking; in the meantime, prices go up, interest rates fluctuate, and the couples continue to throw away rent on apartments. In each of these cases, people delay getting started on things because the first step seems so monumental. By making the first step easier, they could get started more quickly and build up the momentum they need to accomplish the tasks.

Choose steps that are the right size for solving the problem, neither too small nor too large. Most problems require a number of steps for their solution, and some consideration beforehand as to how large these steps should be can greatly facilitate your problem solving. The "step size" may not be the same throughout the problem-solving process: for example, you may start off with small steps, proceed to larger ones, and end up with smaller ones again. When you choose steps that are too large, you may find yourself unable ever to solve the problem; at each step you are biting off more than you can chew. However, choosing steps that are too small can result in your taking what seems to be forever to solve the problem and in your becoming frustrated or losing interest before you get very far.

Some years ago, when I entered into a contract to train intellectual skills among Venezuelan college students, I knew no Spanish at all; but it quickly became clear that I would have to acquire at least a working knowledge of the language. I bought myself a "learn Spanish quick" book, which guaranteed results within just a few weeks. After a few days I realized that I was never going to learn Spanish this way. The book went much too fast and would never give me the working knowledge of Spanish it promised in such a brief period of time. I then hired a graduate student to tutor me in Spanish once a week. After a year I had a pretty good working knowledge of Spanish. I realized that there was no quick fix to learning Spanish in a usable way and that the only way I would learn it would be to take it in small but progressive steps.

Consider alternative steps to a solution before choosing any one set of them. In his famous book *Administrative Behavior* Herbert Simon describes a strategy called "satisficing," frequently used by people solving problems.[7] When people use this strategy, they choose the first minimally acceptable course of action rather than considering the available alternatives and then settling on the best. Satisficing is clearly a suboptimal strategy; it does not allow you to consider whether there might be an easier or a better way to solve a particular problem. Although it is usually not possible to consider all of the ways of solving a problem, it is generally better to consider some alternatives before rushing into any one of them.

I learned this the hard way when purchasing a car several years ago. Having settled on a Mazda GLC as the model I wished to buy, I went to the two local Mazda dealers and bought my car from the one that offered the better price. Soon thereafter, I discovered that my membership in an automobile association entitled me to a substantial discount on the Mazda. Had I considered the alternatives, I would have saved several hundred dollars.

Here's another case of looking at alternatives. Each year, tens of thousands of couples get divorced. Usually they rush to lawyers, who end up slugging out matters in the courts, with the courts basically deciding who gets what. Most of these couples never look into an alternative set of steps for solving their problems—namely, divorce mediation. Through mediation it is possible for the couple to arrive at a settlement that they, not the courts, have worked out. By using the judicial system, they lose the opportunity to resolve their dispute in a more amicable and rational way. Not all couples, of course, could settle their differences through mediation, but by not even considering it, many couples lose what could have been, for them, a superior opportunity to reach a settlement.

Strategy Selection: Ordering the Steps for Problem Solution

When solving a problem, it is necessary not only to pick the right steps but to order them in the right way. Even if you decide on the right steps, you can undermine your problem solving by ordering them incorrectly.

Often people have to persuade others of the validity, or at least the acceptability, of their own points of view. A pacifist might try to persuade people that war is wrong, or a salesman might try to persuade people that his brand is the best. Research on persuasion indicates that the order in which an individual presents his arguments has a large effect on just how persuasive they are.[8] In particular, you should put your strongest arguments first and last and your weakest arguments in the middle. Frequently, however, people order their arguments randomly, putting some of their stronger points in the middle, where they are least likely to be remembered. As a result, they lose arguments or sales that they might otherwise have won.

Here's an example of how things in the wrong order ruined a vacation: Several years ago, I planned a trip to Europe. I let a ticket agent convince me that I should purchase train tickets well in advance, thereby taking advantage of discount fares between various cities. When I got to Europe,

I found that I had to plan my sightseeing around the tickets I had bought, rather than planning the train schedule around the sights I wished to see. Although I took the right steps, I put them in the wrong order, and the trip was not nearly as much fun as it might otherwise have been.

In making purchases, people sometimes put the cart before the horse: they see why they need a product only after they have bought a product that isn't right for them. Many people today are buying personal computers for home use. They shop around and then buy the computer that seems to give them the most for the least money. Unfortunately, they do not always consider their needs, for different computers tend to be good for different purposes. For example, computers that are highly suitable for games are not necessarily the best for word processing, and vice versa. By considering first the uses to which they plan to put the computer, they can buy the one that is best suited to their purposes.

There are several steps you can take to improve your strategy for ordering the steps of problem solving:

Don't immediately assume the "obvious."   We often assume the obvious in ordering the steps of problem solving, only to realize later that the obvious was not the optimal. Consider alternatives before rushing for the "obvious" order.

When I took high-school geometry, I encountered many proofs that were difficult for me to solve. Gradually I realized a strategy that would make many of these proofs much easier. Instead of working forward from the premises to the conclusion, I worked backward from the conclusion to the premises. Many of the problems I could not solve working forward I was easily able to solve working backward. Sometimes it's better to start at the end and work toward the beginning rather than working from beginning to end.

Similarly, I assumed what seemed obvious in writing this book: I should start with chapter 1 and move on. But I was uncertain as to just what the first chapter should look like; I pondered over it a long time, considering and reconsidering what should go into it, and becoming more and more frustrated. Finally, I decided to start by writing some of the chapters in the middle of the book. As I wrote them, the first chapter became clearer and clearer to me. Had I insisted on starting with the first chapter, I might still be trying to write it. Likewise, I have discovered that when writing journal articles, I should always write the summary or abstract that precedes the articles last rather than first. Although it comes at the beginning, not until after I have written the article am I able to summarize just what the article says.

Make sure that your sequencing of steps follows a natural progression toward the goal you wish to reach. Some orderings are more natural than others, and it pays to consider the most natural ordering before actually attempting to solve a problem. For example, many couples who are having marital problems think that having a child will help to settle their differences. Unfortunately, most of the time it only makes things worse: by having a child *before* they resolve their problems, they're only increasing the stress on their marriage.

Don't "self-terminate" prematurely. People often make errors in problem solving because they believe they have solved the problem before they actually get to the end. This is called "premature self-termination."

People who write test items are aware of this tendency and use it to the test-takers' disadvantage, particularly on mathematical ability tests. Consider, for example, multiple-choice mathematical aptitude tests. Such tests usually consist of a set of problems each followed by four or five alternative responses. Upon reaching a solution that appears as one of the options, many test-takers rush to select that option. After all, they figure, what are the chances of their reaching a solution that appears as an answer option, given the infinite number of mathematical solutions they might have reached? The problem is that the solver does not always complete all of the steps necessary to solve the full problem. The test constructor has provided "sucker" options that represent solutions to incomplete versions of the problem. As a result, the individual solves the problem incorrectly.

The same thing can happen with psychotherapy. People often experience a noticeable improvement after just a few sessions; some of them stop at this point, convinced that they can now take matters into their own hands. When their situation deteriorates and they find themselves back where they started, they conclude that the psychotherapy was worthless rather than that they terminated it prematurely.

Here are three classic psychological test problems that show the importance of ordering one's steps in problem solution.

Searching the field. Figure 6 depicts an irregularly shaped field. Somewhere in that field is a valuable gold coin. Your problem is to set up a systematic search strategy that will assure you of finding that gold coin by walking along some pattern through the field. Try to devise a systematic search strategy that would guarantee your finding the coin.

The critical element for solving this problem is that the search strategy you set up is ordered. Randomly roaming around the field or even unsystematic attempts to look at different parts are unlikely to yield the

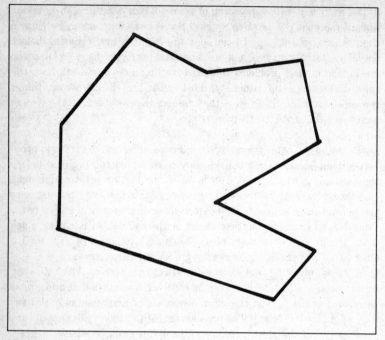

Figure 6. The searching-the-field problem.

gold coin. Note that the solution shown in figure 16 in the Appendix is one that is highly likely to reveal the coin.

A variant of this problem occurs when we lose something in our homes. My son never seems to be able to find his shoes when he needs them. He looks around the house but without any particular system. As a result, he looks in the same place many times but misses other places altogether. I am known to do the same thing when I lose my glasses. Almost anyone who has been through this experience of searching for a lost item can remember with chagrin looking several times in one spot but failing to look in the right place.

The permutation problem.   Piaget has used as a measure of advanced intelligence—what he calls "formal operations"—a variant of what is known as the permutation problem. This problem is difficult to solve correctly.

Consider the four letters A, B, C, D. Provide a listing of all the possible permutations (orders) in which these four letters could be written. For example, A, B, C, D is one permutation, and D, C, B, A is another.

This problem can be either quite easy or quite difficult, depending on the strategy you use to solve the problem. If you simply try to solve the problem in an unsystematic fashion, the chances of listing all of the possible permutations are quite slim. However, if you devise a systematic strategy, the chances of listing them all are quite good. In fact, when this problem is used as a measure of advanced reasoning, the important thing the examiner looks for is not so much the number of permutations listed as the strategy that is used to generate these permutations. In other words, the ordering of steps is the critical feature the examiner uses for rating performance on the problem.

One systematic way of obtaining the entire list is to hold one letter constant and to vary subsequent letters systematically, going through each of the successive letters in doing so. For example, the strategy applied to the present problem might yield:

1. A B C D
2. A B D C
3. A C B D
4. A C D B
5. A D B C
6. A D C B

Note how the first letter, A, is held constant in each of these six permutations and variation is created from the right end moving toward the left. In other words, first the last two letters, C and D, are interchanged with each other, and only then is B interchanged with C and D. As a result, there are six permutations beginning with the letter A, consisting of two permutations with each of B, C, and D in the second position. It stands to reason that, similarly, there will be six permutations starting with B, six starting with C, and six starting with D. By proceeding systematically, all twenty-four permutations can be methodically generated. See if you can complete the list before looking at the solution in the Appendix.

People who are familiar with this type of problem know that the number of permutations for n different elements equals the product obtained by multiplying together all the counting numbers from n down to 1. For example, for three items, there are $3 \times 2 \times 1$, or six permutations. In the current instance, the number of permutations is $4 \times 3 \times 2 \times 1$, or 24. This knowledge is helpful, of course, in preventing premature self-termination; however, even without knowing the formula, a person approaching the problem systematically is bound to get the correct answer.

The missionaries-and-cannibals problem.   One of the most famous problems requiring careful ordering of steps is the so-called missionaries-and-cannibals problem, which has been part of the problem-solving folklore for many years. It goes like this:

Three missionaries and three cannibals are on a riverbank. The missionaries and cannibals need to cross over to the other side of the river. They have for this purpose a small boat that will hold just two individuals. There is one problem, however. If the number of cannibals on either side of the river exceeds the number of missionaries, the cannibals will eat the missionaries. How can all three missionaries get across to the other side of the river in a way that guarantees they all arrive alive and uneaten? Try to solve this problem before looking at the solution in figure 17 in the Appendix.

When you do so, you will see that the solution of the problem is almost linear in nature. There are only two points at which there are actually alternatives for problem solving, and these alternatives can lead to the correct solution. The errors people make tend to be either of two kinds. One is making an illegal move, resulting in more cannibals than missionaries on one side of the river. As a result, the cannibals can eat the missionaries. The other kind of mistake is a move going backward rather than forward, returning to a previous state rather than progressing forward to the next. The missionaries-and-cannibals problem is an example of how taking things one step at a time in a logical progression can lead to the correct solution.

Deciding How to Represent Information About the Problem

An important part of problem solving is the way in which information is represented. The representation can be either external (a table, figure, or chart, for example) or internal (a mental image or a set of propositions). Problems that can be solved easily using one form of representation often can be solved only with great difficulty or not at all using another form of representation. Representations can differ in complexity as well as in kind.

Patricia Linville has looked at the relationship between the way we represent information about other people and our stereotypes about and prejudices toward these people.[9] One of her findings is that simple mental representations about other people tend to lead toward extreme judgments about these people, whether favorable or unfavorable. The converse also holds: extreme judgments, and especially prejudicial ones, tend to imply simple representations about people. This makes sense, because almost inevitably a complex representation simply will not support the prejudice. This finding gives credence to the view that one of the best ways to fight prejudice is through fighting ignorance. It has often been noted that prejudice tends to be directed toward groups rather than individuals: once we get to know an individual well, it is hard to maintain a stereotype about him.

Linville also discovered a connection between the simplicity of mental representations of unfavorable events and the depression that often follows them. People who become depressed after a particular event, such as the loss of a love, tend to view it in very simple terms. As the complexity of their view increases, their depression decreases. Consider an example involving depression after loss of a lover. Susanna was very depressed after her lover left her for someone else. A counselor helped her realize that there was much more to her life than just her relationship with her boyfriend and that part of her depression resulted from her simplistic view of herself. Once Susanna realized the diversity in her life, and the multiple possibilities open to her, her depression began to lift. She became involved in new activities, and eventually she started a relationship with another man.

Complexity of representation is an important factor not only in human relations but, more generally, in skill acquisition. A number of psychologists have studied just what it is that seems to distinguish experts from novices in a variety of domains, ranging from playing chess to fixing cars.[10] A consistent finding is that experts have more complex representations of information than do novices. For example, experts on Russian affairs have stored in their memories a wealth of information regarding the ways in which the Soviet Union has responded to various kinds of world crises and, when asked to predict how the USSR will respond in a new crisis, can draw upon this vast and complex knowledge base.

Another difference between the experts and the novices is in the degrees to which they can "chunk" information about a given domain. Chunking of information refers to putting items of information together into a single, unified, and coherent representation. For example, what might seem to me to be five unrelated facts about the way a car works may seem to an expert to be just one network of interrelated items. This difference applies not only to novices versus experts but to younger versus older children and to children versus adults.

In my study with Bathsheva Rifkin (mentioned earlier), we presented individuals roughly seven, nine, eleven, and eighteen years old with picture analogies that required them to see various kinds of relationships between the images. One of the more striking findings was that the mental representations of the children changed with increasing age. The youngest children tended to represent information about the pictures "separably": they encoded each of the attributes of the picture separately, retaining separate representations for each of these attributes in their heads. For example, each shape, size, shading, and gender of the people in the pictures was viewed independently. In contrast, the older children tended to represent information about the pictures "integrally": although the attributes of the pictures may have been encoded separately, they were integrated, or chunked together, when they were represented mentally and stored in the head. The advantage of the integral representation for the pictures is that it consumes less working memory space. Because they chunked the information more efficiently, the older children were able to hold more information in their heads and to process it more effectively. Other such studies of children's encoding strategies and working-memory capacities, such as ones by Micheline Chi,[11] have tended to suggest that younger children differ from older ones not in the number of "slots" that they hold in working memory but rather in the amount of information that they can place into each of these slots.

In yet another domain, it has been found that people of the same age will often solve cognitive problems differently, depending on their particular pattern of abilities. As I noted earlier, good mental self-managers—and hence, effective problem solvers—tend to be people who capitalize on their strengths and compensate for their weaknesses in solving problems. Thus, it is important to know what these strengths and weaknesses are. In the realm of mental representation of information, for example, some people tend to be better at representing information spatially, or in the form of mental imagery; other people tend to be better at representing the same information linguistically, or in the form of sentences or propositions.

Consider the so-called sentence-picture comparison task. In this very simple type of task, individuals are asked to compare the contents of a sentence to the contents of a picture and to say whether or not they match. For example, the individual might be presented with the sentence "Star is below plus" and the picture * +. In this particular case, the answer is no—the contents of the sentence and the picture do not match. Another, somewhat more complicated example of the sentence-picture comparison problem is "Star is not below plus," * +. Here, the correct answer is yes— a match.

Colin MacLeod, Earl Hunt, and Nancy Mathews, studying the strategies used in solving this kind of sentence-picture-comparison problem,[12] reported that people employed two basic kinds of strategy. The first entails representing information about the sentence verbally: taking the sentence and summarizing its contents in the form of a propositional string, such as "star above plus." In the second kind of strategy, information from the sentence is represented spatially: the verbal information is converted into an image, which then is compared with the actual picture presented. MacLeod and his colleagues found that whether people represented information verbally or spatially was in part a function of respective ability levels in these two domains. People who were "more verbal" were more likely to represent information linguistically; people who were "more spatial" were more likely to represent information spatially. Thus, they were adopting the mental representations suiting their own patterns of abilities.

Unfortunately, people do not always do this. For example, in a study of linear-syllogistic reasoning (that is, reasoning for problems such as "John is taller than Pete. Pete is taller than Sam. Who is shortest?"), Evelyn Weil and I found that although there exist both linguistic and spatial strategies for problem solution, as well as a strategy that combines elements of the two, people do not tend to select the strategy that is most suited to their pattern of abilities.[13] Perhaps because of the greater complexity of these problems relative to the sentence-picture-comparison problems, the optimal strategy is less obvious. Indeed, in these problems people usually are not initially aware of the availability of alternative strategies. Thus, use of better mental representation could facilitate problem solving.

What kinds of steps can you take to help yourself better represent problems? Here are three.

Know your pattern of abilities for representing information. It helps to gain a sense of what kinds of representations you use most effectively. For example, I teach several statistics courses in which it is possible to gain an understanding of the statistical techniques through either geometric or algebraic representations. I find quite a bit of diversity in which route students choose. I teach the conceptual basis for most of the techniques both ways. To this day, I have trouble teaching the geometric style of problem solving, because I have so much difficulty with it myself. But if a student knows what her pattern of abilities is, it is easier for her to capitalize on this information to facilitate learning statistical techniques.

Occasionally I visit someone's house for the first time. When people give me verbal directions to get there, I usually have no trouble; but if someone draws a map for me, I have considerable difficulty reading it, especially if I try to do it while driving. Using these maps, I used to get lost frequently in trying to find the person's house. Eventually, I learned that if I am given a map, I need to sit down in advance and write out the directions verbally. (I have also learned to be helpful to others—I now have a set of directions to my own house that includes both a map and a set of verbal instructions for getting there!)

Use multiple representations whenever possible.   In problems in which multiple representations of information are possible, it often helps to use at least two of them. If you know you are better at representing information in one way than in another, then you can designate one of the representations as primary and the other as secondary. The advantage to using multiple representations is that even if they are formally equivalent, they may not be equivalent psychologically. Sometimes you see aspects of a problem when representing it in one way that are not obvious when the problem is represented in another.

Consider the problem of mutual arms reduction. One of the major obstacles to achieving this goal has been the inability or unwillingness of two major powers, the United States and the Soviet Union, to see things from each other's point of view. When each side attempts to solve the problem from its own point of view, the attempt invariably fails, because the solution depends on mutual steps toward reduction, which in turn depend on mutual understanding. International relations in general often are compromised because one side cannot appreciate the other's point of view.

One of the best-selling products in the personal computer marketplace has been the Apple Macintosh. It was clear from the beginning that somehow the Macintosh was responding to a need unmet by other computers: the need for pictorial as well as verbal representation of commands. Many people had difficulty relating to the verbal commands on earlier computers. Some of these commands employed mnemonics that seemed to make no sense at all. With both pictorial and verbal mnemonics available on the Macintosh, the user has a greater choice in the way she chooses to represent information, and in many instances she can represent information both verbally and pictorially.

Use external representations.   Many complicated problems become much simpler when you don't rely totally on mental representations to solve them. For example, algebra problems often seem easier if you draw a diagram representing the relations among the different terms. Sometimes, just writing a problem out puts it into a perspective that you can't see when you're trying to work everything out in your head.

External representations may be used to solve the kinds of problems employed in psychological research and testing. Consider the following:

Bill is taller than Tom. Pete is taller than Sam. Pete is shorter than Tom. Bill is shorter than Mike. Sam is taller than Jack. Who is tallest?

The easiest way to solve this problem is through the use of a linear array. Try using such an array before looking at figure 18 in the Appendix. Notice how the use of the array as an external representation solves two problems: representing the spatial relations among the heights of the different individuals in the problem, and avoiding working-memory overload in trying to remember all of the different people and their interrelations.

Three men—Henry, Louis, and Pete—differ in their levels of wealth. The last names of these three men are Toliver, Gray, and Masters, but not necessarily in that order. Pete is not as wealthy as Henry. Pete is wealthier than Louis. Toliver is wealthier than Gray. Masters is not as wealthy as Gray. What is the full name of the least wealthy individual?

Solution of this problem hinges upon the formation of two spatial arrays, one of which relates each first name to each other first name, the other of which relates each last name to each other last name. The problem can then be solved by correctly linking up the first names to the last names so that they correspond in wealth. Before looking at the solution in figure 19 in the Appendix, try solving the problem on your own.

Three women—Joan, Patty, and Sandy—have among them three children—Sam, Louise, and Dave. Sam likes to play with Patty's son. Sandy occasionally babysits for Joan's children. Who is Louise's mother?

This problem requires that you notice both who cannot be whose mother, and how many children each woman has. Try solving the problem on your own before looking at the solution in figure 20 in the Appendix.

Gina, Barbara, and Elaine are a housewife, a lawyer, and a physicist, although not necessarily in that order. Gina lives next door to the housewife. Barbara is the physicist's best friend. Elaine once wanted to be a lawyer but decided against it. She is glad not to be a housewife. Gina has seen Barbara within the last two days, but has not seen the physicist. Indicate the respective occupations of Gina, Barbara, and Elaine.

This problem is best worked out by creating a table. A table might have Gina, Barbara, and Elaine as rows and housewife, lawyer, and physicist as columns. Use the process of elimination to put x's in cells that represent impossible combinations of women with jobs. The solution appears in figure 21 in the Appendix.

Allocating Mental and Physical Resources to Solving the Problem

Perhaps no executive process is more important to successful problem solving, and even to successful living in general, than resource allocation. People are constantly making decisions about resource allocation that have significant and even profound effects on their lives.

For example, Frank had a good job as a bank manager. This was fortunate, because he had two passions in life: going on semiannual vacations to faraway places with his wife, Martha, and buying new cars as often as was expedient. He and Martha traveled twice yearly, leaving their three children behind with an aunt; and every third year they bought a new car. It's an oft-told tale but true: when the time came for Frank to put his children through college, he didn't have the money. Moreover, the scholarship aid he had counted on did not come through, for his income was just too high. When Frank had to borrow large amounts of money for his children's college education, he realized that he should have saved at least some of the money that so thoughtlessly went into cars and vacations.

Resource allocation is critical at every level of society: individual, family, community, state, and country. The wisdom with which resources are allocated can have a tremendous impact on both the short-term and the long-term future. For example, certain companies are reluctant to allocate funds for basic research, figuring that the payoffs will come only in the distant future. But the large majority of great discoveries have resulted from basic research, and failure to fund it has proven time and again to be shortsighted. Whereas applied research may indeed be more useful in the short run, it is rarely so in the long run.

In a research study, I investigated how students allocated their time in a complex analogical reasoning task.[14] The basic task was to solve verbal analogies correctly in as little time as possible. The standard analogy takes the form A is to B as C is to D_i, where D_i represents a variety of different answer options. For example, LAWYER is to CLIENT as DOCTOR is to (a. MEDICINE, b. NURSE, c. PATIENT, d. STETHOSCOPE) is a typical verbal analogy. The analogies in my experiment differed from standard analogies, however, in that it was possible for more than one analogy term to be missing and for positions of missing terms to vary from one problem to another. Either two or three alternative answer options were substituted for each missing analogy term. An example of such a problem is MAN is to SKIN as (a. DOG, b. TREE) is to (a. BARK, b. CAT). In this particular example, the last two terms are presented in a forced-choice format, and the examinee has to choose the correct options, which are TREE and BARK. Subjects were timed while they solved these problems. I used mathematical techniques in order to determine how much time subjects spent on two aspects of the strategy-planning metacomponents: global planning and local planning.

Global planning is the overall strategy that is used to solve a set of problems, regardless of the particular characteristics of any individual problem. For example, in the complex analogies, global planning is that planning relevant to all of them, regardless of format. Local planning is the formation of a strategy tailored to the format of a particular problem. In complex analogies, different local planning would be needed for each item format. Note that the concepts of global and local planning are applicable well beyond any one particular task. For example, global planning is used to set up the list of tasks to be accomplished in a given day, whereas local planning is used to set up the performance of each of those tasks as it occurs. In planning out a career, global planning would take into account the long term, whereas local planning would apply only to the short term.

In analyzing our experimental results, we found that better reasoners tended to spend relatively more time on global planning than did poorer reasoners, whereas poorer reasoners tended to spend relatively more time on local planning. Although the better reasoners were faster problem solvers on the average, overall speed would have hidden the difference in executive processing between the two groups. The better mental self-managers knew to put more time into global planning in order to facilitate and thereby speed up their local planning.

Earl Hunt and Marcy Lansman have studied the allocation of attention in the simultaneous performance of two tasks.[15] Participants in their experiments are asked to solve a difficult task, such as an analogical-reasoning task, at the same time that they are asked to solve another, usually simpler task, such as a probe-reaction-time task. The former task requires complex reasoning, whereas the latter task merely requires one to push a button on hearing a particular sound. The participants have to press the button as quickly as possible after hearing the signal. Thus, although they allocate most of their mental processing resources to the difficult task, they nevertheless have to allocate at least some of their processing resources to the simpler one. Hunt and Lansman have found that more intelligent individuals are better able to divide their attention between the two tasks, indicating that they allocate their mental resources more effectively.

Sarah Goldin and Barbara Hayes-Roth studied allocation of resources in planning.[16] They were particularly interested in what makes a person a good planner. Consider, for example, the problem of performing a number of errands on a single journey. Often you have only limited time to perform the errands, and the order in which you do them needs to reflect both the importance of each errand and the locations where they can be performed. Goldin and Hayes-Roth found that (a) better planners tend to spend relatively more time on higher-level planning, especially given the importance of each of the errands and the proximity of the various places in which the errands can be performed; (b) better planners exhibit more flexibility in allocating their attention; and (c) better planners make more use of world knowledge in their planning.

There are several steps that you can take to improve your allocation of mental and physical resources. Here are some of them:

Be willing to spend relatively large amounts of time on global, high-level planning. All of the results reported above suggest the importance of a person's willingness to spend large amounts of time on high-level planning. Notice the use of the term "willingness." Many people who could be better planners aren't simply because they are unwilling to spend the time it takes to be a good planner. They impulsively jump into tasks before they are ready to perform them, with the result that they do not perform the tasks as well as they might have. Thus, they often have to go back and make up for the time that they should have spent planning to do the task.

Allocation of resources can save a vacation from disaster. Ed and Marti couldn't wait for their dream vacation to Florida. They had been saving up money for several years and were looking forward to an exciting trip. They decided to play things by ear, so they didn't do much planning in advance besides buying their round-trip plane tickets. When they arrived in Miami—during the tourist season—they were unable to rent the car that they had been hoping to rent because all the compacts were taken; instead, they had to spend money they hadn't budgeted on a luxury car. They found that their hotel of choice had vacancies only in the most expensive rooms; again, they had to spend much more money than they had bargained for. They discovered at several of the tourist attractions that they could have saved money by purchasing tickets in advance at their home travel agency. A week before their trip was scheduled to end, they found themselves running out of money and realized that they would probably have to go home early. They then discovered that changing their return-trip plane ticket would involve an extra expense as well. As a result of poor global planning, Ed and Marti's dream vacation turned into something of a nightmare.

Allocation of resources applies importantly in testing situations. Sam was taking the Miller Analogies Test as part of his application for graduate admission in clinical psychology. The test allowed fifty minutes to solve one hundred items. Sam could have figured out that the time limit meant that he could afford to spend, on the average, only thirty seconds per item. But whenever he came to a difficult item, he spent a considerable amount of time attempting to work out the correct answer. As a result of his failing to allocate his time, he finished only sixty-five of the hundred items. Had he skipped over the more difficult items and left them for later, he could at least have attempted more or all of the items on the test.

Make full use of your prior knowledge in planning and in allocating your resources.   Although people differ greatly in the amount of knowledge that they bring to a task, they differ at least as greatly in the extent to which they utilize that knowledge. Your allocation of resources will be much more effective if you use all of the information you have available in order to plan and allocate time effectively.

I discovered the importance of this fact when I was involved in editing *Child Development*, a professional journal. When I started out, I devoted a considerable amount of time to each and every manuscript submitted. Because I was handling only one manuscript a day, the work kept piling up until I found that there was simply no way I could continue to read each manuscript with consummate care. Fortunately, I had the comments of outside referees, all of whom had read each paper carefully, to guide me. I decided to read closely only the good manuscripts and the ones about which the referees disagreed; it was simply not worth my while to devote great attention to manuscripts that the referees agreed were of poor quality. I thus learned to allocate my time in a more effective way.

Consider a very different slice of life—stealing cars. Experience can improve time allocation in this antisocial occupation. The car thief, once he has decided on a car to steal, has relatively little time in which to do it so as not to call attention to himself. The experienced car thief is aware of the different modes of entry and allocates his time effectively to the fastest method of breaking in. The less experienced thief has to fumble around and hence is more likely to be caught. Experience enables the car thief to budget his time more effectively so as to make a clean getaway.

Be flexible and willing to change your plans. Even the best-laid plans can go astray, so it is important to maintain flexibility in implementing them. If a given strategy or allocation of resources begins to fail, you should be ready to change to another plan or set other priorities.

Some years ago, I decided that I really ought to learn the LISP programming language for computers, which is commonly used in writing computer programs that simulate human performance. I set aside the time to take a course in LISP. After several sessions, it became clear that the course was an utter waste of time: the teaching was terrible, and I wasn't learning a thing. I realized that although I had planned to allocate a substantial block of time to learning the language that semester, that time would be wasted if I continued with the course. I dropped it and used the time to better advantage.

Flexibility can be essential when people enter the real-estate market. Consider its relevance for acquiring a down payment on a house. When Harry and Jean moved to California, they had allocated a substantial amount of money for the down payment on a house. On arriving in the Bay Area, they discovered that the cost of housing exceeded even their worst expectations: there was no way they could afford a house on the money they had budgeted. They would have to either extend themselves well beyond their means or else rent for a few years until they saved enough to make a down payment on a house they liked. They decided to rent.

Be on the lookout for new kinds of resources. People often come to take for granted the resources that are available for accomplishing a given task; they fail to consider the possibility that new resources will improve their performance. But we should always be on the lookout for new ways of getting things done.

For many years, I did my writing directly on a typewriter. I would write each page and revise it as many times as needed until I got the page just the way I wanted it. The result was a fairly polished "first" draft but also a lot of wasted paper. When personal computers entered the scene, I was reluctant to switch over from my typewriter. I had become so used to a particular writing routine that I could not imagine any other style would suit me better. After repeated urgings from my colleagues, I eventually decided to try writing with a word-processing program on a microcomputer. To my surprise, I found that the speed with which I could write increased at least twofold. I could make all of the changes I needed directly on a given page without starting the whole page over.

Being on the lookout is crucial in shopping for a car. Biff tried out various models and talked to a number of salespeople but realized that he really knew next to nothing about the quality of the different cars. He was about to base his judgment on the most convincing sales pitch. Then a friend mentioned that *Consumer Reports* evaluated the quality of cars feature by feature. Biff was able to make a more informed decision on the basis of this additional resource.

There are many exercises you could do to develop your skills in resource allocation, but the best exercises are the ones that pertain to your own life. Think, for example of the major categories of activities that you do daily: working, eating, sleeping, playing, relaxing, and so on. Estimate the number of hours you spend on each one during a typical week, then calculate the percentage of your total time each of them consumes. If you relate better to graphs than to numbers, try a pie (circle) graph representing your allocation of time among these various activities. Now write down percentages of time or draw a pie graph representing the way in which you ideally would like to allocate your time among these activities. Consider how you might be able to change your life for the better so that your actual distribution of time corresponds more closely to your ideal distribution of time.

Now try the same exercise with your individual or family take-home income. Consider how you might be allocating your priorities in spending to make your actual allocation of resources better correspond to your ideal.

Monitoring the Solution to the Problem

When you are solving a problem, it is important to keep track of where you are and of how things are going. Monitoring the solution presupposes that some of the initial decisions you make may be wrong, but not irrevocable. You should generally view your initial decisions as tentative and be prepared to change them if the need arises. It is one thing to make an incorrect decision at the start of problem solving; this happens frequently, and there is nothing wrong with it. It is another thing to persist in a wrong decision, either because you are unaware of the error or because you're unwilling to rectify it.

Monitoring solutions is crucial in government. When the United States first became involved in the war in South Vietnam, many Americans thought that the decision was a proper one; sooner or later, however, most people concluded that military involvement was a mistake. The United States was not winning the war, which had ground down to a grueling stalemate with massive casualties on both sides, and nothing much seemed to be happening in terms of either military accomplishment or political change. Yet the United States remained in Vietnam long after the mistake became obvious. The factors that impelled continued involvement included national pride and desire to meet a commitment to another government. But whatever the reasons for staying, the reasons for leaving far outweighed them. In this case, monitoring of the solution to the problem of perceived Communist involvement in South Vietnam simply broke down.

Solution monitoring applies as much to individuals as it does to government. Carl went to an interview for a job that he really wanted. He was nervous, and at first he said little. However, in monitoring the interviewer's response to his silence, Carl became convinced that his silence was being perceived as lack of interest, even dullness, and he made an effort to speak more. Once he got started, he was able to carry on a reasonable conversation. Although ultimately he did not get the job, he realized that in future interviews he would have to get started on a surer footing. He got the next job for which he interviewed.

This last example points to a particularly important aspect of monitoring behavior in our everyday lives. During our interactions with others, we are almost continually receiving feedback, which is sometimes subtle, about the kind of impression we are making. Some of this feedback may be verbal; the rest is nonverbal. An astute conversationalist will monitor the feedback and act upon it so as to increase the probability of obtaining the goals set out for that conversation, whatever they may be.

In my own work, I frequently have to give presentations to diverse audiences. Before giving any talk, I ask my sponsors about the composition of the audience: the number of people expected, their background, their interests, their reasons for coming to hear me speak. I then attempt to tailor my presentation to meet the needs and background of the audience. Occasionally I misjudge, but I try to recognize my misjudgments during the talk rather than after it. When I become aware that a talk is not going over, I try to change it to suit the audience as much as possible. Obviously, once you start giving a talk, you lose flexibility in making it the best talk for a given audience, but it is often possible to make some changes that will make at least a moderate success out of what otherwise would have been a failure. Thus, I see my job as a speaker as partially one of monitoring audience reaction.

The same monitoring applies in teaching: a talented teacher tries to stay aware of whether her students are understanding the material presented and are interested in it. If understanding or interest are waning, she should attempt to figure out why and correct her presentation. The kinds of things I look for are teacher-class eye contact, the absence of obviously irrelevant side conversations, questions that show mental engagement with the material, and interested facial expressions.

The need for monitoring is also evident in psychological research. One striking example has been shown in children's reading of text. Ellen Markman presented children with reading passages in which material later in the passage contradicted material earlier on.[17] To her astonishment, and the astonishment of many of those who have read her articles, the children often failed to notice these contradictions. Apparently, their monitoring of their reading comprehension was inadequate, with the result that they were unable to see the contradictions. Even more unbelievable is the finding that adults display the same failure in comprehension monitoring.[18]

It's clear that the decision-making process in problem solving does not end once the initial decision of how to solve the problem has been made. Rather, the process must continue throughout the solution and not terminate until you are wholly satisfied with the result.

There are several steps you can take to improve your monitoring in problem solving. Here are some of them.

Be aware of the need for solution monitoring and act upon this need. The most important step you can take is simply to be aware of the need to monitor your solution strategies, and then to act upon this awareness.

For example, Traci sought psychotherapy for depression. After three months she felt no improvement at all. The therapist assured her that this was normal and that it might be another three months or more before she felt any improvement. In monitoring her subsequent progress, however, Traci concluded that there just wasn't any. She switched to another therapist and within a few weeks was starting to feel better.

Monitoring is a must in dealing with book and record clubs, but people often fail to do it. In fact, many of these clubs make their profits by betting on people's failure to monitor. You may have wondered how the clubs can afford their attractive initial offers. One of the things they count on is that once people are enrolled they won't bother to quit, even if they are dissatisfied with the products or the service that they are receiving. Many clubs automatically send a book or record every month unless the members instruct otherwise. The strategy here is that most people simply will not bother to return the postcard to say no. And though the clubs often offer refunds on returned items, they bank on the fact that wrapping up a book or a record and mailing it back is enough of an inconvenience to prevent many people from bothering to do it. In other words, the companies count on a failure in the monitoring process to bring them profits.

Beware of "justification of effort."   Social psychologists studying human behavior have found that justification of effort is a powerful force in human thought and action. Once an individual has invested a substantial amount of time or other resources in a given course of action, he seeks reasons to justify this investment. The greater the investment, the harder it is to write it off.

Jeanne, for example, invested in a glamorous stock that her broker assured her was a good investment. She did a great deal of research on the stock and concluded that her broker was right. At first the investment paid off well, but after a while the company began to slide. Jeanne was unwilling to sell the stock, because to do so would be admitting that she had made a mistake. Her need to justify herself resulted in a substantial financial loss.

Justification of effort is frequently applied in interpersonal relationships: Alice and Rick had been involved for five years; they were living together and had anticipated getting married. Things were not going well, however, and Alice was seriously considering leaving the relationship. She decided not to, because she couldn't stand the thought that all the effort she had put into the relationship would go for naught. The outcome was unhappy: the couple got married, but the marriage survived less than a year. Alice's justification of effort proved to be an enormous mistake.

A few years ago, a graduate student and I did a study on reading that yielded excellent results. Before publishing the study, we decided that we ought to make sure that we could replicate the findings. We did a second study, and the results were equivocal: it just was not clear whether it did or did not support the first. We then did a third study that clearly failed to replicate either the first or the second study. Finally we did a fourth study, and the results came out differently again. Clearly, there was something going on that we did not understand. We had invested a considerable amount of effort in the research, but it had become evident that there was no point to continuing until we better understood what was going on. Attempting to justify our efforts probably would have resulted in more studies with ambiguous results that would have told us very little about the reading processes we wished to study.

Avoid impulsiveness in solution monitoring.   It is good to be on the alert for errors in strategies or decisions and to backtrack as necessary. But it's important to realize that solution monitoring is just like problem solving: it is susceptible to error. Before changing strategy, be careful to make sure that it is indeed the original problem-solving strategy and not the solution monitoring that is in error.

An interesting finding in the literature on testing pertains to students' behavior on multiple-choice examinations. After choosing one response, the student later decides it is in error, erases the original response, and chooses another. Studies of this behavior have shown that when a first answer is erased and a new one put in its place, the first answer is often right and the new answer wrong. In other words, it is at least as likely that the solution monitoring was in error as that the original problem solving was in error. Impulsive behavior can actually result in a wrong answer.

The increasing use of word processors has made control of certain kinds of impulses a must. After writing several pages on his word processor, Will became disgusted and impulsively deleted the entire file. He soon realized that a few minor changes might have effected an enormous improvement. But his word-processing program did not have a backup for deleted files; he lost all of the writing he had done and had to start over.

Be open to but evaluative of external feedback. We often receive external feedback (comments or criticisms) on our problem solving, from a variety of sources. This external feedback can be helpful in monitoring our problem solving, for others may pick up errors that we miss. It is important, however, to evaluate external feedback just as carefully as you evaluate your own internal feedback. You need to consider the probable reliability of the source and the usefulness of the feedback. All of us have received feedback from someone who knows less about the problem than we do. Such feedback is not necessarily worthless, but its source needs to be considered. It is most important, however, to avoid defensiveness in receiving feedback. Remember, no one should expect you to be perfect; you can't expect it from yourself. Try to take the attitude that you can learn from your mistakes. The smart person is not the one who never makes mistakes; rather, it is the one who does not repeat the same mistakes. Defensiveness almost inevitably works against high-quality problem solving. First, it blinds you to the problems in your problem solving. Second, it discourages others from offering feedback. If others realize that you only act defensively, they may be reluctant to comment on your performance.

I had a student who was really quite capable but was simply unwilling to accept criticism. Whenever her work was criticized, she immediately jumped to the conclusion that the critic had an ulterior motive or simply didn't understand. At first I tried to be helpful in giving her feedback, but eventually I just gave up. The result was that she was much less successful in her career than she might have been had she been willing to learn from her mistakes.

Openness to constructive external feedback is a must in making a go of a marriage. Tim and Sandy had a good marriage, but it certainly was not perfect. Sandy tried to discuss their problems with Tim, but he was unable to take criticism. He seemed to feel that he could do no wrong; and whenever Sandy criticized him, no matter how constructively, he reacted defensively. Eventually, Sandy gave up and started an affair with a man who was much more open and willing to accept criticism. Although Sandy did not leave the marriage, she was less than ideally happy with it, and it was never as good as it could be because of Tim's unwillingness to accept criticism.

Actively seek external feedback. Don't just wait for it to happen. People are often reluctant to criticize others; as a result, you may never find out what other people think of your efforts.

In this chapter, I have discussed the importance of executive processes in mental self-management. But executive processes are not enough to solve problems. It is one thing to plan what you are going to do, to monitor it while you are doing it, and to evaluate it after it is done; it is another thing actually to solve the problem itself. Higher-order executive processes issue instructions that can be executed only by lower-order performance processes. The next chapter considers the role of performance processes in problem solving.

6

Performance Components: The "Blue Collar" Processes of Mental Self-management

In problem solving, one might view metacomponents as the executives and performance components as the workers taking their instructions. Problem solving requires both metacomponents and performance components for successful completion; the two must work together in mental self-management.

An Overview

This chapter concentrates on the performance components of inductive reasoning, the kind of reasoning we most often use in our lives. Inductive reasoning requires us to infer a general principle from specific information. Consider a concrete use of performance components in inductive reasoning—solving analogies. The ability to solve analogies is measured in one form or another on almost every intelligence test. I have tried to discover the processes underlying reasoning by analogy and to figure out why the ability to solve analogies is such a good indicator of general intelligence. I've included a number of exercises that will give you the opportunity to use what you have learned. The exercises generally follow the model for intellectual-skills instruction I present in my course Intelligence Applied, although the problems themselves are generally not the same ones that appear in that course.

Let's look at how performance components work on a typical analogy:

WASHINGTON is to ONE as LINCOLN is to: (a. FIVE, b. TEN, c. FIFTEEN, d. FIFTY).

To begin with, a person must *encode*, or think about, the various terms of the analogy, identifying each and retrieving from long-term memory the attributes that may be relevant to a solution. Examples of possible encodings for WASHINGTON are: he was a President of the United States; he is portrayed on a piece of currency; he was a Revolutionary War hero. Some people fail to solve the analogy simply because they neglect (or are unable) to encode the proper attributes. For example, those who do not encode either Washington or Lincoln as having his portrait on currency will be unable to solve the analogy.

Next, a person *infers* a relationship between the attributes of the first two terms of the analogy, WASHINGTON and ONE. Here, we may infer that Washington was the first President or that he is portrayed on a one-dollar bill. Failure to infer that ONE can refer to the portrait of Washington on a one-dollar bill is a common error.

Now a person *maps*, or connects, the higher-order relationship that links the first half of the analogy, headed by WASHINGTON, to the second half, headed by LINCOLN. Both halves deal with relationships originating with Presidents of the United States, portraits on currency, and war heroes. Failing to connect WASHINGTON with LINCOLN as portraits on currency leads to failure in analogy solution.

Then a person *applies* the relationship inferred between the first two terms (WASHINGTON and ONE) from the third analogy term, LINCOLN, to each of the possible answers. Whereas Washington is portrayed on a one-dollar bill, Lincoln is portrayed on a five-dollar bill. We may not recognize this relationship, however, either because of a failure in application or because of a failure in an earlier component. For example, we may mistakenly recall Lincoln on a twenty-dollar bill. In that event, an additional, optional component is needed—what we may call justification. A person attempts to *justify* one answer option as preferable to the others, even if it is not ideal. The person checks previous components for errors, and if none is found, selects one option that seems to be the most likely answer. After failing to encode WASHINGTON and LINCOLN as portraits on currency, for example, we may try to solve the analogy on the basis of the ordinal positions of the presidencies. We may recall that Lincoln was the sixteenth President, but if we are not entirely sure, we may well choose FIFTEEN as the preferred response, figuring that there is something slightly amiss with our memory (or with that of the test maker!).

Finally, a person *responds* with the answer that seems best to complete the analogy.

A Detailed Analysis of Three Performance Components

The number of performance components used in problem solving is quite large. Which performance components are used in solving a problem depends largely on the kind of problem one is confronting and the content of that particular problem. It would be impossible and unnecessary to list and describe all of the possible performance components here. Instead, I shall concentrate upon three—inference, mapping, and application, described briefly earlier—that research has shown to be particularly important in mental self-management. As you will see, these components are used in a large variety of everyday situations.

INFERENCE

If you were to select one performance component as most important of all, it would be inference—the discovery of one or more relationships between objects or events. For example, when you hear that a friend is in the hospital, you are likely to infer that the friend is either ill or injured. It may be that nothing in what you have heard directly confirms this: it is possible, for example, that the friend is merely visiting someone in the hospital or has taken a job there. But unless you have evidence to the contrary, you are likely to infer that there is a problem and to become concerned.

Inferences can be of many different kinds. Moreover, there are many different classification schemes for analyzing them. The scheme described here is one that I have used for classifying the kinds of inferences between pairs of words used on the Miller Analogies Test. Remember that this scheme applies to inferences between pairs of words; other schemes would be needed for inferences between pairs of pictures or between various kinds of events. (Some of these are discussed later in the book.)

Similarity. These relationships are between synonyms or words that are nearly the same in meaning, such as SILLY : FOOLISH.

Contrast. These relationships are between antonyms or words that are nearly the opposite in meaning, such as STRONG : WEAK.

Predication. These terms are related by a verb or verb relationship: A is caused by B; A makes B; A rides on B; A eats B; A is a source of B; A induces B; A studies B; A is made of B; A uses B. An example of a predication relationship is TRAIN : TRACKS. A TRAIN rides on TRACKS. Another example is HORSE : NEIGHS; a HORSE performs the action of NEIGHING.

Subordination. These relationships are those in which object A is a type of B, such as DEER : MAMMAL.

Coordination. The two terms are a single type of thing—that is, they are members of the same category, such as OATS : WHEAT.

Superordination. These relationships are those in which A is a category in which B falls, such as INSECT : MOSQUITO.

Completion. In this case, each term is part of a complete expression, such as DES : MOINES.

Part-whole. These relationships are ones in which A is a part of B, such as INCH : YARD.

Whole-part. These relationships are ones in which B is a part of A, such as CHAIN : LINK.

Equality. These relationships involve mathematical or logical equivalence. An example is ONE TWENTIETH : FIVE PERCENT.

Negation. These relationships involve logical or mathematical negations, such as TRUE : UNTRUE.

Word relationships. These inferences involve grammatical relationships between words, such as ARE : WERE. In this case, WERE is the past tense of ARE.

Nonsemantic. In these relationships, words are related to each other in a way that capitalizes on their nonsemantic properties. An example of such a relationship is HEEL : FEEL. In this case, the words happen to rhyme. Another kind of nonsemantic relationship capitalizes on the letters in the word, for example, LIAR : RAIL. In this case, LIAR is RAIL spelled backward.

Although these relationships may seem quite straightforward and obvious, their importance arises not only in recognizing kinds of inferences but in solving more complex kinds of problems that require inferences as part of their solutions—for example, analogies. An obscure analogy may become easier once you recognize the inferential relation on which it is based.

Below is a list of fifteen pairs of words. For each pair of words think of how the two words are related to each other and then classify the pair of words in terms of the thirteen categories of relations just presented. This exercise will accustom you to thinking in terms of the various kinds of inferences. The answer key appears in the Appendix.

WORD PAIR	RELATIONSHIP	CLASSIFICATION
1. SLEEVE : SHIRT	_____	_____
2. BLUE : THREW	_____	_____
3. PENCIL : WRITE	_____	_____
4. PLIERS : WRENCH	_____	_____
5. NATURAL NUMBER : COUNTING NUMBER	_____	_____
6. GIGANTIC : ENORMOUS	_____	_____
7. DRAWER : REWARD	_____	_____
8. SMOOTH : ROUGH	_____	_____
9. ORCHARD : TREE	_____	_____
10. PRIME : NONPRIME	_____	_____
11. WORSE : WORST	_____	_____
12. CHAIR : FURNITURE	_____	_____
13. FRENCH : HORN	_____	_____
14. VEHICLE : BUS	_____	_____
15. MAGICIAN : TRICKS	_____	_____

Inferential fallacies. Although people make inferences all the time, at least some of these inferences are generally incorrect, or at least not justified by the data at hand. For this reason, it is important to study not only kinds of inferences but the inferential fallacies people commit when their inference process goes astray. The best way to avoid committing these fallacies is to become aware of what they are, to see examples of them, and then to practice spotting examples of fallacious reasoning. Philosophers and semanticists as well as psychologists have attempted to classify and study the various kinds of fallacious inferences that people can make. The classification system described here is by no means the only one possible or even necessarily the best; but Susan Nolen-Hoeksema and I have found it useful in understanding the kinds of fallacies people commit in their everyday reasoning behavior. This list is based on the research and writings of both philosophers[1] and psychologists.[2]

Consider these inferential fallacies, and a couple of examples of each:

Representativeness. Sometimes we believe that the cause of some event must resemble that event. For example, a great event must have a great cause. When we decide that two or more things or events are related simply because they resemble each other, we have committed the fallacy of representativeness.

Walter was a top athlete but a very poor student. His mother always was asking him why he couldn't do better in school. "After all," she said, "Josh down the street is a very good athlete, and he's also a good student. If he can do it, you can do it."

Anne was never quite satisfied with her dentist, Dr. C. When he recommended an expensive gum procedure, she sought a second opinion from Dr. R., who had top credentials and an outstanding reputation. When he confirmed Dr. C.'s diagnosis, Anne thought, "Dr. R. is no help at all. He looks so much like Dr. C. he's probably a lousy dentist too." Anne assumes that the physical resemblance between the two dentists indicates a resemblance in their professional skills. She has no logical basis for making this assumption.

Irrelevant conclusion. The fallacy of irrelevant conclusion is committed when the conclusion that follows a line of reasoning is irrelevant to that line of reasoning.

Lou was caught leaving a department store with a flashlight he hadn't paid for. He was taken to the store manager, protesting all the way. She demanded an explanation. He replied, "I'm completely innocent. I just forgot to pay for it. I would have come back as soon as I noticed. Besides, it's not like I stole a gold watch or something."

Jack was born on Christmas Day. When his parents asked him why he wanted an expensive computer—which they couldn't afford—for Christmas, he replied, "I deserve a computer because my birthday is on Christmas, and a computer is a good double present." Jack has created a cause-effect relationship that exists only in his head. From his parents' standpoint, and most people's, his birthday on Christmas does not of itself merit a present they cannot afford, no matter how many other reasons there might be to get him one.

Division. The fallacy of division is committed when we assume that what is true of the whole is necessarily true of each individual part of the whole.

Barb and Carrie were discussing their basketball team. Barb remarked, "Kay has to be most valuable player." Carrie disagreed. "No way," she said. "Jane is nearly a foot taller."

Cal went to see his school guidance counselor, Mrs. Watson, about making plans for college. He hoped to get a scholarship or financial aid from a private university. On learning that Cal's father was a lawyer, Mrs. Watson said, "Forget about financial aid, Cal. Your family is much too well off to qualify." Mrs. Watson is assuming that because lawyers often make a lot of money, Cal's family therefore must be well off. But Cal's father may not have an especially high income, and the family may have many expenses, such as paying college tuition for several other children. In fact, Cal may qualify for financial aid.

Labeling. To attach some label to yourself or to others is a distorted thought process when the label is unjustified by the circumstances, or when the label is inappropriately utilized as a reason for behavior or lack of behavior.

Michelle was a loner. When Jay asked her to the junior prom, she turned him down, saying, "Only popular kids go to the prom."

When Harry retired, he started to think of himself as being old. When he forgot about a lunch date with a friend, he thought, "I must be getting senile." Harry has committed the fallacy of labeling because he is highly sensitive about his age. Of course, everyone forgets now and then. Unless he is abnormally forgetful, the term "senile" is hardly justified.

Hasty generalization. When committing the fallacy of hasty generalization, we consider only exceptional cases and quickly generalize to a rule that actually fits only those exceptional cases.

Bill worked at a bakery. He usually made eight blueberry pies per day. One day the bakery sold five blueberry pies by nine a.m. Bill said, "I'll make thirty blueberry pies today. At this rate we'll need at least that many."

Marilyn and Ken were in an expensive restaurant. "I'm having the shrimp," said Marilyn. "What about you?" "I never eat shrimp," answered Ken. "I tried them once at a cafeteria and they tasted horrible." Ken has rushed to the generalization that he hates shrimp just because he hated them the one time he tried them, at a cheap restaurant where they may have been of poor quality or badly prepared.

Skill, not chance. In situations in which an outcome is controlled entirely and always by chance, it is fallacious to assume that any skill on the part of an agent is involved in the outcome.

Barry bought a lottery ticket at Bargain Drug and won a thousand dollars. The next week Clarence won five hundred dollars on a lottery ticket bought at Bargain Drug. The next week Sam bought his lottery ticket at Bargain Drug instead of at his usual spot, concluding that he would improve his chances that way. Sam's chances are equal, of course, no matter where he buys his ticket.

On the day before Sheila took a transcontinental flight to France, a flight from Canada to France crashed. Her mother asked if she was worried about her flight. "No, Mom, just the opposite," Sheila explained. "Who ever heard of two plane crashes happening right in a row?"

Personalization. If you see yourself as the cause of some event for which you were not primarily responsible, you have committed a distorted personalization. Taking personally a statement that is not directed toward you is also an inappropriate personalization.

Ingrid sent her ten-year-old son to the corner store to buy bread and milk. He returned without the food, tired and dirty, having run away from the neighborhood bully. "It's all my fault," apologized Ingrid. "I never should have sent you out alone."

Ned read a newspaper article that suggested that adopted children had a higher rate of juvenile delinquency than the general population. "Oh no," thought Ned, who was adopted. "Now nobody will trust me." Ned is taking the information too personally. He assumes that even people who already know him would change their opinion of him based merely on a newspaper article that makes a broad generalization.

Appeal to authority. The pattern of the appeal-to-authority fallacy is to argue that a claim is true because authority X supports it. An argument that appeals to authority is a fallacy whenever that authority is not suitable to give evidence.

"Star Trek" was Eugene's favorite TV show. He was especially impressed by Mr. Spock, the relentlessly logical, brilliant science officer played by Leonard Nimoy. Years later, Nimoy narrated a TV series called "In Search Of . . . ," which presented unexplained scientific phenomena.

Eugene was watching "In Search Of . . . " with his girlfriend, who commented that the theories proposed were highly speculative. "Nonsense," replied Eugene, "he would never say them unless they were perfectly logical."

Chris was being interviewed at the seminary he wished to attend the next year. The interviewer asked Chris why he thought he would make a good minister. Chris replied, "Well, my father is a doctor, but he always wanted to be a minister. He's always told me I'd make a good minister, and I respect his opinion in this matter."

Magnification/minimization. People sometimes magnify or minimize their negative or positive characteristics. In such cases, the people are illogically evaluating their role in a situation.

Newtown College could not afford to hire another professor to teach botany, so it asked Professor Hires, whose expertise was in zoology, to teach the botany course. Professor Hires said, "Well, since I'm one of the world's greatest experts in zoology, surely I will teach the botany course just as well as I teach zoology, which is just about perfectly." Whether or not Professor Hires is exaggerating his expertise in zoology, he's almost certainly exaggerating his ability to teach the botany course.

Pam signed up to be a Big Sister, which entails being friend and role model to an underprivileged child. She encouraged her friend Doug to become a Big Brother. "Why should I?" answered Doug. "I don't get good grades like you, I'm not very popular, and I'm not even any good in sports. What could I possibly have to offer?"

Composition. A fallacy of composition is committed when you reason that what is true of parts of a whole is necessarily true of the whole itself.

When Groveton started a professional orchestra, the new conductor was interviewed on the radio. "I personally auditioned each member of the orchestra," he said, "and these musicians rank with the nation's best. Groveton should soon possess one of the best symphony orchestras in the United States." The conductor is assuming that the quality of each musician will carry over to the orchestra as a whole. There is no guarantee, however, that the members will work well together. Even if the conductor is also top-notch, the musicians may be unmotivated or uncooperative.

Jimmy asked his babysitter to make him a sandwich. The babysitter asked him if he'd rather have peanut butter or salami. Jimmy answered, "I like them both, so make me a peanut-butter-and-salami sandwich. That will be best of all."

"Should" statements. "I must do this," "I should feel that," and "They should do this" are examples of "should" statements. Such statements are irrational when they are used as the sole reason for behavior.

Jason sat his teenage son down for a talk. "Everyone in our family has gone to college," Jason told him. "You must carry on the family tradition." Children often gain unrealistic expectations for themselves simply because of their parents' unrealistic expectations.

Joan didn't usually bring work home, but one evening she did, remembering that her husband had a class that evening. When his class was cancelled, he suggested that they go to a concert together instead. "I can't," she said. "I brought a whole briefcase full of work home, so I really should do it."

False cause. An event occurs and a cause for it is sought. If the mere fact of coincidence or temporal succession is used to identify the cause, the fallacy of false cause has been committed.

Julie invited Ross to a party, but then she couldn't go. She encouraged Ross to go anyway. Ross arrived at the same time as a group of guests who were greeted enthusiastically by the host. The host took their coats but didn't offer to take Ross's. Ross thought, "The host resents that I'm crashing his party, so he's not taking my coat in hopes that I'll leave soon." Ross is assuming that the host intended to slight him. It is possible, of course, that he is correct; then again, the host simply may have been distracted.

Donna and Lynn were top students in high school. Lynn, who was black, was accepted by Princeton, whereas Donna, who was white, was rejected. Donna griped to her parents, "I'm sure Lynn got in because of Affirmative Action, and that Princeton didn't accept me because they hardly ever take two students from the same school."

Invalid disjunction. If you consider only two solutions to a question or situation when there are actually more than two possible solutions, and if you believe that these are the only solutions that could possibly be relevant, you have committed the fallacy of invalid disjunction.

Miriam, one of Ron's co-workers, asked him where his family was from. "Morocco," he answered. When they ran into each other a few weeks later at a synagogue, Miriam exclaimed, "Ron! What are you doing here? I thought you said you were Moroccan!" She assumed that you can be either Moroccan or Jewish but not both. (In fact, until recently Morocco had a substantial Jewish population.)

Penny was updating her address book. She got stuck when she was about to write in her friend Juanita Perez. "I always think of Juanita as

Juanita, but all my listings are by last name. I know that if I put her under J I'll look for her under P, but if I put her under P I'll look for her under J."

Availability. We commit the fallacy of availability by accepting an explanation that comes quickly to mind without considering other, less obvious or less readily available, explanations.

Ray owned a bookstore in which he employed fifteen people. He had discovered that in the past month several dozen mystery novels had been stolen. One day he noticed two mystery novels sitting in the back room next to Patty's purse. "Patty!" he shouted. "You stole all those mysteries!" In fact, someone else may have left the books there, or Patty might have set them aside in order to buy them later. Ray has no real evidence of Patty's guilt but jumps to an unwarranted conclusion simply because of circumstantial evidence: Patty happens to be readily available to Ray's field of observation and hence tops his list of suspects.

As Norma and Nick took their seat at a teen movie, they noticed a woman in her fifties enter alone and take a seat further down the row. During the movie, Norma saw an usher scolding a noisy youngster who was sitting next to the older woman. Norma whispered to Nick, "That lady must have complained about the kid to the usher."

Argumentum ad populum. The reasoning behind argumentum ad populum is "If everyone else thinks this way, it must be right."

Frank and Glen were picking out a paper at a newsstand. "Let's get this one," said Frank, pointing to a tabloid with an enormous headline. "Why not this one?" said Glen, indicating a more traditional-looking paper. "No, that paper's no good," answered Frank. "Only half as many people read it." A newspaper that has a larger circulation is by no means guaranteed to be the better paper.

Peg asked Jackie why she wanted so much to go out with Cliff. Jackie said, "I want to go out with him because he's the most popular guy in school. If everyone likes him so much, I bet he'd be a fantastic boyfriend."

Argument from ignorance. This fallacy is committed whenever it is argued that something is true simply because it has not been proven false, or that it is false simply because it has not been proven true.

Ralph and Nate were discussing religion. Ralph said, "I am an atheist because no one has ever scientifically proved the existence of God." He concludes that God does not exist because God's existence has never been proven by science. But science has often failed to prove things for lack of the proper approach or instrumentation. Furthermore, it is not clear that science is capable of proving (or disproving) the existence of God.

Les and Audrey saw on the news an account of a murder trial in which the defendant had been found not guilty. Les remarked, "I was sure that he was the murderer, but I was wrong. If they couldn't convict him, he must be innocent."

Mental filter.   A person using a mental filter picks out one small aspect of a situation, often a negative aspect, and focuses on that aspect to such an extent that the larger picture is distorted. It is as though all incoming events were perceived through the filter of that small aspect.

Mary was showing Kathleen her new apartment. "Look at this," Mary said, pointing to a reproduction of a van Gogh on the wall. "I just bought it today. Like it?" "Not much," said Kathleen. "It's the stars—as an astronomer, I know that van Gogh's stars are inaccurately painted, so I just can't enjoy the painting." Kathleen's technical knowledge has prevented her from appreciating the artistry of van Gogh.

Stan invited Clara to see a spy movie, saying that *Playboy* had recommended it highly. Clara said, "I hate *Playboy* because of their attitude toward women. I'm sure I wouldn't want to see a movie that any of their reviewers liked."

Emotional reasoning.   This occurs when an individual uses his emotions as tangible evidence of a truth. "This is true because I feel it is true" is the paradigm of emotional reasoning.

Sue had just broken up with George, and George was crushed. Tom, George's best friend, suggested that George go to a singles brunch at their church. "Why should I go?" George asked. "I'll never meet anyone like Sue, and I'll just be miserable." Feeling sorry for himself, he concludes that the brunch isn't worthwhile. He can't know whether or not he'll meet anyone interesting there.

Angela stayed up most of the night writing a history paper due the next day. The next evening, exhausted, she went to a performance by a popular comedian. The comedian poked fun at people who wait until the last minute to do things. Everyone but Angela laughed. Later, she met a friend who asked her how she liked the show. "What an awful comedian!" Angela answered. "He was so dull I could hardly keep my eyes open."

Argumentum ad hominem.   In this type of fallacious reasoning, aspects of a person's character, lifestyle, race, religion, sex, etc., are submitted as evidence for a conclusion, even when these circumstances are irrelevant to the situation being examined. The argument is against the person rather than against the person's position on a matter.

Dr. Conway was furious when the IRS audited his accounts and found a minor error, which cost him thirty dollars. "I'm sure that petty auditor who found the mistake was really out to get me because I make five times as much money as he does," he thought to himself. Dr. Conway concludes that the auditor must have been motivated by envy; in fact, he has no way of knowing what the auditor was thinking.

Jan went to a computer store to buy a computer for her business. She saw two salespeople: a slim young man with thick glasses and a fashionably dressed young woman without glasses. Jan directed her questions to the salesman, thinking, "Boy, he looks like a brain. I bet he really knows about computers."

It is important to note that these nineteen types do not form an exhaustive list of the possible fallacies one could commit in reasoning; nor do they constitute a mutually exclusive list. A given example of fallacious reasoning can often involve more than one kind of fallacy. The important thing is to be aware of the kinds of fallacies people can commit, both in formulating your own reasoning and in evaluating the reasoning of others. If you are more aware of the kinds of fallacies people can commit, you'll be less likely to commit them yourself and more likely to spot them in the reasoning of others.

Practice in detecting fallacies. Below are twenty vignettes presenting examples of everyday reasoning. Some of them involve fallacies; others do not. For each vignette, first determine whether the everyday reasoning is valid or invalid; then, if it is invalid, try to characterize the nature of the fallacy. Remember that there is often no unique characterization of a fallacy; hence, there may be more than one correct answer. The answers appear in the Appendix.

1. Stella was hesitant to go water skiing with her husband and his friends, but she agreed to go anyway. The first time she tried, she remained standing only a second or two. When she climbed back into the boat, she said to her husband, "Let's go home. I'm no good at this."

2. Andrew had been in the nursing home two years. While he was napping, a nurse started to tidy up his personal things on the night table. Andrew awoke and snapped, "Please don't touch those without asking! You should have more respect for my privacy."

3. Jill and Alison were talking in the hall after auditioning for the second-grade play, *Alice in Wonderland*. Jill said, "I think Mrs.

Howard will pick me to be Alice." "No, she'll pick me instead," Alison replied. "I have long blond hair like in the book—and besides, everyone already calls me Alison Wonderland."

4. Joanne entered a local baking contest. She selected a well-tested family recipe and bought the finest ingredients. Yet the cake was burned on top and mushy inside. "Maybe the oven's on the blink," she said to her boyfriend.

5. Alan and Ed were discussing cars and agreed that Rolls-Royce produced the best. Ed said, "The reason Rolls-Royces have to be better than the rest is that each piece is individually inspected."

6. John, Gino, and Charlie planned to spend Sunday at the beach. But it rained on Sunday, so they canceled their plans. "I thought it would rain," Gino said. "Whenever I plan something on my day off, it rains."

7. Karen couldn't forgive herself after her roommate, May, attempted suicide. "It was all my fault," Karen told her friends. "Just this morning May said she wanted to talk to me, and I said I didn't have time until after classes. By then it was too late."

8. Adam had a hernia operation and had been out of the hospital for three days. Overnight a foot of snow fell, and Melanie shoveled the driveway in the morning. Adam fumed, "You should have let me do it, Melanie. I'm perfectly fine—there's no reason for you to treat me like an invalid."

9. The first time Hal drove to Appleton, traffic was backed up on route 31 because of an accident. The next time, traffic was greatly slowed on route 31 due to construction. From then on, Hal always took the back roads to Appleton, saying, "I never take route 31 anymore. It's always so slow."

10. Ian was an antiques dealer who displayed a large variety of merchandise at shows. He had things of all prices and sizes, all of which sold at about the same rate. After eight years in the business, he said to himself, "From now on I'm going to stock mainly the smaller, more expensive items. I make more money on them, they're easier to transport, and I can show more items at a time."

11. Doreen worked for four years as a lab technician, then for five years as a dental hygienist. After she quit that job, she applied for a position as a medical technologist. She was confident of getting the job, thinking, "I got my other two jobs on my first try. I should get this one on the first try too."

12. Paul had recently gotten into the habit of jogging every day in the late afternoon. Sally invited him to go to a lecture on space travel, a subject that interested him. "I'd like to go," he told her, "but I really should go jogging."

13. Gerry went shopping for summer clothes in October to take advantage of an end-of-season clearance sale. He found two pairs of shorts that fit, one green and one tan. He needed only one pair, so he bought the green ones, thinking, "Both the tan and the green match three of my T-shirts, but the green shorts also match my winter jacket."

14. Daphne was babysitting at the Millers'. After she put the kids to bed, she went to the kitchen, hoping to make herself a salami sandwich. Although the refrigerator was nearly full, she found no salami, nor did she see meat of any kind. Looking in the well-stocked cabinets, she saw plenty of grains and canned goods, but not even the soups contained meat. "The Millers must be vegetarians," she concluded.

15. Don played golf for the first time when his friend Dave, a better-than-average amateur, dragged him along. It was immediately clear that Don had a real talent for the game, and in a few months he was among the best local golfers. "You should try to go pro," Dave told him. "Come off it, Dave!" Don said. "Who ever heard of a pro golfer who first played at age forty-five?"

16. Theresa played bingo every Thursday night. She hadn't won in months. On the last game of the evening, she needed only B-9 to win. "I'm bound to win," she thought. "I haven't won in ages, and besides, B-9 hasn't been called all night. It's about time."

17. Tina's car kept stalling, so she took it in to a nearby garage. Three days later she phoned, and the mechanic hadn't even started working on it. A week later the job still wasn't done. She stopped in and spoke with the mechanic. "Sorry about the delay," he told her, "but what do you want—a quick job or a good job?"

18. Sylvia looked forward to introducing her friend and law partner, Shari, to Maureen, an old friend from back home. When the three of them met for lunch, Shari and Maureen quickly got into a heated argument that lasted through the entire meal. Sylvia was crushed. She thought, "Now Shari and Maureen will both think that I have no taste in friends."

19. On Wendy's first day of work at the bank, she ate lunch with Jack, another teller. She mentioned to him that she had studied English in college. "I'd better watch my grammar," said Jack.

"I did awful in English in high school, and I'm sure you'll be taking note of my every mistake."

20. Kevin, a meteorologist, had had a terribly hard day at the weather station. When he got home, his wife greeted him and said, "Larry and Amanda just phoned. They invited us to come along to Hurricane Jim's Steakhouse for dinner." "Ugh," replied Kevin, "how could I possibly enjoy eating at a restaurant with a name like that?"

MAPPING

Mapping, another inductive process, is the recognition of a relationship between two relationships. Thus, it is related to, but nevertheless different from, inference, which is the recognition of a relationship between two terms or single items. For example, recognizing the relationship between YELLOW and LEMON requires an inference. Recognizing the relationship between YELLOW and LEMON on the one hand and GREEN and LIME on the other hand—that both are about colors of fruits—requires mapping.

Let's consider two examples of mapping.

When the United States sent troops to Lebanon a few years ago, many Americans related the event to the commission of troops to Vietnam. To the extent that the higher-order relationship between the two interventions held, the implication was that the intervention in Lebanon would be a failure. In fact, it did not prove to be very successful, and the United States withdrew its troops from Lebanon with much the same malaise as accompanied the withdrawal of troops from Vietnam.

Jim and Jan were in trouble in their relationship—at least, that was Jim's interpretation of what was happening. Several years before, his former girlfriend had left him. Right before she left the relationship, she had indicated a desire to date other men, "just to see what it's like." Now Jan had indicated the same desire. Jim found that although there were many differences between the two relationships, the analogy between the two was inescapable. Unfortunately, Jim did not give sufficient credence to the differences between the two relationships. Unlike Diane, Jan was not planning to leave the relationship, but Jim's anxiety created a self-fulfilling prophecy, and eventually Jim and Jan split up.

Psychological research has shown that, on the average, performing inferences is easier than performing mappings, and that the ability to perform inferences develops earlier in children than does the ability to perform mappings. For example, Bathsheva Rifkin and I, in a study we published in 1979, showed that whereas children solving analogies can perform inferences as early as the second grade, or at roughly seven years of age (which was the lowest age level used), children cannot map relations until, at earliest, roughly the fourth grade (or at nine years of age). In Jean Piaget's well-known theory of intelligence, the ability to map second-order relations is a hallmark of entrance into what Piaget calls the "formal-operational period," which begins at roughly eleven or twelve years of age. The ability to infer relations, however, begins much earlier.

Mapping is essential to the solution of most kinds of analogies. Indeed, one might argue that mapping forms the essence of an analogy, in that analogical reasoning and problem solving require one to see the relationship between two relationships. Consider a simple analogy, such as PLUM is to PRUNE as GRAPE is to RAISIN. The essence of the analogy is the recognition that plums are dried to make prunes, just as grapes are dried to make raisins.

Below are fifteen sets of pairs of terms. See if you can figure out the relationship between the first two terms and the second two terms. In the above example, the relationship is that the first item, PLUM or GRAPE, is used as a basis for producing the second item, PRUNE or RAISIN. Note that the first-order relations must be inferred before the second-order relations are mapped, and that the first-order relations can be classified according to the kinds of inferences described earlier in the chapter. Note also that the inferences and mappings required by verbal items can often require substantial knowledge as well as an ability to reason well. The answers appear in the Appendix.

First Relation	Second Relation	Relation Between Relations
1. ENGAGEMENT : PROBABLE	WEDDING : CERTAIN	_____
2. FRENCH : POODLE	GERMAN : SHEPHERD	_____
3. NOON : TWELVE	MIDNIGHT : TWELVE	_____
4. SHORTEST : MAY	LONGEST : SEPTEMBER	_____
5. COFFEE : MUG	WINE : GOBLET	_____
6. MOM : DAD	383 : 121	_____

7. SEAGULL : FLOCK	WOLF : PACK	_____
8. TURQUOISE : BLUE	SCARLET : RED	_____
9. WARTS : STRAW	LIVED: DEVIL	_____
10. SOCKS : PAIR	BEER : SIX-PACK	_____
11. FRESHMAN : YOUNGEST	SENIOR : OLDEST	_____
12. CABBAGE : COLE SLAW	POTATOES : FRENCH FRIES	_____
13. ASIA : CONTINENT	CHINA : COUNTRY	_____
14. TRIP : STRIP	LIME : SLIME	_____
15. DISCUS : THROW	GLOVE : WEAR	_____

APPLICATION

Yet another inductive process, application, involves applying a relation that has been previously inferred. For example, in the simple analogy PLUMBER is to PIPE as ELECTRICIAN is to _____, one has to infer the relationship between PLUMBER and PIPE, map it to the new domain headed by ELECTRICIAN, and then apply the relation so as to generate the best possible completion—namely, WIRE. Sometimes, instead of being asked to generate the correct response, a person will be asked to choose the correct response from among multiple answer options. So, for example, the sample analogy might have read PLUMBER is to PIPE as ELECTRICIAN is to (a. REPAIR, b. TOOL, c. WIRE, d. OUTLET).

Now let's consider some concrete examples of the inductive process of application.

Alex had taken three years of Latin in high school and slowly came to the conclusion that it had been a waste of time. He had not been able to find one instance in which his knowledge of Latin had been useful to him. Then, one day, he finally found a situation in which he was able to apply his knowledge. Reading a book, he came across the word "meliorate." He didn't know what the word meant, but he remembered that the word "melior" in Latin meant "better." He was able to apply his knowledge of Latin to figure out the meaning of the new word—correctly, as it turned out.

Real-world applications of one's knowledge can be difficult. Ben and Darlene were about to have a baby. In order to prepare for the big day, they took a course in the Lamaze method. When she went into labor,

Darlene found the method invaluable in controlling her pain. Although it had been easier to apply the principles in her class than it was during the actual birth, she had learned them well enough to apply them with only minimal difficulty.

PRACTICE PROBLEMS USING THE COMPONENTS OF INDUCTION: ANALOGIES

Analogies can be expressed in verbal or figural form. In the case of figural analogies, the problem solver's task is the same as in verbal analogies, except that the possible relations are different. Thus, the mental processes of encoding, inference, mapping, application, and justification need to be used, but they need to be used on a different kind of stimulus. Typically, geometric analogies involve additions, deletions, and transformations of geometric figures or portions of such figures, and the problem solver's task is to figure out what these additions, deletions, and transformations are.

Consider, for example, the sample figural analogies in figure 7. In each analogy, there are three terms in the stem (givens) and four answer options. Your task is to figure out which answer option best completes the analogy. Look at the first sample analogy. In the first term (1) of the analogy, there are two triangles, one inside the other. In the second term of the analogy, only the larger triangle appears. What was done to the first term in order to arrive at the second? You can probably *infer* that the relation between the first term and the second is one of deletion. The smaller triangle has been deleted from the first figure in order to create the second. One therefore needs to *map* this deletion relation to the second half of the analogy. In the third term, however, there are two large triangles, each with a smaller triangle inside. In order to *apply* the relation inferred in the first half of the analogy, what you must do is to delete each of the smaller triangles. Doing this generates answer (c)— the correct one.

Now look at the second sample analogy. The relation you are likely to *infer* between term 1 and term 2 is one of addition of a part—the diagonal line. So you'll need to *map* this addition relation over to the second half of the analogy, and *apply* the relation you inferred above. The best answer option is (d), with two dark circles connected by a line. Notice that the line connecting the two dark circles is vertical rather than diagonal. This analogy provides an example of the need for the *justification* process. To many people the best of the answer options would seem not quite correct, but it nevertheless is the best choice available.

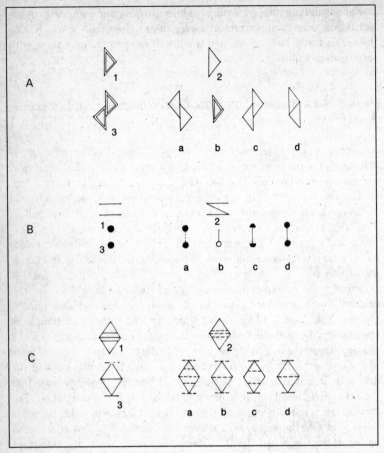

Figure 7. Sample figural analogies.

Now consider the third sample analogy. The relation to be *inferred* between term 1 and term 2 is one of transformation: the solid horizontal lines have been transformed into broken lines. This relation now needs to be *mapped* to the second half of the analogy. Term 3 involves the same diamond, but with horizontal lines at the top, middle, and bottom. *Apply* the relation inferred above and the best answer is (b), the completion with three broken horizontal lines.

You have thus seen three sample analogies, each involving a different type of inferred relation: *deletion*, *addition*, and *transformation*. Below are fifteen verbal analogies for you to solve, followed by fifteen figural analogies (see figure 8). The figural analogies involve various combinations of addition, deletion, and transformation in the relations between terms. Doing these problems will give you practice in using and combining the various kinds of inductive performance components that you will need to think inductively—to see analogies, make predictions, classify things, and the like. The answers to both types of problems appear in the Appendix.

1. STATUE is to STONE as SHOE is to (a. PAIR, b. SOCK, c. LEATHER, d. FOOT)

2. PARENT is to FATHER as CHILD is to (a. UNCLE, b. ADULT, c. SON, d. BROTHER)

3. ¼ is to 175% as ³⁄₂₅ is to (a. 3%, b. 12%, c. ²⁵⁄₃, d. ⁴⁄₇)

4. RODIN is to THE THINKER as DA VINCI is to (a. ART, b. ITALY, c. MONA LISA, d. RENAISSANCE)

5. CABINET is to CARPENTER as NOVEL is to (a. BOOK, b. AUTHOR, c. SHELF, d. WRITING)

6. BREEZE is to GALE as SHOWER is to (a. RAINDROP, b. WIND, c. WEATHER, d. CLOUDBURST)

7. COWARDICE is to YELLOW as ENVY is to (a. GREEN, b. HATRED, c. FEAR, d. JEALOUSY)

8. TOUCH is to NUMB as SIGHT is to (a. BRIGHT, b. OPTICAL, c. CLEAR, d. BLIND)

9. EGGS is to BEAT as CREAM is to (a. PIE, b. CHEESE, c. WHIP, d. POUR)

10. WATER is to STEAM as FIRE is to (a. CHIMNEY, b. WOOD, c. SMOKE, d. ARSON)

11. COMPASS is to DIRECTION as WATCH is to (a. STRAP, b. CLOCK, c. SIGHT, d. TIME)

12. CHAIRMAN is to MEETING as JUDGE is to (a. TRIAL, b. LAWYER, c. CRIMINAL, d. SENTENCE)

13. REPEL is to LEPER as REMIT is to (a. BANKER, b. ENVELOPE, c. CANCER, d. TIMER)

14. FLOUR is to BREAD as WOOL is to (a. SWEATER, b. SHEEP, c. COTTON, d. KNIT)

15. SOUND is to SILENCE as MOTION is to (a. SPEED, b. RATE, c. DECORATION, d. STILLNESS)

SERIES COMPLETIONS

The performance components of inference, mapping, application, and justification apply to other kinds of inductive-reasoning problems besides

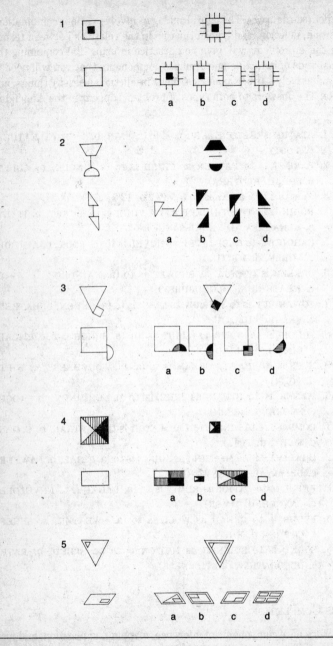

Figure 8. Figural analogies.

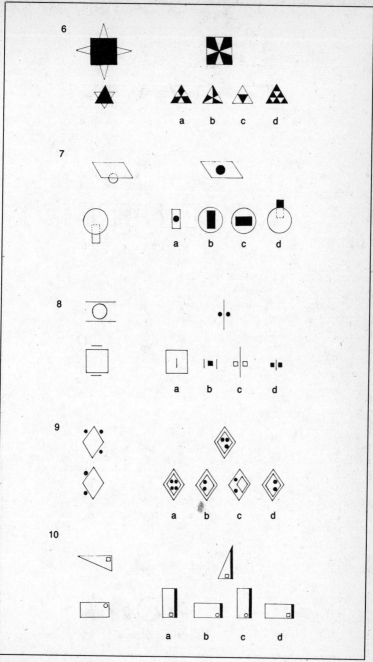

Figure 8. (Continued)

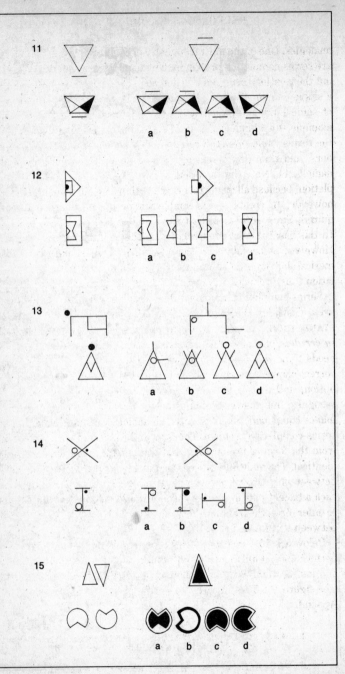

Figure 8. (Continued)

analogies. One of the most frequently encountered types of such problems are series-completion problems. Unlike analogies, where you are figuring out the relations between two domains, here you make predictions within a single domain. You are usually given several terms that form a series of some kind, and your task is to complete the series. Consider, for example, the simple series 2, 5, 8, ___. In this problem, you must *encode* the terms, then *infer* the relation between each successive pair of numbers, and then *apply* this relation to generate a correct completion—namely, 11. Note that mapping is not needed in this form of series completion, because all of the terms are within a single domain. It is possible, however, to create series-completion problems where mapping is required. Suppose instead that the problem had read 2, 5, 8, 11 : 29, ___. In this case, the inferred relation is the same as before—namely, +3. However, before applying this relation, you must *map* it to a new numerical domain, one starting with the number 29. *Applying* the +3 relation thus produces an answer of 32 in this form of the problem.

Series-completion problems, like analogies, can involve words or figures. Consider the following series-completion problem: LIE, KNEEL, STAND: HIGH, (a. TALL, b. HIGHER). In this problem, the relation to be *inferred* is one of progressively greater vertical height. This relation needs to be *mapped* to the term HIGH and then applied so as to yield a correct answer. You may or may not perceive HIGHER as an ideal answer option, and if it is not so perceived, then *justification* is required to recognize this answer option as better than TALL. Note that the performance components used to solve an analogy are here being applied to a series-completion problem. The form of the problem is somewhat different from the form of the analogy, but the mental operations are practically identical. The main difference is that instead of having to infer the relation between only two terms, you have to infer successive relations between each adjacent pair in a set of three terms. Thus, in the sample, you have to infer first the relation between LIE and KNEEL, then the relation between KNEEL and STAND.

Below are fifteen verbal series completions that require you to use the performance components of encoding, inference, mapping, application, and justification. They are followed by fifteen figural series completions (see figure 9). The answers to both types of problems appear in the Appendix.

1. SEED, SEEDLING, SAPLING : TEENAGER, (a. ADOLESCENT, b. CHILD, c. ADULT, d. INFANT)
2. KNUCKLE, WRIST, ELBOW : KNEE, (a. FOOT, b. LEG, c. TOE, d. HIP)

3. ALWAYS, USUALLY, SOMETIMES : POSSIBLE, (a. UNLIKELY, b. PROBABLE, c. CERTAIN, d. CHANCE)

4. BEE, SEA, DEE : PEW, (a. POD, b. OWE, c. CUE, d. BEAN)

5. BROOMSTICK, PENCIL, TOOTHPICK : NAIL, (a. HAMMER, b. METAL, c. BOLT, d. TACK)

6. CLEVELAND, OHIO, UNITED STATES : FRANCE, (a. EUROPE, b. COUNTRY, c. PARIS, d. GERMANY)

7. FOG, DRIZZLE, SHOWER : FLURRY, (a. BLIZZARD, b. SNOW-FLAKE, c. DRIFT, d. ICE)

8. ECLAIR, PASTRY, DESSERT : FRUIT, (a. APPLE, b. FOOD, c. VEG-ETABLE, d. BANANA)

9. GRANDFATHER, FATHER, BROTHER : SISTER, (a. PARENT, b. DAUGHTER, c. MOTHER, d. CHILD)

10. ELEMENTARY SCHOOL, JUNIOR HIGH, HIGH SCHOOL : 18, (a. 0, b. 10, c. 65, d. 22)

11. LUXURY CAR, FAMILY CAR, JALOPY : COTTAGE, (a. HOUSE, b. CHEESE, c. HUT, d. MANSION)

12. NORTH MINNESOTA, EAST CONNECTICUT, SOUTH NE-BRASKA : SIX O'CLOCK, (a. NINE O'CLOCK, b. MIDNIGHT, c. ALARM, d. HOUR)

13. ANTHEM, KICKOFF, FIRST QUARTER : LAST ACT, (a. INTERMIS-SION, b. OVERTURE, c. ACTORS, d. CURTAIN CALL)

14. REPRIMAND, SUSPENSION, EXPULSION : ROBBERY, (a. CRIMI-NAL, b. MURDER, c. THEFT, d. MISDEMEANOR)

15. ANIMAL, VERTEBRATE, REPTILE : TREE, (a. PLANT, b. FOREST, c. WILLOW, d. BRANCH)

CLASSIFICATIONS

In series completions, you predict what element comes next in a given series. In a related kind of problem, the classification, you figure out which elements belong in the given domain in the first place.

Classification problems require essentially the same set of performance components as do analogy and series-completion problems and, like them, can come in a variety of forms. In one form, a person is presented with a set of terms, one of which does not belong with the others. The person's task is to figure out which term does not belong. For example, in the problem PESO, POUND, DOLLAR, CURRENCY, RUPEE, the word "Currency" does not fit with the rest because it is superordinate to the other terms. A peso, a pound, a dollar, and a rupee are all units of currency. In another form of problem, you may receive a set of terms followed by

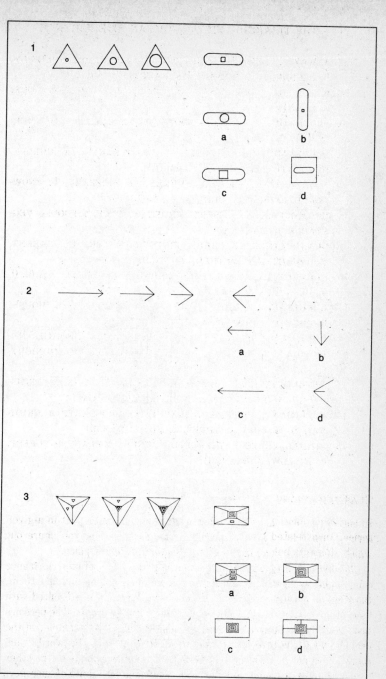

Figure 9. Figural series completions.

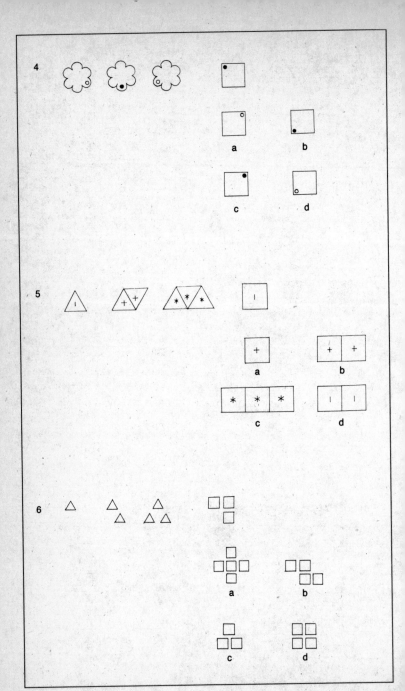

Figure 9. (Continued)

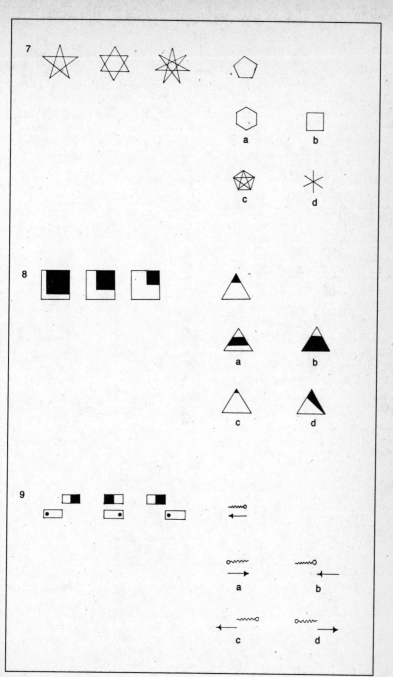

Figure 9. (Continued)

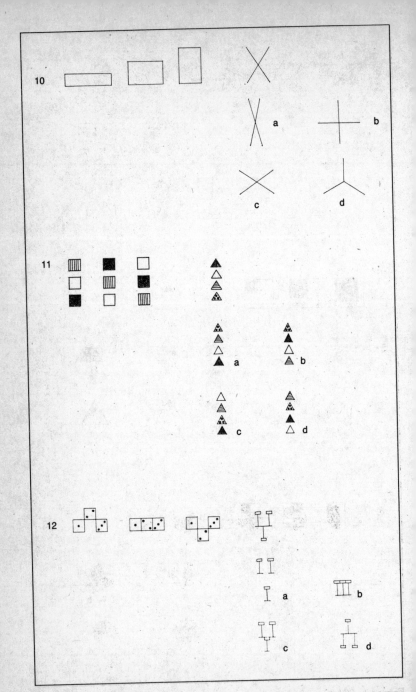

Figure 9. (Continued)

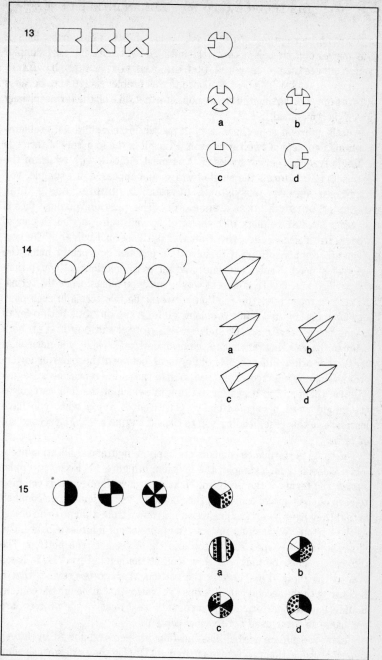

Figure 9. (Continued)

a set of answer options. In this task, your job is to figure out which of the answer options belongs with the initial set of terms. So, for example, you might see the problem LION, DOG, GIRAFFE, FOX, (a. BIRD, b. WHALE, c. TUNA, d. WASP). The best response to this problem is WHALE, because it is the only one among the answer options that, like all the terms initially given, is a mammal.

Another format sometimes used in presenting classification problems contains four sets of two terms each. Preceding the four sets of terms is a single term appearing by itself. You must indicate with which of the four sets of two terms the single term should appear. For example, you might see SECRET, (a. VISIBLE, OBVIOUS; b. HIDDEN, CONCEALED; c. SILENT, QUIET; d. LIKELY, PROBABLE). The question you must face is whether SECRET belongs with the first, second, third, or fourth pair of words. In this case, the correct answer is the second pair (b). The performance components used to solve this problem are pretty much the same ones used to solve analogies and series completions, although they are applied in a slightly different way. First, you must *encode* the terms. Next, you must *infer* the relation between the two terms in each pair. For example, in the sample problem, VISIBLE and OBVIOUS both refer to things being easy to see or understand. HIDDEN and CONCEALED both refer to things being difficult to see or understand. Next, you must *map* the higher-order difference or differences between the pairs of lower-order relations inferred. You need to map these differences because you will use them as the bases for deciding in which of the four categories the single word belongs. Finally, you need to *apply* what you have learned—in this case, leading you to classify SECRET with the second set of terms.

The same performance components apply to figural classification problems. Consider, for example, the problem in figure 10. First, you must *encode* the terms of the problem. Next, you must *infer* what is common to each of the pairs of terms. In this example, what seems to be common is that they have a vertical line extending down from a shape to an object at the bottom. What differentiates the four sets of figures? Apparently, it is the set of shapes at the top and the objects at the bottom. The differences must be *mapped*. Now look at the single term (1). It has a star at the top and a square at the bottom. *Application* reveals that it belongs with the second pair of terms (b). Notice that although the content is different, the performance components used to solve the problem are the same as those used with verbal content.

Below are fifteen verbal classification problems, followed by fifteen figural classification problems (see figure 11). Use the performance components of encoding, inference, mapping, and application to solve them.

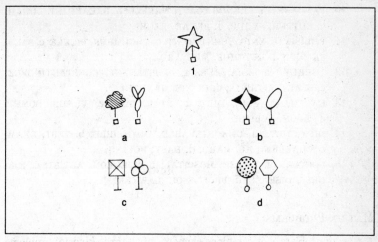

Figure 10. Sample figural classification problem.

In some instances, the single word or picture will not seem to fit perfectly with any of the option pairs; you must use the performance components of *justification* in order to decide which of the four classes of terms provides the best, although not ideal, fit. Answers to both types of problems appear in the Appendix.

1. BOOK, (a. CHAPTER, PAGE; b. MAGAZINE, LETTER; c. PUBLISHER, PRINTER; d. SHELF, LIBRARY)

2. BURGUNDY, (a. SCARLET, CRIMSON; b. WINE, BEER; c. PARIS, FRANCE; d. BOTTLE, CORK)

3. THREAD, (a. NEEDLE, PIN; b. STRAND, SPOOL; c. SEWING, MENDING; d. ROPE, STRING)

4. STOMACH, (a. DIGESTION, CIRCULATION; b. ESOPHAGUS, INTESTINES; c. ULCER, OPERATION; d. NECK, LUNGS)

5. RING, (a. CHIME, BELL; b. CIRCLE, SPHERE; c. BRACELET, NECKLACE; d. JEWELRY, MONEY)

6. HAIR, (a. BLOND, BRUNETTE; b. FUR, COAT; c. SHAMPOO, HAIRCUT; d. TEETH, NAILS)

7. CHIMPANZEE, (a. BABOON, GORILLA; b. TREE, ZOO; c. OSTRICH, ANTELOPE; d. JUNGLE, AFRICA)

8. JACK, (a. TIRE, REPAIR; b. CARD, DECK; c. ACE, SEVEN; d. RABBIT, POT)

9. COMPASS, (a. MAGNET, NEEDLE; b. STENCIL, RULER; c. DIRECTION, BEARING; d. NORTH, SOUTH)

10. PANCAKE, (a. FRENCH TOAST, WAFFLE; b. BREAKFAST, LUNCH; c. BUTTER, SYRUP; d. BREAD, BAGEL)

11. RELISH, (a. ENJOY, SENTIMENT; b. CUCUMBER, PICKLE; c. SALT, PEPPER; d. KETCHUP, MUSTARD)

12. TURKEY, (a. ASIA, RUSSIA; b. ISTANBUL, CONSTANTINOPLE; c. SPAIN, ALGERIA; d. GOOSE, GANDER)

13. EARTH, (a. SOIL, DIRT; b. STAR, SUN; c. VENUS, COMET; d. MOON, ECLIPSE)

14. DIFFICULT, (a. UNACHIEVABLE, IMPOSSIBLE; b. TEST, EXAM; c. CHALLENGING, HARD; d. EASY, BORING)

15. DOCTOR, (a. NURSE, HOSPITAL; b. SURGEON, ARTIST; c. ILL-NESS, DISEASE; d. PROFESSOR, LAWYER)

MATRIX PROBLEMS

A type of problem that combines elements of all three kinds of problems we have just considered—analogies, series completions, and classifications—is the matrix problem, which requires inductive reasoning in two dimensions rather than just one.

In a matrix problem, there are typically nine small squares, or cells, embedded in one large square. In each of the small squares is a figural design that is part of several patterns. The patterns go horizontally across the matrix and vertically down the matrix. Usually, one of the cells of the matrix is blank—most typically, the cell at the lower right. The test taker's task is to figure out what figural design ought to go in the empty cell in order to finish the various patterns. Keep in mind that if, for example, the bottom-right cell is empty, the figure that is placed in it must fulfill the constraints of the horizontal and the vertical patterns embedded in the matrix. Matrix problems have been found to provide particularly good (although limited) tests of general intelligence; indeed, one of the most famous intelligence tests, the Raven Progressive Matrices, is composed exclusively of matrix problems.

Here are some sample matrix problems for you to try (See figure 12). The first one has been worked out for you. In the first sample problem, only things unique to the two uppermost boxes in each column appear in the bottom row. ("Unique" means that they appear in one box but not in the other.) Things common to the two boxes are dropped in the bottom row. In the left-hand vertical column, the center and lower-left circles are unique to the two boxes 1 and 4. So they are added together in 7. The upper-right circle is common to both 1 and 4, so it is dropped from 7. In the center vertical column, the lower-left, center, and upper-right circles are unique to boxes 2 and 5; therefore, they both appear in box

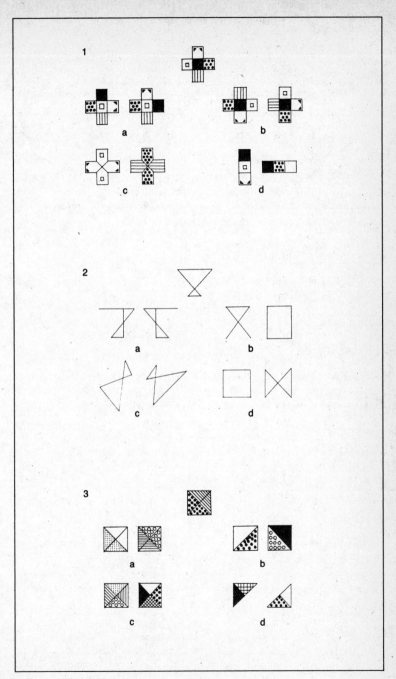

Figure 11. Figural classification problems.

Figure 11. (Continued)

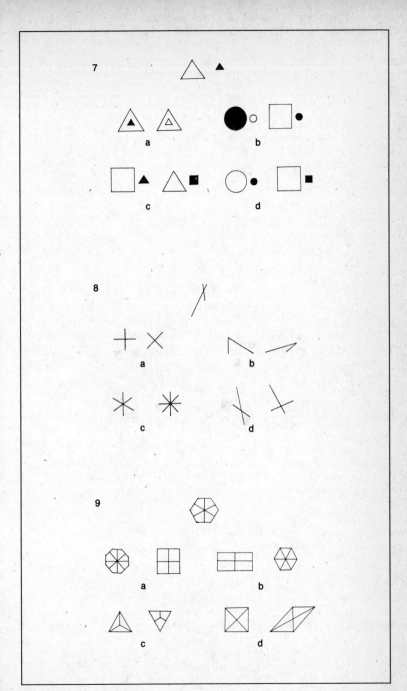

Figure 11. (Continued)

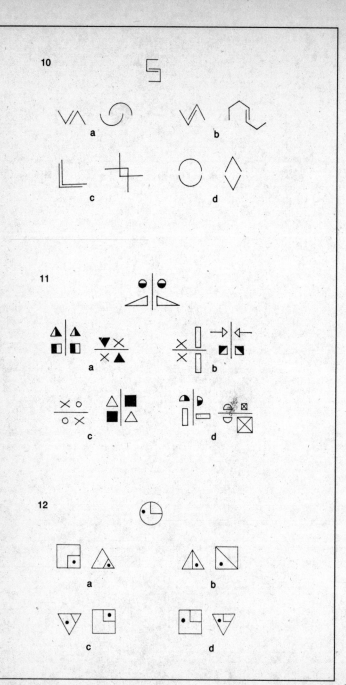

Figure 11. (Continued)

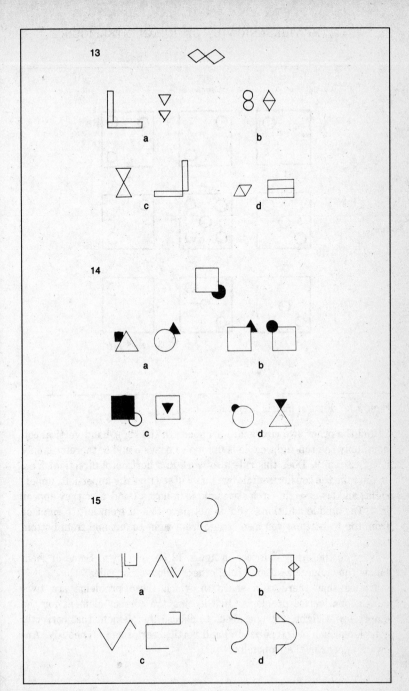

Figure 11. (Continued)

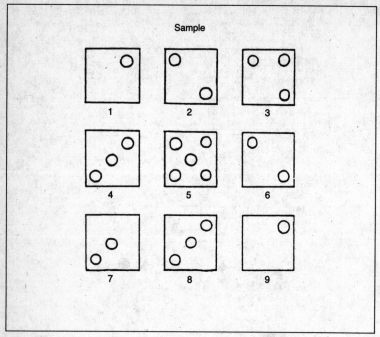

Figure 12. Figural matrix problems.

8, and the other two circles are dropped. In the right-hand vertical column, only the top-right circle is unique to boxes 3 and 6; therefore, only it appears in 9. Does this rule also work in a horizontal direction? Yes. If you take the top horizontal row, you will see that the upper-left, upper-right, and lower-right circles are unique in boxes 1 and 2, so they appear in 3. In "unique addition," you do not have to add from left to right or from top to bottom; you also can go from right to left and from bottom to top.

Now do the other matrices in figure 12 on your own. Some of them follow the "unique addition" rule; others follow other rules.

Notice that there is a sense in which these problems are two-dimensional series problems. In choosing the correct element for the empty lower-right cell, one needs to choose the element that correctly completes each of the horizontal and vertical series simultaneously. Answers appear in the Appendix.

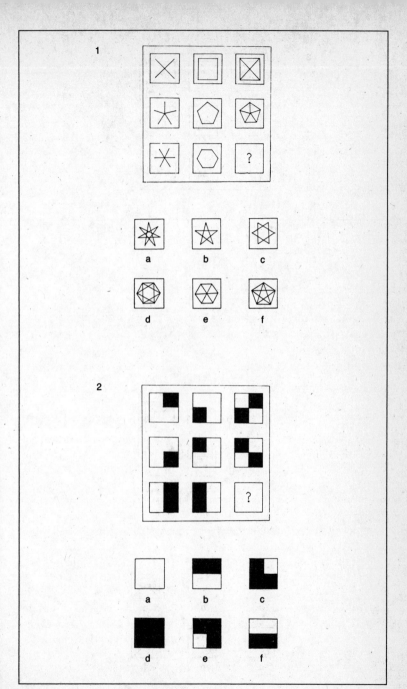

Figure 12. (Continued)

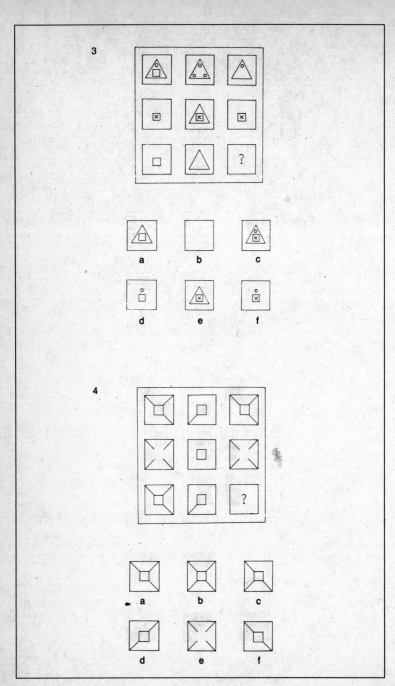

Figure 12. (Continued)

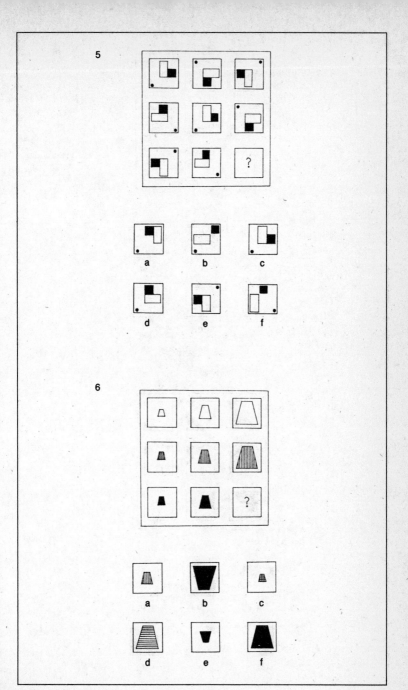

Figure 12. (Continued)

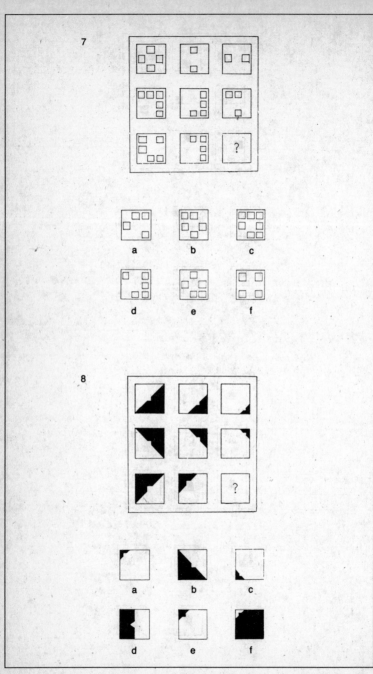

Figure 12. (Continued)

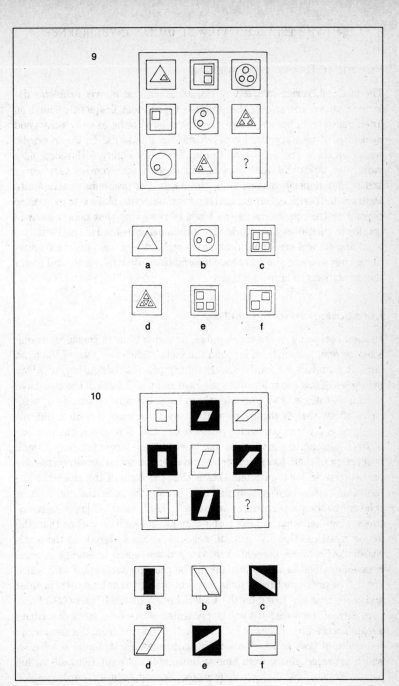

Figure 12. (Continued)

PRACTICAL REASONING PROBLEMS

The analogy, series-completion, classification, and matrix problems described above are among the problem types most frequently found on intelligence tests because they have been found to be exceptionally good measures of intelligence, by psychometric standards. In other words, scores on these problems tend to correlate very highly with scores on a variety of kinds of intelligence tests and with achievement test scores and academic performance. Still, these kinds of problems remain quite abstract and testlike. Our goal in training intellectual skills is to generalize beyond testlike problems to the kinds of reasoning that people need to employ in their everyday world. The problems presented in this section—legal and clinical reasoning problems—make use of such practical situations; they require you to *encode* information, *infer* relations, and *apply* these relations to new situations.

LEGAL REASONING PROBLEMS

In legal reasoning, a lawyer, a judge, or a client has to consider, among other things, principles of law and the facts of the case. One of the most difficult problems the legal reasoner confronts is that of figuring out which principles of law are relevant to the case and which facts of the case have legal implications. For example, there exist literally thousands of principles of law that might be relevant to any given case; it is often difficult to figure out which particular principles to use. Moreover, the number of facts relating to a given case can be extremely large, but only a small proportion of them have legal consequences. A frustration often faced by participants in legal embroilments is that the facts of the case that are relevant from a legal standpoint may not be the ones that seem most relevant to the participants. For example, settlements of lawsuits sometimes hinge on what appear to be minor technicalities rather than the major injustices that the plaintiff believes he has suffered. In the legal-reasoning problems presented below, you are asked to engage in legal reasoning, albeit in a simplified form. The principles and cases with which you will be presented are in some respects similar to the kinds of principles and cases that are found on the Law School Admission Test (LSAT).

In each of the cases, you will be presented with a brief story describing a legal proceeding, followed by some facts extracted from the case, some principles of law, and a choice of two outcomes. First, figure out (*infer*) which principle of law from among those given is most relevant to this particular case, and indicate your choice. Second, identify (*encode*) which fact this principle most directly bears upon, and again indicate your response. Finally, use (*apply*) the selected principle in order to decide the outcome of the case, and indicate the response that you believe to be correct for this particular case. Although, of course, the reasoning that will be required of you here is a gross simplification of the kind of reasoning lawyers and judges employ in an actual case, it will give you the flavor of what is required in legal reasoning, and particularly of how the performance components of induction can be applied in a real-world setting.

Please keep in mind that the principles given below, as well as the facts of the particular cases, are imaginary, even though the kind of reasoning you need to apply is not. Answers appear in the Appendix.

CASE 1

Mr. Dolan sold ten tables to Mrs. Roscoe, a careful buyer who inspected all ten tables carefully before agreeing to buy them. Five tables had wide cracks, plainly visible to the naked eye, where the legs joined the tabletops. Mrs. Roscoe appeared critical of the tables as she looked at them, but when she noted the low price for the total of ten, she bought them. In fact, the other five tables were poorly glued in certain hidden parts, and within a week or two they became useless. Mrs. Roscoe asked Mr. Dolan to take the ten defective tables back and to refund the price paid. He refused. Mrs. Roscoe then took legal action against Mr. Dolan to recover the cost of the five tables with the defective glue. Will Mrs. Roscoe win?

PRINCIPLES

1. If there are hidden defects in a product not noticed by an inspecting buyer, and if the defects make the product unfit for use, the purchaser may recover his cost.
2. If there are open and visible defects in a product, the buyer cannot assume an implied warranty of fitness against such open defects.

FACTS

1. Mrs. Roscoe inspected all ten tables carefully before agreeing to buy them.
2. The price for all ten tables was very low.
3. Five of the tables had visible cracks.
4. Five of the tables had hidden defects in gluing that made them useless.

OUTCOMES
1. Mrs. Roscoe will lose.
2. Mrs. Roscoe will win.

CASE 2

Oliver owned a roadside diner. He leased it to Stanley for a term of five years, with the understanding that Stanley would continue to run the diner. Shortly after Stanley took over the diner, one of the wooden steps leading into the diner rotted through, but Stanley carelessly failed to notice it.

Two days later, Mr. and Mrs. Dickey stopped at the diner. Mrs. Dickey, rushing to the bathroom, ran up the steps without mishap, but as she entered the bathroom she tripped over an unusually high doorstep. Oliver had known the concrete doorstep was dangerously high when he leased the diner to Stanley, but he decided it was not worth the expense to level the floor. Mrs. Dickey fell forward, striking her head against the partly opened door. Hearing his wife's scream, Mr. Dickey ran up the steps and put his foot through the rotten board, breaking his ankle. Mrs. Dickey was not seriously injured, but Mr. Dickey was. He sued Stanley for damages. Will Mr. Dickey win?

PRINCIPLES

1. Where premises are leased for use involving the admission of many patrons of a tenant, the owner is liable for injuries caused by unreasonable defective conditions which he knew about, if he should have realized that the tenant would probably not remedy them.

2. A tenant must keep his premises in such condition that they will be reasonably safe for those who enter there, and he is liable for injuries caused by defects in the premises that could have been remedied by the exercise of reasonable care.

FACTS

1. Stanley carelessly failed to notice the rotten board.
2. Oliver knew that the doorstep was dangerous and should have realized that Stanley would not repair it.
3. Mrs. Dickey tripped on the doorstep and struck her head.
4. Mr. Dickey put his foot through the rotten board and broke his ankle.

OUTCOMES
1. Mr. Dickey will lose.
2. Mr. Dickey will win.

CASE 3

Al, a football player, was driving his car one afternoon. He saw Ellen, a friend, walking down the street and offered to give her a ride. She accepted. After Al drove safely for several miles, he lost control of the vehicle and it hit a tree. Al's leg was broken and he was knocked unconscious. Ellen suffered serious cuts and bruises. It was eventually discovered that Al had lost control of the vehicle because of a concussion that he had unknowingly sustained in a touch football game in which he had participated that afternoon, prior to football practice. Al had never blacked out before, and he was feeling all right at the time he picked Ellen up. Al was insured through his school for injuries he might sustain while participating in authorized high-school athletic activities. Al sued his insurance company for expenses related to his broken leg. Will Al win?

PRINCIPLES
1. An insurer's liability includes only those injuries sustained by the insured party while participating in an insured event, or which can reasonably be said to be caused by participation in an insured event.
2. The owner of a vehicle is liable for accidents caused by persons driving with his permission.

FACTS
1. Al received the concussion while participating in an uninsured activity.
2. Al drove the car with all reasonable care.
3. Al's broken leg was the result of the concussion.
4. Ellen suffered serious cuts and bruises.

OUTCOMES
1. Al will lose.
2. Al will win.

CASE 4

Mogul was a pawnbroker. Every Friday he took all the cash from the week's receipts to the bank. Wishing to prevent a possible robbery, he contacted the Magnum Armed Guard Service. Magnum's ad showed a picture of a guard with a pistol. They entered into a contract which stated that Magnum would provide Mogul with one of its pistol-equipped professional armed guards every Friday from 1:00 p.m. to 3:00 p.m. for the sum of $50 per day.

The next Friday, Bruno, one of Magnum's employees, showed up at 1:00 p.m. He was armed with a billy club but had no gun. Mogul was apprehensive about Bruno's not having a gun, but he started to go to the bank, anyway. Halfway there, two men attempted to rob Bruno and Mogul. Mogul sued Magnum Armed Guard for breach of contract. Will Mogul win?

PRINCIPLES
1. If a contract is impossible to perform, its nonperformance does not constitute breach of contract.
2. When a contract has been entered into, the performance required to satisfy the contractual obligation must be substantially equivalent to the performance contracted for. Anything less is considered a breach of contract.

FACTS
1. Magnum's ad pictured a guard with a pistol.
2. Magnum provided a guard at the specified time.
3. The guard was not armed with a pistol.
4. The guard's presence did not prevent a robbery attempt.

OUTCOMES
1. Mogul will lose.
2. Mogul will win.

CASE 5
Mr. Crump owned a piece of real estate which he wanted to sell. He sent a letter in duplicate via registered mail to Mrs. Rails; it read: "I have a lot, size 40' x 200', that I am interested in selling for $10,000. If you are interested I would like to hear from you. Details attached." The details were attached.

Mrs. Rails decided she wanted the lot, so the day after receiving the letter she wrote "accepted" and signed her name to both copies of the letter. She returned one copy by registered mail to Mr. Crump.

Shortly thereafter, the lot increased in value and Mr. Crump decided he wanted $15,000 for it. Mrs. Rails brought suit against him to require him to sell it for $10,000. Will Mrs. Rails win?

PRINCIPLES

1. An offer to sell property must be accepted in writing by the offeree within a reasonable time and communicated to the offerer within a reasonable time to constitute an agreement enforceable in law.

2. An offer to sell property must be unqualified and definite. An invitation to negotiate cannot be treated as an offer to sell, and the courts will not enforce a mere offer to negotiate even though the same is accepted in writing.

FACTS

1. The offer of the lot was an invitation to negotiate.
2. Mrs. Rails accepted the offer within a reasonable time.
3. Mrs. Rails communicated her acceptance in a reasonable time.
4. The lot increased in value.

OUTCOMES

1. Mrs. Rails will win.
2. Mrs. Rails will lose.

CLINICAL REASONING PROBLEMS

People often think of lawyers and doctors as being similar in little other than their professional status and income. However, there are striking similarities in the kinds of reasoning they need to do on the job. Medical diagnosis problems are in many respects similar to legal reasoning problems. The problems presented below will require you to make clinical inferences for a test that is often used in psychiatric diagnosis, the Rorschach Inkblots Test. Please keep in mind that the principles given below, as well as the facts of the particular cases, are imaginary, even though the kind of reasoning you need to apply is not.

In each hypothetical case, you will receive a protocol of a patient (i.e., the patient's response to the presentation of an inkblot), where the patient's task is to describe what he sees in it. You will also be presented with some principles of interpretation for the Rorschach test, some fragments of the response summarized from the entire protocol, and some alternative diagnoses. Your task will be, first, to *infer* which principle is most relevant for making a clinical diagnosis in this case; second, to *encode* the fragment from the protocol to which this principle most directly applies; and, third, to *apply* the principle to the fragment in order to select the correct diagnosis. In reality, of course, a clinician would not make a diagnosis based on the application of a principle of test scoring to a single response. As with the above legal reasoning problems, this task represents a simplification of the reasoning in which professionals must engage. Nevertheless, it gives you some idea of the kind of reasoning in which clinicians must engage when making their diagnoses. Note that the structure of these problems is parallel to the structure of the legal reasoning problems. As noted above, for all the difference in content, the inductive reasoning processes required for clinical diagnosis are quite similar to those required for legal reasoning. Thus, you will practice using the same processes in a different domain. Answers appear in the Appendix.

SUBJECT 1

"Well, I see a ribbon in the white space there, all tied up nice. The knot is in the middle there. And right underneath it is a crab. It has two pincers by its nose, and more pincers on its legs. Those pincers can really hurt a person. That line going down the middle must be its backbone or whatever."

DIAGNOSE: Hypomania or not

PRINCIPLES
1. When a subject sees aggressive or threatening animal figures on the sides of the blot, hypomania is indicated.
2. Hypomanic responses are always characterized by excessive concentration on isolated black areas, such that only black areas that are completely surrounded by white ones are used.

FACTS
1. The two objects that are seen are both in the middle of the blot.
2. The ribbon is completely surrounded by white space.
3. The crab is not completely surrounded by white space.
4. The crab has pincers that are capable of hurting people.

OUTCOMES
1. The subject has hypomania.
2. The subject does not have hypomania.

SUBJECT 2

"It's a dark gloomy forest—a big tree in the middle, and a lot of branches and undergrowth along the sides. And there are two women hiding from each other, one on each side of the tree. They're the white in the black. Looks like they're pressing their faces against the tree, hiding from each other. Here are the heads . . . they have on skirts . . . they don't have hands."

DIAGNOSE: Dementia praecox or not

PRINCIPLES
1. Use of white areas to define forms is an indication of dementia praecox.
2. Figures lacking heads counterindicate dementia praecox.

FACTS
1. The women are hiding from each other.
2. The women have heads but not hands.
3. The women's bodies are formed by the white spaces.
4. The forest is dark and gloomy.

OUTCOMES
1. The subject does not have dementia praecox.
2. The subject has dementia praecox.

SUBJECT 3
"I see two vultures . . . well, they're vultures but they're also people . . . two men. They look like they're in pain . . . they're clutching their stomach. They're back to back and their legs are bent. The pain makes them double up."

DIAGNOSE: Psychosis or not

PRINCIPLES
1. If the response involves bodily mutilation, psychosis is indicated.
2. The subject has psychosis if, and only if, two separate ideas are fused into one.

FACTS
1. The subject sees people and vultures at the same place on the card.
2. The men are back to back.
3. The men double up.
4. The men are clutching their stomachs in pain.

OUTCOMES

1. The subject does not have psychosis.
2. The subject has psychosis.

SUBJECT 4

"Well, I see two elephants, two itty-bitty miniature elephants, fighting over a roach—a cockroach—in the middle. They're both kind of standing sideways. I see their ears flying out, and their legs. And they have their trunks, or whatever you call them, wrapped around the cockroach. And the cockroach is the central figure. You see the two little—uh—pincer things on the top of his head."

DIAGNOSE: Hysteria or not

PRINCIPLES

1. Distortion of real-world size relationships indicates hysteria.
2. If an aggressive figure is seen in the middle of the blot, hysteria is not present.

FACTS

1. The elephants have their trunks wrapped around the cockroach.
2. The elephants are approximately equal in size to the cockroach.
3. The cockroach is in the middle of the blot.
4. The elephants are on either side of the blot.

OUTCOMES

1. The subject does not have hysteria.
2. The subject has hysteria.

SUBJECT 5

"The two things on the sides at the top look like people falling through space. They're dead people. They're falling upside down. I have the impression they're being dropped. They're falling. They look dead 'cause they're just kind of all stretched out like a fluid—like something flowing. They look like they have no control of their body. They're just falling. I think they're women."

DIAGNOSE: Paranoia or not

PRINCIPLES

1. If only one small central area is elaborated on, paranoia is counterindicated.

2. Human movement can generally be taken as a sign of mental health, but passive movement is a sign of paranoia.

FACTS
1. The two black areas on the upper sides are dead people.
2. The dead people are limp.
3. The sex of the dead people is probably female.
4. The dead people are falling through space.

OUTCOMES
1. The subject has paranoia.
2. The subject does not have paranoia.

This chapter has concentrated on a sampling of some of the most important performance components in mental self-management—namely, the performance components of inductive reasoning. These processes are used to make sense of the present and to predict to the future, as when you see analogies between things, classify objects or ideas into groups, or complete a series. In combination with the metacomponents, they provide a powerful means for solving a variety of the problems we encounter in everyday life. What neither the metacomponents nor the performance components provide is a means to learn how to solve these problems in the first place. That is the job of knowledge-acquisition components, which are discussed in the next chapter.

7

Knowledge-Acquisition Components: The Students of Mental Self-management

We would live our lives, psychologically, as perpetual newborns were it not for the work of knowledge-acquisition components. Consider, for example, the following brief passage, which illustrates the major way in which you learn new words and concepts—namely, from the use of knowledge-acquisition components to learn from context: "Do you suffer from phalacrosis? If so, there is now hope for you. A new chemical compound has been discovered that will restore to you the youthful appearance, self-esteem, and general good looks you may have lost when your hair started to fall out."

How do you figure out what "phalacrosis" means? How do you determine, as you very likely did, that this word refers to baldness? In this chapter, we consider the ways whereby you learn meanings of new words and concepts presented to you in everyday context. In particular, we discuss the *knowledge-acquisition components* of intelligence, the processes of learning. Learning can occur in many different forms, but one of the most exciting forms of learning is insightful learning, the primary subject of this chapter.

An Overview

Before departing from San Francisco on a flight to New York recently, a colleague picked out some reading to test his wits. A professor of some accomplishment, he expected to make short work of the problems in *Games for the Superintelligent* and *The Mensa Genius Quiz Book*. By the time he crossed the Rocky Mountains, however, he had realized that he was neither a genius nor, as *The Mensa Genius Quiz Book* puts it, "a secret superbrain who doesn't even know it." By the time he crossed the Mississippi River, he knew that he wasn't "superintelligent," either.

More often than not, the puzzles stumped him. How could two men play five games of checkers and each win the same number of games without any ties? He couldn't figure it out. How could you plant a total of ten trees in five rows of four trees each? He drew several diagrams, and none of them worked. But he couldn't put the books down.

This colleague wasn't alone in his frustration. Mental puzzles have been a staple of the publishing industry for years. Martin Gardner's mathematical puzzles, from the monthly column he used to write for *Scientific American*, have been collected in ten different books, with total sales of more than half a million copies. *Solve It*, *Games for the Superintelligent*, and *More Games for the Superintelligent*, all by James Fixx, have together sold nearly one million copies.

Puzzles can certainly be fun, and great ego boosters for those who eventually get the right answers. According to Fixx, many people use mental puzzles to "strengthen their thought processes" and to "tune up their minds." Others use them to test or measure their own intelligence. In fact, *More Games* and *The Mensa Genius Quiz Book* actually contain what are supposed to be short IQ tests.

Many of the problems in these books require flashes of insight or "leaps of logic" on the part of the solver, rather than prior knowledge or laborious computation. Janet Davidson and I wondered just how people approach such puzzles—which are commonly called insight problems—and whether they provide a valid measure of a person's intelligence.[1] To answer these questions, we examined the literature on problem solving and then conducted a mini-experiment to measure the relationship between performance on insight problems and scores on standard intelligence tests.

On the basis of our research, we identified three types of knowledge-acquisition processes that, separately or together, seem to be required in solving most insight problems: selection and "encoding" of relevant information—that is, understanding what information is relevant to solving the problem and *how* it is relevant; combination of different and seemingly unrelated bits of useful information; and comparison of the problem under consideration with problems previously encountered. For example, in solving the problem of the checker players, faulty encoding would lead you to assume that the two men were playing each other.

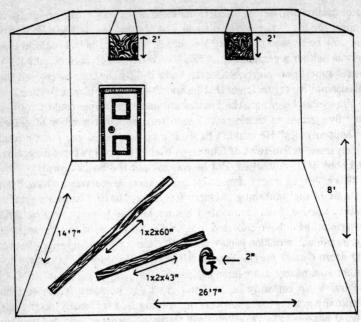

Figure 13. The hat-rack problem.

Correctly combining the facts that there were no ties and that each player won the same number of games should lead to the conclusion that they couldn't be playing each other.

Similarly, to plant ten trees in five rows of four trees each, you must get away from the idea of making the five rows parallel. People who are accustomed to thinking in geometric terms will usually imagine several other patterns, until they hit on the correct one—a pentacle, or five-pointed star.

The literature on how people solve insight problems is meager, and it includes almost no reports on research relating solution of these problems to intelligence. One of the few studies of this sort was done by Norman Maier and Ronald Burke at the University of Michigan.[2] Maier and Burke compared people's scores on a variety of aptitude tests with their skill at solving the "hat-rack problem" (see figure 13). The problem calls on them to build a structure sufficiently stable to support a man's overcoat, using only two long sticks and a C-clamp. The opening of the clamp is wide enough so that the two sticks can be inserted and held together securely when the clamp is tightened. Participants are placed in a small room and are asked to build a hat rack in the center of the room. The solution is shown in figure 22 in the Appendix.

When the researchers compared people's ability to solve the hat-rack problem with their scores on the Scholastic Aptitude Test, the correlations were all insignificant. In other words, whatever insight people needed to build the hat rack seemed to be unrelated to their scores on standardized intelligence tests. Burke and Maier concluded that the abilities needed to solve insight problems may be different from those required to solve problems of the kinds found on such tests. Their study is of limited value, however: they used only one problem and scored the responses only in terms of "right" or "wrong."

Davidson and I did find in the research literature some theoretical basis for the lack of relationship between intelligence and performance on the hat-rack problem. Kjell Raaheim, a psychologist at the University of Bergen in Norway, wrote in *Problem Solving and Intelligence* that "it is unreasonable to expect intelligence to be an important factor of success in solving tasks which are totally unfamiliar to the individual facing them."[3] According to Raaheim, problems will best measure intelligence if they present a situation that is *intermediate* in its degree of familiarity to a problem solver. Problems presenting situations that are either too familiar or too unfamiliar will provide poorer measures of a person's intelligence.

In an ingenious set of experiments, Robert Weisberg and Joseph Alba of Temple University asked people to solve a set of insight problems.[4] One was the familiar nine-dot problem discussed in chapter 5, in which people were shown a three-by-three array of nine equally spaced dots and asked to connect the nine dots using four straight lines without lifting pencil from paper. The solution requires an approach similar to that used to plant the five rows of trees.

What is unique about Weisberg and Alba's study is that participants were actually given the insight they needed to solve the problem: they were told that it could be solved only by drawing the lines beyond the boundaries formed by the dots. Even so, they had considerable difficulty in solving the problem. Weisberg and Alba interpreted the results as suggesting that such problems may really measure not insight but, rather, problem-specific prior knowledge. Our interpretation is a bit different. As Davidson and I see it, subjects not only needed to know that they could draw the lines outside the boundaries; they also had to know how to combine the portions of the lines outside the dots with the portions within. Performance on these insight problems therefore might not correlate with performance on intelligence-test problems.

Even though classic insight problems may not truly measure insight alone, we believed that problems could be found that do provide fairly accurate measures of insight, and that performance on such problems would be correlated with intelligence as it is typically measured by standardized tests.

To test this view, we compiled a set of twelve insight problems from a number of popular books. The problems varied in difficulty, in trickiness, and in the number of possible approaches that could be taken to reach a solution.

We recruited thirty people from the New Haven area by means of a newspaper advertisement that invited them to take part in a problem-solving experiment at Yale. Though not selected by scientific criteria, our small sample—nineteen men and eleven women—represented a fairly typical cross-section of urban residents, with a wide range of ages, occupations, and educational backgrounds.

First, we gave them a standard IQ test (the Henmon-Nelson Test of Mental Ability), including questions of vocabulary, math, and reasoning. None of the problems were quite like our insight problems. A typical reasoning problem, for example, might require the person to solve an analogy such as CAR is to GASOLINE as HUMAN is to (a. OIL, b. ENERGY, c. FOOD, d. FUEL); or a number series such as 3, 7, 12, 18, (a. 24, b. 25, c. 26, d. 27). The IQ test problems were multiple-choice, whereas the insight problems we used required people to generate their own answers.

The average IQ score of our sample on this test was 112, 12 points above the national average. (Elevated average IQs are typical in such experiments, because those who volunteer for studies on problem solving are likely to be of above-average intelligence. People with very low IQs may not read newspapers and probably wouldn't volunteer for experiments on problem solving even if they did.)

Second, we gave our subjects a deductive-reasoning test on nonsense syllogisms, with problems such as "All trees are fish. All fish are horses. Therefore, all trees are horses. Please indicate whether the conclusion is logically valid or not." (This one is.) Third, in a test of inductive reasoning, we presented our subjects with five sets of letters (for example, NOPQ, DEFL, ABCD, HIJK, UVWX) and asked them to choose the set that was based on a rule different from the rule used as a basis for the other four sets.

We included these two specific tests, as well as the more general IQ test, to judge the accuracy of a prediction we had made: if our problems genuinely measured insight, they should be more highly correlated with the inductive test, which requires an individual to go beyond the information given, than with the deductive test, which merely requires him to analyze the given information and draw the proper conclusion. Normal arithmetic or logic problems, for example, require primarily deductive rather than inductive reasoning skills.

Our subjects found the insight problems fun but sometimes frustrating, because the items varied considerably in difficulty. The easiest item, answered correctly by 73 percent of our sample, was this: "Next week I am going to have lunch with my friend, visit the new art gallery, go to the Social Security office, and have my teeth checked at the dentist's. My friend cannot meet me on Wednesday, the Social Security office is closed weekends, the art gallery is closed Tuesday, Thursday, and weekends, and the dentist has office hours only on Tuesday, Friday, and Saturday. What day can I do everything I have planned?" Reaching the answer (Friday) is easy, because one can simply check off which days don't work.

The hardest item, answered correctly by only 7 percent of our subjects, was this: "A bottle of wine cost ten dollars. The wine was worth nine dollars more than the bottle. How much was the bottle worth?" People probably had a hard time coming up with the answer (fifty cents) because they misunderstood the word "more."

The average score on our insight-problem test was 37 percent. There was no difference between the average scores of the men and the women. The time people spent solving the problems ranged from eleven minutes to forty-seven minutes, with an average of twenty-eight minutes.

When we examined the relationship between scores on the set of twelve insight problems and scores on the mental-ability tests, we found relatively high correlations between the insight-problem scores and the scores on the IQ tests (.66 on a scale from 0 to 1, on which a correlation of 0 means no relationship and a correlation of 1 means a perfect relationship) and inductive reasoning (.63), and only a moderate correlation with the scores on the test of deductive reasoning (.34). (All of the correlations were statistically meaningful; in other words, they were highly unlikely to represent merely chance associations between the tests.) These correlations suggest that performance on insight problems does provide a good index of intelligence, and that such performance may be more closely related to inductive than to deductive reasoning.

We then looked at the relationship between the test scores and time spent on the insight problems and found that people who spent the most time working on the problems tended to have a higher number of correct solutions and higher IQ scores. (The correlation between time spent and number of insight problems correctly solved was .62. The correlation between time spent and IQ was .75, which is remarkably high.) Why did smart people take longer on this task? Although we can only speculate, we suspect it is because they became more absorbed in the problems and more motivated to solve them. Our observations suggested that the less bright people either were too quick to choose the seemingly obvious but wrong answers on trick questions, or simply didn't know how to get started on the tougher problems and gave up more quickly.

When we looked at the correlations between the test scores on the insight problems and the scores on the standardized intelligence test, we found that the individual problems varied considerably in their relation to IQ. The problem of which day to schedule a lunch date with a friend had almost no correlation with IQ. The problem that proved to predict IQ scores best was this: "Water lilies double in area every twenty-four hours. At the beginning of the summer there is one water lily on a lake. It takes sixty days for the lake to become covered with water lilies. On what day is the lake half covered?" To find the answer, people must realize that since the water lilies double in area every twenty-four hours, the lake will be half covered on the fifty-ninth day in order to be completely covered on the sixtieth.

What made some items better measures of IQ than others? We discovered two patterns among the "good" and "bad' indicators of IQ that we thought were striking, at least as preliminary hypotheses.

The best indicators of IQ seemed to be those problems that presented both relevant and irrelevant information: the key to success was the ability to distinguish the two. For example, people with high IQs tended to realize that "water lilies double in area every twenty-four hours" was an important clue to solving this problem. People with low IQs frequently ignored this information and tried to solve the problem by dividing the sixty days by two.

Our interpretation of performance on the problems supports the theory that the ability to detect and use clues embedded in the context of what you read plays an important role in solving verbal problems. When reading a text—whether it is a newspaper, a science book, or a verbal or mathematical problem—much of the information may be irrelevant to your needs; often the hard part is figuring out what is relevant, and how.

The problems that proved to be poor indicators of IQ were the "trick" problems in which errors were due primarily to misreading the problem situation—fixating on the apparent question rather than on the actual question. Take the following problem: "A farmer has seventeen sheep. All but nine break through a hole in the fence and wander away. How many are left?" People making errors generally failed to comprehend exactly what "all but nine" meant; many assumed that the nine had escaped and thus subtracted the number from seventeen to get the number of sheep that remained behind.

If, as we have shown, insight problems do provide a good measure of intellectual ability—at least when they require you to make inductive leaps beyond the given data and when they require you to sift out relevant from irrelevant information—we must ask: Just what is insight? The reason that others have not found any common element in the various insights they have studied is that no one model works for all cases. Davidson and I have identified three basic kinds of cognitive processes of insightful performance, one or more of which may be required to solve a given problem: selective encoding, selective combination, and selective comparison.

SELECTIVE ENCODING

This kind of insight occurs when you perceive in a problem one or more facts that are not immediately obvious. It is important to be able to sort out relevant from irrelevant information. This skill can provide the solver with a basis for selective encoding.

A famous instance of selective encoding in science was Sir Alexander Fleming's discovery of penicillin. Fleming was doing an experiment in which he was growing bacteria in a petri dish. The experiment was spoiled: mold grew in the medium used to grow the bacteria. But Fleming noticed something that most scientists would have ignored or passed off as irrelevant: the mold had killed the bacteria—and bacteria are hard to kill! Thus, what had started off as an experiment in one thing had become an experiment in something else, and it had become a much more important experiment as well. Fleming's selective encoding of the mold killing the bacteria led to the isolation of the antibiotic penicillin from the mold penicillium.

Let's consider a more everyday use of selective encoding. Sara, a curriculum specialist in a large school district, had decided that she would like to advance to the superintendency of at least a small school district. Over the past few years she had busily filled out applications for superintendencies. She had not gotten any job offers, however, nor had she even been interviewed for a position. She was at her wit's end trying to figure out why she was not being seriously considered. There were many things that distinguished her from most of the successful applicants, and she had trouble putting her finger on just what made the difference. She had considered sex discrimination, but at least two of the jobs had gone to women. Finally, she was able to selectively encode the relevant data: unlike Sara, all of the individuals hired for the superintendencies had experience as a school principal. She realized that before she got a superintendency, she would have to gain experience as a school principal.

Now let's consider another use of selective encoding, this one in the domain of interpersonal relationships. Mitch was very interested in Susan. Susan, however, did not seem very interested in Mitch. At first

Mitch could not understand why. He was handsome, or at least so he was told; he was easy to get along with; he was reasonably bright; he shared a lot of interests with Susan. He began to look for the pattern in the men Susan dated. Eventually, he was able to selectively encode what seemed to be the relevant fact, and a disappointing fact it was: all of the men were blond-haired and blue-eyed, or at least a close approximation of it; they all had the same "look." Mitch did not look like this at all. Mitch ended up being pretty disgusted with Susan, and realized he would not be happy with a woman who selected men on the basis of a certain kind of physical appearance.

Consider the following problem: "If you have black socks and brown socks in your drawer, mixed in the ratio of four to five, how many socks will you have to take out to make sure of having a pair the same color?" Subjects who failed to realize that "mixed in the ratio of four to five" was irrelevant information consistently came up with the wrong solution. (The correct answer is three.) In the hat-rack problem, noticing the relevance of the floor and the ceiling as elements in the problem is also an example of selective encoding.

SELECTIVE COMBINATION

This type of insight takes place when you see a way of combining unrelated (or at least not obviously related) elements, as you must do in the following problem: "With a seven-minute hourglass and an eleven-minute hourglass, what is the simplest way to time the boiling of an egg for fifteen minutes?" Our subjects had all the necessary facts, but they had to figure out how to combine the two timers to measure fifteen minutes. In the hat-rack problem, figuring out how to combine the use of the floor, the ceiling, the C-clamp, and the two sticks constitutes a similar insight of selective combination.

A famous scientific example of selective combination is Darwin's formulation of the theory of evolution. The data needed to formulate the theory had been around for a while and were available to others besides Darwin. What Darwin saw was how to put the data together. His selective combination of data led him to postulate the principle of natural selection, or survival of the fittest.

Now consider a more mundane example of selective combination: Ned had grown up in Arizona and had spent his whole life there. At age twenty-two, he left the Southwest for the first time and moved to Buffalo, New York. The very first day he arrived, the sky was gray, the humidity was high, there was a thickness in the air, and it was colder than anything he could ever remember. It wasn't hard for him to combine this information to reach the conclusion that he was about to see snow for the first time.

Here is another example of a selective combination, this one in the domain of careers. Roger had worked hard during his seven years at his law firm and was hoping to be promoted to partner. He knew that he would be hearing any day now. One day, he thought he noticed a partner of his law firm avoiding eye contact with him. A day later, he had the feeling that the partners were avoiding him, and when he suggested a lunch to the one partner with whom he had any real social relationship at all, the partner politely declined. Roger started putting two and two together and became convinced that he had not been made a partner. Unfortunately, he found out the next week that he was correct.

SELECTIVE COMPARISON

This kind of insight occurs when you discover a nonobvious relationship between new and old information. It is here that analogy, metaphor, and models come into play.

A famous scientific example of a selective-comparison insight is Friedrich Kekulé's discovery of the structure of benzene. Kekulé had been seeking out this structure for some time, without success. One night, he had a dream in which he visualized a snake dancing around and biting its tail. When he woke up, he saw a connection between the dream and his scientific quest: the snake biting its tail was a visual metaphor for the structure of benzene, which proved to be a ring. Kekulé's selective comparison was in realizing the relevance of the dream for his scientific work.

Now consider an example of selective comparison as it applies in a very different domain, psychotherapy. Although he had been a psychiatrist for almost ten years, Saul was at a loss as to how to handle Jill, one of his patients. Jill's phobia for dogs simply did not seem to be responding to the psychodynamic therapy that Saul was attempting to use. Then Saul remembered some behavior-therapy techniques he had once read about that apparently had been successful in treating phobias. Although Saul was committed to the psychodynamic point of view, he decided that Jill desperately needed some immediate relief, so he brought his knowledge from the past to bear upon the present situation. In fact, Jill was helped considerably within only a few weeks. At that point, Saul was able to resume psychodynamic therapy in order to better understand the origins of Jill's phobia.

Now let's examine a final example of selective comparison. While riding in their car, the Warner family heard a loud noise that sounded almost like an explosion. Mr. Warner realized that he had nearly lost control of the car and tried as best he could to steer it gradually toward the break-down lane of the highway. Eventually, he was able to bring the car to a stop. Mr. Warner knew from his past experience what had just happened to him for the second time in his life: he had had a blowout of one of his tires.

Consider another type of selective comparison. If someone doesn't know a word on a vocabulary test, he often can figure out its definition by thinking of words he does know that have the same word stems. For example, if you don't know the word "exsect," you might be able to guess its meaning by thinking of a word that has the same prefix (such as "extract," where "ex" means out) and a word that has the same root (such as "dissect," where "sect" meants cut). This information might help you realize that "exsect" means to cut out.

Note the critical role of selection in each kind of information processing. In selective encoding, you must choose the right elements to encode among the often numerous and irrelevant bits of information presented by the problem. In selective combination, there may be many possible ways for the encoded elements to be combined or otherwise integrated; the trick is to select the right way of combining them. In selective comparison, new information must be related to one or more of many possible old pieces of information. There are any number of analogies or relations that might be drawn; the trick is to make the right comparison(s). Thus, what the three kinds of insight have in common is the importance of selection to each of them.

Psychologists in the past have attempted to view insight as a single process, and the result has been a great deal of confusion. Much of the confusion in the literature on problem solving stems from a failure to recognize the existence of and differences among these three kinds of insight, which together seem to account for the mental processes that have been labeled as insight, and which are involved in everything from solving problems in puzzle books to making major scientific break-throughs.

Although we have focused on the importance of insight in problem solving—and also in intelligence—insight alone is not enough to solve problems. Certain other essential ingredients count, including:

Prior knowledge. Even apparently simple problems often require a store of prior knowledge for their solution; complex problems can require a vast store of such knowledge. Consider the problem of the seven-minute and eleven-minute hourglasses. If people have used hourglass timers before and remember that they can turn them over at any point, that knowledge will certainly help.

Metacomponents (executive processes). These are the processes, discussed in chapter 5, used to plan, monitor, and evaluate your performance in problem solving.

Performance components. To solve insight problems, you must be able to execute the basic steps needed to take you from the beginning to the end of each problem.

Motivation. Really challenging problems often require a great deal of motivation on the part of the solver. Successful problem solvers are often those who simply are willing to put in the necessary effort. Indeed, in our mini-study, we found that the better problem solvers were more persevering than the poorer ones. Indeed, part of what made them good problem solvers was probably their willingness to persevere.

Style. People approach problems with different cognitive styles. In particular, some tend to be more impulsive and others more reflective; most people follow just one style or the other. The most successful problem solvers are those who manage to combine well both impulsive and reflective styles. At certain points in the problem-solving process, they act on impulse; at other times, they act only after great reflection. The hard part is knowing which style will pay off at which point.

Successful problem solving involves a number of different abilities. For many problems, one kind of insight may provide the key to a quick solution. But most problems are like the apartment doors in large cities: they have multiple locks requiring multiple keys. Without combining different kinds of insights, as well as prior knowledge, executive processes, motivation, and style, the problems remain locked doors.

A Detailed Look at the Three Processes of Knowledge Acquisition

SELECTIVE ENCODING PROBLEMS

Consider the following problem. As you do so, think about how selective encoding can help you to solve it.

Many scientists have offered explanations for the total extinction of the dinosaurs and other creatures sixty-five million years ago. One of the facts agreed upon by most geologists is that the earth was struck by a huge asteroid or comet approximately ten kilometers in diameter. The data that support this theory rest on the fact that a thin layer of iridium, an element found mainly in meteors, is present in geological strata throughout the world. (Scientists know that the iridium itself did not cause the extinction of dinosaurs and plants; it is simply proof that some catastrophic event involving meteors took place.)

The scientists explain that an asteroid crashed into the earth and caused huge amounts of dust and dirt to fly into the atmosphere. The dust blocked the sunlight, according to scientists, for approximately three months to a year, which caused the land to cool. Many animals died from starvation and from the cold.

Until recently, one of the puzzles has been why the ocean ecology died. The ocean—which was then even larger than it is now—did not change in temperature as drastically as the earth did. In view of the evidence, scientists have come up with an explanation. What might it be?

In order to find relevant information, you might want to go through the following steps, at least mentally.

First, restate the problem. An example of such a restatement would be: "A meteor crash caused many land animals to die. Why might a meteor crash also kill ocean plants and animals?"

Second, consider the information in the problem. What exactly are all the potentially relevant pieces of information? In this problem, such information would include that: (a) dinosaurs and other animals died suddenly sixty-five million years ago; (b) the earth was struck by a huge asteroid ten kilometers in diameter; (c) a layer of iridium, mainly an element from meteors, is embedded throughout the earth; (d) when the meteor crashed, huge amounts of dust and dirt were thrown into the atmosphere; (e) the dust blocked sunlight for three months to a year; (f) the land cooled, and animals presumably died from cold; (g) the ocean mass is much larger than the land mass; (h) the temperature change was not important to the ocean.

Third, eliminate information that is probably irrelevant in solving the problem. In this case, information about the land dinosaurs is probably not directly relevant to this problem.

Fourth, list the information that is relevant to solving the problem. In this problem, such information would include facts that might explain the results of the crash of the meteorite: that it threw large amounts of dust out into the atmosphere; that the dust blocked sunlight for three months to a year; that the land cooled in the darkness, so that animals starved and died from cold; and that the ocean temperature did not change significantly.

Fifth, think about what you might be able to infer from the given relevant information. For example, the fact that large amounts of dust were thrown into the atmosphere would result in air pollution and blockage of sunlight. What effect might a blockage of sunlight have upon the ocean ecology? What effect might pollution have on this ecology? What effect might the death, due to pollution, of even a small subset of the animals in the seas have on the total food chain upon which all animals in the sea depend?

These same steps can be applied to very practical kinds of problem solving, such as deciding what kind of automobile to buy. First, you need to state the problem as you see it. Is it just one of buying *any* car, a family car, a sporty car? Second, decide what kinds of information are relevant: price? gas mileage? color? weight? Third, eliminate any irrelevant information. A salesman may push a car because of its sporty look—which you don't care about. Fourth, simply list the information that you have decided is relevant. Finally, see whether you can infer any new information from the given information before you make your decision. If the salesman refuses to give you a test ride, for example, you might be led to question what kind of a ride you would get when you take the car on the road.

Let's consider the application of selective processing in a more academic problem. The socks problem, presented earlier, is a good example of how selective encoding plays an important role. People who answer the problem incorrectly tend to focus on information in the problem that is actually irrelevant to the problem's solution—namely, that the socks of two colors are mixed in a ratio of four to five. There are at least three reasons why this information would *seem* to be relevant, at first reading. First, we often assume that all of the quantitative information given in a mathematical problem will be relevant to solution. This assumption, however, is incorrect. Second, there is so little quantitative information in this particular problem that we might assume that whatever such information is given must be relevant, even if we do not always make this assumption. Yet this problem can be solved with only the information that there are two colors of socks in the drawer and that you need to pick out a pair of the same color. Third, people often start to solve problems of this kind by figuring out how to use the quantitative information in the problem, before they even consider whether it is relevant to the solution. Thus, people who answer the problem incorrectly often do so because they are misled by the irrelevant information in the problem.

In some cases, such as the dinosaur problem, the use of selective encoding is on a fairly large scale, and the need for it may therefore suggest itself immediately, at least to some people. In other cases, selective encoding needs to be applied on only a very small scale, but its application may nevertheless determine the correct answer to a problem. Consider the following problem: "A teacher had twenty-three pupils in her class.

All but seven of them went on a museum trip and thus were away for the day. How many of them remained in class that day?" This problem again requires selective encoding for its correct solution. People frequently immediately subtract seven from twenty-three to obtain sixteen as their answer. But this answer is incorrect. The critical word in the problem is "but." It is not the case that seven students went on the museum trip but rather that "all *but* seven" went on the trip. Thus, the fact that there are a total of twenty-three students in the class actually becomes irrelevant, even though it is one of only two numbers in the problem. The correct answer to the problem is actually the only one of the two numbers in the problem that is relevant to the solution—namely, seven.

A famous problem that is similar to the museum problem and similar in its selective encoding requirements is the following: "An airplane crashes on the U.S.–Canadian border. In what country are the survivors buried?" The correct solution to this problem requires careful reading and selective encoding of the word "survivors." Unless you read the problem very carefully, you will not come up with the correct answer that the survivors are not buried. People taking standardized tests often answer items incorrectly because they have not carefully read the terms of the problems and end up answering questions other than the one asked.

Each of the following problems requires selective encoding for its solution. First list the relevant information for solving each problem (selective encoding). Then solve each problem. Solving these problems will give you practice on careful selective encoding. The answers to the problems appear in the Appendix.

1. Calendars made in England do not show Lincoln's birthday, of course. Do these calendars show the fourth of July?

2. In a country that allows polygamy, a man married three women. Each woman had only one husband, and each woman had a legitimate child. Yet none of these children were at all related to each other. How is this possible?

3. A man was putting some finishing touches on his house and realized that he still needed one thing. He went to the hardware store and asked the clerk, "How much will sixteen cost me?" The clerk in the hardware store answered, "They are a dollar apiece, so sixteen will cost you two dollars." What did the man buy?

4. In a certain city, .05 percent of the people are totally deaf. Shortly before an election, a local political party contacted ten thousand people by phone and reminded them to vote. How many of these people can be expected to be totally deaf?

5. In the Howard family, there are four sisters, and each sister

has one brother. If you count Mr. Howard, how many males are there in the Howard family?

6. Julie took a city bus from home to work one morning. The traffic was heavy and the bus's average speed for the entire trip was just twenty-five miles per hour. The total time of the trip was eighty minutes, and Julie paid a fare of $1.50. That afternoon, Julie's mother visited her at work, then took the city bus to Julie's home. Julie's mother was a senior citizen, so she got a 25-percent fare discount. The bus returned along the same route that Julie had taken that morning and traveled with the same average speed. But this time the trip took an hour and twenty minutes. Can you explain why?

7. An appliance store ordered forty toasters. Each toaster cost the manager $15. The total bill was $600. After she placed the order, the store manager discovered that had she ordered fifty or more toasters, she would have received a 10-percent discount. If she had ordered five more toasters, how much more would she have had to pay?

8. A customer gives a twenty-dollar bill to a jeweler for a watch priced at $12. Because he is short of change, the jeweler changes the twenty-dollar bill at a store next door. He gives the watch and $8 to the customer. Later, the neighboring storekeeper, discovering the twenty-dollar bill to be counterfeit, returns it to the jeweler. If the jeweler sold the watch for twice what he paid for it, how much did he pay for the watch?

9. Al starts biking at the beginning of Shoreline Road and continues north toward Gull Beach, averaging five miles per hour. An hour later, Dave starts biking at the same place and heads north on the same route, averaging ten miles per hour. It is twenty-five miles from the beginning of Shoreline Road to Gull Beach. Which bike is nearer to Gull Beach when they meet?

10. Eggs that are laid on Tuesday at Taunton Farms appear on the shelves of Best Market on Thursday morning. Mrs. Connelly always buys these eggs on Thursday afternoon. She then hard-boils any eggs left over from the previous week. Eggs in the Connelly household are always eaten up within two weeks of purchase. One Saturday her son Jeff eats egg salad for lunch. How many days ago did a rooster lay this egg at Taunton Farms?

The problems presented in this section have given you an overview of the use of selective encoding in fairly well-structured mathematical and logical problems. Many problems in everyday life, however, are less structured and require you to evaluate the relevance of successive bits of information—say, when you keep hearing new things about a car you're thinking of buying. The information-evaluation problems below will give you some practice in distinguishing relevant from irrelevant information.

Information-evaluation problems. In each of the following problems, you are presented with a question and a number of facts taken from a story. Mark each fact as either relevant (R) or irrelevant (I) for answering the questions. In some cases, two pieces of information may be relevant only when considered in conjunction with each other. In such cases, both pieces of information should be marked as relevant. You should therefore read all of the statements before marking any of them as relevant or irrelevant. When you have read all of the statements, go back and reread the statements, marking each as relevent or irrelevant. Answers appear in the Appendix.

1. How do desert animals withstand the heat of the desert?
   a. Most desert animals cannot tolerate temperatures above 150 degrees Fahrenheit.
   b. Desert animals are often nocturnal and live inside underground tunnels during the day.
   c. A typical burrow does not get any hotter than 80 degrees Fahrenheit.
   d. The burrows of desert animals have high relative humidity, which comes from the animals' own water vapor.
   e. The burrows prevent animals from becoming dehydrated.
2. Why do television sets with cable connections get better reception than televisions with antennas?
   a. Televisions flash pictures on a screen at a rate of thirty pictures per second and so produce the effect of continuous motion.
   b. At the broadcast station, a television image must be analyzed into 200,000 electrical charges.
   c. Each of the 200,000 charges is discharged thirty times per second and transmitted to the viewers.
   d. The picture can be transmitted by a coaxial cable, which travels directly from the broadcast source to the viewer.
   e. Most television pictures are transmitted by waves (high-frequency short waves) similar to those used by radio stations.
   f. High-frequency short waves can travel only in straight lines; they cannot bend to follow the earth's surface. Their range is limited to the visual horizon.

3. Why is it necessary to add detergent to water in order to wash clothes?
   a. The combination of detergent and water allows the detergent to penetrate between the clothes and the dirt.
   b. One hundred pounds of domestic washing is soiled with between two and four pounds of dirt.
   c. Most dirt cannot be dissolved by water alone.
   d. One hundred pounds of domestic washing typically has 0.9 pound of protein-free organic matter (waxes, alcohol), 0.3 pound of protein (hair, skin), 0.15 pound of grease and sweat, as well as sand and dust.
4. Where do space satellites get the electricity to run their electronic equipment?
   a. Weather satellites, communication satellites, and probes are unmanned.
   b. The storage batteries of U.S. satellites are kept charged by current generated in solar cells.
   c. Satellites can alter their courses with control jets when they receive commands from earth monitoring stations.
   d. In 1965, the space probe *Mariner 4* took twenty-one pictures of the planet Mars from a distance of 6,000 miles.

Now that you have had some practice in discerning the relevance of various bits of information, you will have a chance to see whether you can use your information-evaluation skills. All of us have to solve mysteries in our lives—figuring out what a person is like or why a car won't start, diagnosing ailments, and so on. Here are some mystery problems that involve fictitious crimes.

Mystery problems. The prototypical situation for the application of insights is the situation faced by a detective trying to solve a crime. Selective encoding can be particularly important in detective work. Consider each of the following four mystery stories, and solve them, using selective encoding as your primary basis for solution. Answers appear in the Appendix.

MYSTERY 1
Trying to fight his seasickness, Detective Ramirez followed the ship's captain through the long corridor that would take him to the cabin of his favorite actor, Kevin Stock.

The cabin door was open and Ramirez saw Stock's body slumped over the desk. A small gun lay in his right hand. Approaching the desk, Ramirez could see some loose papers on it, splattered with blood. Among them was a suicide note in which Mr. Stock explained why he had suddenly decided to end his life. A pen without its cover was also on the desk.

Having read the suicide note, Ramirez still could not understand how a famous actor such as Stock could have committed suicide. His death upset Ramirez very much.

Ramirez shifted his eyes from the note to Stock's body, which was lying on its left side. Stock was a slim man in his fifties whose thick dark hair made him look much younger and nearly masked a small scar near his right ear. He was wearing a well-cut summer suit that showed the actor's taste for the good things in life. "What a loss," Ramirez thought.

A noise in the background reminded Ramirez that there were two other people in the cabin: Stock's niece, Ms. Landry, who had discovered the body, and the ship's captain. Detective Ramirez asked Ms. Landry to tell him everything she had heard or seen regarding the incident.

"We came back to Mr. Stock's cabin shortly after dinner," she said. "Uncle Kevin told me he wanted to be alone. He wanted to write a letter. So I left the cabin and went directly to my own cabin, across the hall."

"What happened after that?" asked Ramirez.

"Shortly after I left, I heard a shot," Ms. Landry continued, "and when I came in, I saw Uncle Kevin's body slumped on the desk. I called his name but I got no reply, so I moved closer to see why he didn't answer. Then I noticed the bullet hole through his left temple."

"Did you touch anything?" asked Detective Ramirez.

"No, I did not. I left everything the way it was."

Ramirez was certain that the apparent suicide was in fact a murder. "You'd better tell me the whole truth," he said to Ms. Landry.

How did Detective Ramirez know that Mr. Stock's death was murder, not suicide?

MYSTERY 2

It was a hot midsummer evening, and Detective Ramirez was just finishing a late dinner. He was considering dessert when the clock struck ten and the phone rang. It was his boss, Chief Inspector

Finley, who asked Ramirez to go immediately to a second-floor apartment in a well-off neighborhood. On the way, Ramirez noticed that the night sky was particularly clear.

As soon as Detective Ramirez met Finley, he asked him what the problem was.

"This is Mr. Harlow," said Finley. "He can explain everything better than I can."

"Well?" said Ramirez to a very nervous man, who seemed to be in shock.

"We came back from the movies around eight," said Mr. Harlow. "My wife went directly to our bedroom while I read the paper in the den. An hour later I went to go to bed and I found our bedroom locked. I knocked but my wife didn't answer. I thought she had forgotten to unlock the door and was taking a bath, so I went back to the den and read some more. When I returned to the bedroom and still got no response, I started to worry and called the police."

"Show us the room," said Ramirez.

Once there, Ramirez tried, unsuccessfully, to force the door. He asked Harlow if there was another way to enter the room. Harlow took Ramirez outside the building and showed him the bedroom window. Ramirez put a ladder to the window and climbed up. The window was slightly open. When he finally entered the room, he could barely see well enough to find the switch to turn on the light. He then opened the door to let Finley in. Mrs. Harlow's body was slumped over her desk, a suicide note under her hand. The handwriting was erratic and the lines sloped down to one side. The pen was still firmly grasped by the woman's hand. In a very unclear way, the woman explained why she had taken her life.

Just at that moment, the Harlows' only son arrived home. When he saw a policeman, he asked at once what was going on. There had been a death, he was told; his mother had committed suicide. When the young man heard this, he rushed up and found Detective Ramirez, Inspector Finley, and Mr. Harlow reading the note. They were talking about the difficulty of reading the woman's handwriting.

"If only she had written a more legible note," said Mr. Finley. To which the young man replied: "Mother could never see very well in the dark."

Ramirez lit a cigar, looked at the young man, and asked him where he had been earlier in the evening. Between sobs, the young man said to Ramirez, "I was at the public library. I left home around six thirty. When the library closed, I took a walk in the park and then came home to find this terrible event."

Ramirez looked at the young man and said, "I would like you to come with me to the police headquarters. I do not believe this was suicide. It was murder."

Why did Ramirez suspect Harlow's son?

MYSTERY 3

Sitting in his office, smoking a big cigar, Detective Ramirez was ready to question Mr. Springer about his friend Mr. Wilson's death when the phone rang.

It was the coroner, reporting the cause of Mr. James Wilson's death. "The body has bruises everywhere, but James Wilson died from a blow to the back of his head," he said.

As soon as Ramirez hung up the phone, Mr. Springer started to tell in his very soft voice his version of what had happened to his friend.

"Yesterday we started hiking back from the campsite where we stayed the night before. It was a difficult hike; the ground was wet and slippery, and the wind was against us strongly the whole way. I started getting tired, so I slowed down. But Jim got very impatient and said he would go on ahead and meet me at the next shelter. He started to run. I called after him to be careful and slow down, but by this time he was so far ahead of me that, although his voice was strong, I could hardly hear him shout back angrily that he knew how to hike. I then lost sight of him. Shortly after I passed the place where I had last seen him, I saw him on the rocks at the bottom of the cliff. By the time I got down to him, he was already dead."

Detective Ramirez smiled as he booked Mr. Springer as a murder suspect.

Why did Detective Ramirez arrest Mr. Springer?

MYSTERY 4

It was noon, and Detective Ramirez was on his way to a house on Southwood Avenue. A few minutes before, Inspector Finley had phoned to inform him of a death and to ask him to come to the house where the death had occurred. As soon as Ramirez arrived at the posh three-story house, Inspector Finley told him what he knew.

"This morning, just before I called you, the cleaning woman called me and told me about the incident."

"Is she still here?" said Ramirez. "I would like to ask her some questions."

As soon as Ramirez met the cleaning woman, he asked her to explain everything she knew about the incident.

"As usual," she explained, "I came here at eight o'clock and let myself in with the key that Mrs. Ewing gave me. She's usually eating breakfast by then, but her bedroom door was closed and the radio was on, so I decided not to disturb her. So I went back downstairs and started cleaning the living room. Then I went down to the basement and started cleaning there; that's a project she's wanted me to do for a while. About eleven thirty, when I had finished all the rest of the cleaning, I went upstairs to do the bedrooms. Everything was quiet, and her door was still closed. I thought that maybe she had left without my hearing her. So I opened the door and there I saw her lying on the bed. She was very pale and her eyes were lifeless. I got scared and called the police."

"Let's go to the room," said Ramirez.

Detective Ramirez entered Mrs. Ewing's room and saw her lying on her bed, dead. Everything was quiet; there was no sign of any violent struggle or damage caused by somebody breaking into the room. Everything seemed to be in perfect order. Certain details in the room showed Detective Ramirez some features of the deceased's personality. Several well-kept plants hung in front of the window. Family photos sat on the night table. The closet was open, revealing a large selection of fashionable clothes. There was an ornate Oriental fan on the bureau. In Mrs. Ewing's right hand there was a covered bottle of sleeping pills; only two were left. It looked like a typical suicide.

Touching the deceased's body, Detective Ramirez said, "This woman has been dead for many hours." He asked the inspector, "Did you remove anything in this room?"

"No, nothing at all!"

"There is something odd here, and I am going to find out what it is," said Ramirez, looking at the cleaning woman. "I will need to talk with you a little longer."

Why did Detective Ramirez think there was something odd going on?

You have now solved a variety of problems requiring the skill of selective encoding—deciding what information is relevant for the solution of a given problem. Sometimes, however, the biggest problem we face is not deciding what information is relevant but putting relevant information together in a meaningful way. Problems that require this skill are called selective-combination problems.

SELECTIVE-COMBINATION PROBLEMS

Here are some of the kinds of selective-combination problems one may encounter, starting again with well-structured arithmetical and logical problems.

There were one hundred politicians at a meeting. Each politician was either honest or dishonest. We know the following two facts: First, at least one of the politicians was honest; second, for any two politicians at least one of the two was dishonest. Can you tell how many of the politicians were honest and how many were dishonest, and if so, what are the respective numbers of each?

In this particular problem, selective encoding of information is not particularly difficult. Indeed, the relevant clues—that at least one politician was honest and that for any two politicians at least one was dishonest—are even emphasized. The problem is to figure out how to combine these clues.

The first clue tells you that there is at least one honest politician. From it, you can infer that there are possibly ninety-nine dishonest politicians—of course, there may be fewer. The second clue tells you that if you take any two politicians, you are guaranteed that at least one of them (and possibly both of them) will be dishonest. Combining these two clues gives you an answer to the problem. The second clue tells you that if you take the honest politician in the first clue and match that politician with any other of the 99 politicians, at least one of the two will be dishonest. Now, since you know that the politician from the first clue is honest, it follows that the other 99 must be dishonest. There is no other way of guaranteeing that at least one politician in each pair will be dishonest. You can conclude, then, that there is one honest politician and there are ninety-nine dishonest politicians.

Now, consider another selective-combination problem that many people find to be quite difficult, despite its simple appearance.

I bought one share in the Sure-Fire corporation for $70. I sold that share for $80. Eventually, I bought back the share for $90, but later I sold it for $100. How much money did I make?

As in the preceding problem, the information that is relevant for solution is quite obvious. Indeed, all of the numerical information in this problem is relevant. The question is, how does one combine it? There are actually two ways to arrive at the answer. The first involves considering the first buying-selling sequence. When the share of stock is sold the first time, I make a profit of $10. When I sell the share the second time, I again make a profit of $10. My total profit, therefore, is $20. Another way to solve this problem involves simply adding up the amount of money I pay in purchasing shares ($70 + $90 = $160) and subtracting that sum from the total amount involved in my selling of the shares ($80 + $100 = $180). The difference, again, is $20, my profit on the transactions.

Each of the following problems requires selective combination for its solution. Although there may be other difficulties to each problem, the primary one is figuring out how to combine pieces of information. See if you can solve each problem below. Answers appear in the Appendix.

1. How many flowers do I have if all of them are roses except two, all of them are tulips except two, and all of them are daisies except two?

2. Janine's three children are home for lunch. They must finish quickly so they can be back at school on time. They each want one slice of French toast. Janine's frying pan, however, is big enough for only two slices at a time. Janine thinks, "It takes six minutes to prepare a slice of French toast—three minutes on each side. So it'll take six minutes to prepare the first two slices, and another six minutes for the third slice. That makes twelve minutes in all." How can Janine finish all three slices of French toast in just nine minutes?

3. Dale worked at the library twenty hours per week. On busy weeks his boss asked him to work twenty-five hours, but he always refused, saying he was too busy. Finally his boss asked him why he was always so busy. Dale answered, "Well, I work twenty hours per week. I sleep eight hours at night, or fifty-six hours per week. I spend three hours a day eating—that's another twenty-one hours per week. Weekends take up forty-eight hours per week. Night school, including homework, takes up another fifteen hours per week. I spend another five hours visiting my parents. Altogether that's 165 hours. Since there are only 168 hours in a week, that leaves me just three hours a week for recreation, shopping, and laundry. So how could I possibly work another five hours?" Dale's boss was puzzled. Can you help her find the error in Dale's calculations?"

4. You have three boxes of checkers: one labeled "red checkers," one labeled "black checkers," and one labeled "red and black checkers." Unfortunately, each label is on a wrong box. By

taking only one checker from one box, how can you label each box correctly?

5. You arrive in a country that has two types of people: truth tellers and liars. The truth tellers always tell the truth, and the liars always lie. Your tour guide, a native, tells you that the country's prime minister just admitted to being a liar. Is your tour guide a liar or a truth teller?

6. On October 1 you go to the first lecture in a weekly series of four lectures. On what date will the final lecture take place?

7. Since it was founded in 1860, the town of Harwood has doubled in population every twenty years. In 1980 the population of Harwood was forty thousand. In what year did Harwood have half as many people as it did in 1980?

8. A camera costs $100, including the case. The camera costs $80 more than the case. How much does the case cost?

9. A cookie recipe calls for three cups of flour. You have only a two-cup container and a seven-cup container, both of which are otherwise unmarked. How can you measure out exactly three cups of flour using only these two containers?

10. Sarah has $60 and Joe has $40. How much money must Sarah give Joe so that they have the same amount of money?

SELECTIVE-COMPARISON PROBLEMS

Finally, consider the last of the three "selective" processes, one by which new information is related to old. This process, called selective comparison, is used to bridge the gap between what you already know and what you are learning. Analogies are good examples of such problems because they require you to draw upon prior knowledge but also require you to infer a relation and then to use the relation to complete a new one. Most analogies, however, are quite familiar in type. As previously mentioned, the problems that best test intelligence present moderately unfamiliar or novel situations.

Novel analogies. It is possible to create novel analogies by proposing altered states of the world. Consider the analogies below. In solving these analogies, assume that the statement given before the analogy is true, whether or not it actually is. Then solve the analogy, taking this assumption into account. Sometimes the assumption will be true in the real world; other times it will be false. Sometimes the assumption will affect the solution you reach; other times it will not. The important thing is to assume the statement is true, regardless of its actual truth or falsity, and then to use the assumption, where needed, to solve the analogies. Answers appear in the Appendix.

1. LEMONADE is carbonated.
   CINNAMON is to SPICE as LEMONADE is to
   SODA   GLASS   STRAW   ORANGE JUICE

2. VIOLINS are made of plastic.
   PIANO is to KEYS as VIOLIN is to
   TUNE   INSTRUMENT   STRINGS   WOOD

3. LAME people cannot see.
   DEAF is to EAR as LAME is to
   RACE   LEG   CANE   EYE

4. OCEANS have fresh water.
   DESERT is to DUNE as OCEAN is to
   SALT   SAND   WAVE   SEA

5. THUNDER makes noise.
   LIGHTNING is to VISIBLE as THUNDER is to
   SCARY   AUDIBLE   CLOUDY   DANGEROUS

6. The CHINESE drink tea.
   GERMAN is to EUROPEAN as CHINESE is to
   ENGLISH   JAPANESE   KOREAN   ASIAN

7. PESSIMISTS expect the worst.
   OPTIMIST is to HOPE as PESSIMIST is to
   DEPRESSION   CONFUSION   DESPAIR   FEELING

8. BEDS have sheets.
   BUILDING is to DOME as BED is to
   CANOPY   PILLOW   HOTEL   ROOM

9. TYPEWRITERS use paper.
   TELEPHONE is to DIAL as TYPEWRITER is to
   MARGIN   KEYBOARD   OFFICE   CORD

10. SIAMESE is a variety of cow.
    DALMATIAN is to PUPPY as SIAMESE is to
    CALF   ANIMAL   KITTEN   CAT

11. A SWING is a hanging weight.
    SEESAW is to LEVER as SWING is to
    PENDULUM   CHILD   SLIDE   PLAYGROUND

12. RACCOONS eat meat.
    HUMANS is to HANDS as RACCOONS is to
    PAWS   STRIPES   FUR   FOOD

13. DOGS have three legs.
    TRAIN is to CABOOSE as DOG is to
    COLLAR   TAIL   EARS   PAW

14. PIGS are pet birds.
    GOLDFISH is to BOWL as PIG is to
    FEATHERS   CAGE   STY   MUD

15. LIMOUSINES are long.
    JET is to PILOT as LIMOUSINE is to
    PASSENGER   CHAUFFEUR   MANSION   WEALTH

SCIENTIFIC-INSIGHT PROBLEMS

Now, combine the use of the three insight skills—selective encoding, selective combination, and selective comparison—in solving the scientific-insight problems that follow. Answers appear in the Appendix.

1. Every morning, millions of microscopic crustaceans in the world's lakes and oceans migrate to water many fathoms deep. Late each afternoon, they surface again. For them, this is an expensive round trip to commute, requiring enormous amounts of energy and time, and students of migration have wondered for years what such zooplankton gain by spending their days in cold, dark waters, where food is scarce, and where they cannot reproduce quickly.

   To find out, two scientists spent a year observing two species, *Daphnia hyalina* and *Daphnia galeata*. Both species spend the night near the surface, but in the morning, *D. hyalina* departs for the depths, rejoining *D. galeata* only when shadows lengthen in early evening.

   All day long, *D. galeata* enjoys the benefits of warmth and abundant food near the lake's surface while, far below, *D. hyalina* is deprived. Under such conditions, one would expect *D. galeata* to thrive and multiply until it drove its neighbor out.

   Not so, the scientists report. Even though *D. galeata* grows and reproduces faster, its population is equaled—and often outnumbered—by *D. hyalina*.

   Please explain why.

2. There is at least one known instance of a jet fighter pilot's shooting his own plane out of the air, using his own guns. Amazing as it seems, a supersonic jet fighter can catch up with the fire from its own guns and shoot itself down. If a plane flying at 1000 mph fires a burst from 20-millimeter guns, the shells leave the plane with an airspeed of about 3000 mph.

Why won't a plane that continues to fly straight ahead fly into its own bullets?

3. Napoleon surrendered to the British in 1815. The British sent him into exile on the island of St. Helena because they wanted to eliminate any possibility that he would rebuild his army. Napoleon and a few attendants were sent to Longwood House, a moldy, damp house, which, as their only concession to the once-powerful emperor, the British repapered in green-and-gold wallpaper.

Over the past few years, Dr. Stan Forshufrud has studied the medical accounts of Napoleon's last months on St. Helena. The scientist developed a theory that Napoleon was deliberately and systematically poisoned with arsenic by his enemies. Napoleon's symptoms were classic for arsenic poisoning: shivering, swelling of the limbs, and repeated gastric upsets. Napoleon's companions in exile also suffered from these symptoms.

Another scientist, Dr. David Jones, has been studying the uses of arsenic over the years. This is his report:

By 1800, a popular and cheap dye, "Scheele green," was used in paints, fabrics, and wallpapers. The dye was arsenic. As long as the wallpaper, fabric, or paint was dry, it was quite harmless. But once it got wet—from condensation, rising damp, or whatever—it could go moldy. To survive on the wallpaper, the mold must somehow get rid of the arsenic. Many molds convert it to a vapor.

What do you think might have caused Napoleon's death?

4. In 1960, Dr. Wooton, a doctor and professor of medicine at the University of Tennessee, was surprised to see a young man walk into his office. The young man was orange.

Dr. Wooton was even more surprised when the man said that his problem was a stomach pain, but made no mention of his color. Quickly, Dr. Wooton recalled various medical disorders that could cause skin color to change. Liver damage turned a victim yellow; heart disease turned a victim blue; pituitary disease turned a victim paper-white. But he couldn't imagine what turned a person orange.

After examining the patient, Dr. Wooton discovered the patient had an abnormal pancreas, which could mean cancer. He scheduled the young man for tests at the hospital and took a detailed history. One of the doctor's questions was "When did you turn orange?" The man said he hadn't realized he was turning orange, because it had happened so gradually. The doctor found nothing else unusual in the man's background, except for his diet. He ate lots of vegetables—carrots, rutabagas, squash, beans, spinach—as well as oranges and eggs, and he drank gallons of tomato juice each day.

The man went to the hospital and had tests performed. They showed that his stomach pain was not cancer but a simple cyst that could be easily removed. It was not responsible for the strange color of his skin.

Dr. Wooton did more research into the problem of the man's skin color and finally found documented proof that food could change a person's color. Foods like carrots, oranges, and eggs contain carotene, which turns a person yellow but not orange. Then he found reports that tomatoes contain lycopene, a red dye. But tomatoes were not known to turn a person orange.

What do you think caused the man to turn orange?

5. Heat pumps, air conditioners, and refrigerators are very similar machines. What each of them does is to pump heat from one place into another. Heat pumps move heat from air that is outside a house into the inside of a house. (Even when it is cold outside, the air still has some heat.) Air conditioners move heat from inside a house to the outside of a house. Refrigerators take heat from inside a refrigerator and move it outside of the refrigerator.

On a hot afternoon, if you opened the door of your refrigerator, do you think it would significantly cool off your kitchen? Why?

THE USE OF SELECTIVE ENCODING, SELECTIVE COMBINATION, AND SELECTIVE COMPARISON IN VOCABULARY ACQUISITION

It is often said that what separates humankind from other animal life is the ability of humans to learn and use language. By almost any standard, this ability is an impressive one. People regularly use, with only minor flaws, a grammatical system that to this day linguists and psychologists do not fully understand. They apply this grammatical system to vocabularies that, for adults, are usually estimated to exceed fifty thousand words, and that for educated adults may exceed seventy thousand or eighty thousand words. The prodigious size of people's vocabularies becomes even more amazing when you consider that only a very small proportion of these words were ever directly taught. In early school years, an individual is probably more likely to have formal instruction in spelling than in vocabulary, and what vocabulary is directly taught seems most likely to be forgotten later. However we acquire the tens of thousands of words in our vocabulary, it is clearly not primarily on the basis of direct instruction.

The skills we use to acquire our vocabularies would seem to be critical as building blocks of our intelligence. As discussed earlier, psychologists have found vocabulary to be perhaps the best single indicator of a person's overall level of intelligence. The importance of vocabulary to the measurement of intelligence is shown by the prevalence of vocabulary items on both of the major individual scales of intelligence—the Stanford-Binet and the Wechsler—and on many group-administered tests of intelligence. In an effort to understand and increase your intelligence, you should understand the basis of vocabulary acquisition and then work on improving your vocabulary-acquisition skills.

The point of view advanced here, and one believed by many other psychologists as well, is that most vocabulary acquisition proceeds as we learn the meanings of words by encountering them in context. In many instances, the individual may not even be fully aware of this process. Suppose, for example, you are reading a book or a magazine and encounter a word that is either unknown or only vaguely familiar in meaning. At this point you may consult a dictionary, but chances are you won't bother. More likely, you'll try to figure out the meaning of the word through the context. Quite often, the context provides a wealth of information about the word in question. However, the contextual information must first be located, and individuals differ in their skills in finding and using this information.

In learning the meanings of new words embedded in context, you have to separate helpful, relevant information from extraneous material that is irrelevant to or may actually obstruct the words' meanings. Moreover, you must combine the selected information into a meaningful whole, using past information about the nature of words as a guide. Deciding what contextual cues are useful and how to use them does not occur in a vacuum. Rather, these processes are guided by the use of old information. The reader constantly seeks to connect the context of the unknown word to something familiar. Thus, processing the available information requires three distinct operations: (a) locating relevant information in context, (b) combining this information into a meaningful whole, and (c) relating this information to what you already know—in other words, selective encoding, selective combination, and selective comparison, respectively.

Selective encoding involves sifting out relevant from irrelevant information. When an unfamiliar word is presented in context, cues relevant to deciphering its meaning are embedded within large amounts of unhelpful or possibly even misleading information. The reader must sift out the relevant cues. Metaphorically, the wheat must be separated from the chaff. Most readers selectively encode information without even being aware that they are doing it. By becoming more aware of this process, you are in a better position to use it effectively.

When you encounter an unfamiliar word, imagine the word to be the center of a network of information. Seek out cues concerning the word's meaning that appear in the same sentence as the unknown word. Then, expand your systematic search, incorporating the sentences surrounding the sentence containing the unknown word.

Consider the brief passage presented in box 1.

BOX 1

At the zoo, they were just starting to eat their lunch at one of the picnic tables when they saw the *macropodida*. The children were fighting over which sandwich they each wanted. Not thirty feet away, the *macropodida* suddenly hopped closer. A typical marsupial, she was carrying a young baby, called a joey in Australia, in her pouch. When the children ran over toward her, she stopped chewing on a piece of vegetation and bounded away.

Even in this rather obvious example, there is much information to weed out. For instance, in order to figure out the meaning of *macropodida*, we need not know that the family in the passage was eating their lunch or that the children were fighting over food. In a systematic search for relevant information, it helps to realize that irrelevant information will relate to something in the context other than the unknown word. For instance, most of the irrelevant data in the above example relate to the children in the story, whereas the helpful cues relate directly to the word *macropodida*.

In the first sentence, there are two important cues: (a) they saw a *macropodida*, so *macropodidae* must be visually perceptible, and (b) they were in a zoo, so that *macropodidae* are found in zoos. The second sentence does not contain any particularly relevant information; the facts of the sentence relate to the children, not to the unknown word. The next sentence informs us that *macropodidae* hop. In the fourth sentence, we learn that a *macropodida* is a marsupial and is carrying her young in a pouch. Finally, the last sentence tells us that *macropodidae* eat vegetation and can jump fast.

It should be noted here that normally you would not selectively encode all of the available information before proceeding to combine and compare the relevant facts. Usually, you would shift from one process to another as you proceed through the paragraph. The listing of relevant data above is merely an attempt to show you the kinds of information that can be selectively encoded.

Selective combination involves combining selectively encoded information in such a way as to form an integrated, plausible definition of the previously unknown words. Simply sifting out the relevant cues is not enough to arrive at a tentative definition of a word: you must know how to combine these cues into an integrated representation of the word. Typically, the available information can be combined in many ways; and inevitably, two different individuals will produce slightly different combinations. Usually, however, there is one optimal combination of information. You can imagine an analogy to the job of a detective. First, the detective has to decide what the relevant clues are to figuring out who perpetrated a crime (selective encoding). Once the detective has figured out some relevant clues, he begins to combine them selectively in such a way as to build a plausible case against the suspect. Combining the clues improperly can result in a false lead and, ultimately, the apprehension of the wrong suspect. Like a detective, you have to track down the meaning of the word that is appropriate in the given context.

Consider how the process of selective combination can be applied to the *macropodida* example. Combining the information encoded earlier, we now know that *macropodidae* are plant-eating animals that can hop rapidly and that may carry their young in a pouch (typical of marsupials). We now have a fairly extensive network of information about the word *macropodida*. Putting all the information together in a systematic manner yields a definition of a *macropodida*. All that is left to do is to replace *macropodida* with its synonym "kangaroo."

Box 2 contains a passage with a relatively uncommon word. Read the passage and note all portions of the text that seem to you to be relevant to figuring out the meaning of the unknown word. Try to be conscious of how each relevant item relates to the target word. Then define the word.

Try to figure out the meaning of the word *neolagnium* before reading on. As you may have noticed, there are many helpful pieces of information relating to the target word. First, we learn that *neolagnium* is a period

---

BOX 2

Physically and psychologically, the years of *neolagnium* are filled with the growth and development of the individual. The young person's efforts to understand this changing self are often unpleasant and alarming to adults; his or her explorations of new social, sexual, and intellectual possibilities may seem more a challenge to the parents' authority than part of the process of *neolagnium*. The young person's boasting about his or her adventures and misadventures serves to strengthen the parents' tendency to respond to such activities as moral issues. The sinner who is vocally proud of his or her sin is generally regarded with greater distaste than the discreet offender. Misunderstandings abound, fed by the lack of diplomacy on the part of the young and the fear of changing times on the part of the adults.

---

of years of development of the individual. This period of change affects young people physically and psychologically. We learn that adults—in particular, parents—often find this period unpleasant and alarming. Later on in the passage, we are informed that *neolagnium* is a period of misunderstandings, marked by fear of change on the part of adults. From all this information, it is reasonable to infer that this period of life comes before adulthood—that is, adolescence.

In box 3 is another passage that will give you a chance to exercise your skills in selective combination. Locate the available cues in the passage (selective encoding), and then see if you can combine these cues into a meaningful definition or sentence describing the unknown word.

This is an easy passage on which to practice your skills. Not only is there a wealth of helpful cues, but these cues are easily combined as well. One way of combining concrete information such as this is to attempt to form a visual image of what the object, in this case an animal, could look like. Before too long, the visual image that you form, as you combine into it more and more information, is quite likely to look like a camel, which is what an *oont* is.

Selective comparison involves relating new information to information acquired in the past. As a reader decides what information to encode and how to combine this information, what is already known about the topic can be quite useful as a guide. No contextual information, no matter how relevant, can be at all useful unless it can somehow be related to past knowledge. Without previous knowledge, the helpful hints that would normally lead the reader to the definition of an unknown term will be meaningless, and they will probably not even be recognized as relevant information. New information can be related to old information, and vice

---

BOX 3

Haro took great care of his *oont*, his one means of survival in the great desert of Africa. Whenever water in one area got scarce, everyone would load up their *oont*s and travel to a new water hole. Haro was fond of his *oont*, with her long, shaggy coat, humped back, and long, graceful neck. After being unloaded, she would settle down in the desert sand, chew her cud, and spit or bite anyone who annoyed her. As is typical of *oont*s, once she made up her mind, there was no budging her. She would sit out a sandstorm before she would change her mind. No wonder people called her kind the "ship of the desert"!

---

versa, by the use of similes, metaphors, analogies, and models, but the goal is always the same: to give the new information meaning by connecting it to old information that is already known.

Now return once again to the passage in box 1 in order to analyze how selective comparison operates. In selective comparison, we try to establish how the new word is similar to and different from old words that we already have stored in memory. We may end up deciding either that the new word is a synonym for an old word that we already know or that a new concept has to be constructed that expands on our old concepts. In the case of the *macropodida*, the more information we get, the more restricted is the range of things that it might be. Initially, it might be anything one might see in a zoo. That leaves a very large list. Later, we are able to reduce our list as we learn that a *macropodida* is something that hops. We can restrict our list of possibilities further when we learn that it is a marsupial that eats vegetation. If our original list of animals found in a zoo included things such as lions, tigers, giraffes, kangaroos, koalas, seals, and hippopotamuses, our developing list could no longer include all of these things. In fact, by the time we are done with the passage, the only item on this list that could be described in the passage is the kangaroo. Thus, the process of selective comparison includes a whittling-down process whereby large numbers of possibilities are successively reduced. Eventually, if only one possibility remains, that possibility is a likely synonym for the unknown word. If no possibilities remain, then we probably have to form a new concept that is related to, but different from, all old concepts we have stored in memory.

Consider the sample passage in box 4. The passage contains two unknown words. As you read the passage, try to be conscious of the background knowledge that you are bringing to bear. Create a list of possible meanings for each of the two unknown words, based on the selective comparisons that you make. As you progressively encode and combine more information, eliminate meanings from your lists that do not seem to fit the descriptions of each of the two words.

BOX 4

Convict DiHoti had been incarcerated in a Mexican prison for selling contraband. Three weeks later, his *famulus*, Pancho Sanza, cleverly engineered his liberation from the hellish jail. Sanza provided DiHoti with a strong Persian horse while he himself rode on his donkey, named Dribble. Covered by darkness, they began their journey home. At dawn, as they were passing a large mansion, an explosion shook the house, glass shattered everywhere, and Sanza's *jennet* was struck in the hindquarters. Dribble lay down, dying.

The sound of the explosion alarmed the police, and the two outlaws could hear the approaching sirens. DiHoti pleaded with Sanza to flee, but Sanza would not abandon his stricken *jennet*. While they argued, the police arrived and, recognizing the two, arrested them both.

This passage has two target words, each of which must be analyzed separately. Start with the word *famulus*. We are told that Sanza is DiHoti's *famulus* and that he helps DiHoti to escape from jail. Together they ride away in the direction of home. Combining this information we can infer that they work and live together. Consider again the fact that Sanza provides DiHoti with a large Persian horse but only rides a donkey himself. Comparing this with prior knowledge, we would surmise that Sanza is the subordinate and DiHoti is the leader. Combining all the information about the word *famulus*, we can conclude that the word means sidekick, partner, or servant.

The word *jennet* is also fairly easy to define, given the amount of information available. First, we learn that a *jennet* has hindquarters and that it belongs to Sanza. When the *jennet* was struck in its hindquarters, Dribble lay down dying; a quick check of the beginning of the passage shows that Dribble is the name of the donkey that Sanza is riding. Later in the passage, reinforcing our definition of the word, we learn that Sanza will not abandon his stricken *jennet*. The link between the donkey Dribble and *jennet* is now complete—a *jennet* is a donkey (in fact, a female one).

Now use what you have learned about selective encoding, selective combination, and selective comparison to try to define the two uncommon words in the passage in box 5.

BOX 5

City police today reported the arrest of Matilda Jones, suspected of robbing the Pottstown Savings and Loan on November 23 and escaping with $75,000 in cash and with jewels and securities of undisclosed value. Jones will be held without bond until her trial next month. The bank has not yet recovered its *exinanition*, although police are following several leads. The crime has been hailed as the most carefully planned small-town robbery of the century. There were no witnesses to the crime; the security cameras had apparently malfunctioned; no fingerprints were left; and the alarm system had been tampered with. Jones would probably have remained unidentified, except that an ex-boyfriend reported her *jactancy* that she had found the perfect way to make money that was "quick, easy if you're clever, and tax-free."

Were you able to use selective encoding, selective combination, and selective comparison to figure out that *exinanition* is loss or theft and that *jactancy* is boasting or bragging? (Most people find the first word easier to figure out than the second.)

As we have seen in this chapter, knowledge-acquisition components are used to learn new information. Together with metacomponents and performance components, they enable us to solve a wide variety of problems. By now, perhaps you can see how the three kinds of components work together. You need metacomponents to decide what to do (performance components) and what to learn (knowledge-acquisition components). You need the other two kinds of components to execute the instructions of the metacomponents. The execution of these instructions provides feedback to the metacomponents, which, in effect, learn from their mistakes.

Thus, the three kinds of components work together to make intelligent thought and action possible. One example of relevant problems is the kind found in management. In the next chapter, we will consider how these components can be combined to form a basis for a critical aspect of management—"executive intelligence."

Applications of the Triarchic View

CHAPTER
8

Executive Intelligence

Intelligence is used in many aspects of our daily lives, and one of the most important of these is on-the-job performance. For those whose job is managerial in nature, the effective use of intelligence can make or break a career. But the intelligence used in managerial jobs is a far cry from the kind of intelligence required in academic situations, as measured by conventional intelligence tests. I refer to this different kind of intelligence as "executive intelligence."

Executive intelligence is the application of the skills of mental self-management to business situations. In our work on executive intelligence, Richard Wagner and I have attempted to understand executive intelligence in terms of the metacomponents, performance components, and knowledge-acquisition components of mental self-management.[1] Other researchers have also focused on executive intelligence, and their findings concur with those of Richard Wagner and myself. John Kotter, for example, studied fifteen general managers in nine United States corporations, and found that senior managers emphasize five activities in their work, all of which require the planning, monitoring, and evaluation activities of the metacomponents:[2]

1. Setting goals, policies, and strategies in the face of high uncertainty
2. Balancing their time and energy across different business functions
3. Controlling diverse activities so as to identify and solve a variety of problems rapidly

4. Developing an agenda that can be used to implement the tasks the manager needs to get done
5. Developing and maintaining a network of interpersonal relationships that can be used to collect information and carry out an agenda.

Daniel Isenberg has also studied the thinking of managers.[3] Isenberg's theory of executive intelligence emphasizes the importance of "opportunistic thinking," which has four main elements:

1. Responding to opportunities—even unexpected ones
2. Developing ideas and evaluations before the complete picture of a situation has been formed, and before you truly have a firm basis for judgment
3. Making inferences based on readily available information, with only minimal search for information
4. Applying this kind of thinking to your actions, attitudes, and beliefs.

Siegfried Streufert and Robert Swezey of Pennsylvania State University emphasize what they call "differentiation" and "integration" as bases for managerial thinking.[4] Good managers are able to break down a problem into its many parts, correctly understand the dimensions of the problem (differentiation), and then combine this information in a useful way (integration). According to these investigators, good managers have a reasonable degree of cognitive complexity—that is, they can see many elements of a given problem and put them together. They are not oversimplifiers.

Perhaps the greatest emphasis on metacomponential thinking comes from the work of Elliot Jaques of Great Britain, who emphasizes the time span for which an individual is able to plan.[5] Jaques believes that better managers are those who are able to plan ahead for a longer period of time.

Theorists of executive intelligence also consider performance components important. Isenberg notes the importance of "sense making," or what we have called "encoding" in this book—getting the sense of the information available. Isenberg also stresses the considerable importance of reasoning, and particularly of inference, in executive functioning. He further notes that successful executives are ones who use informal, plausible reasoning: they do not require certainty in their decisions, but they make decisions on the basis of what is likely to occur. George Klemp and

David McClelland also note that good managers are effective at coming up with and combining concepts.[6]

Tacit Knowledge and Intelligence in the Everyday World

We commonly assume that competence in many real-world pursuits is not fully attained on completion of one's formal training. If important knowledge and skills accrue from the application of knowledge-acquisition components to experience in real-world pursuits, what is the nature of such knowledge and skills, and what is their relation to practical intelligence?

Academic and Practical Intelligence

Ulric Neisser of Emory University argued that the tasks typically found on IQ tests and in school settings are measures of *academic intelligence*.[7] According to Neisser, tasks such as these are formulated by other people, are of little or no intrinsic interest, have all needed information available from the beginning, and are distant from an individual's ordinary experience. To these characteristics, Richard Wagner and I have added that academic tasks usually are well defined, have but one correct answer, and often have but one method of correct solution. IQ tests, then, measure skills in problem solving that are relatively different from the skills required to solve problems in the everyday world.

In contrast to academic intelligence, Neisser defines "intelligent performance in natural settings," which we consider to be *practical intelligence*, as "responding appropriately in terms of one's long-range and short-range goals, given the actual facts of the situation as one discovers them." In other words, you respond to situations in ways that help realize, or at least do not get in the way of, attaining your goals. Emotions may accompany this kind of intellectual performance. For example, deciding what kind of car to buy is partially an intellectual decision based on your objective needs for a car—but the decision also has strong emotional elements.

That "academic" intelligence is insufficient for successful performance in real-world settings is suggested by the low typical correlation (about .2 on a scale from 0 to 1) between occupational performance and performance on either IQ or employment tests reported by several researchers.[8] Correlations of this magnitude indicate that hardly any variance (only about 4 percent) in occupational performance is accounted for by IQ level. Stated simply, IQ provides only very modest prediction of performance on the job. Whether these typical correlations are good estimates of the true relationship between performance on IQ tests and performance in real-world pursuits is difficult to determine. Whereas Frank Schmidt and John Hunter argue that these correlations run low because of sources of error of measurement,[9] McClelland argues that they run high because of the joint effect of factors such as social-class status on both test and job performance (i.e., higher-status individuals score higher on the tests and are rated as better performers on the job by employers who share their status).[10]

It is also informative to compare performance on intelligence tests with performance in on-the-job training programs. The typical correlations between the tests and performance in on-the-job training situations are roughly double (.4) the typical correlations between the tests and actual job performance (.2), on the 0 to 1 scale. That the tests predict training performance better than job performance suggests that the tests measure only a subset of the competencies required for real-world success.

Approaches to Measuring Real-World Abilities

If traditional IQ and employment tests neglect abilities important to performance in real-world settings, how might such real-world competencies be measured?

The approach Richard Wagner and I have taken is based on the *knowledge-based approach* used by cognitive psychologists and others in their study of the ways in which "experts" differ from "novices" in task performance in their field of expertise. Examples of tasks examined with this approach include chess, physics problems, and computer programming. As discussed earlier, the consistent finding has been that experts differ from novices primarily in the amount and organization of their knowledge about the task rather than in underlying cognitive abilities.

Whereas the knowledge-based approach has been applied mostly to tasks of the "academic intelligence" variety, we sought to apply it to practical tasks faced by individuals in several real-world pursuits.

We commonly assume that competence in many real-world pursuits requires much more than formal training. What is the nature of the knowledge and skills we gain from real-world experience, and what is their relationship to everyday intelligence?

Wagner and I believe that much of the learning important to success in real-world pursuits happens in the absence of formal instruction. Furthermore, we view traditional IQ tests as measuring only a subset of the abilities required for maximal learning and performance in everyday situations. Our approach to isolating some of the abilities ignored by the developers of IQ tests has been to study differences in practical knowledge between "experts" and "novices" in the fields of academic psychology and business management. The major claim we make is that much of the knowledge on which performance in real-world settings is based is *tacit knowledge:* knowledge that is not openly expressed or stated.[11]

Tacit knowledge is considered to be practical rather than academic, informal rather than formal, and usually not directly taught. Knowing how best to get along with your colleagues or your boss is an example of tacit knowledge. By our use of the word "tacit" we do not wish to imply that such knowledge is completely inaccessible to conscious awareness, unspeakable, or even unteachable, merely that it usually is not taught directly. Much tacit knowledge may be disorganized and relatively inaccessible, making it potentially ill suited for direct instruction.

An Exercise in the Use of Tacit Knowledge

Below is a section of our tacit-knowledge questionnaire for business managers. Answer the questions, putting yourself in the position of a business manager. Then look at the solutions in the Appendix. The questions ask you to rate the importance you would assign to various items in making work-related decisions and judgments. Use a rating scale of 1 to 7: a 1 should signify "not important," whereas a 7 should signify "extremely important." Try to use the entire range of the scale when responding, although not necessarily for each question. For example, you may decide that none of the items listed for a particular question are important, or that they all are. There are, of course, no "correct" answers. You are encouraged to scan the items of a given question briefly before responding, to get some idea of their range of importance. Remember, you are being asked to rate the importance you personally would assign each item in making the judgment or decision mentioned in the question.

1. It is your second year as a mid-level manager in a company in the communications industry. You head a department of about thirty people. The evaluation of your first year on the job has been generally favorable. Performance ratings for your department are at least as good as they were before you took over, perhaps even a little better. You have two assistants. One is quite capable; the other just seems to go through the motions and is of little real help.

Although you are well liked, you believe that in the eyes of your superiors there is little to distinguish you from the nine other managers at a comparable level in the company.

Your goal is rapid promotion to the top of the company. The

following is a list of things you are considering doing in the next two months. You obviously cannot do them all. Rate the importance of each by its priority as a means of reaching your goal:

_____ a. Participate in a series of panel discussions to be shown on the local public television station.

_____ b. Find ways to make sure your superiors are aware of your important accomplishments.

_____ c. As a means of being noticed, propose a solution to a problem outside the scope of your immediate department that you would be willing to take charge of.

_____ d. When making decisions, give a great deal of weight to the way your superior likes things to be done.

_____ e. Accept a friend's invitation to join the exclusive country club that many higher-level executives belong to.

2. Your company has sent you to a university to recruit and interview potential trainees for management positions. Rate the importance of the following student characteristics by the extent to which they lead to later success in business:

_____ a. ability to set priorities according to the importance of your task

_____ b. motivation

_____ c. ability to follow through and bring tasks to completion

_____ d. ability to promote your ideas and to convince others of the worth of your work

_____ e. the need to win at everything, no matter what the cost.

3. A number of factors enter into the establishment of a good reputation in a company as a manager. Consider the following factors and rate their importance:

_____ a. critical thinking ability

_____ b. speaking ability

_____ c. extent of college education and the prestige of the school attended

_____ d. no hesitancy to take extraordinarily risky courses of action

_____ e. a keen sense of what superiors can be sold on.

4. Rate the following strategies of working according to how important you believe them to be for doing well at the day-to-day work of a business manager:

_____ a. Think in terms of tasks accomplished rather than hours spent working.

_____ b. Be in charge of all phases of every task or project you are involved with.

_____ c. Use a daily list of goals arranged according to your priorities.

_____ d. Carefully consider the optimal strategy before beginning a task.

_____ e. Reward yourself upon completion of important tasks.

5.   You are looking for several new projects to tackle. You have a list of possible projects and desire to pick the best two or three. Rate the importance of the following considerations when selecting projects:

_____ a. The project should prove to be fun.

_____ b. The project should attract the attention of the local media.

_____ c. The project is of special importance to me personally.

_____ d. The risk of making a mistake is virtually nonexistent.

_____ e. The project will require working directly with several senior executives.

In related research, Richard Wagner and I have sought to identify the "rules of thumb" managers use to solve problems such as those above and in order to succeed at their jobs. These "rules" fit well into the framework of the triarchic theory of intelligence; in other words, they can be categorized as corresponding to metacomponents, performance components, and knowledge-acquisition components.

An example of a rule of thumb is to "find ways to recognize problems as they arise before they become serious." This rule corresponds to the metacomponent, discussed earlier, of "recognizing the existence of a problem." Managers who fail to do so can pay a heavy price. For example, during the gas crunch of the 1970s, many people found themselves waiting in interminable lines for gasoline. Once they finally got to the pump, sometimes it would shut down right before they got their gas! Prior to the gas lines, there were relatively few imported cars in the United States, and what imported cars there were tended to be Volkswagens. Today, the market is flooded with imports, and they are not all Volkswagens. The flood started during the gas crunch. Japanese manufacturers had recognized that people would start wanting smaller, more fuel-efficient cars. The Detroit manufacturers, however, apparently did not see the problem on the horizon, and the result was that they lost a substantial share of their market.

A second example of a rule of thumb is that you should "know what the problem is before you tackle it." The entertainment business is a good example of an industry in which problem definition is key. Executives have to decide what films will appeal to public taste. But it is difficult to define just what the public's taste is at a given time, and, moreover, that taste can change. The movie *ET*, for example, was originally rejected by one studio, and yet it proved to be overwhelmingly popular. Book publishers face the same problem. They try to define what the public's taste in books is, but they do not often guess right. The famous mystery writer Elmore Leonard found his first novel rejected by many publishers, but today he is a bestselling author.

A third example of a rule of thumb is to "make sure the company's resources you expend are commensurate with the importance of the problem." Remember the Edsel, a major product of the Ford Motor Company in the 1950s? This total disaster, in terms of sales, was the result of a major misallocation of resources. Other white elephants, such as the Apple III computer and automobiles that speak to their owners, are also the end results of misallocated resources.

Research and development firms are perhaps most keenly aware of the rule of thumb—also relevant to resource allocation—that you should "balance short-term losses against long-term gains," and vice versa. Long-term research projects tend to be those that have the greatest payoff over time but are often expensive in the short run, with no measurable short-term gain. Short-term projects, on the other hand, provide immediate benefits but often offer fewer long-term payoffs.

Evaluation of feedback is an important metacomponential skill, and one of the rules of thumb that follow from it is that you should "learn from your mistakes and those of others." The Chrysler Corporation was recently caught in an embarrassing fix. It was discovered that Chrysler executives were using cars with the odometers disconnected, so that when they were sold to the public, the cars would seem new. Even worse, some of the cars had been in accidents, and they were repaired and then sold as new cars. When the scandal broke, Lee Iacocca, chairman of the Chrysler Corporation, did not make the same mistake many other leaders of industry have made—to try to engage in a cover-up. On the contrary, he took out full-page ads in newspapers, admitted the mistake, and promised that it would never happen again. This decisive action resulted in the scandal's blowing over, rather than its staying around to haunt the corporation, year after year.

Another rule of thumb is to "take a second look at first impressions." This rule applies in hiring; managers sometimes hire people who make a good first impression, or fail to hire those who do not look so good, and then regret their decision. The rule also applies to product development. One of the most practical, widely used paper products these days is the stick-on notepaper that can be attached to another sheet of paper. The stick-on, usually a small yellow sheet of paper with a strip of weak adhesive on the back, almost never saw the light of day. The engineer at the 3M Corporation who developed the product had a terrible time convincing his bosses that there was any use for a weaker, rather than stronger, adhesive than those currently in use. Fortunately, his attempts at persuasion succeeded.

It's clear that rules of thumb form an important part of management, and adherence to them can make the difference between greater and lesser success. The following outline is a complete listing of the rules of thumb Richard Wagner and I have derived from the theory of mental self-management.

Rules of Thumb for Managerial Tacit Knowledge

I. Componential
    A. Metacomponents
        1. Recognizing the existence of a problem
            a. Find ways to recognize problems as they arise before they become serious.
        2. Defining a problem
            a. Know what the problem is before you tackle it.
            b. Find out whether others in authority agree with how you have defined the problem.
            c. Make sure the level at which you define the problem can lead to a solution.
            d. If the problem seems insoluble, try reformulating it.
        3. Selecting a strategy for problem solution
            a. Formulate strategies with built-in flexibility.
            b. Get approval of the strategy from those who matter so they don't try to sabotage it later.
            c. Make sure the people who should know, do know.
        4. Allocating resources
            a. Make sure the time you put in is commensurate with the importance of the problem.
            b. Make sure the company's resources you put in are commensurate with the importance of the problem.
        5. Solution monitoring
            a. Step back on occasion to take stock of the situation.
            b. Seek hard, concrete data regarding how the solution is going.

    c. Set up multiple independent tests to see how the solution is going.

    d. Monitor results frequently enough to redirect if you need to.

6. Solution evaluating

    a. Have a built-in evaluation procedure for the strategy.

    b. Make sure others will accept the tests as valid.

7. Using feedback

    a. Seek out feedback on your performance from those who matter.

    b. Evaluate the utility of the feedback you receive.

    c. Selectively use the feedback you receive.

B. Performance Components

1. Balance short-term losses or inefficiencies against long-term gains, and vice versa.
2. Make sure you hear what someone is saying.
3. Take a second look at first impressions.
4. Consider doing the opposite.
5. Seek to understand things from other points of view.
6. Follow through on your commitments.
7. Know when to let people off the hook.
8. Learn from your mistakes and those of others.
9. Use humor to defuse difficult situations.
10. Know when to admit your mistakes.
11. Know the cababilities, interests, and values of those with whom you are working.
12. Figure out ways to turn crises into opportunities.
13. Know when to wait and when not to wait.
14. Accept criticism nondefensively.
15. Admit when you don't know something.
16. Know when to seek help.
17. Know whom you can and whom you cannot trust.
18. Know when and how to criticize.
19. Know what people expect of you.
20. Know when to give up and when not to give up.
21. Know the weaknesses as well as the strengths of your positions.
22. Find ways of getting around your weaknesses, such as delegating.
23. Know what you need to know and what you don't need to know.
24. Let others save face.

      25. Treat others the way you would like to be treated.
   C. Knowledge-Acquisition Components
      1. Selective encoding
        a. When barraged with information, ask yourself what the important parts are.
      2. Selective combination
        a. Put together disparate sources of information.
      3. Selective comparison
        a. Draw upon past experience, but recognize its limitations as well as its domains of generalization.
 II. Experiential Subtheory
   A. Coping with novelty
      1. Ask yourself whether there are better ways of doing things that are now done in ways you take for granted.
   B. Automatization
      1. Devise effective standard operating procedures for handling routine activities.
III. Contextual Subtheory
   A. Adaptation
      1. Know your managerial strengths.
      2. Make the most of your managerial strengths.
      3. Know your managerial weaknesses.
      4. Find ways to compensate for your managerial weaknesses.
   B. Selection
      1. Try to place yourself in an environment that matches your interests, abilities, and values.
   C. Shaping
      1. Determine the extent to which the environment can be shaped into what you want it to be.

Wagner and I performed two experiments to study the role of tacit knowledge and its associated rules of thumb in job performance. We selected two very different fields: academic psychology and business management. The procedure was the same in the two experiments: subjects were professionals in the field, graduate students in the field, or undergraduates. The subjects took a paper-and-pencil test, similar to the one you completed earlier in this chapter, which presented job-related situations with a number of possible responses for each. We then examined how test performance correlated with subjects' expertise and with the level of actual job success among the professionals in the field. The results of these experiments supported the relationship between tacit knowledge and competence in both academic psychology and business management. Three major findings in business management were:

1. Expert-novice differences in tacit knowledge about managing self, others, and career were found for groups of individuals whose members differed in amount of experience and formal training. People with more training and experience have, on the average, greater tacit knowledge than those with lesser training and experience. But this difference is only *an average*. What truly turns out to matter is not how much training or experience a person has but how much the person has learned from it.

2. Differences in tacit knowledge were consequential for performance in professional and managerial careers. In each experiment, relations were found between tacit-knowledge scores and a variety of performance measures. The relationships between overall tacit knowledge and career performance were surprisingly strong: many of the correlations were significant, and some were of a magnitude (.3–.5) about double that of correlations typically found between performance on ability tests and performance on the job. Thus, tacit knowledge can predict things like performance ratings for executives, numbers of employees supervised, and merit salary increases.

3. Tacit knowledge was not related to verbal intelligence as measured by a standard verbal reasoning test. In other words, tacit-knowledge tests are not just fancy IQ tests: they measure a different set of skills. Of course, the lack of relationship between IQ and tacit knowledge has been shown to hold only within the normal range of IQs for business executives; with a wide enough range of IQs, there might be some relationship. But with a very wide range of IQs, almost anything predicts IQ—for example, ability to tie shoelaces!

Categories and Orientations of Tacit Knowledge

On the basis of the results just presented and further theorizing, our initial tacit-knowledge framework has recently been revised and extended.[12] A new method for quantifying tacit knowledge has been developed, in which an individual's performance is compared with a prototype derived from the responses of an expert group. Here's a brief sketch of this framework, followed by the results of two experiments recently carried out to evaluate it.

This tacit-knowledge framework consists of three categories of tacit knowledge—managing self, managing tasks, and managing others—and two orientations—local and global. ("Orientation" as used here refers to an individual's perspective in a given work-related situation.)

THREE CATEGORIES OF TACIT KNOWLEDGE

Tacit knowledge about *managing self* refers to knowledge about self-motivational and self-organizational aspects of performance in work-related situations, such as knowing how best to overcome the problem of procrastination.

Tacit knowledge about *managing tasks* refers to knowledge about how to do specific work-related tasks well. An example in an academic setting is knowing the value of beginning a manuscript by telling the reader what major points you plan to make. An example in a business setting is knowing how to evaluate the potential worth of new products.

Tacit knowledge about *managing others* refers to knowledge about managing one's subordinates and interacting with peers, such as knowing how to reward subordinates so as to maximize both productivity and job satisfaction.

TWO ORIENTATIONS OF TACIT KNOWLEDGE

A *local orientation* of tacit knowledge refers to a focus on the short-term accomplishment of the specific task at hand. No consideration is given to reputation, career goals, or to the "big picture."

A *global orientation* refers to a focus on long-range, career-related goals when making work-related judgments and decisions.

This tacit-knowledge framework, then, consists of three categories of tacit knowledge—managing self, managing tasks, and managing others—which are "crossed" with two orientations—local and global. This framework is portrayed in figure 14. I will illustrate each cell in the diagram with a brief example.

Consider the previously mentioned problem of procrastination. Forcing yourself to spend at least ten minutes on a task is a strategy that works for some individuals who find that once they have begun they will keep working at their task. According to the above framework, knowledge that this strategy works for you is an example of tacit knowledge about managing self with a local orientation. However, if the task at hand is to write a report for your boss, reminding yourself that getting promoted may hinge on finishing the report may help you to overcome your procrastination. Knowing that this strategy works for you is an example of tacit knowledge about managing self with a global orientation. Strategies

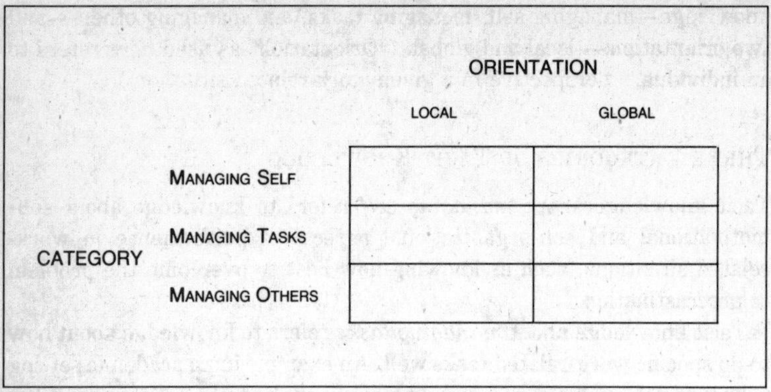

Figure 14. Categories and orientations of tacit knowledge.

such as these are considered to be general across tasks but possibly specific to individuals. Some individuals may simply be unable to force themselves to spend even five minutes at a task, and others, by reminding themselves that a future decision with important career implications may hinge on their timely completion of the task, may procrastinate even more!

Next, consider the task of how to begin a manuscript. An example of tacit knowledge about managing tasks with a local orientation is knowing that it helps to inform readers in advance about what you plan to say. Knowing where to submit your manuscripts so as maximally to publicize your work is an example of tacit knowledge about managing tasks with a global orientation.

Recognizing that the time has come to let an employee go because of inadequate performance is an example of using tacit knowledge about managing others with a local orientation. Knowing that you should not let the employee go even though he deserves it, because you have terminated more employees than your colleagues and terminating employees is discouraged by your company, is an example of tacit knowledge about managing others with a global orientation.

Actualities and Ideals

The comments of respondents in Wagner's and my experiments suggested the need to distinguish between two additional kinds of tacit knowledge: tacit knowledge about competence in the real world (that is, how good a given response alternative *actually is*, given the realities of the situation) and tacit knowledge about competence in an ideal world (that is, how good a given response *should be*). Simply stated, the distinction is between *what does work* and *what ideally should work*. The use of "ideally" here refers to a judgment about the quality of a course of action without regard to its practicality in an actual job situation.

For example, an assistant professor of psychology attempting to get tenure in a prestigious department would probably be making a serious mistake by devoting most of her time to perfecting her lectures for her introductory-psychology class. Given the realities of how tenure decisions are made, such a strategy would be less than optimal. But outstanding introductory-psychology classes might conceivably attract more and better students to major and go on to graduate school in psychology, thereby yielding a long-term but perhaps dramatic payoff to the field. The point is that the value of devoting most of one's time to teaching introductory psychology might differ in the real, versus an ideal, world. Similarly, in business, an executive might feel committed to the development of a new product he considers to be promising but have to abandon the project because of top management's unwillingness to support it.

Two additional experiments were carried out to evaluate the tacit-knowledge framework. The domains examined were again academic psychology and business management. These experiments facilitated more rigorous evaluation of the tacit-knowledge framework, including how the different kinds of tacit knowledge are related to one another and to career performance. As before, the tests were administered to subjects of varying levels of training and experience, who selected responses to job-related situations. The results of the study of business managers are more relevant to our quest to understand executive intelligence.

A Prototype of Tacit Knowledge in Business Management

There were three groups of subjects, differing in amounts of formal training and experience in the field of business management. The *business professional* group consisted of sixty-four managers from a nationwide sample of companies of various levels of prestige. The *business graduate student* group consisted of graduate students from seven business schools of varying rank. The *undergraduate* group consisted of sixty Yale undergraduates.

We found that individuals with more experience in management were closer to the "prototype" for business managers, meaning, the more training and experience the individual had, the more she resembled, on the average, the experienced executive. These expert-novice differences were found for each category of tacit knowledge, for each orientation, and for both the actual and the ideal ratings.

For the business professional group, overall tacit knowledge was related to years of management experience. No reliable relations were found between tacit knowledge and total financial resources of an individual's company or years of schooling beyond high school. Salary was related reliably to tacit knowledge about managing tasks. Whether or not a business student was currently employed was also related reliably to global tacit knowledge.

In general, the correlations between tacit knowledge on the ideal scale and success in the field were similar to and somewhat stronger than correlations to the actual scale. The strong correlation between job success and responses on the actual (practical) and ideal scales suggests that an awareness of both the practicality and the quality of alternative courses of action is important to success in business management. These findings concerning the "ideal" ratings are important because they indicate that high levels of tacit knowledge are not just a reflection of a person's willingness to conform to existing rules and regulations. When an individual rates an ideal company as opposed to an actual one, a strong relationship is maintained between test scores and job performance.

Members of the undergraduate group were given both the psychology and the business tacit-knowledge tests. Thus, it was possible to examine the generality of tacit knowledge, at least for the undergraduate group, by comparing performance on the two tests. The correlations obtained between scores on the psychology and business tacit-knowledge measures were moderate (on the order of .5 for each category, on a 0–1 scale).

The results of an attempt to replicate directly the Wagner and Sternberg results in the domain of business management produced similar (although not identical) results.

General Issues

The results of these experiments largely supported the usefulness of the tacit-knowledge framework and measurement operations. Consider why.

First, by using this framework, it was possible to construct measures of tacit knowledge for the two quite different fields of business and academic psychology. Tacit knowledge can be measured, and it has been shown to be important in two different domains.

Second, in two experiments carried out in two domains, expert-novice differences were found for groups whose members differed in level of professional advancement. In both experiments, performance on the tacit-knowledge measures increased reliably across groups as a function of level of professional advancement. Follow-up analyses indicated that these expert-novice differences were present for each of the categories of tacit knowledge (managing self, managing tasks, and managing others) and for each of the orientations (local and global) proposed by the framework.

Third, in two experiments carried out in two domains, within-group differences in tacit knowledge were related to career success. Correlations with success (.3–.5) were about double those typically found between performance on ability tests and performance on the job. For example, for psychology faculty, performance on the tacit-knowledge measure was related favorably to a variety of research-related criteria, including number of citations, number of publications, rated scholarly quality of departmental faculty, and percentage of time spent in research. Performance on the tacit-knowledge measure was related unfavorably (negatively) to non-research-related criteria, such as percentage of time spent in teaching and percentage of time spent performing administrative duties.

Comparing the performance of undergraduates in tacit knowledge for academic psychology and business management yielded correlations in the .5-to-.6 range. These results suggest that at least some tacit knowledge is general to both academic psychology and business management. People who have high tacit knowledge about one of the domains also tend to have high tacit knowledge about the other.

Tacit knowledge applies in domains of business other than management. One of the more interesting of these is sales, especially commission sales. Commission salespeople basically depend on their ability to sell for their livelihood. Whereas an incompetent manager may be able to retain his job indefinitely, the incompetent commission salesperson will be quickly out of a job, if only because he won't make enough money on which to live.

Richard Wagner, Carol Rashotte, and I have studied tacit knowledge in salespeople, looking at "rules of thumb for selling anything to anyone." We have found that more experienced salespeople follow, and in many cases develop, rules of thumb that less experienced salespeople are unaware of. Some examples are: targeting sales goals in terms of number of units sold, not dollars; setting goals that are measurable and specific; playing hunches and asking if the salesperson suspects a competitor has entered the picture; being selective in targeting promotional efforts; asking customers to provide leads; using the fact that customers associate price with quality to the salesperson's advantage if the salesperson's price is higher than the competition's; and so on.

We gave tacit-knowledge questionnaires embodying these rules of thumb to individuals differing in sales experience and found that the rules are predictive of sales success. They are also predictive of other measures, such as years of selling experience and awards received for selling. In other words, the concept of tacit knowledge applies in sales at least as much as in the domain of management.

Some concerns might understandably be raised about our principles and procedures for measuring tacit knowledge. Let's consider two:

Can individuals "fake good" on our tacit-knowledge measures? Might respondents have given "socially desirable" responses rather than responses indicating what they actually would do? "Faking good" on tacit knowledge is impossible, though, because knowing what a good response is, regardless of whether the individual would do it, is precisely what we set out to measure. A limitation of our approach, however, is that we do not measure an individual's ability to do what he knows should be done. Still, the strength of the correlations between tacit-knowledge scores and job success does suggest that those who know what to do are indeed capable of doing it.

Whose values should be used to evaluate criterion performance? Determining how good an individual is as an academic psychologist or business manager is not easily done. For an academic psychologist, how much weight should be given to research, teaching, and other aspects of the profession? Should the weighting be the same, regardless of the nature of one's position? Our strategy in handling this very difficult problem was, to the extent to which we were able, not to impose our own values but to adopt the values of the field, on the basis of those items that differentiated statistically among groups of individuals varying in amount of experience and formal training in that field. Not all individuals may share the dominant values of the field, however, and there certainly may be identifiable subgroups within a field that share different values. The strategy of adopting the dominant values of a field obviously limits the generalizability of the results to those who share these values or who are judged by them.

SOME CONCLUSIONS ABOUT THE NATURE OF TACIT KNOWLEDGE IN PRACTICALLY INTELLIGENT BEHAVIOR

Experts in real-world domains differ from novices in, among other things, having acquired tacit knowledge in their field. Furthermore, such tacit knowledge can be measured by presenting individuals with descriptions of work-related situations and asking them to rate the quality of alternative responses. In other words, we can measure how much a person knows regarding the critical information about job performance that is not directly taught. At least some of the tacit knowledge people acquire is good across jobs. This conclusion is based on finding, in each of five experiments across two real-world domains, reliable expert-novice differences in tacit knowledge.

Differences in tacit knowledge are related to differences in domain-related performance. In each of the experiments, performance on measures of tacit knowledge was related to a wide variety of measures of career performance. Many of these relationships were much stronger than those typically found between IQ or employment tests and job performance.

Tacit knowledge of the sort examined in the present experiments is more than simple "careerism." In other words, knowing how to promote one's career appears to be just one aspect of the tacit knowledge acquired through experience in fields such as academic psychology and business management. Higher levels of professional advancement were associated with increased tacit knowledge useful both for accomplishing a wide variety of short-term tasks and for attaining one's long-range career objectives. The scope of tacit knowledge extended to work-related situations that required skill at managing oneself, managing tasks, and managing others, and encompassed judgments about the quality (i.e., How good is this?) as well as the practicality (i.e., Will this work?) of responses to work-related situations.

Acquisition of tacit knowledge does not appear to be closely related to performance on traditional measures of verbal intelligence. Tacit-knowledge scores were related more to standard measures of job performance (such as number of employees supervised) than to scores on the standardized test of verbal intelligence, and in most cases the correlations between tacit-knowledge scores and verbal-intelligence test scores were insignificant.

There are at least two possible explanations for the relative lack of relations between tacit-knowledge scores and verbal intelligence as measured by a standard psychometric test. First, individuals in professional pursuits represent a relatively narrow range of verbal ability, having been selected on the basis of academic aptitude. Restricting the range of a variable tends to reduce its correlation with any other variable. Second, we agree with Neisser's contention that traditional IQ tests are better measures of "academic" rather than "practical" intelligence.

Individual differences in tacit knowledge appear to be general rather than specific in nature. The strong correlations between the types of tacit knowledge, and their fairly consistent correlation with real-life performance, suggest that the types of tacit knowledge are not independent factors but suggest an underlying general fund of knowledge and skill.

Similar findings for academic tasks led Charles Spearman, and later many others, to propose g, a construct representing a general ability that is measured to a greater or a lesser degree by most academic tasks. Might there be a comparable general ability for practical tasks?

Evidence in favor of a general ability for practical tasks from our experiments includes the strong correlations among scales that are constructed to measure distinct categories and orientations of tacit knowledge; between performance on the actual and ideal scales; between undergraduate performance on the tacit-knowledge measures for academic psychology and business management; and between job performance and the tacit-knowledge measures for academic psychology and business management. However, it is important to note that the tacit-knowledge measures were limited in scope to two professional domains.

Although g seems to underlie performance on academic tasks, the evidence for a similar general ability for social intelligence or competence has been mixed at best.[13] The issue of a general ability for social intelligence is difficult to resolve because there are few valid instruments for measuring social intelligence. It will remain difficult to determine the generality of knowledge and skills in practical and social domains until instruments are available for these domains that share the psychometric sophistication of instruments used to assess academic performance.

The results of the work described indicate that the first step in understanding competence in real-world settings has been taken. The theory of tacit knowledge shows that performance levels are a function of level of expertise of the examinees—something that few, if any, traditional measures of mental abilities have shown. The second step—understanding the nature of tacit knowledge and its role in competent performance in real-world settings—has yet to be completed, although some progress has been made. Attempts to take the third step—accelerating acquisition of tacit knowledge and ultimately improving performance—should be in the foreseeable future: I am teaching a course on tacit knowledge in Yale's psychology department. This course is perhaps the first of its kind.

Who's Intelligent? People's Conceptions of the Nature of Intelligence

It is now time to go beyond the triarchic theory of human intelligence and consider some broader issues. One such issue, covered in this chapter, is how people conceive of intelligence. Another issue, also covered here, is where intelligence leaves off and other psychological phenomena, such as wisdom and creativity, begin. In order to understand intelligence fully, we need to know what it *is not*, just as we need to know what it *is*.

A third issue is how intelligence develops. Why do some people grow up to be more intelligent than others, and what sorts of factors in the environment influence the intelligence a person shows as he matures? These issues are covered in chapter 10.

The issues covered in chapter 11 go beyond intelligence to the *use* of intelligence: how do people use or manifest their intelligence in their everyday lives? This interface between intelligence and personality is referred to as an "intellectual style." The final issue, covered in chapter 12, is how mental self-management can fail. This chapter outlines behaviors and attitudes which can impede the proper use of intelligence.

How Is Intelligence Perceived?

When experts try to define intelligence, they generally consult one another or their own intuition. But to the layman, the definitions they come up with often seem to be rarefied abstractions, unconnected with real people or real life. And formal IQ tests frequently seem unfair or beside the point.

Almost everyone likes to think that he pretty much knows what intelligence is and how to judge who has more or less of it. Indeed, people make informal judgments about others' intelligence all the time, and don't need intelligence tests to do so. One could argue that the bulk of intelligence testing is not the kind that takes place in schoolrooms and psychologists' consulting rooms but the kind that goes on in face-to-face encounters between people: in job and admission interviews, in classrooms and meetings, at cocktail parties, during coffee breaks, and in initial encounters with strangers. As Ulric Neisser of Emory University has pointed out, psychologists have done many studies of intelligence as measured by IQ tests but practically none of intelligence as judged by people in everyday encounters.[1] And it turns out that there are striking commonalities in what people mean by intelligence and how they judge it in themselves and others. But consider first how experts have defined intelligence.

DEFINITIONS OF INTELLIGENCE

The best-known example of the experts-only approach to defining intelligence is a symposium published in the *Journal of Educational Psychology* in 1921, in which fourteen psychologists and educators gave their views on the nature of intelligence.[2] Lewis M. Terman said that intelligence is "the ability to carry on abstract thinking." Herbert Woodrow called it "the capacity to acquire capacity." S. S. Colvin said that a person "possesses intelligence insofar as he has learned, or can learn, to adjust himself to his environment."

Three years later Edward L. Thorndike offered yet another definition. "Let intellect," he wrote, "be defined as that quality of mind (or brain, or behavior if one prefers) in respect to which Aristotle, Plato, Thucydides, and the like, differed most from Athenian idiots of their day, or in respect to which the lawyers, physicians, scientists, scholars, and editors of reputed greatest ability at constant age differ most from idiots of the age in asylums."[3]

ASKING PEOPLE ABOUT INTELLIGENCE

Some research that my colleagues and I have done was designed to find out what laymen mean when they speak of intelligence. Our main conclusion is a simple one: ordinary people have very definite ideas about what intelligence is, and their ideas are not too different from those of experts. Moreover, the conception of intelligence held by scientists and nonscientists alike is not abstruse or unrealistic but is firmly and clearly anchored in the real world. Thus, the scientists have a more realistic conception of intelligence than is often reflected by their theories and tests.

In 1978, Barbara Conway, Jerry Ketron, Morty Bernstein, and I began asking laymen for their views on intelligence. In a series of experiments carried out over a year and published in 1981,[4] we personally interviewed or questioned by mail 476 men and women, including students, commuters, supermarket shoppers, and people who answered newspaper advertisements or whose names we selected at random from the phone book. To compare the ideas of our lay subjects with those of experts, we later also sent questionnaires to 140 research psychologists specializing in intelligence.

We did not think it would be useful to ask laymen directly for their definitions of intelligence. Such a request seemed less likely to elicit genuine convictions than to produce platitudes: stale ideas dredged up, perhaps, from memories of old courses taken in school or college, or from articles read long ago. We decided instead on an indirect approach. In our first experiment, for instance, we gave people a blank sheet of paper and asked them to list behaviors that they considered to be characteristic of "intelligence," "academic intelligence," "everyday intelligence," or "unintelligence."

We found our subjects in everyday settings. Sixty-three of them were commuters about to board trains at the New Haven station; 62 were housewives and others about to enter a New Haven supermarket; and 61 were students studying in a Yale library. Almost no one had trouble with our request; people were apparently convinced that certain kinds of behavior indicated certain kinds of intelligence—or the lack of it.

From people's responses, we compiled a master list of 250 behaviors, 170 that had been named as characteristic of intelligence and 80 that had been called signs of unintelligence. Some of the behaviors most frequently listed as intelligent were "reasons logically and well," "reads widely," "displays common sense," "keeps an open mind," and "reads with high comprehension." For unintelligence, the most commonly listed behaviors included "does not tolerate diversity of views," "does not display curiosity," and "behaves with insufficient consideration of others." The great diversity of the behaviors cited showed that our subjects held eclectic views of intelligent and unintelligent behavior, and suggested that people probably do not consider any one-dimensional scale adequate for measuring intelligence.

A study of this kind runs the risk of finding some idiosyncratic responses that reflect just one or two people's peculiar notions. For example, one person listed "bores others" as characteristic of an intelligent person, whereas another person listed "is fun to be with"—almost the opposite. In order to deal with this problem, we had 28 people from the New Haven area—nonstudents answering a newspaper advertisement—rate on a scale of 1 (low) to 9 (high) how characteristic they thought each of the 250 behaviors on the master list was of an ideally intelligent person, an ideally academically intelligent person, and an ideally everyday-intelligent person. We then applied the statistical technique of factor analysis described in chapter 3, which allowed us to determine the few basic factors underlying people's diverse and, in a few instances, highly unusual responses. The result was to give us, in effect, a simple characterization of intelligence as viewed by our subjects.

CONCEPTIONS OF INTELLIGENCE, ACADEMIC INTELLIGENCE, AND EVERYDAY INTELLIGENCE

It turned out that people conceived of intelligence as having three facets, which we labeled (in descending order of perceived importance) practical problem-solving ability, verbal ability, and social competence. Comparable facets for academic intelligence were verbal ability, problem-solving ability, and social competence, and for everyday intelligence were practical problem-solving ability, social competence, character, and interest in learning and culture—again in order of perceived importance. The facets for academic intelligence were almost the same as for intelligence, except that their ordering of importance changed. The facets for everyday intelligence were somewhat less similar to those for intelligence in general but had more of an everyday slant.

Our study showed that the resemblance between the views of scientists and nonscientists is surprisingly clear. On the whole, what psychologists mean by intelligence seems to correspond generally to what people untrained in psychology mean by intelligence. On the other hand, what psychologists study corresponds to only part of what people mean by intelligence in our society, which includes a lot more than IQ tests measure, such as everyday competence and common sense in the conduct of our lives.

Then we compared experts' and nonexperts' views on intelligence in another study in which two questionnaires were sent to a group of laymen and to a group of recognized authorities in the field of intelligence. The two questionnaires named the 250 behaviors on our master list. One questionnaire asked respondents to rate how characteristic each behavior was of an ideally intelligent, an ideally academically intelligent, and an ideally everyday-intelligent person. The other asked respondents to rate how important each behavior was to defining the respondents' conceptions of each of these three kinds of people.

Expert Versus Nonexpert Views

The correlation between ratings of the experts and those of laymen was .82 (on a scale where 0 indicates no relationship and 1 indicates a perfect correspondence), indicating close but not perfect agreement between the experts and the laymen. There were two main differences between the groups. One was that the experts considered motivation to be an important ingredient in academic intelligence—an ingredient that did not emerge when we factor-analyzed the responses of the laymen. Behaviors central to this motivational factor included "displays dedication and motivation in chosen pursuits," "gets involved in what he or she is doing," "studies hard," and "is persistent."

The second difference was that laymen seemed to place somewhat greater emphasis on the social-cultural aspects of intelligence than did the experts. Whereas laymen emphasized behaviors such as "acts politely," "displays patience with self and others," "gets along well with others," "is frank and honest with self and others," and "emotions are appropriate to situations," experts typically emphasized "reads with high comprehension," "shows flexibility in thought and action," "reasons logically and well," "displays curiosity," "learns rapidly," "thinks deeply," and "solves problems well." The experts thus emphasized *intra*personal competence in an individual context; laymen emphasized intelligence as an *inter*personal, social phenomenon.

Another way of comparing the views of experts with those of laymen is to ask in what specific ways laymen's informal conceptions of intelligence resemble formal scientific theories. Some theorists, like most laymen, do consider social competence to be an element of intelligence. In addition, many theorists have proposed a fundamental distinction between problem-solving abilities (also called, in the psychological literature, "fluid" abilities) and verbal abilities (also called "crystallized" abilities). This distinction is basic to the conception of intelligence held by our lay subjects.

Why, if we know people's informal theories of intelligence, do we need formal scientific theories at all? Because descriptions merely label behaviors without really explaining them or even defining what goes into them. What does it mean, psychologically, to reason logically and well, or to read with high comprehension? What makes some people reason or read better than others? These are the kinds of questions psychologists must address in their scientific theories, and some of them are considered in this book. Thus, the informal theories of laymen can be seen as setting up a framework within which scientists can work; the details can be filled in only by scientific research.

Yet another comparison can be made by considering how people's conceptions of intelligence correspond to what IQ tests measure. The correspondence is striking, up to a point. Behaviors such as "reads with high comprehension" are measured by tests that ask people to remember facts and make inferences from short reading passages. "Is verbally fluent" is measured by word-fluency tests, such as those that ask people to think of as many words as they can beginning with the letter r in a brief time period. "Displays a good vocabulary" is directly measured by vocabulary tests. "Displays a good memory" is measured by memory tests like those that ask a person to remember a string of digits such as 3-5-1-8-6-2. "Is knowledgeable about a broad range of things" is measured by tests of general world knowledge, which ask people questions about history, politics, finances, and the like. "Works puzzles well" is measured by tests such as anagrams, which present scrambled words (rtdooc) to be unscrambled (doctor). "Solves problems well" is measured by tests such as arithmetic word problems. But people's conceptions of intelligence go beyond what conventional intelligence tests examine.

DIFFERENCES AMONG LAY GROUPS IN CONCEPTIONS OF INTELLIGENCE

A fine-grained analysis of our data reveals not only differences between experts and laymen but also distinguishable subpopulations among laymen. Students, predictably, gave greater weight to academic ability as a component of general intelligence than commuters did. Commuters, on the other hand, considered everyday intelligence more important.

Although the present study did not divide adults by age—either the raters or the ratees—another series of studies did.[5] A group of people varying in age from roughly thirty to seventy was asked to characterize the intelligence of a prototypical thirty-, fifty-, and seventy-year old. We found that "practical" as opposed to "academic" aspects of intelligence received higher weights with increases in the ages of both the raters and the ratees. In other words, the practical side of intelligence seems to become increasingly important in later life.

The differences in conceptions of intelligence become much greater if we move outside our own culture, as we will do in the next chapter. Mallory Wober, an African psychologist, investigated conceptions of intelligence among members of different tribes in Uganda and found considerable variation.[6] The Baganda, for example, tended to associate intelligence with mental order, whereas the Batoro associated it with some degree of mental turmoil. When Wober asked his subjects to associate descriptive words with intelligence, he found that members of the Baganda tribe thought of intelligence as persistent, hard, and obdurate, whereas the Batoro thought of it as soft, obedient, and yielding.

LETTERS OF RECOMMENDATION

Just as psychologists administering IQ tests can measure intelligence on the basis of some (at least allegedly) scientific theory of what intelligence is, so ordinary people should be able to assess intelligence—their own and others'—on the basis of their own theories. Indeed, we found that laymen not only have internalized conceptions of intelligence but make good use of them in evaluating intelligence.

To find out whether or not what people say they think about intelligence is actually reflected in their judgments of intelligence, we sent lay subjects a series of character sketches of fictitious people, employing behaviors taken from our master list. Here are two typical sketches:

I. Susan
   a. She keeps an open mind.
   b. She is knowledgeable about a particular field.
   c. She converses well.
   d. She shows a lack of independence.
   e. She is on time for appointments.

II. Adam
   a. He deals effectively with people.
   b. He thinks he knows everything.
   c. He shows a lack of independence.
   d. He lacks interest in solving problems.
   e. He speaks clearly and articulately.
   f. He fails to ask questions.
   g. He is on time for appointments.

The respondent's task was to rate the intelligence of each person on a scale of 1 to 9. Our task was to find out whether or not the respondent's ratings were consistent with our earlier study in which we asked subjects to rate the degree to which each of the 250 master behaviors is characteristic of intelligent or unintelligent people. "Keeps an open mind," for example, had been rated 7.7, while "shows a lack of independence" was worth 2.7. Averaging the ratings for each fictitious person, we came up with a score of 6 for Susan and of 4.3 for Adam. By comparison, our respondents rated Susan's intelligence at 5.8 (above average) and Adam's at 4.3 (below average). Overall, when we calculated the correlation between the two sets of ratings, it was an extremely high .96 (on a scale where 1.00 would mean a perfect relationship). In other words, laymen's ratings of people's intelligence are firmly grounded in their theories about intelligence.

In the course of doing this part of our study, we found that unfavorable characterizations of people—"fears the unfamiliar," "likes to argue but not to think about arguments," "is slow to learn," "acts indecisively," and "succumbs to propaganda"—carry more weight than do favorable characterizations. That is, ordinary people can be very harsh in their judgments of unintelligent behavior; when people do something stupid, others may brand them as stupid without giving them full credit for the intelligent things they do.

As for people's ability to assess their own intelligence, we found a correlation of .23 between self-ratings on general intelligence and actual IQ. That correlation is not impressive; it is higher than chance, but it shows that most people have only a very modest ability to assess their own measured intelligence, which, of course, is not the same as their actual intelligence.

A BEHAVIORAL CHECKLIST

We found that people's self-descriptions can tell us much more about their intelligence than their global self-ratings on a 1–100 scale. Specifically, we discovered that if we presented people with our master list of 250 intelligent and unintelligent behaviors and asked them to rate how characteristic each behavior is of themselves, we could then estimate from their responses not only their overall IQ but their subscores on such aspects of intelligence as problem-solving ability, verbal ability, and social competence. The correlation between overall scores on the checklist for intelligence and IQ was .52, more than twice as high as the correlation of self-ratings of intelligence with actual IQ. Moreover, this figure compares favorably with correlations obtained by psychologists using "cognitive measures," such as the time it takes to complete intellectual tasks—for example, analogies and anagrams. In other words, we seem to have found a potential measure of intelligence that could supplement, although not replace, conventional IQ tests. This kind of measure, the checklist, we think is a major value of our research. An abbreviated checklist follows.

Rate on a 1 (low) to 9 (high) scale the extent to which each of the following behaviors characterizes you.

I. Practical problem-solving ability
_____ a. Reasons logically and well.
_____ b. Identifies connections among ideas.
_____ c. Sees all aspects of a problem.
_____ d. Keeps an open mind.
_____ e. Responds thoughtfully to others' ideas.
_____ f. Sizes up situations well.
_____ g. Gets to the heart of problems.
_____ h. Interprets information accurately.
_____ i. Makes good decisions.
_____ j. Goes to original sources for the basic information.
_____ k. Poses problems in an optimal way.
_____ l. Is a good source of ideas.
_____ m. Perceives implied assumptions and conclusions.
_____ n. Listens to all sides of an argument.
_____ o. Deals with problems resourcefully.

II. Verbal ability
_____ a. Speaks clearly and articulately.
_____ b. Is verbally fluent.
_____ c. Converses well.
_____ d. Is knowledgeable about a particular field of knowledge.
_____ e. Studies hard.
_____ f. Reads with high comprehension.
_____ g. Reads widely.
_____ h. Deals effectively with people.
_____ i. Writes without difficulty.
_____ j. Sets aside time for reading.
_____ k. Displays a good vocabulary.
_____ l. Accepts social norms.
_____ m. Tries new things.

III. Social competence
_____ a. Accepts others for what they are.
_____ b. Admits mistakes.
_____ c. Displays interest in the world at large.
_____ d. Is on time for appointments.

_____ e. Has social conscience.

_____ f. Thinks before speaking and doing.

_____ g. Displays curiosity.

_____ h. Does not make snap judgments.

_____ i. Makes fair judgments.

_____ j. Assesses well the relevance of information to a problem at hand.

_____ k. Is sensitive to other people's needs and desires.

_____ l. Is frank and honest with self and others.

_____ m. Displays interest in the immediate environment.

In general, higher ratings on these items are associated with greater intelligence. The estimates of intelligence that we can calculate from the master list of behaviors are only fairly accurate, not absolutely so. For that reason, I would only go so far as to suggest that the checklist does have several desirable features as a supplementary measure of intelligence. First, its questions deal with typical performance rather than with the maximal performance required by IQ test questions. There are few situations in life that require quite the expenditure of mental effort that is involved in taking an IQ test. Second, the checklist is not stressful, or at least it is much less stressful than an IQ test, making it especially appropriate for people who, for one reason or another, do not show their true abilities in an IQ testing situation. Third, the items on the checklist deal with real-world behaviors rather than with the highly artificial behaviors required by IQ tests.

Fourth, the checklist is more wide-ranging in the kinds of behaviors it inquires about than are IQ tests. For example, the checklist includes items assessing the kinds of social competence all but ignored by IQ tests. Moreover, the checklist can be tailored to different cultural groups by constructing and scoring it on the basis of behaviors that members of that group consider to be important ingredients of intelligence. Both the content and the scoring are thereby made culturally relevant for the particular person whose intelligence is being assessed. Finally, the circumstances of administering the checklist would not have the inherent biases found in IQ testing situations, which place a premium on rapid solution of test items little resembling the tasks in ordinary people's lives.

One might attempt to dismiss the behavioral checklist by arguing that people would simply rate themselves as showing a maximum of desirable behaviors and a minimum of undesirable ones. But such a dismissal would be ill advised. The scoring system we have developed calls for figuring out how much resemblance there is between a person's self-description and other people's descriptions of the ideally intelligent person: the greater the resemblance, the higher the real person's IQ. Thus, what matters is not the level of people's responses (on the 1-to-9 scale) but the *pattern* of responses. Moreover, we know that subjects do not, in fact, simply check off for themselves the "ideal" pattern; no subjects came anywhere near depicting themselves as ideal.

On a theoretical level, our research can help enrich scientifically based theories of intelligence with intuitively based ones. The two kinds of research are complementary. Conducted in tandem, with each informing the other, they can provide greater understanding of the nature of intelligence than can either kind pursued alone. At the very least, the research we have done on people's conceptions of intelligence has taught us that what psychologists study as "intelligence" does have some connection with what people mean by "intelligence" in everyday life.

Thus far we have considered people's conceptions of the nature of intelligence. Two related but distinct constructs are wisdom and creativity. But just how do people understand these, both as they are similar to and as they differ from intelligence? Consider my studies on how people conceive of intelligence, wisdom, and creativity, and their interrelations.

Beyond Intelligence to Wisdom and Creativity

What do we mean when we say that Einstein was "intelligent," Solomon was "wise," or da Vinci was "creative"? Or, to take some more mundane examples, what does it mean to say, "Anne may be intelligent, but she just isn't creative," or "If only the President's wisdom matched his intelligence, we might have averted this mess," or "My grandfather—a self-educated man—might not have done well on intelligence tests, but he had more wisdom than all Harvard professors combined."

In each of these statements, some assertion is made about a person's intellectual abilities. Clearly, the intention is to make a different statement about each of the people. Indeed, we know that although Einstein, Solomon, and da Vinci are all renowned for their extraordinary mental feats, the nature of these feats differs in each case. But what are intelligence, wisdom, and creativity, and how do they differ? Furthermore, can the three abilities be reliably distinguished from each other?

I believe that wisdom and creativity do differ in kind from intelligence, and that our preoccupation with the nature, measurement, and training of intelligence to the exclusion of wisdom and creativity is a mistake. There are several reasons why it is important to study wisdom and creativity as well as intelligence and to distinguish each of these constructs from the other.

First, although our society is preoccupied with the measurement of intelligence to predict future success, major contributions to virtually all fields of endeavor seem to derive primarily from creative enterprise. During the school years, it may well be the children with high levels of intelligence who stand out. The tasks required in school and the values of the society place a premium on rapid learning time, good reasoning, good problem solving, and many of the other skills that contribute to what we refer to as intelligence. But in the remaining three-quarters of people's lives, it appears to be creativity rather than intelligence that distinguishes many exceptional performers from the more mundane ones. If you look at the contributions of the truly distinguished, and even of those who do not reach the ranks of Mozart, Picasso, or Tolstoy, you find that what sets these individuals apart from others is their creativity, not merely their intelligence.

An interesting example of the difference between intelligence and creativity is provided by Peter Shaffer's play *Amadeus* and the recent film adaptation of it. Shaffer portrays the competition between Mozart and Salieri for recognition of their musical accomplishments. Both men are obviously intelligent. Had each been given a standard intelligence test suitable for the times, it is unlikely that the test scores would much have distinguished their relative levels of musical expertise. But Mozart was far more creative than Salieri, and in the long run this difference has been easily recognized.

Howard Gardner[7] might, of course, say that Mozart was more "musically intelligent" than Salieri. But such a comparison would not do justice to the precise nature of the difference between the two men. What, exactly, is musical intelligence? Is it pitch discrimination, memory for tones, the ability to perform well on a musical instrument or to sing well, the ability to learn or understand musical theory, the ability to compose, or some combination of these skills? In the case of the Mozart-Salieri comparison, the critical difference was not in musical skills in general but in the creative force of Mozart's work, which was absent in Salieri's.

The difference can be seen in many other fields as well. In my own field, for example, there are any number of psychologists who are universally considered to be bright in the sense of having high levels of intelligence; but for some of them the question is often asked, "How can someone be so intelligent and yet so uncreative?" Indeed, there are a few cases in which the most outstanding feature of the individual seems to be his IQ or SAT scores. High test scores seem to be these people's last distinguished accomplishment!

Second, it becomes clear merely by looking at history that, in many walks of life, intelligence without wisdom is not enough—indeed, can be a dangerous thing. Nowhere is this more evident than in the field of government. No one would question the intelligence of most of our recent Presidents, for example. To take one from each of the major political parties, consider for a moment John Kennedy and Ronald Reagan. These men showed no lack of intelligence in the traditional sense, yet each made certain decisions that from almost any point of view were ill advised. Kennedy's decision to invade the Bay of Pigs was certainly so and resulted in one of the major fiascoes of his administration. Reagan's decision to visit the cemetery at Bitburg, Germany, where Nazi SS officers are buried, was considered unwise by many people.

You need not look to national government to observe the difference between intelligence and wisdom. Almost all of us know at least one person who, though not exceptionally intelligent in any traditional sense, shows the wisdom that traditional notions of intelligence simply do not encompass. Even modern, broader conceptions of intelligence, including my own, do not seem fully to encompass our notions of what it is that makes a person wise and distinguishes him from one who is merely intelligent.

It's clear that our understanding of human mental capabilities is going to be limited so long as we remain preoccupied with intelligence to the exclusion of wisdom and creativity. Certainly, the time has come to understand all three of these psychological dimensions and the ways in which they interrelate. But just how should we go about doing this?

Intelligence, wisdom, and creativity have each been studied in their own right, but not in ways that make them easy to compare. Most often, they have been studied by different investigators using different methods of research to study different populations. As a result, it has been difficult to compare one study to another. The amount of theory and research on each of these attributes also differs widely. There are innumerable studies of intelligence and many studies of creativity, but relatively few studies of wisdom. Might it be possible to study these three in a way that would help illuminate their interrelationship? In a series of investigations, I have attempted to do just that.

The studies I will describe seek to discover people's conceptions, or implicit theories, of the nature and interrelationship of intelligence, wisdom, and creativity. The studies address several questions: How do we conceive of intelligence, wisdom, and creativity? Are these conceptions the same regardless of endeavor? How are these conceptions interrelated? Are these conceptions related to scores on "objective" tests? Do people use these conceptions in their everyday evaluations of themselves and others?

THE INTERRELATIONS OF INTELLIGENCE, WISDOM, AND CREATIVITY

I started off by sending questionnaires to professors of art, business, philosophy, and physics, asking them to list behaviors characteristic of people who are highly intelligent, wise, or creative in their respective fields. A comparable questionnaire was given to lay persons—people from the New Haven area who answered an advertisement in a local newspaper. The number of individuals responding averaged 25 per group. The number of behaviors listed averaged 130 for each of the three attributes of intelligence, wisdom, and creativity, so that the listing procedure generated quite a large number as well as a variety of behaviors for each attribute.

A new questionnaire was then sent out to different people within the same subject population. These new people were asked to rate on a 1-to-9 scale how characteristic each of the set of behaviors was of an ideally intelligent, wise, or creative individual in their own occupation. A rating of 1 meant "extremely uncharacteristic," and a rating of 9 meant "extremely characteristic." The average number of subjects per group was 65, and all subjects provided all three ratings (for intelligence, wisdom, and creativity), although in different orders, so that, for example, some of the people would provide ratings for intelligence first, some second, and some last. The ratings obtained in each of the groups proved to be highly reliable, meaning that there was substantial agreement among the members of the various groups as to what constituted intelligent, wise, or creative behavior.

First, we found that, in general, intelligence and wisdom are perceived as most closely related, intelligence and creativity as next most closely related, and wisdom and creativity as least related. The only departure from this pattern was for philosophers, for whom intelligence and creativity were more closely related than were intelligence and wisdom.

Second, all of the interrelationships were positive, meaning that higher amounts of intelligence were associated with higher amounts of wisdom, higher amounts of wisdom with higher amounts of creativity, and higher amounts of intelligence with higher amounts of creativity. There was one exception to this trend, however. The business professors saw greater amounts of wisdom as associated with lesser amounts of creativity—in other words, in business, the wiser people are seen as less creative, and vice versa.

These patterns of correlations tell us about the interrelations of intelligence, wisdom, and creativity. A second study was designed to say something about the internal structure of each attribute.

THE NATURE OF INTELLIGENCE, WISDOM, AND CREATIVITY

In the second study, forty college students were asked to sort three sets of forty behaviors into as many or as few piles as they wished on the basis of which behaviors are "likely to be found together" in a person. These behaviors were from the listings for intelligence, wisdom, and creativity from the first study. Only the top forty behaviors (that is, behaviors rated by lay persons as highly characteristic of ideally intelligent, wise, or creative individuals) were used in each sorting task. The same subjects did the sortings for intelligence, wisdom, and creativity in different orders.

A method of data analysis called nonmetric multidimensional scaling was used to analyze the sortings. This method enables us to determine the underlying structure in a set of sorting or rating data. In other words, we could ascertain the mental categories people use in understanding intelligence, creativity, and wisdom. Underlying categories were determined for each of the three attributes.

The results for intelligence yielded six basic categories in people's conceptions of intelligence. These basic categories, with examples, are:

1. *Practical problem-solving ability* (tends to see attainable goals and accomplish them; has the ability to change directions and use another procedure; is able to apply knowledge to particular problems).
2. *Verbal ability* (can converse on almost any topic; has demonstrated a good vocabulary; has a good command of language).
3. *Intellectual balance and integration* (has the ability to recognize similarities and differences; listens to all sides of an issue; is able to grasp abstract ideas and focus attention on those ideas).
4. *Goal orientation and attainment* (tends to obtain and use information for specific purposes; possesses ability for high achievement; is motivated by goals).
5. *Contextual intelligence* (learns and remembers and gains information from past mistakes and successes; has the ability to understand and interpret his environment; knows what's going on in the world).
6. *Rapid thinking* (has a thorough grasp of mathematics and has good spatial ability and hence can mentally manipulate images; has a high IQ level; thinks quickly).

The multidimensional scaling for wisdom also revealed six basic elements in people's conceptions of wisdom:

1. *Reasoning ability* (has good problem-solving ability; has a logical mind).
2. *Sagacity* (considers advice; understands people through dealing with a variety of people; feels she can always learn from other people; is fair).
3. *Learning from ideas and environment* (attaches importance to ideas; is perceptive; learns from other people's mistakes).
4. *Judgment* (acts within own physical and intellectual limitations; is sensible; has good judgment at all times; thinks before acting or making decisions).
5. *Expeditious use of information* (is experienced; seeks out information, especially details; learns and remembers and gains information from past mistakes or successes).
6. *Perspicacity* (can offer solutions that are on the side of right and truth; is able to see through things—read between the lines; has the ability to understand and interpret his environment).

The multidimensional scaling for creativity also yielded six major elements:

1. *Lack of conventionality* (makes up rules as he goes along; has a free spirit; is unorthodox).
2. *Integration and intellectuality* (has the ability to recognize similarities and differences; is able to put old information, theories, etc., together in a new way).
3. *Aesthetic taste and imagination* (appreciates the arts; can write, draw, or compose music; has good taste).
4. *Decisional skill and flexibility* (follows gut feelings in making decisions after weighing the pros and cons; has the ability to change directions and use another procedure).
5. *Questioning spirit* (questions societal norms, truisms, assumptions; is willing to take a stand).
6. *Drive for accomplishment and recognition* (is motivated by goals; likes to be complimented on work; is energetic).

This study provided a good sense of just what people mean by "intelligence," "wisdom," and "creativity." But do the ways in which people use these terms correspond at all to the kinds of things that have been and can be measured by conventional kinds of tests? In other words, do people's conceptions of intelligence, wisdom, and creativity correspond in any way to scientific notions as manifested in conventional tests? A third study was designed to answer this question.

PEOPLE'S CONCEPTIONS AS A BASIS FOR MEASURING INTELLIGENCE, WISDOM, AND CREATIVITY

Can people's conceptions of intelligence, wisdom, and creativity serve as a basis for the measurement of these attributes, and if so, do these measurements relate to more traditional measures?

Thirty New Haven–area adults were administered four psychometric tests, two measuring cognitive intelligence as it is traditionally defined and two measuring social intelligence. The social-intelligence tests measured interpersonal judgments in social situations. Psychometric tests of creativity were not employed because of my view (and the view of many others in the field) that such tests capture at best only the most trivial aspects of creativity. In addition, participants in the study were asked to fill out all three of the questionnaires from the first study—those for intelligence, wisdom, and creativity—as they pertained to themselves, rather than as they pertained to an ideal individual. The same participants filled out all three questionnaires in varied order, so that effects of order of administration of questionnaires would be balanced out. Only those questionnaire items were retained that had been shown in the first study to provide good measurement of each of the constructs. Subjects rated themselves on a 1–9 scale for each item and were given as long as they needed to complete the questionnaires.

Questionnaires were scored by correlating each subject's response pattern on each questionnaire (intelligence, wisdom, and creativity) with the "prototype" questionnaire obtained from the lay persons in the first study. The prototype contained the set of ratings for the hypothetical ideal individual with respect to intelligence, wisdom, or creativity. Thus, the correlation measured the degree of resemblance between the subject in this experiment and the hypothetical ideal individual emerging from the first study.

We predicted that scores on the intelligence behavioral questionnaire would correlate substantially with scores on the tests of cognitive intelligence, whereas scores on the wisdom behavioral questionnaire would correlate substantially with scores on the tests of social intelligence. Underlying this set of predictions was the notion that wisdom comes close to being intelligence applied to social-practical settings, whereas intelligence as measured by standard psychometric tests is more cognitive in nature. The predicted pattern of results held up: the correlations of the intelligence behavioral questionnaire with the cognitive measures were higher than with the social measures, whereas the correlations of the wisdom behavioral questionnaire were higher with the social measures than with the cognitive measures. Moreover, these differences were both statistically significant and substantial. The creativity behavioral questionnaire did not correlate with either kind of test, as would be expected if creativity is indeed distinct from both intelligence and wisdom.

These results show that people's conceptions of intelligence, wisdom, and creativity are not merely frivolous or scientifically vacuous. Rather, they correspond fairly well to the patterns of scores that would be expected on more conventional psychometric measures. Obviously, you would not wish to test for people's intelligence, wisdom, and creativity solely on the basis of questionnaire measures that involve self-descriptions. Nevertheless, the results suggest that such measures have at least some external validity, and that people's implicit theories underlying the measures are related to the experts' notions, although I believe that the implicit theories go well beyond these conventional notions in their breadth and possibly their depth.

EVALUATING THE INTELLIGENCE, WISDOM, AND CREATIVITY OF OTHERS

Our third study showed that people use their implicit theories of intelligence, wisdom, and creativity in evaluating their own levels of each of these attributes. Do they use these same implicit theories in evaluating the attributes of others? In other words, when given a behavioral description of someone, will people bring to bear their implicit theories in evaluating the described person's level of intelligence, wisdom, and creativity? A fourth (and last) study addressed this question.

Forty individuals, all of them New Haven–area adults, were presented with 54 attributes culled from simulated letters of recommendation. Two typical lists of attributes would be:

I. Gerald
   _____ a. He possesses ability for high achievement.
   _____ b. He has the ability to grasp complex situations.
   _____ c. He has good problem-solving ability.
   _____ d. He attaches importance to well-presented ideas.

II. Doris
   _____ a. She is motivated by goals.
   _____ b. She questions societal norms, truisms, and assumptions.
   _____ c. She thinks quickly.
   _____ d. She is not materialistic.
   _____ e. She is totally absorbed in study.

Descriptions were generated so as to vary predicted levels of intelligence, wisdom, and creativity. Each description was either four, five, or six sentences in length, and was paired equally often with names of males and females. A given subject, however, saw a given description only once—with either a male name or a female name. The subject's task was to rate the intelligence, wisdom, and creativity of each of the described individuals. Ratings were made on a 9-point scale. Order of ratings was varied across subjects in the study.

It was possible to obtain predicted ratings of intelligence, wisdom, and creativity by summing up the ratings of lay persons from the first study on each attribute for each subject and then dividing by the number of attributes given for the hypothetical individual. Averages rather than sums of ratings were used because the number of behaviors was not the same for each of the descriptions.

The more closely the description of the hypothetical individual represents the ideal of the first study on each of the three attributes of intelligence, wisdom, and creativity, the higher should be the the rating that the hypothetical individual receives in the present study.

Average ratings of the hypothetical individuals were highest for intelligence, intermediate for wisdom, and lowest for creativity. The ratings were highly reliable, meaning that there was good agreement among subjects as to who was relatively more intelligent, wise, or creative. Intercorrelations (degree of relationship) of ratings were extremely high between intelligence and wisdom, high between intelligence and creativity, and moderately high between wisdom and creativity. Thus, the rank order of the correlational relations was the same as that in the past studies, although in this study intelligence and wisdom were almost indistinguishable. Use of male versus female names had no effect: the average ratings and patterns of ratings were essentially identical regardless of whether the described individual was listed as male or female.

The observed ratings and predicted ratings (derived from the first study) were extremely similar. In each case, the correlation between the predicted and observed values for a given attribute was extremely high (about .9 on a -1-to-1 correlational scale). Thus, people seem not only to have implicit theories of intelligence, wisdom, and creativity but to use them in predictable and somewhat distinguishable ways to judge others.

It is possible, then, to predict people's evaluations of others on the basis of knowledge about their implicit theories. And despite the omnipresence of standardized tests in our society, most evaluations of people's abilities are still done informally—through casual conversations, interviews, letters of recommendation, secondhand comments, and the like. Psychometric tests tell us nothing about how these informal evaluations are made. But the results of implicit-theoretical evaluations do. For this reason, it is important to identify people's implicit theories and to know how they use them.

Psychologists have put a great deal of effort into understanding intelligence because of its importance in both the academic and the "real" world. Traditional conceptions of intelligence have been too narrow, and the triarchic theory of intelligence was formulated to remedy this deficiency. But formal theories don't tell us much about how people in general view and use psychological constructs. Analyses of people's conceptions of these constructs, such as those presented in this chapter, do. But we need to go beyond even our broader conceptions of intelligence to understand mental self-management, because other constructs, such as wisdom and creativity, are clearly important, too.

CHAPTER
10

The Socialization of Intelligence

Where does our intelligence come from? Are we born with it, or do we acquire it in our interactions with the environment? Probably both heredity and environment matter some, but I argue in this chapter that the effects of environment are extremely powerful. My basic claim is straightforward: intelligence is in part a product of socialization—the way a person is brought up. Accounts of the development of intelligence stressing heredity view intelligence as a product of the genes with which you are born. They ignore the major effect of differences in socialization on the development of intelligence. Socialization is defined here as the interaction between the social environment and the way an individual develops as a person. Given this definition, there must be differences in socialization in different cultures and at different levels of society. What Australian Aborigines learn to be intelligent in their culture is different from what we learn to be intelligent in ours.

My goal here is to show how socialization processes affect intelligence and its development. I draw on evidence from studies both within and across cultures supporting the view that intelligence is largely a product of socialization. To lend coherence to the presentation, my own triarchic theory of intelligence will be used to provide a framework within which the effects of socialization will be demonstrated. You will see how people's—especially parents'—implicit theories of intelligence affect the way they "socialize" children to be intelligent.

The Socialization of Intelligence: Componential, Experiential, and Contextual Aspects

How does socialization affect the development and manifestation of intelligence? In other words, is it possible that almost all parents and communities raise their children to be intelligent in accordance with their conception of what it means for a child to be intelligent? This section of the chapter will deal with this question, drawing mainly on Shirley Heath's 1983 study of language development in three communities in the Piedmont Carolinas.[1] Heath surveyed language acquisition among lower-class blacks (the Trackton community), lower-class whites (Roadville), and middle-class whites (Gateway). But whereas her interest was in how language develops, mine will be in how intelligence develops—especially, how each community seeks to develop the intelligence of its children in a different way. Further evidence will be drawn from Ochs and Schiefflin's 1982 cross-cultural study of language socialization in white middle-class America, Papua New Guinea, and Western Samoa,[2] and from Ray McDermott's 1974 study of sources of school failure among ethnic and racial "outgroups."[3]

THE COMPONENTIAL SUBTHEORY

Components of intelligence operate in all cultures, although their specifics may differ cross-culturally. According to cultural norms, for example, some strategies may be preferred to others (suggesting differential "weighting" of metacomponents), or specific resources (such as time) may be more or less carefully allocated. Components vital to success in a society will develop readily, whereas others may tend to be inhibited.

Metacomponents. Metacomponential functioning is the kind of intellectual processing most heavily involved in thinking of many kinds. Consider four metacomponents and how their use is socialized through the environment.

A critical metacomponent is *understanding the nature of tasks with which one is confronted.* The assumption in school, of course, is that children will accept the tasks as given and appreciate their value. The upbringing of children in Trackton (the lower-class black community) scarcely prepares them to recognize the usual tasks.

Heath found that children in Trackton start off on the wrong foot by not being able to answer even so simple a question as to whether they are present in class. They have grown up with nicknames different from those on their birth certificates and often do not know their formal names—hence, their failure to respond. Moreover, even having found out these names, they dislike being called by them, and are reluctant to answer to them. Teachers, however, object to using names like "Frog" and "Red Girl" and often insist on using the formal names.

Furthermore, in Trackton, questions for which the questioner has or expects specific information are rare. A question such as "What's my name?" or "What's your name?" is not expected to yield a literal answer but, rather, recognition of a social relationship. The name given will depend on who asks the question and on why it is asked. In even so simple a situation as responding to one's name, therefore, the Trackton children appear stupid because of their unwillingness or inability to respond appropriately.

The problem of Trackton children goes beyond mere naming. Trackton children do not expect adults to ask them questions in general, because in Trackton children are not seen as information givers or as question answerers. As a result, the very act of being asked a question is strange to them. When Heath assigned tasks to the Trackton children, the children often protested, seeing no reason why they should do these tasks. Trackton children particularly have trouble dealing with indirect requests, such as "It's time to put our paints away now," because such unfamiliar kinds of statements may not even be perceived as requests. These children have particular difficulty with "why" questions, because adults in Trackton do not engage children in conversations in which such questions are asked.

Roadville children (lower-class whites) also confront a problem in naming, although of a very different kind. Here, a very small number of first names—such as Robert and Elizabeth—tend to be favored, with the result that many schoolchildren of the same age have the same name. The obvious solution, to use additional initials (such as the middle or the last), is resisted by the children, causing frustration for teachers and students alike.

In Roadville, adults see themselves as teachers and thus ask and answer questions, including "why" questions. By the time Roadville children go to school, they have had considerable experience with both direct and indirect requests. Unfortunately, once the children start school, their parents more or less abdicate their role as teachers, leaving the job to the school. Gateway parents, in contrast, continue to see themselves in the role of teacher, and continue to intervene in their children's educational process.

Once a problem is understood, it still must be solved. Two other important metacomponents involve *deciding upon steps in accomplishing tasks* and *putting these steps together to form a strategy*. But the ability to do these things depends in large part on prior familiarity with the kinds of steps and strategies that are appropriate to a given task. Middle-class children are familiar with typical kindergarten toys, which often have parts that need to be coordinated and then pieced together in some way. Trackton children usually have not experienced such toys before and thus may have great difficulty in playing with them. Nor have they been given books, puzzles, manipulative toys, or blocks, unless the materials happened to be brought from outside the community. Thus, whereas the Gateway child will know right away what the task is—to put together the puzzle, to manipulate a given toy in a certain way, to play with blocks—the Trackton child may find this kind of play unfamiliar and strange. It is much more difficult for him to figure out how to play with these toys than it is for the middle-class child who is familiar with the toys.

The situation in Roadville is quite different from that in Trackton. Although it, too, is a lower-class community, parents are aware of the importance of a rich environment for their children's development, and they make it a point to surround even newborns with mechanical, musical, and constructional toys. The children hear nursery rhymes recited and are expected to learn the stories. Objects in the environment promote exploration of color, shape, texture, and the like. Children receive educational toys and from the start are taught how to use them.

Another example of different strategies affecting task performance comes from Judith Kearins's 1981 study of visual-spatial memory in Aboriginal and Anglo-Australian children.[4] Aboriginals have been shown to remember spatial displays better than Anglo-Australians, an ability sometimes explained as adaptive for the survival of a nomadic people. Kearins sought to identify the behavioral aspects of this ability by examining how the two groups went about remembering, and then reproducing, the arrangement of items in a three-dimensional display. During the thirty-second observation period, the Anglo-Australians typically moved around the display, picking up the objects and naming them. The Aboriginals, on the other hand, chose a single position from which to view the display and then sat motionless before it, apparently trying to "burn" the image of the display into their minds. In reproducing the display, the Anglo-Australians would replace the first few items very quickly, then proceed much more slowly, often moving items they had already placed. The Aboriginals worked at a more constant pace, deliberating before placing each item and rarely moving one that had been positioned. When asked how they had performed the task, many Anglo-Australians mentioned verbal strategies, whereas the Aboriginals showed a reliance on their visual memory, saying they remembered the "look" of the display. Clearly, each group tended to use strategies that were appropriate for the tasks most familiar to them: the Anglo-Australians used verbal (school-appropriate) strategies, and the Aboriginals used visual (desert-nomad-appropriate) strategies.

Another critical metacomponent is *allocation of resources*. In Western societies, time is one of the resources most carefully apportioned. We live out our lives under the external constraints imposed by clocks and timetables; the Bible teaches us "To every thing there is a season." A comparison of the lifestyles of American and Kipsigi (Kenyan) infants, however, shows the differences in time allocation across cultures.[5] Kipsigi infants are socialized into a culture where time allocation is much less important than in most Western cultures. Whereas the children of middle-class American parents must learn to deal with a rigid schedule and limited access to their parents, Kipsigi infants are not subject to such restrictions. During the day, they are carried by their mothers in a sling; by night, mother and baby sleep in the same bed. Because the agricultural economy of the Kipsigi allows for flexible work schedules, the babies' needs can be attended to at any time. If a baby needs to be fed three times during the night, the Kipsigi mother sleeps later in the morning; an American working mother cannot afford herself such luxury, and either baby or mother loses out to the demands of a nine-to-five schedule.

Heath suggests that the importance of resource allocation differs in the three communities she has studied. One of the ways American schools prepare children for a schedule-dominated adulthood is through the expectation that the schools' fairly strict schedules will be observed. Place constraints are equally important. Things are expected to go in their proper place at the proper time. In Trackton, however, the flow of time is casual. There are no timed tasks at home, and few tasks that are even time-linked. For example, people eat when they are hungry, and there are few constraints on what is eaten when during the course of the meal. There are few scheduled activities, and routines such as going to bed may happen at very different times on different days. The children are used to a flow of time in which their wants and needs are met when there is someone there to meet them, and when the provisions needed are available. It is thus odd for the Trackton child to adhere to a schedule that appears to be arbitrary and capricious. Timed tests, of course, seem even stranger than school schedules: before entering school, the child may have had literally no experience with being timed in the performance of a cognitive task. In Trackton, things get done, basically, when they get done.

The Trackton child has similar difficulties with space allocation. Being told to put things in a certain place has little or no meaning. She is used to putting things down when done, but the place may vary. The child has so few possessions that finding the object later is generally not a problem. The Trackton child's relatively poor handling of time and space becomes a basis for teachers' unfavorable judgments almost from the start of school.

In contrast, children from Roadville and Gateway have a very strict sense of time and place. In Roadville, even the stories maintain a strict chronological order, emphasizing sequences of events. In Gateway, life is strictly scheduled, and even babies are expected to adjust. Things have a time and a place, and children are expected to learn what these are, just as they later will be expected to do in school.

As we have seen, the same metacomponents are socialized in a broad variety of environments, but in different ways. These ways vary in how effectively they prepare children for school. The same applies to performance components.

PERFORMANCE COMPONENTS

Consider the skills needed to *understand similarities and differences between objects*, so important in school and so critical on typical intelligence tests.

Trackton children almost never spontaneously volunteer to list the attributes of two objects that are similar to or different from each other. They have been taught to view objects holistically, comparing the objects as wholes rather than attribute by attribute. Although they may be sensitive to shape, color, size, and so on, they do not use these attributes to judge similarities and differences. Their holistic approach and their unfamiliarity with abstraction impede progress in reading as well as in reasoning. If the print style, type font, or even the context of a printed word changes, the Trackton child notices the change and may become upset. He fails to realize the symbolic equivalence of the print under these transformations, which, although relevant to the child, are irrelevant to the meaning of the printed word. Each new appearance of a word in a new context results in a perception of a different word.

The holistic perceptual and conceptual style of the Trackton child also interferes with his progress in mathematics, where one object plus one object may be perceived as yielding one object—the two objects are viewed as a new whole rather than as two discrete parts resulting in a sum. Rather than carrying rules over from one problem to another, children may see each problem as a distinct whole, needing new rules rather than the transfer of old ones.

The situation is quite different in Roadville. Adults encourage children to label things, and they talk to the children about the attributes of these things. Adults give the children toys that encourage them to match attributes such as color, shape, and size. Gateway parents, too, give their children educational toys from an early age. Children are encouraged to note points of similarity and difference between objects, and to label differences as they are encountered. Gateway parents talk to children about names of things in books as well as in the world, discussing matters of size, shape, and color as they arise.

Like the Trackton children, who sometimes suffer from a holistic perspective, the Kpelle (the African tribe whose sorting patterns we discussed in chapter 2) seem to view certain kinds of problems holistically, which inhibits the transfer to problem-solving skills to other contexts. Cole and his associates showed that the Kpelle were completely stymied by one problem that utilized an unfamiliar apparatus, but successfully solved an analogous problem that involved familiar objects.[6]

Trackton children are disadvantaged as much by attitudes toward reading as they are by their perception of the reading material. In Trackton, reading is strictly a group affair. An individual who chooses to read on her own is viewed as antisocial. Solitary reading is for those who are unable to adjust successfully in the Trackton social milieu. Moreover, there are few magazines, books, or other reading materials in the community, so that children have little opportunity to practice reading or to be read to. Whereas Roadville parents frequently read to their children, especially at night, such a practice would be most unusual in Trackton.

McDermott also notes that reading is an act that aligns the black child with the wrong forces in the universe of socialization. Reading is a part of the teacher's agenda, a game the teacher wishes the students to play. By not reading, Trackton children are accepting their peer group's games over the teachers'—just the choice they are likely to make.

Attitudes toward reading are different in both Roadville and Gateway. Once children start school, parents in Roadville generally stop reading to them, expecting the school to take on this task. Adults encourage children to watch "Sesame Street" to pick up reading, but they themselves scarcely set examples to model: Heath notes that in Roadville, everyone *talks* about reading but few people actually read. Unlike Trackton homes, Roadville homes do have reading matter—mostly magazines, which usually pile up unread and are then thrown away in periodic house cleanings.

In Gateway, children are coached before they enter school in both reading and listening behaviors. Children are encouraged to read, to learn the structures of stories, and to use what they learn in their lives. They generally can model their behavior after their parents, who often read.

Children in different environments not only plan things differently (metacomponents) and do them differently as well (performance components); they differ in the ways they learn. These differences impact on their school performance, favoring, on the average, the white middle-class child.

Knowledge-acquisition components. Cross-cultural studies of classification, categorization, and problem-solving behavior illustrate the effects of selective encoding, combination, and comparison. *Selective encoding* is at issue in studies of attribute preference in classification tasks. In these tasks, a subject may be shown a red triangle, a blue triangle, and a red square and asked which two things belong together. The child could classify on the basis of either color or form; different children show different preferences. In Western societies, very young children choose color as the decisive (or relevant) basis for classification but shift their preference to form by about age five.[7] Cross-cultural studies, however, often fail to show this color-to-form shift. Michael Cole and Sylvia Scribner suggest that the preference for form versus color may be linked to the development of literacy (where alphabetic forms acquire tremendous importance), which differs widely across cultures.[8]

Another investigator, Alexander Luria, provides an illustration of *selective combination* in a categorization task.[9] Shown a hammer, a saw, a log, and a hatchet, an illiterate Central Asian peasant was asked which three items were similar. He insisted that all four fit together, even when the interviewer suggested that the concept "tool" could be used for the hammer, saw, and hatchet but not for the log. The subject in this instance combined the features of the four items that were relevant in terms of his culture and arrived at a functional or situational concept (perhaps "things you need to build a hut"). In his failure to combine the "instrumental" features of the tools selectively into a concept that excluded the log, however, the subject was not performing intelligently—at least, from the perspective of the experimenter's culture.

In many of Luria's studies, the unschooled peasants have great difficulty in solving the problems given them. Often they appear to be thrown off by an apparent discrepancy between the terms of the problem and what they know to be true. For example, take one of the math problems: "From Shakhimardan to Vuadil it is three hours on foot, while to Fergana it is six hours. How much time does it take to go on foot from Vuadil to Fergana?" The subject's response to this problem was "No, it's six hours from Vuadil to Fergana. You're wrong . . . it's far and you wouldn't get there in three hours." In terms of *selective comparison*, performance suffered precisely because the subject was comparing incoming data to what he knew about his world, which was irrelevant to the solution of the problem. As Luria put it, the computation could readily have been performed, but the condition of the problem was not accepted.

Components are not the only aspect of knowledge acquisition that can differ in their application across cultures and subcultures; modes of knowledge acquisition differ considerably as well. These differences across the communities Heath investigated have powerful effects upon later performance in school.

In Trackton, there is a heavy emphasis on nonverbal transmission of knowledge. Adults pay little or no attention to a baby's words, even sounds that are clearly linked to objects. In contrast, they pay careful attention to the baby's nonverbal responses and praise responses such as coos and smiles that seem appropriate to a situation. People talk *about* babies but rarely *to* them. During the first six to twelve months of their lives, babies are not even directly addressed verbally by adults. Signs of aggressive play in children are acknowledged and generally encouraged. Babies sit in the laps of mothers and other adults frequently during the first year, and during that time the child literally *feels* the nonverbal interaction of the conversationalist. Children are expected to pay close attention to nonverbal responses to their actions and to act accordingly. When older children show younger children how to do things, most often they do not describe the required actions in words; rather, they simply exhibit the behavior and tell the younger children to do it in the way they are seeing it done. Watching and feeling how to do things are viewed as more important than talking about how to do them.

In Roadville, there is much more stress on verbal interaction and development. When babies respond to stimuli verbally, adults notice these responses and ask questions and make statements directed at the baby. When the children start to combine words, usually between eighteen and twenty-two months, adults respond with expansions of these combinations. Children are encouraged to label things and, as importantly, to communicate their needs and desires verbally.

Habits of verbal learning in Roadville, despite these desirable features, do not very closely match up with what will later be expected in school. Home teaching and learning are modeled on modes of knowledge transmission in the church, not in the schools. Children are expected to answer questions with prescribed routines. The measure of a child's understanding of things is his ability to recite back knowledge verbatim. The style of learning is passive: one listens and repeats back and thereby is expected to learn. The sign of learning is memorization, not understanding. Even in their play, Roadville children use language in the same way: they tell stories in strict chronological order and do not embellish them with either evaluations or creative fictions.

When the goal of learning is verbatim recall, the techniques used by Roadville mothers are extremely effective. In Islamic cultures, for example, memorization of lengthy passages from the Koran is a goal unto itself. According to Cole and Scribner,[10] Nigerian children in Koranic schools are trained to memorize the Koran in Arabic, a language they do not speak or understand. In Nigeria, as in Roadville, the mode of learning is geared to what is to be learned; the result is perfectly acceptable in its immediate context but may not be ideal in other situations.

In Gateway, modes of learning are again different. As in Roadville, early language use is encouraged and reinforced. Mothers talk to babies and assume that the babies are listening and will want to respond. Parents believe that a child's success in school will depend in part on the amount of verbal communication directed to and received from the child. But while Roadville parents discourage fantasy, Gateway parents encourage it, and praise children's imaginary tales. When children ask questions, adults answer at some length and probe the children's knowledge in order to assess just what is known and what needs to be known. The goal is to encourage understanding rather than verbatim recall.

THE EXPERIENTIAL SUBTHEORY

Consider now how socialization affects the use of the various components of information processing in two different kinds of tasks and situations, those that are relatively novel and those that are so familiar that they are in the process of becoming automatized.

Novelty. In school and in later life, children will encounter many novel situations, and a measure of their intelligence will be their ability to cope with them. Children in all three environments—Trackton, Roadville, and Gateway—learn to deal with novelty, but novelty of very different kinds.

Children in Trackton need to acquire flexibility from an early age. Indeed, flexibility is a key element of success in this community. By the time they are a year old, Trackton children learn to play out roles in the community, and it is crucial for them to learn to gauge community members' reactions to their actions. They have to interpret cues, know what to say when, and adjust their behavior as needed. As boy toddlers become a part of the Trackton milieu, they are teased and challenged, both verbally and nonverbally, and successful responses to these challenges are taken as a sign of intelligence. Clever putdowns win praise: Heath notes that by the age of four, a child is usually able to come up with the right level and content of ridicule in one-liner responses to aggressive challenges. The use of insult, and especially rhyming insult, is strongly reinforced by peers right through early adolescence. Because preschoolers are physically unable to meet aggressive challenges, they must learn to outwit their aggressors, dealing with novel challenges as they go along. Later on, they will be very quick at besting teachers in verbal combat, but this skill in coming up with novel and quick retorts will probably not elicit the same admiration from the teachers that it does from peers and even from elders in Trackton. The Trackton child acquires considerable flexibility and ability to deal with novelty, but in a domain that will not be reinforced, or will be punished, in later schooling.

Storytelling is another important aspect of Trackton life. A good story is one that is creatively fictionalized in a way that expands on real events—even to the extent that the outcome has little resemblance to what actually happened. All that is required is that the story have some seminal basis in fact. The best stories are "junk," which consists of highly exaggerated and fictionalized narrative. Stories are intended not to convey actual events but to promote social interaction and to enhance the reputation of the storyteller, whose accomplishments, victories over adversity, cleverness, and personal power they exalt. The audience gladly accepts the embellishments in the stories without any need for the truth to be acknowledged. Unfortunately, the schoolteacher does not react the same way at all. Stories that would be accepted in the community may well be perceived as deliberate lies, attempts to deceive the teacher or other school authorities. Again, the creative abilities developed in Trackton do not provide the Trackton student with a needed edge in school, because of the very thin line that is drawn between truth and fiction.

The situation in Roadville is entirely different. Stories are intended to recount events as they actually happened. There are rigid rules of chronology and factuality in stories, and children are thus discouraged from exercising creativity in invention of narrative and from exploring alternative ways of creating stories. Children are not expected to evaluate characters' actions or to elaborate on their inner emotions. It is considered inappropriate for the child to introduce fictional characters or any element of fancy into a story.

As a result, by the time they enter nursery school, Roadville children have had little or no experience with creative storytelling. When the children are asked to tell stories, they do not create or repeat fictional or fanciful stories. In order for Roadville children to accept such stories, a distinct frame of mind must be created where departures from reality are allowed—and even then, their fictional stories often fail to set the scene, to introduce characters, or even to have any particular point. The Roadville child is simply unable to form coherent stories of the kind that the school expects. This situation is scarcely surprising, as the stories that are requested in schools would be received at home as lies and probably would cause the child to be punished.

The attitude of Roadville children toward stories also emerges in their play. Although these children are very conscientious about following rules, they have trouble doing so when the play turns from realism to fantasy: they simply do not know how to engage in fantasy play. Eventually, Roadville children were observed to stop playing in those areas of the classroom where they could not utilize their play habits from home. Just as a child from Trackton may easily be perceived as a liar, a child from Roadville may easily be perceived as utterly lacking in spontaneous creativity. Thus, the encouragement of creativity in Trackton and the discouragement of it in Roadville both lead to unfortunate ends when a child enters school.

The situation in Gateway is different still. Children's imaginary tales are acknowledged and praised, so long as they take the form of fantasy and are clearly introduced with the signals appropriate for fictional stories. Children are encouraged to mix fact and fiction, but only so long as it is clear both to child and to listener which is which. Children learn the difference between fictional and nonfictional accounts and develop the ability to generate each with relative ease. Stories by Gateway children have neither the exaggerations of the Trackton children's stories nor the extreme, formulaic literalism of the Roadville children's. Gateway children learn to balance their synthetic and creative abilities with their analytic and critical ones in a way that later will be praised and rewarded in the school.

Automatization. Now let's consider the effects of socialization on the automatization of information processing.

Although experimental psychologists disagree on criteria for detecting automatization, we may make some inferences about automatization based upon the relative familiarity or novelty of specific tasks or situations. Studies of perception suggest that features of an individual's everyday environment are perceived automatically, whereas unusual features require more deliberate processing.[11] Thus, Trackton children entering school for the first time need to expend considerably more cognitive energy on mentally taking in the books and educational toys than their Roadville and Gateway counterparts do. Their progress in school may be impeded from the first by this initial disadvantaged position—a situation recognized by the developers of the Head Start program.

The novelty or familiarity of a task also affects how readily information is processed. One problem in cross-cultural experimentation is that many tasks that are relatively familiar to most Americans are completely novel to people in other cultures. The task may be as complex as the evaluation of syllogisms or as basic as the perception of depth in two-dimensional pictures.[12] What is of importance here is that experience influences the automatization of intellectual processing, which is often a key to effective use of intelligence.

THE CONTEXTUAL SUBTHEORY

Finally, consider how socialization affects the use of components in experience in order to adapt to, shape, and select everyday environments.

Adaptation. Whereas the cognitive processes required to be intelligent may be the same from one culture to another, adaptation may be directed toward radically different goals. Clearly, for example, what constitutes adaptive behavior differs across the subcultures of Trackton, Roadville, and Gateway. In the previous sections, some of these differences have been alluded to. Here they will be further elaborated.

Trackton children are born to relative disadvantage, in that few provisions are made for them beforehand. When a child arrives home from the hospital, there are no boxes of toys, no cribs, and possibly few toys. This lack of planning contrasts with the situation in Roadville and Gateway, where a great deal of attention goes into the preparation of the baby's room and of materials for the baby. Attitudes toward children are also quite different in the various communities. In Roadville and Gateway, parents take ultimate, and usually sole, responsibility for the early upbringing of their children. In contrast, Trackton children are viewed almost as community property. Although this system provides the children with a large number of interested parties, it also diffuses responsibility so that certain aspects of caretaking may never be attended to. Because Trackton adults believe that they should know what the baby needs, they are insensitive to the baby's verbal utterances, whereas in Roadville and Gateway adults are very sensitive.

Differences in attitudes toward children increase as the children grow older. In Trackton, children are regarded as entertainers, and a great deal of the child's adaptive resources are channeled into entertaining others. Children must learn to give performances and to play parts that fit the multiple contexts in which they find themselves. Telling stories is done for entertainment of others as well as for self-aggrandizement. The successful story is one that accomplishes both of these goals. Unfortunately, this attitude carries over into school, where the Trackton child views herself as a source of entertainment and behaves in ways that are inappropriate to school. In Roadville and Gateway, children are viewed as learners, and are not expected to entertain as they do in Trackton.

Perhaps the clearest case of the role of adaptation in the socialization of intelligence is in the match (or mismatch) of home values to school values, which in turn affects teachers' evaluations of children's general progress. Let's consider some examples.

In Trackton, people look ahead to improving their lot in life. Getting ahead is a major topic of conversation. Hence, Trackton children are by no means unambitious. At the same time, they quickly fall into a pattern of failure in school. Many of them begin to work or to raise families while still in school. Their highly contextualized and holistic intellectual styles do not serve them well in the lower grades, where they need to work with abstractions and to begin thinking analytically. Ironically, their contextualized abilities, as well as their creative talent, might serve them better in the upper grades; but by that time their pattern of failure is so entrenched and their levels of accomplishment so low that it is just too late for them to capitalize on their skills. Indeed, it is the child who fails in the Trackton milieu who may best succeed in school, so opposite are the values of Trackton from those of school. The behaviors required for adaptation are so different in the two milieus that successful adaptation to one almost excludes successful adaptation to the other.

McDermott argues that the pariah status of schoolchildren from Trackton-like communities is largely attained; it is not merely ascribed by the authorities. Such a status results from initial miscommunications and mismatches of values between students and teachers, and from the cycle of mutually destructive and regressive actions and reactions that follow.

The situation in Roadville is somewhat different. Roadville children tend to start off well in school. Home and school seem to match well. The Roadville child's experience with memorization and with obedience to authority serves him well in learning initial academic skills and patterns of socialization. But sooner or later things start to fall apart. As the role of reasoning increases and the role of rote learning decreases, the children of Roadville find themselves successively less able to cope with the school environment. The children have the memory skills but not the creative abilities to succeed. By junior high school, most of the Roadville children are eager to leave, and many do so as soon as they turn sixteen, the age at which they can legally quit school.

A major problem of the Roadville child is the separation between school and home habits. Home teaching ends once school teaching begins. School habits are not discussed at home, and ways in which school might help at home are not considered. Indeed, both children and adults do what they can to keep the domains of home and school separate. Roadville children and parents cannot understand the ultimate purpose of school activities or where these activities lead. Students do the minimum amount of work needed to get by and do not engage in school activities with their full mental or emotional effort. By the time they have reached high school, they view school as threatening their social lives and as interfering with their job prospects. They are eager to leave school not only because of their marginal performance but to get on with setting up households, working and making money, and planning to get ahead.

The situation in Gateway is completely different. The townspeople are strongly school oriented and believe that academic success is a prerequisite to success in later life. Moreover, they view the values of the school and of the home as perfectly consonant: whereas in Trackton and Roadville the connection between school and home is fragile, in Gateway it is close and strong. Indeed, the school teaches the values that the child will need to succeed in later life.

Like Heath and McDermott, Ochs and Schiefflin have described how children adapt to their environment according to the culture into which they are socialized.[13] The attitude toward children taken by the Kaluli of Papua New Guinea, for example, is very different from that of middle-class Americans. The Kaluli perceive their infants as "soft," helpless, and without understanding; they view their responsibility toward children as one of helping them "harden" into mature members of society. Because everyday life in Kaluli culture is "overtly focused around verbal interaction,"[14] language learning is an important aspect of "hardening." The speech of parents around Kaluli infants differs in several ways from American "motherese." Although Kaluli mothers explicitly teach their children specific words, they do not expand on their children's utterances or guess about their meaning. The Kaluli avoid interpretation, saying that "one cannot know what another thinks or feels."[15] One result of this tendency is that "the responsibility for clear expression is with the speaker,"[16] even when the speaker is a child of two. The Kaluli mothers' expectation that their children adapt to their social and verbal environment is strikingly different from middle-class American motherese,[17] which emphasizes a willingness to accommodate to children through "rich interpretation." The Kaluli children's need to adapt goes beyond making themselves clear; they must extract meaning from the utterances of people who are not simplifying their vocabulary or syntactic forms for their sake. Whereas American mothers typically attempt to enhance their communication with young children by repeating themselves (sometimes with variation) and by using a simplified lexicon, Kaluli mothers believe that doing so would result in the acquisition of a babyish language—clearly a counterproductive move in the effort to "harden" the child. Socializing Kaluli children, then, means "fitting (or pushing) the child into the situation rather than changing the situation to meet the interests or abilities of the child."[18] This is dramatic evidence of the extent to which a child may be required to adapt in being socialized into a way of life.

The linguistic socialization of children in Western Samoa bears some resemblance to Kaluli upbringing: children are initially talked *about* rather than *to;* the conversation around them tends to involve many people; and they are responsible for expressing themselves clearly to their elders. The underlying belief systems are quite different, however. Whereas the Kaluli are an egalitarian people, the Samoans live in a rigidly stratified society: Samoan children are responsible for making themselves clear, not because interpretation is discouraged, but because they are lower-ranking members of society. (If a high-ranking Samoan says something ambiguous or unintelligible, lower-ranking hearers must decide on the meaning for themselves.) Like the Kaluli, the Samoans encourage their children to repeat words, but the intent is to teach children memorization skills, so that they can begin serving as verbatim messengers. The stratification of Samoan society is reflected in caretaking practices as well. Normally, a child will be cared for by a number of people of differing social rank, ranging from older siblings through unmarried aunts to parents. Interpretations of the infant's gestures and vocalizations typically filter up through the hierarchy from lowest- to highest-ranking care giver, with subsequent instructions filtering back down to the lowest-ranking care giver (as in Western military protocol).

This system has two important consequences for language learners. First, if a message such as "Pesio's hungry again" is repeated by two or three care givers on its way to the child's mother, Pesio will have been exposed to the phrase several times in a single context and likely will learn its meaning quickly, as well as learning that the meaning is maintained in the words even though the voices are different. Second, children learn the "chain of command" quickly and soon begin to voice their requests directly to the highest-ranking person present, without necessarily expecting the response to come from that person. This knowledge of the appropriate routing of utterances is vital to becoming a viable member of the hierarchical Samoan society. In fact, the stratification of Samoan society, combined with the belief that children are naturally persons of lower rank, determines the Samoan attitude toward child care and development. In teaching children to fit into the hierarchy and to interact socially with people of various ranks, "the Samoan way is to encourage the child to meet the needs of the situation, i.e., to notice others, listen to them, and adapt one's own speech to their particular status and needs."[19]

Cultural differences in adaptation to the environment certainly apply to domains other than the language socialization emphasized in our ethnographic examples. For example, John Berry has found that individuals from low-food-accumulating societies, in which food is scarce and hard to come by (in particular, the Eskimo), tend to be superior on spatial-ability tests and measures of cognitive differentiation to individuals from high-food-accumulating societies, where food is more plentiful and easier to come by (in particular, the Temne, who live in Africa). People in the former kind of society typically depend on hunting and fishing for their food and hence need, from an early age, to develop their spatial skills as fully as possible. People in the latter kind of society are not as dependent on spatial skills and hence have less need to develop them.

Another culture where the development of spatial skills is highly adaptive is that of the Puluwat, who inhabit the Caroline Islands in the South Pacific. Individuals able to master knowledge domains including wind and weather, ocean currents and the movements of the stars, and to integrate this knowledge with mental maps of the islands, become navigators and are highly respected in their world.[20]

Although many conventional tests favor white over black examinees (which is no surprise, given the culture that has generated the tests), not all such assessments yield these results. For example, Geber[21] found that Baganda infants are superior to Western ones in sensorimotor skills, and this finding has been replicated by others.[22]

Heath's work showed that differential patterns of socialization lead to different cognitive as well as social outcomes, affecting performance on tests. These effects extend beyond American subcultures. For example, Durganand Sinha has shown how populations in India are disadvantaged in conventional testing.[23] The Indians concentrate on the social rather than the cognitive context of testing and try to please the examiner. Unfortunately, the result is that the Indians—following their cultural conventions—do worse on the tests and ultimately end up pleasing the examiner less.

Shaping. People sometimes choose not to adapt to their environment but, rather, to shape it. How does socialization affect this choice?

Although the account of child rearing in Papua New Guinea rightly suggests that it is the children rather than the adults who do the accommodating, Kaluli children are also successful at shaping their environments—within culturally prescribed boundaries. The Kaluli make extensive use of rhetorical and affective devices, such as shaming or teasing retorts and begging behavior. Children quickly learn how to use these features of social interaction to their advantage, and shape their environment by applying them ruthlessly, which leads to prompt rewarding by adults, who delight in their socially adept children.[24] Kaluli children are not trapped in an inflexible environment from which they can escape only by uttering the magic (adult) words their mothers are waiting for; through the judicious use of confrontational rhetorical language, they can gain a measure of control over their elders.

Children in Trackton, Roadville, and Gateway attempt to shape their environment as well, but their efforts take very different forms. In Trackton, shaping consists largely of paying close attention to the behavior of others and calculating adjustments in one's own behavior so as to maximize gains from social interactions. In a typical interaction, the Trackton child learns to assess jointly his own strengths and the weaknesses of the other person and then to respond in a way that makes the most of this assessment. Perhaps this is why a child from Trackton-like communities can be so successful in irritating his teacher—he knows exactly how the teacher is vulnerable and what will irritate her most. For example, as children grow older, their insults, songs, and stories involve numerous instances of double-entendre. The primary meaning is usually quite innocuous, whereas the secondary meaning often carries sexual or aggressive connotations, as in "banging on your door." Although teachers and other authority figures are aware of these double meanings, they find themselves powerless to do anything about them, because the child can and does deny that he intended the second meaning. The child shapes the environment more successfully than the teacher, but the child pays the consequences in terms of teacher disapproval.

In the school environment, there is generally a mix between individual and group activities, but the individual is expected to learn for herself and to engage in many learning activities independently. In Trackton, however, almost everything is done in groups. About the only things that are not subject to group negotiation are matters of sexual activity, finances, and knowledge that may give an individual an edge in the struggle to survive. The consequence for school activity is that the Trackton child tries to turn almost everything into group activities, even if the teacher intends certain things to be done individually. Again, the child's attempt to shape the environment is in direct opposition to the teacher's plans. Consider, for example, writing, which is often an individual activity. But for Trackton children, talking is a necessary concomitant of writing: if they write something, they also communicate it orally to others. This pattern of behavior may not serve the student well if the teacher intends the class to write quietly.

Roadville children and adults also seek to shape their environments, but in different ways. Roadville residents frequently compare themselves with the middle-class inhabitants of Gateway and elsewhere, and the adults seek to work toward membership in the middle class. They are eager to obtain the money that will propel them upward, and they educate themselves as to why middle-class children succeed in school whereas their children do not. But certain viewpoints and values get in the way of their climb upward. For example, they have very definite notions about how to get ahead, with men and women retaining fixed, traditional roles. Accordingly, women, but not men, are supposed to be interested in their children as good students; men follow more carefully their children's success in other domains, such as sports.

For the men and women of Roadville, work equals money. If they want to obtain more middle-class possessions, then they have to work harder, taking second jobs or odd jobs in order to improve their incomes. Because the children adopt this value as well, they, too, are eager to work to get ahead and accumulate wealth. Indeed, the young often look to those who have left Roadville and moved up in the world as role models. But because the young do not see much connection between school and the accumulation of wealth, success in school has only the vaguest connection, in their minds, to getting ahead.

As young children, Roadville tots have surprisingly little opportunity to shape their own environments. For example, when Roadville adults remember language-learning experiences, they tend to remember "learning to say the right thing," and their preoccupation with their own children's learning to say the right thing results in relatively narrow and rigidly prescribed standards of conduct for the children, in other domains as well as in learning language. When visitors come, for example, children have little or no choice in what or how to recite to show off—and the impression they make is through recitation rather than through creative storytelling or other flexible forms of enterprise. If children tell a story, their story, like those of adults, has a fixed format—it must be factual, maintain strict chronological order, contain a moral, avoid exaggeration, and so on. Thus, even in one of the domains that children often use most freely to create their own worlds, whether real or fantasy, Roadville children have relatively little freedom. Moreover, the de-emphasis on the development of the analytic and synthetic abilities of the children in favor of memory abilities is not likely to serve them well in school after the first few years, as reasoning becomes more and more important to school success.

In Gateway, adults do what they can to shape the environments of their children to maximize the school grades and the test scores that together will largely determine where their children go to college. Children learn that the actions they take can have a substantial effect on their future. They expect their actions of the present to bear on future life events; thus, they attempt to succeed in school. This attitude can emerge only from a consistent sequence of cause-event chains: certain behaviors need to lead to predictable consequences. It is interesting to compare this situation with that in Trackton, where adults make little attempt to be consistent with their children. Reward and punishment, for example, emerge inconsistently, and the actions and reactions of others to oneself are relatively unpredictable. It is no wonder, then, that Trackton children are likely to see themselves as relatively helpless in what they can do to attain long-term success: they just do not see consistent links between their behavior and the outcomes that emerge.

Selection. When adaptation or environmental shaping does not work, an alternative is environmental selection.

Consider how paths of selection are affected by socialization. The range of environments from which members of "developed" cultures may select is not generally available to members of traditional, nonspecialized societies. Kaluli tribespeople rarely leave their tropical rain forest, and because they are a small society (total population approximately 1,200), all members must participate fully to ensure their survival. The situation is similar for the Samoans, who are constrained by the hierarchical nature of their society as well as by their traditional values: perpetuation of the tightly knit family and cooperation among families in a village requires that individuals take their appointed places in society.

In contrast, a goal, and perhaps the ultimate goal, of the socialization process in Western societies is to allow the child as many degrees of freedom as possible in the selection of an environment—occupation, residence, style of living, and so on. It is here that we must add up the effects that the various socialization processes discussed above have on the children of Trackton, Roadville, and Gateway. The effects, we believe, are clear. Gateway youngsters will have considerable opportunity to select the life course they wish to pursue. Roadville children will have less opportunity, in part because they tend to leave school early and often start families and work while still in school. The lack of choices in these children's lives may also ill prepare them with the decision-making strategies needed in later life. Trackton children will be in the poorest position to select their own environments, if only because, from the start, they have been perceived as failures by school authorities and, academically, by themselves as well. They are the children most likely to live lives of poverty—perhaps in Trackton, perhaps in other Trackton-like communities—and to continue the cycle of failure that has stalked their progenitors for generations.

Some Conclusions

The main message of this chapter is simple: *levels and patterns of intelligence, and their manifestations in intellectual performance, are substantially affected by socialization processes.* Because of the vast differences in socialization processes that occur across cultures and subcultures, intelligence is not quite the same thing for everyone.

The elements of the triarchic theory—the components of intelligence, the experiential facets of intelligence, and the need for contextual fit—all apply and are the same in all cultures and subcultures. But these elements are manifested differently in different settings. Children in Trackton, Roadville, and Gateway all need to adapt, to shape, and to select their environments, but what constitutes such behavior differs radically across the three subcultures. Moreover, as the children grow up, what is novel in one subculture will be routine and possibly highly automatized in another, and vice versa. What the review of Heath's analysis makes clear is that conventional intelligence tests favor the socialization of intelligence that occurs in standard middle-class environments such as Gateway. Children in Trackton and Roadville develop many sophisticated adaptive skills. Indeed, the subtlety of thought and action required for social success in Trackton exceeds in many respects that required for success in Gateway. But not only do schools and intelligence tests not reward the kinds of subtlety that Trackton children need to develop; they punish it. The outcome of the socialization processes of Trackton is, if anything, diminished success in school relative to either Gateway or Roadville.

Traditional schooling and intelligence testing are based on the notion that intelligence is the same thing for everyone. But intelligence and its measurement can only be properly viewed as culture-dependent. Because context strongly influences performance, the instruments used to measure cognitive functioning must be calibrated—or transformed, where necessary—to fit the appropriate context.

Consider musical ability. People might seek to evaluate musical ability in a number of different cultures. But there might be a culture where the expression of musical ability was forbidden for religious reasons. In such a culture, development of musical ability would be maladaptive and hence unintelligent. Because musical ability is relevant to intelligence in one culture and irrelevant in another, the requirements for intelligence in the two cultures would differ. For a comparison of intelligent behavior across cultures, a model of intelligence is needed that takes cultural context into account.

If our goal in intelligence testing is to discover the true intellectual potential of children from cultures or subcultures other than the standard United States middle-class one, then we need to take very seriously the implications of a view of intelligence that takes into account its partial cultural relativity. We need to use ethnographic evidence such as that collected by Heath and McDermott to decide just what would be an appropriate test of intelligence as it has been socialized in a given environment. Such a test may actually be a poorer predictor of school success than are conventional intelligence tests, because the conventional tests share the biases of the schools in terms of what constitutes intelligent performance, and hence are likely to predict school performance better. It is ironic that it is this shared bias that has led Arthur Jensen to conclude that intelligence tests are unbiased![25]

New, fairer tests need to be constructed. If you wish merely to predict future success in institutions oriented to and controlled by the middle class, existing tests are sometimes partially appropriate, although narrow. If your goal is to assess a person's intelligence—regardless of how you define intelligence and taking socialization experiences into account—new tests are needed.

It is important to note that the view of intelligence and its assessment presented here is not one of radical cultural relativism, in which intelligence is viewed as a wholly different entity in each culture. Although intelligence is not exactly the same thing across different cultures and subcultures, neither is it wholly different. The three subtheories of the triarchic theory are alleged to apply equally well in all cultures and subcultures. What change are not the components of intelligence, the experiential facets of intelligence, or the modes in which contextual fit may be achieved, but rather the environments and behaviors in environments to which these aspects of the theory apply. Thus, adaptation will always be required, but what constitutes adaptation may differ drastically across environments. Because intelligence tests cannot be, according to the contextual subtheory, totally decontextualized, it is necessary to generate culturally appropriate tests that go beyond mere translation of test items from one language or dialect to another. Intelligence is largely the result of a socialization process, and our understanding and assessment of intelligence must seriously take into account the nature of this process.

PART
IV

The Roles of
Personality and
Motivation

11

Intellectual Styles

We have dealt hitherto primarily with the cognitive side of mental self-management. But intelligence is expressed through personality as well as cognition, and so we now turn to the interface between cognition and personality—intellectual styles. These styles can be used to explain and predict aspects of performance in school, on the job, and in personal life that cannot be directly attributed to intelligence.

We have discussed adaptation to, selection of, and shaping of environments, and we know that people approach these life tasks in different ways. The basic claim of this chapter is that a person's response to these tasks is largely the result of his repertoire of intellectual styles, his ways of approaching the world intellectually. The more wide-ranging and flexible this repertoire is, the likelier it is that a person will be able to fit successfully into his environment. But certain intellectual styles provide better fits to particular kinds of tasks and situations than do others. In order fully to understand intellectual styles, we need to understand not only the person and the situation themselves but also the interaction between them.

Consider a particular form of mental self-management—namely, self-government. The basic idea here is that actual governmental structures may be external, societal manifestations parallel to basic psychological processes, which are internal and individual. Seeds of this notion can be found in the writings of political theorists such as Hobbes, Locke, and Rousseau, whose political theories were based on psychological theories of what people are like. The difference here, perhaps, is that rather than attempting to understand governments in terms of the psychology of human beings, we will try to understand the psychology of human beings in terms of governments. From this point of view, government in society is a large-scale, externalized mirror of the mind. People are systems, just like societies, and they need to govern themselves just as do societies. Mental incompetence results from a breakdown of self-regulating functions, and high levels of mental competence derive in part from superior self-regulation.

The view of mental self-government presented here focuses more on styles than on levels of intelligence.[1] In standard theories of intelligence, including recent ones such as Howard Gardner's and my own, the emphasis is on levels of intelligence, of one or more kinds. In measuring intelligence, we typically seek to assess how much of each ability the individual has. In contrast, the governmental model leads to assessment not of how much intelligence the individual has but, rather, of how that intelligence is directed or exploited. Two individuals of equal intelligence by any of the existing theories of intelligence might nevertheless be viewed as intellectually quite different because of their intellectual styles—the ways in which they organize and direct that intelligence. A style, then, is not a *level* of intelligence but a way of using it, a propensity. When we are talking about styles rather than levels, we cannot talk simply about better or worse. Rather, we must speak in terms of "better" or "worse" *for what*. How might we use the concept of style, as well as the application of styles to problems, to generate a theory of how styles differ in terms of mental self-governance?

Governments have many aspects: function, form, level, scope, leaning. Three major *functions* of government are the legislative, the executive, and the judicial. Four major *forms* of government are the monarchic, the hierarchic, the oligarchic, and the anarchic. Two basic *levels* of government are the global and the local. Two *domains* in the scope of government are the internal (domestic affairs) and the external (foreign affairs); and two *leanings* are the conservative and the progressive. Let's consider the implications of each of these aspects for understanding intellectual styles.

The Functions of Government

Governments may be viewed as having three primary functions: legislative, executive, and judicial. These functions are reflected both in the types of mental processes and problems that utilize them and in terms of the styles that they generate. Similarly, individuals favoring one function or another will also tend to favor those mental processes that partake of the corresponding function.

THE LEGISLATIVE FUNCTION

The legislative function involves the creation, formulation, and planning of ideas, strategies, and products. Legislative *processes* in task performance are information-processing components involved in formulation and planning; a legislative *style* in a person corresponds to a predilection for formulation, planning, and creation.

Legislative processes are wide-ranging, including the processes involved in various forms of creation, formulation, and planning. Some examples are those metacomponents, or higher-order mental processes, used in various phases of planning for task performance: defining a problem, deciding on the lower-order processes needed to solve it, combining them into a coherent strategy, formulating a mental representation for information, and allocating the mental and physical resources necessary for a solution.

Consider, for example, a problem such as combating terrorism. If you wish to legislate and then execute a strategy for such action, you must first decide how to define the problem—whether it originates with Libya (possibly leading, as in recent American history, to a decision to bomb Libya), with Syria (leading, perhaps, to behind-the-scenes negotiation, because an attack on Syria is perceived as too dangerous), with misguided revolutionaries (in which case you might decide to bomb revolutionary headquarters, as Israel has attempted to do), or with indigenous self-help groups (in which case you might do nothing but applaud the terrorist actions). Legislation begins with the definition of a problem, and the way you define the problem will affect the processes selected to solve it, which in turn will affect both the strategy and the representation of the problem and how resources are allocated toward the solution.

The legislative style characterizes individuals who enjoy creating, formulating, and planning for problem solution. Such individuals tend to gravitate naturally toward legislative activities. In general, they tend to be people who like to create their own rules and enjoy doing things their own way. They prefer problems that are not prestructured or prefabricated, and like to build structure as well as content in deciding how to approach a problem. They prefer creative and constructive planning-based activities (such as writing papers, designing projects, and creating new business or educational systems) and enter occupations that enable them to utilize their legislative style (such as creative writing, science, art, architecture, and investment banking). The legislator's idea of perfection is a superior creation for which he is responsible.

THE EXECUTIVE FUNCTION

The executive function is involved in carrying out the plans formulated by the legislative function. It is important to note that the term "executive" is used here as it is used in government rather than as it is used in contemporary psychology. Here, "executive" refers to those mental functions involved in *implementing* cognitive and other activity, not in *planning* it. The executive branch of intellectual style executes rather than plans for execution.

Executive processes are those that carry out legislative plans. Included among them are performance and knowledge-acquisition components that encode, combine, and compare information. For example, the decision as to what strategy to use in solving a problem (legislative) will determine in part what aspects of a stimulus or set of stimuli should be encoded to solve that problem. Thus, legislative activities would be involved in deciding on a research topic, whereas executive activities would be involved in encoding the information relevant to that topic, combining the collected information, and comparing that information to what you already know in order to put together new and old information in an expeditious way. Similarly, with respect to terrorism, how you define the problem of terrorism will affect your planned strategy for combating it, which will in turn affect the actions taken to combat it.

The executive style applies to individuals who are implementers. They like to follow rules, to figure out which pre-existing means they should use to get things done. They prefer problems that are prestructured or prefabricated, and to fill in content within existing structures; they like activities that are already defined for them (such as solving algebraic word problems, applying rules to prestructured engineering problems, giving talks or lessons based on others' ideas, and enforcing rules) and executive-type jobs (such as lawyer, policeman, soldier, surgeon, manager, and builder—from others' designs). The executive's idea of perfection is an assigned task flawlessly completed.

THE JUDICIAL FUNCTION

The judicial function involves activities of judging. Such activities may start before a given path to problem solution is ever instigated and continue as a person monitors the solution during its course and then evaluates it after it is completed.

Judicial processes are information-processing components, such as those metacomponents that involve monitoring and evaluating internal and external feedback in problem solving. For example, judicial processes would be involved in recognizing that a term paper is getting off track or that an answer to a math problem does not make sense. Judicial processes would also be involved in evaluating the success of a response to terrorism.

The judicial style involves judgmental activities. Judicial types like to evaluate rules and procedures and to judge existing structures, both for form and for content; they prefer problems that analyze and evaluate existing things and ideas, and activities that exercise the judicial function (writing critiques, giving opinions, judging people and their work, evaluating programs). They tend to gravitate toward jobs involving large amounts of judicial activity (judge, critic, program evaluator, admissions officer, grant or contract monitor, systems analyst, consultant). The judge's idea of perfection is an evaluation that aptly characterizes the strengths and weaknesses of the ideas, objects, or persons being evaluated.

GENERAL ISSUES REGARDING THE FUNCTIONS OF MENTAL SELF-GOVERNMENT

It is important to note that people do not have one style or another exclusively—rather, they tend to specialize, some people more than others. For example, one person might be strongly legislative and only weakly executive and judicial, whereas another might be approximately equally balanced among the three functions. Thus, people differ not only in their direction of specialization but in the amount of specialization they show in the first place. Because people encounter problems involving all three kinds of functions at some point in their lives, at least some balance is desirable. But the issue of fit between persons and problems should not be sidestepped: a person will gravitate toward problems whose solutions emphasize her preferred style of functioning. She may also use certain styles in the service of others. A primarily legislative type, for example, may use judicial functions primarily to further legislative ends.

A person's proclivity toward one or more styles must be distinguished from her ability actually to implement these styles. It seems likely that most people will prefer styles that capitalize on their strengths, but there is no logical or psychological reason why preferences and abilities should always correspond. Some people may prefer styles that are not as well suited to their abilities as are others. In measuring styles, it will be important to measure both the predilection toward a given style and the ability to implement it. As a result of such measurement, it will be possible to determine for each individual the extent to which her predilection matches the corresponding ability. My collaborator, Marie Martin, and I are currently devising style measures.

The match between people's styles and preferred tasks is important in job performance. Two people with equal levels and profiles of intelligence, regardless of the theory of intelligence used, may perform differently in a job not because of difference in ability or even in motivation, but because of differences in style. For example, two university professors come to mind, both of whom are sometimes thought of as underachievers in their chosen occupations. The theory of styles has something to say about why this might be true. One of them is clearly a judicial type. He enjoys writing critiques, reviewing and editing articles, and serving on grant-evaluation panels. But in his academic field, the greatest rewards come not for judicial activities but for legislative ones—for coming up with ideas for theories and experiments. Similarly, the second professor seems greatly to enjoy collecting his own data, analyzing them, and writing up articles, but he seems less interested in the experiments he actually runs. His executive penchant might be more appreciated in a field where the rewards are for executing the ideas of others rather than for coming up with ideas of one's own. But in the field of both professors, executive and judicial processes must be used in service of legislative ones, as when one implements experimental ideas and then evaluates the results.

An important implication of these differences is that although style is independent of level of intelligence in general, it probably is not independent of level of intelligence within a particular domain. The same individual thought to be a brilliant scientist because he is a legislative type might be thought somewhat duller in a field, such as business management, that emphasizes executive skills. It is important to fit not only level and profile of intelligence, but level and profile of style, to jobs.

Sometimes, the very same career can call for different styles. Consider, for example, the career of university professor. It often has occurred to me that despite the fact that a professor of comparative literature or history and a professor of biology or psychology are both given the same job title, their jobs are quite different. A comparative literature or history professor needs to be more judicial, as this kind of professor builds a reputation on the basis of analytical (judgmental) skills; in contrast, skills of theory or experiment generation (legislative ones) are more important to the scientists. This is not to say that either kind of job is unidimensional. Scientists must judge their own ideas and those of others; literary theorists must build as well as critique systems. But the emphases in their work are clearly different. Similarly, two military officers might have the same rank, but one might be serving in the field and the other at a desk.

In general, different styles may work differentially well at various points within a given career path. Lower-level managers, for example, need to be more executive in style, but higher levels of management call for more legislative and judicial functioning. The fact that stylistic needs may change as a function of level of career raises serious issues about how we select and filter people through career ladders. The so-called "Peter Principle" is often interpreted as meaning that people are sometimes promoted above their level of competence. But the problem may not be one of competence but rather one of style: their style may suit lower but not higher levels within a given career path. In research and development centers, for example, brilliant scholars often have nowhere to go within the organization in terms of research; they become managers, but less than successful ones. Some of the new biotechnology firms faced this problem: they found that while scientists were not always the best managers, managers without scientific backgrounds did not always understand the minds of the scientists. This is not surprising, as managers tend to be more executive and scientists more legislative. Within companies formed by entrepreneurs, it often has turned out that the same style that was so successful in forming the company and managing it during its early days does not work nearly as well once the company is more established.

Some occupations have optional career-path switches built in to accommodate those whose styles do not quite match their jobs. So, for example, lawyers of a more judicial bent may become judges later in their careers. Executive-minded scientists may become managers in research and development organizations or administrators in universities. In the university setting, administrators frequently have trouble going back to research after their administrative stint has ended, having discovered that they are in fact more executive than, say, legislative in their preference. But being of a certain type at the wrong time in one's career can be fatal. For example, unless the scientist has some legislative ability, he may never get tenure and hence never make it into the administrative ranks within the university. Or a manager who is too judicial early in her career may end up stepping on so many toes by judging peers and even superiors that she never makes it to the higher ranks, where such judgments might be more appropriate occupationally.

Although I have emphasized how people bring certain styles to jobs, it is important to realize that jobs may also affect and possibly modify styles. A legislative university professor who tries a stint in administration may find himself gravitating toward an executive style out of necessity and may increase his executive penchant or even his executive abilities. Leaving the legislative (or any other) style for a number of years may actually suppress it. Just as the job you hold can help increase or decrease the level of various mental abilities, so may intellectual styles. Sometimes the switch may be crucial. Many state and federal legislators, for example, have been lawyers. They may thus actually not be the individuals who would be most comfortable in coming up with new ideas. Indeed, in the political speeches of legislators, the freshness of the ideas is often less than impressive. Some of these legislators hire staff to come up with ideas for them and then essentially become the mouthpieces for the staff, at the same time receiving credit for the staff's ideas. Other legislators may gravitate toward the legislative style and come up with their own ideas. The notion of style makes us consider seriously what kinds of job switches are likely to work better and what kinds are likely not to work so well.

The issues that apply to jobs apply as well to schools. I would argue that schools most reward executive types—children who work within existing rule systems and seek the rewards that the schools value. To some extent, the schools create executive types out of people who might have been otherwise. But whether the rewards will continue indefinitely for the executive types depends in part on career path—one reason why school grades are not very predictive of job success. The ability to get high grades in science courses involving problem solving, for example, probably will not be highly predictive of success as a scientist, an occupation in which many of the rewards are for coming up with the ideas for the problems in the first place. Judicial types may be rewarded somewhat more in secondary and especially tertiary schooling, where at least some judgmental activity is required, as in paper writing. Legislative types, if they are rewarded at all, may not be rewarded until graduate school, where a person needs to come up with her own ideas in dissertations and other research. But some professors—those who want students who are clones, or at least disciples, of themselves—may not reward legislative types even in graduate school, preferring executive types who will carry out their research for them in an effective, diligent, nonthreatening way.

The fit between student and teacher can be critical to the success of the student-teacher relationship. A legislative student and an executive teacher, for example, may not get on well at all. A legislative student may not even get along with a legislative teacher if the teacher happens to be intolerant of other people's ideas. During the course of my career, I have found that although I can work with a variety of students, I probably work best with students whom I now, in retrospect, would classify as legislative. I can work reasonably well with executive types as well. I am probably weakest with judicial students, who to me seem more eager to criticize than to do research. The general point is that an educator needs to take his own style into account in order to understand how it influences his perceptions of and interactions with others. Clearly, certain children benefit from certain styles. A gifted executive-type student might benefit more from acceleration, with material presented at a more rapid pace. A gifted legislative-type student might benefit more from enrichment, with opportunities to do creative projects consistent with the student's preferred style of working.

In general, certain stylistic combinations are probably better than others—at work, at school, and in a person's private life as well. Legislators may find executives boring and uninspiring. Executives may find legislators impractical or "flaky." Both types may tire of judges, who always seem to be evaluating them. And it's understandable that a legislative-executive couple might find it difficult to communicate with one another.

It is necessary that schools take into account not only the fit between teacher style and student style but also the fit between the way a subject is taught and the way a student thinks. A given course often can be taught in a way that is advantageous (or disadvantageous) to a given style. Consider, for example, an introductory or low-level psychology course: it might stress learning and using existing facts, principles, and procedures (an executive style of teaching), or it might stress designing a research project (a legislative style of teaching), or it might stress writing papers evaluating theories, experiments, and the like (a judicial style of teaching). Little wonder that I received a grade of C in my introductory psychology course, taught in the executive style! And little wonder that in my own psychology courses I have almost always made the final grade heavily dependent on the design of a research project— my style of teaching was reflecting my own style of thinking, as it does for others. The general principle that a style of teaching reflects the teacher's preference is not limited to psychology or even science. Writing, for example, might be taught in a way that emphasizes critical (judicial), creative (legislative), or expository (executive) papers.

Sometimes there is a natural shift in the nature of subject matter over successive levels of advancement, just as there is in jobs. In mathematics and basic science, for example, lower levels are clearly more executive, requiring solution of prestructured problems. Higher levels are more clearly legislative, requiring formulation of new ideas for proofs, theories, experiments, or whatever. What is of concern is that some of the students screened out in the earlier phases of education might actually succeed in the later ones, and vice versa.

Perhaps the most important point to be made is that we tend to confuse level of intelligence with style. For example, most current intelligence and achievement tests reward the executive style by far the most—they require solution of prestructured problems. A person can't create his own problems or judge the quality of the problems on the test (at least not at the time of test!). Judicial types get some credit for analytical items, but legislative types hardly benefit at all from existing tests, and may actually be harmed by them. Clearly, style will affect perceived competence; but, as we noted earlier, style is independent of intelligence in general, although not within particular domains. Style ought to count as much as ability and motivation in recommending job placements, although probably not in making tracking decisions that deal with issues of ability rather than style.

Forms of Mental Self-government

We have considered functions of mental self-government. Now let's consider its forms.

Governments come in different forms. Four of these are the monarchic, the hierarchic, the oligarchic, and the anarchic. Corresponding to each in the domain of mental self-government is a set of problems (requiring various kinds of mental processes) and a style. Each style of form can co-occur with any style of function. Logically, any form may be paired with any function, although, psychologically, certain pairings are likely to be more common than others.

THE MONARCHIC FORM

Monarchic problems are problems requiring fulfillment of a single goal or need. Pure monarchic problems are rare, although problems that are not intrinsically monarchic may be approached as though they were: making children literate, for example, or financing an addiction. Often, problems become monarchic not because they are inherently so but because they have been oversimplified by the problem solver. It is important to recognize, here and elsewhere, that problems elicit a certain style largely as a function of the way people represent them. A given problem might seem monarchic to one individual but hierarchic to another. For example, in looking for dates, some men seem to look for physical attractiveness to the exclusion of almost everything else, while others consider a wide range of characteristics.

The monarchic style.   People who exhibit a predominantly monarchic style tend to be motivated by one goal or need at a time. Single-minded and driven, they believe that the end justifies the means; they attempt to solve problems full speed ahead—damn the obstacles. They are relatively un-self-aware, intolerant, and inflexible, and have relatively little sense of priorities and alternatives. They are decisive, often *too* decisive, because they view their decisions in oversimplified terms; and they are systematic, but trivially so, as their system takes into account only those variables pertaining to a single goal or set of needs. The business executive who seeks to maximize profits at the expense of all else is exhibiting a monarchic style.

THE HIERARCHIC FORM

Hierarchic problems   are problems requiring fulfillment of multiple goals, with the goals assigned different weights or priorities: choosing a career, selecting a college or a job, finding a mate, planning a course.

The hierarchic style.   Individuals preferring a hierarchic style tend to be motivated by a hierarchy of goals, with the recognition that not all can be fulfilled equally well and that some are more important than others. They take a balanced approach to problems and seldom believe that the end justifies the means. They seek complexity and view competing goals as acceptable, but they sometimes have trouble if the priorities come too close to each other and thus do not allow for formation of a hierarchy. Self-aware, tolerant, and relatively flexible, they have a good sense of priorities and usually are decisive, unless priority setting becomes a substitute for decision or action, and are systematic in their solution to problems and in their decision making.

THE OLIGARCHIC FORM

Oligarchic problems   are problems requiring fulfillment of multiple, equally important goals. The equal importances of the goals may be perceived rather than actual. Examples of such problems are the teaching of English as a second language with the constraint that the indigenous culture of the learners not be destroyed, reforming an organization without undermining its basic tenets, and the teaching of thinking with the constraint that the students not become "machines." Note that in each of these cases there is a goal, but the fulfillment of the goal has associated with it a constraint such that if the constraint is not fulfilled, the solution is deemed unacceptable. Thus, both the goal and the constraint are of equal importance.

The oligarchic style.   Individuals preferring the oligarchic style tend to be motivated by multiple, often competing goals of equal perceived importance and to have available multiple, possibly competing approaches to problems. They are driven by goal conflict and tension, with the tension arising from the fact that they believe that satisfying the constraints is as important as solving the problem. For them, the end does not justify the means. They find that competing goals and needs tend to interfere with task completion, because each is seen as of roughly equal importance. They seek complexity—sometimes to the frustration point. Self-aware, tolerant, and very flexible, they are rather indecisive and have trouble setting priorities, because everything seems equally important. They are multiply systematic, with the multiple systems competing with each other because of the individual's need to satisfy multiple equally important goals.

THE ANARCHIC FORM

Anarchic problems   are problems that require a breakaway from existing paths and procedures for their solution. They are what I sometimes refer to as "nonentrenched." Some insight problems, such as the nine-dot problem, may best be solved anarchically, because existing solution paths tend to interfere with, rather than facilitate, solution. Such problems require a totally new approach. Radical life changes often require an anarchic approach as well, with the understanding that it is necessary to break away from existing approaches in order to adapt to circumstances.

The anarchic style.   Anarchic stylists tend to be motivated by a potpourri of needs and goals that are often difficult for them, as well as for others, to sort out. They take a random approach to problems and are driven by what seems like a muddle, with sometimes seemingly inexplicable forces behind their actions. They believe that the end justifies the means but are often unclear or unreflective on their goals. They're simplifiers, intolerant, and believe that anything goes. They have trouble setting priorities because they have no firm set of rules on which to base them. They're extreme—either too decisive or too indecisive—and asystematic; indeed, they eschew system.

GENERAL ISSUES REGARDING THE FORMS OF MENTAL SELF-GOVERNMENT

Some general issues arise with regard to forms of mental self-government. Monarchists are often too single-minded for the likes of most teachers and even social acquaintances. But in later life, their single-minded zeal may render them among the most successful of entrepreneurs or goal attainers in general. Often, their memories of school are not fond, because they believe that their talents went unrecognized. Monarchists' single-mindedness can make them difficult to live with.

Hierarchical types probably fare best in solving the widest variety of problems in school life and beyond, because most problems are probably best conceived of hierarchically. They will generally achieve a good balance between thought and action, but it is important for them to remember that the existence of priorities does not guarantee that those priorities are right. When there is a serious bottom line or pressing goal, hierarchists may get lost or sidetracked in their own hierarchies, whereas the monarchist may blitz through and attain the goal.

Oligarchists often frustrate themselves and others, in school and in careers, because of their indecision and hesitation. Because they tend to assign equal weights to competing means and goals, they may appear "lost in thought" and unable to act. They *can* act, but they may need others to set their priorities for them.

Anarchists are at risk of becoming educational as well as social misfits, and their talents may actually lead them into antisocial rather than prosocial paths. Properly nurtured, they may have the potential for truly creative contributions to the world, if their anarchic style is combined with the necessary intellectual talents for creative performance. But proper nurturance may be quite a challenge because of the anarchists' unwillingness to work within existing systems in order eventually to go beyond these systems. Rather than working within existing systems, anarchists may end up attempting to destroy them.

Levels of Mental Self-government

Consider next the levels of mental self-government. Government functions at multiple levels—for example, federal, state (or provincial), county, and city. In general, one can distinguish between global and local levels. Corresponding to these two levels are two aspects of mental self-government.

THE GLOBAL LEVEL

Global problems are general ones, often at a relatively high level of abstraction. Some examples are policy issues, general ideas for experiments (as opposed to the details of the implementation of these experiments), paper topics, and advertising plans. Tasks requiring global processing include formulating an overall instructional policy, coming up with new ideas for business products or promotions, and large-scale theorizing.

The global style. Globalists prefer to deal with relatively large and abstract issues. They don't like detail and often ignore it. They like to conceptualize and work in the world of ideas; they tend to be abstract and sometimes diffuse thinkers and have a tendency to get lost on cloud nine. They see the forest but not always the trees within it.

THE LOCAL LEVEL

Local problems. Local problems are problems involving detail, whether of conception or of implementation, such as the details of experiments, advertising campaigns, or mathematical problems. Examples of local problems are organizing the details of a conference, planning a detailed instructional sequence, preparing tax forms, and writing codes or laws.

The local style. Localists relish detail and often like concrete problems requiring detail work. Oriented toward the pragmatics of a situation, they are down-to-earth and may not see the forest for the trees.

In terms of the three types described earlier, the legislators and the judges probably would tend to be globalists, while the executives would tend to be localists. The local style is not, however, inextricably linked to the executive style. Some executive types may prefer to work at a broader level, accomplishing the main tasks in a project while relegating the local details to others. Similarly, a legislative or judicial type could be more local. For example, in science, some individuals generate ideas for experiments but do not have a clear sense of the global issue that the experiments test. Or a scientist may generate ideas that essentially deal with a smaller rather than a larger picture with respect to a phenomenon under investigation. Thus, the global-local distinction can be crossed with the functions of mental self-government as well as with its forms.

GENERAL ISSUES REGARDING THE LEVELS
OF MENTAL SELF-GOVERNMENT

Preferred levels of processing can logically co-occur with any functions or modes, although, psychologically, certain levels may tend more often to co-occur with certain functions and modes. Although most people have a preference to work at either a more global or a more local level, a key to successful problem solving in many situations is being able to traverse between levels. If one is weak within a given level, it is often helpful to pair up with someone who is not. In particular, we often value the people who are most like ourselves, but actually benefit most from people who are moderately unlike ourselves with respect to preferred level of processing. Too much overlap leads to some levels of functioning simply being ignored. Two globalists, for example, may do well in forming ideas but need someone to take care of the details of implementing them. Two localists may help each other in implementation but need someone to set down the global issues that need to be dealt with. Too little overlap can lead to a breakdown in communication. People who do not overlap at all in level may not be able to understand each other well.

In early stages of careers, where a person is largely self-dependent, the inability to switch between levels may be disastrous. Later, when she has subordinates, it may be possible to delegate tasks requiring levels of functioning different from her own preferred one.

In general, successively higher levels of responsibility demand successively more global functioning. Sometimes, people promoted for their success at more local levels of functioning may be stymied by their jobs as the tasks they confront become more and more global. Unfortunately, some of the globalists will already have been selected out because they could not handle the local tasks required earlier in their careers. Like functions and forms, levels of processing are independent of intelligence in general but not in particular. Certain kinds of tasks may lend themselves to one kind of level, while other kinds of tasks lend themselves to another kind of level.

Scope of Mental Self-government

Governments need to deal both with internal, or domestic, affairs and with external, or foreign, ones. Similarly, people need to deal with both internal and external issues.

INTERNAL SCOPE

Internal problems. Internal scope concerns tasks applying intelligence in isolation from other people. A person may deal with the world of objects or the world of ideas, but other people do not enter in, except perhaps trivially. Solving analytical problems, creating compositions or arts or crafts, and working with machines are examples of internal problems.

The internal style. Internalists tend to be introverted, task-oriented, aloof, socially less sensitive and interpersonally less aware than externalists. They also like to work alone. Essentially, their preference is to apply their intelligence to things or ideas in isolation from other people.

EXTERNAL SCOPE

External problems. External problems require applying intelligence as it pertains to the external world of the individual—the world of others as well as of oneself. External problems thus either are about other people or require work in conjunction with other people, so that the interaction with the people essentially becomes part of the problem. Examples of tasks requiring such a style are directing subordinates, working with supervisors or peers, maintaining friendships, and developing intimate relationships.

The external style. Externalists tend to be extroverted, people-oriented, outgoing, socially more sensitive and interpersonally more aware than internalists. They like to work with others and seek problems that either involve working with other people or are about other people.

In terms of the three types described earlier, the executive and the legislator would tend toward the internal scope of mental self-government, while the judge would tend toward the external. These proclivities should fit with their jobs. For example, an executive might work in corporate law, dealing with legal principles and documents and less with people; a legislator might work with ideas, instantiating them through experiments; a judge might work with other people—as a psychotherapist, for example. It should be realized that there is some degree of situation-specificity involved: in other words, a person who is externally oriented in her social life might be internally oriented in her job.

GENERAL ISSUES REGARDING THE SCOPE OF MENTAL SELF-GOVERNMENT

Some people prefer to work alone and to deal with the worlds of things and ideas on an individual basis. Other people prefer to work with others and to deal with the world of people. The former are called here internalists; the latter, externalists. Again, most people are not strictly one or the other but alternate between them as a function of task, situation, and the people involved. But it is important to realize in education and job placement that a bright individual who is forced to work in a mode that does not suit him may perform below his capabilities.

In management, a distinction is sometimes made between task-oriented and people-oriented managers. This distinction is roughly comparable to that between internalists and externalists. In schooling, we sometimes find students who prefer working individually, while others prefer working in groups. It is worth noting that our system of schooling probably most benefits internalists who have at least some minor external orientation. Indeed, in many settings in school, group work is considered cheating. Ironically, for all the emphasis on individual performance in school, much of people's performance after schooling is over is in groups. Many of these people often have received only minimal experience in how to work with groups. Their individual intelligence may have been nurtured, but not their group intelligence. The imbalance is unfortunate, because group performance may be hindered not by the individuals in it but by their interaction.

Leanings of Mental Self-government

Governments can have various leanings. Optimally, these leanings are represented on a continuum, such as right-wing to left-wing. But for present purposes, two major "regions" of leanings will be distinguished: conservative and progressive.

THE CONSERVATIVE LEANING

Problems and people differ in the degree to which they can be aptly labeled conservative, or emphasizing maintenance of existing goals, structures, and values. Consider each of the problems and people in turn.

Conservative problems require no, or minor, extension of existing principles or practices. Generally, they require solution of the problems based on existing rules and procedures. Some examples of such problems would be computing taxes (legitimately), following or explaining rules, and implementing them.

The conservative style.   Individuals with a predominantly conservative style like to adhere to existing rules and procedures, minimize change, and avoid ambiguous situations where possible. They prefer familiarity in life and work.

THE PROGRESSIVE LEANING

Problems and people may tend toward the progressive rather than the conservative.

Progressive problems   require a major extension or change of existing rules and procedures, and solutions that go beyond these existing rules and procedures: for example, creating a new art style, a paradigm in science, or a marketing campaign.

The progressive style.   Individuals with a progressive style like to go beyond existing rules and procedures. They maximize change, seek (or at least are comfortable with) ambiguous situations, and prefer some degree of unfamiliarity in their life and work.

GENERAL ISSUES REGARDING LEANINGS OF MENTAL SELF-GOVERNMENT

Although individuals, on the average, may tend toward a more conservative or more progressive leaning in their mental self-government, there is clearly some degree of domain specificity involved. For example, an individual who is conservative politically is not necessarily conservative in his personal life. Thus, in evaluating styles, and especially leanings, tendencies within particular domains must be taken into account. Moreover, leanings may well change over time as people feel more or less secure in their environments. Thus, an individual who is new to an environment may tend to adapt conservatively, whereas an individual who has been in that environment longer may feel freer to attempt to shape the environment. This aspect of style may be among the most mercurial.

The styles of intellect proposed here are not, of course, the only ones ever to have been proposed. Theories of intellectual styles abound, and it is not possible to review them exhaustively here. We merely can cite some pertinent examples.

In 1980, Isabelle Myers proposed a series of psychological types.[2] According to her, there are sixteen types, resulting from all possible combinations of two ways of perceiving (sensing versus intuition); two ways of judging (thinking versus feeling); two ways of dealing with self and others (introversion versus extraversion); and two ways of dealing with the outer world (judgment versus perception). In 1985, Tony Gregorc proposed four main types or styles, based on all possible combinations of just two dimensions—concrete versus abstract and sequential versus random.[3] Taking a more educationally oriented slant, Joseph Renzulli and Linda Smith suggested in 1978 that individuals have various learning styles, with each style corresponding to a method of teaching: projects, drill and recitation, peer teaching, discussion, teaching games, independent study, programmed instruction, lecture, and simulation.[4] In 1973, John Holland took a more job-related orientation and proposed six styles that are used as a basis for understanding job interests. These styles are measured on the Strong-Campbell Interest Inventory, a measure used to determine how people's patterns of interests can be matched to jobs.[5] Holland's typology includes six "types" of personality: realistic, investigative, artistic, social, enterprising, and conventional.

These various theories are all different, perhaps at least in part because they deal with slightly different phenomena. The Myers theory is based upon Jung's personality theory; Gregorc's is more cognitive. The theory of Renzulli and Smith is intended to apply primarily to educational settings, while Holland's is intended to apply primarily to occupational settings. My own theory, as presented here, is meant to be placed squarely at the interface between intelligence and personality. It relates to how intelligence is utilized in a person's daily life—in school, on the job, and in one's private life.

When we speak of adaptation, selection, and shaping as important to intelligence, style helps us flesh out just what adaptation, selection, and shaping mean. The argument here is that these functions are not just a matter of level but one of style. In order fully to understand intelligence, we must understand as well its bridge to personality through intellectual styles. Most important, we need to understand both our own preferred styles and those of others.

Where do these various modes of intellectual functioning come from? It seems likely that at least some portion of stylistic preference is inherited, but I doubt that it is a large part. Rather, styles would seem to be partly socialized constructs, just like intelligence. For example, in traditional cultures in which ideas are supposed to emanate from males, boys seem more likely to be socialized into a legislative style than girls. From early on, we perceive that certain modes of interaction with others and with things in the environment are more rewarded than others, and we probably gravitate toward these modes, at the same time that we have built-in predispositions that place constraints on how much and how well we are able to adopt these rewarded styles. To some extent, society structures tasks along lines that benefit one style or another in a given situation. There is a continuous feedback loop between the exercise of a style and how well that style works in a given societally imposed task. It is important to add that some of the rewards as well as punishments for various modes of interaction are probably internal rather than external. We adopt styles not only in relation to external objects and people but in relation to ourselves.

If styles are indeed socialized, even in part, then they are almost certainly modifiable to some degree. Such modification may not be easy. We know little about how to modify intelligence, and we know even less about how to modify intellectual styles. Presumably, when we learn the mechanisms that might plausibly underlie such attempts at modification, we will pursue a path similar to that which some educators and psychologists are using in teaching intelligence. We need to teach people to capitalize on their strengths and to remediate and compensate for their weaknesses. Some remediation of weaknesses is probably possible; but to the extent that it is not, mechanisms of compensation can usually be worked out to help narrow the gap between weak and strong areas of performance. For example, a business executive who does not like detail work may hire someone else to do it for her. Ultimately, we can hope that a theory of intellectual styles will serve not only as a basis for a test of such styles but also as a basis for training that maximizes people's flexibility in their encounters with things, with others, and with themselves.

Some Conclusions

People have intellectual styles that they bring to bear upon the problems they confront in their lives. These styles are independent of abilities in general, but not in particular domains. How well these styles work for a person depends upon the fit of a given style to a given problem, and upon the match between his pattern of abilities and the styles he uses in their expression. The effectiveness of the styles will also depend on how well they are integrated: for example, an executive style may work well in certain kinds of business endeavors but less well if it is combined with an anarchic form for its expression. People do not simply have one style or another but, rather, have preferences among the various possible styles. They exhibit differences in the flexibility with which they can bring various styles to bear upon a variety of problems, with some people exhibiting more flexibility than others. Moreover, certain styles may be used in the service of others, so that an individual who is primarily executive, for example, may occasionally be legislative in order to accomplish her executive goals.

Intellectual styles represent an important link between intelligence and personality, because they probably represent in part a way in which personality is manifested in intelligent thought and action. Attempts to understand academic or job performance solely in terms of intelligence or personality probably have not succeeded as well as we had hoped because they neglect the styles through which personality is manifested through intelligence. Thus, styles represent what may be an important "missing link" between intelligence and personality on the one hand, and between these two constructs and performance in school and on the job on the other.

Styles are probably partially socialized. They also are probably generated in part by ability patterns. Creative people, for example, are probably likely to adopt a legislative style. How well a given individual can modify her style in response to task and situational demands will depend upon her flexibility and responsiveness to feedback both from the outside and from her observation of the outcomes of the application of a particular style. Two major goals in future research will be to devise measures to assess styles and to develop programs that assist people in modifying their styles to better fit the tasks the environment presents. Although the theory of intellectual styles is only in its infancy, it seems to provide a useful way of understanding aspects of intellectual performance that have received less attention than they deserve in contemporary accounts.

Throughout most of this book, I have discussed intelligence in and of itself. Now I have discussed the bridge to personality—intellectual styles. In the next chapter I will consider the role of personality and its relevance to intelligence.

When Mental Self-management Fails

In everyday life, intelligence doesn't seem always to work the way it is supposed to. Why? Because of motivational and emotional blocks that can get in the way of our proper use of intelligence. No matter how adept we are as mental self-managers, our attempts at mental self-management sometimes fail. This chapter deals with the issue of when and why our attempts sometimes fail. I will discuss twenty sources of failure, each of which is an impediment to the full realization of a person's intelligence. It is to everyone's best advantage to be aware of these stumbling blocks and to try to correct them before it is too late.

Lack of motivation. No one is motivated to do everything he has to do all the time. We all go through periods when we just don't feel like working or when the tasks confronting us just seem overwhelming. For example, if a loved one has just died, or if we have just gone through a divorce, chances are excellent that we will not be as highly motivated in our work as we otherwise would be. These kinds of acute motivational problems are a part of life and not something to be worried about. Indeed, worrying about them can compound the problem.

It is necessary, however, to distinguish between acute and chronic motivational deficits. Chronic motivational deficits are ones that persist and seem to be around no matter what the circumstances. They are more serious the more they apply to a range of activities in our daily lives. The employee who never seems to be able to get his work done on time or the way it should be done might be labeled as having a chronic motivational deficit. Chronic motivational deficits not only prevent us from getting our work done but often result in our being labeled as unmotivated, which in business settings is often the kiss of death. This type of person is going to have a hard time remaining on the fast track or getting himself promoted. To me, this is the most serious problem in an employment situation. If I have an employee who lacks certain abilities, I can usually find some kind of work for him to do. But if the person lacks motivation, then there is nothing he will get done in the way I want or in the time span that I am willing to allocate to a given task.

It is useful to distinguish between intrinsic and extrinsic motivation. Intrinsic motivation comes from within, extrinsic motivation from without. People who constantly need prodding or rewards or the fear of punishment to get tasks done are extrinsically motivated. They work not because they want to, but because they believe they have to, or to please others. People who are intrinsically motivated are motivated from within: they work because they want to. I find intrinsically motivated people to be far better bets as employees than extrinsically motivated ones. Moreover, Teresa Amabile, in her studies of creativity, has found that intrinsically motivated people are more creative than extrinsically motivated ones.[1] When I have extrinsically motivated people on my staff, I always have the unpleasant feeling that they are working for a salary or for praise or for enhancement in the eyes of others, rather than because they really enjoy what they are doing. The biggest problem with extrinsic motivation is that it usually disappears when the rewards or punishments do. In other words, little can be expected from an extrinsically motivated person unless a system of rewards and punishments is in place. Hence, it is generally better to be highly motivated intrinsically. If up to now you've motivated youself primarily through extrinsic means, start looking for reasons why you do what you do not just because these things matter to other people but because they matter to *you*.

Lack of impulse control. There are times, of course, when it is perfectly reasonable to act impulsively. Sometimes we have no choice. If a decision must be made quickly or an act performed on the spot, we need to go with our instincts. But some people carry impulsiveness too far and act on impulse routinely. As a result, they never take the opportunities available to them to think things through, time and circumstances permitting. Their lives often seem chaotic to others; and indeed, they seem to create and then revel in this chaos. But their repeated impulsiveness may not only get them into trouble but get others into trouble as well. Louis Thurstone defined intelligence as the ability to withhold an instinctive response.[2] In other words, the intelligent person is someone who may well have an impulsive reaction—smart people, like everyone else, have impulses—but knows when to act on them and when to withhold them and put forth a more reasoned response. Impulsive decisions to marry, divorce, change jobs, move, and so on are generally inferior to well-reasoned and careful decisions.

Lack of perseverance and perseveration. Part of being intelligent is knowing when to persevere and when not to, but people often do not make the right decisions in this regard. It is discouraging to recognize lack of perseverance in others as well as in oneself. I have seen students, for example, who will try a variety of different projects but give up as soon as the going gets tough. I once had an employee who, like these students, was willing to try things but never willing to pursue them to completion if even the slightest difficulty barred her path. Such individuals make neither effective students nor effective employees; they are quitters. One finds such quitters in personal pursuits as well. Some people go after something or someone but, encountering the least discouragement, give up: they never give themselves the opportunity to discover what the outcome would have been had they really tried. I have a friend who has met a number of attractive women with whom he would have liked to pursue a relationship; but at the least sign that things were off an easy course, he terminated the budding relationship. He never gave himself or anyone else the chance to see whether the difficulties could be worked out.

At the other extreme is the perseverator—the person who doesn't know when to quit. Such people are not rare. The suitor who can't or isn't willing to take no for an answer is an example of an individual who perseverates; so is the theorist who proposes a theory and is unwilling to give it up in the face of extensive counterevidence. Sometimes we have goals in our work life or our private life that, for one reason or another, we are not able to meet. The intelligent individual needs to know when to persevere, but also when to stop perseverating and to recognize that these goals will not be reached.

Using the wrong abilities. A central thesis of this book is that an intelligent person is one who capitalizes on strengths and either compensates for or remediates weaknesses. The most successful individuals are usually not ones who are stellar at everything they try; rather, they are people who know their strengths and weaknesses, making the most of their strengths while finding ways around their weaknesses. At the same time, there are potentially excellent performers who do not perform up to their abilities because they capitalize on the wrong ones. The doctor who is afraid of blood, the scientist who is afraid to take risks, the policeman who is afraid to make arrests are all people who might be very successful at something but probably will not be optimally successful in their chosen careers. Capitalization on inappropriate abilities occurs in the personal as well as the academic domain. Someone with a charming personality but only average looks would probably do better to try to win other people over on the basis of charm rather than appearance; but he may not act in an ideally appropriate fashion. In order optimally to use the right abilities, you have to know your strengths and weaknesses. An analysis of your performance on the exercises in different parts of this book should indicate at least some of these. Take, for example, giving or receiving directions. This is an ideal situation in which to capitalize on a strength. If you are more spatially oriented, draw and ask for maps. If you are more verbally oriented, give and ask for sentence directions. In my own case, the kinds of directions I receive can make the difference between whether or not I get to where I need to go. For me, sentence directions, please!

Inability to translate thought into action. Everyone knows someone (maybe himself) who always seems to be coming up with great ideas but never seems to be implementing them. Some people seem simply to be unable to translate thought into action. We tend to think of intelligence as something cognitive—as something that occurs in the mind. But intelligence that never translates itself into action is merely inert; it is of little practical use. We need to learn to behave intelligently as well as to think intelligently. To be fully intelligent, it is not enough just to have good ideas; you have to act on them.

Lack of product orientation. I once had a student who seemed always to be working but never to be getting anything done. After a year of watching this student accomplish little, I tried to analyze what was going wrong. What I discovered was that she had an extreme lack of product orientation. She liked to do research but didn't care about writing up the results or coming up with a finished product. There are people like this in every walk of life. They work hard but produce little. They somehow manage to terminate their efforts prior to coming up with anything that communicates and shows to others the work that they have done. But in most occupations, you are judged by the products, not by the processes. Even if you are observed in your work, it is what emanates from the work that makes the difference. Similarly, in an interpersonal situation, there are people who are always talking about what they will do for their partner but never produce any results. In order for others to take your word seriously, it is necessary to follow through on your promises, not just to make them.

Inability to complete tasks and to follow through.   Every so often I find myself on a committee in which someone promises to accomplish a certain task but never follows through. Lack of follow-through seems to be a trait. Some people are always claiming that they will do things that never get done. People who show a lack of follow-through usually get a reputation for it. They are the ones we know we can't count on. No one wants to hire them; no one wants to work with them; often, no one wants to get into relationships with them, because people know they will not come through. Related to lack of follow-through is the inability to complete tasks. People who don't complete tasks are chronic starters but chronic nonfinishers. They remind me of Zeno's Paradox, in which a man wishes to traverse from point A to point B. Zeno points out that in order to get from point A to point B, one first has to go half the distance; then one has to go half the remaining distance; then one has to go half the remaining distance again; one keeps going half the distance to the completion—and never gets there. In order to get there, one needs to make a leap. So do we all: we need to leap beyond working on things to getting them done.

Failure to initiate.   For some people, the problem is not in finishing projects but in starting them. Some people seem always to be reticent to undertake anything of consequence. They don't want to decide on a job, or a mate, or a place to live. Often these are people who are afraid to commit themselves. They are afraid that if they take a big step, they will close off their options. But they are so concerned with keeping their options open that they never utilize any, and often they fall farther and farther behind. They seem always to be in a prelude to life rather than living life itself. It is understandable that people hesitate before making major commitments, but repeatedly failing to make any commitments solves nothing. Sometimes we need to consider our options carefully, consider the possibilities of a wrong decision, and then jump in. We will never give ourselves or others a chance to see our intelligence unless we initiate the projects in our lives that will give us the opportunities to manifest whatever intelligence we have.

Fear of failure.   One of the most serious obstacles to learning and performance is fear of failure. People will construct elaborate scenarios for themselves and others in order to prevent themselves from undertaking activities in which they are afraid they will fail. Carol Dweck has described two kinds of children: those who are not afraid to make mistakes, because they believe that the only way they can learn is through making them; and those who are afraid to make mistakes, because they believe that making them will show that they are stupid.[3] The latter type of child is clearly one who constantly will be afraid of failure. He will not undertake new and challenging activities because of a fear that the activities will not be accomplished successfully. Of course, adults can be the same way. Almost all of us could count many things that we would like to do that we have not done because we are afraid we will fail at them. Fear of failure makes sense when the result of a failure will be devastating—loss of life, loss of self-respect, and so on. But in most cases we learn from our mistakes, and we will never learn much unless we allow ourselves to make them.

Procrastination.   Almost everyone procrastinates sometime on something. Some degree of procrastination is probably a universal fact of life. The problem is when procrastination becomes chronic rather than acute—a person finds himself procrastinating in almost everything. There will always be students who start their papers the night before they are due; regardless of how long ago the paper was assigned, they always put things off until the last possible minute. The result is that they often receive poorer grades than they would have had they started even a few days earlier. We can pay a steep price for our procrastination—poorer-quality work, stress as we try to complete work in an unreasonably short amount of time, disappointment when we and others find that the work is not as good as it could or should have been. In one of our studies of business executives, Richard Wagner and I examined how business executives fight procrastination in themselves.[4] Less senior executives had a variety of strategies for fighting procrastination; but more senior and more successful executives did not. The reason was that they had no need for these strategies: they knew the cost of procrastination and simply did not indulge in it. Perhaps that is a large part of what made them both senior and successful.

Misattribution of blame.   I once had an employee who never made a mistake. Don't believe me—ask the employee. This individual was an expert at finding other people to blame for anything that could conceivably go wrong. Sometimes I wondered whether the externalizations of blame wouldn't start to wear thin; but if they did, the employee never gave any indications of it. Misattribution of blame can be seriously debilitating in both work and personal settings. In work settings, it is debilitating because you are likely to make the same mistakes again and again, because you never recognize them when they are made. Moreover, neither peers nor bosses are likely to have much tolerance for someone who is always looking for a scapegoat. Of course, spouses, lovers, and other intimates are just as unlikely to want always to be targets of blame. As in the work setting, moreover, you are unlikely to change if you do not acknowledge a fault when it exists. So misattribution of blame is problematical in two respects: it prevents you from correcting your mistakes, and it antagonizes others. When there is blame to be assigned, it is important to know where to assign it, even if it is to yourself.

Excessive self-pity. I know a guy who has led the worst life possible. You wouldn't know it to hear him tell of it, but it must be true, because he is always feeling sorry for himself. When people first meet him, they often feel sorry for him, too. He seems to be a walking fount of misfortunes. But after a while, his self-pity begins to wear thin. People don't want to hear about his trials and tribulations anymore. They especially don't want to hear because most of the trials and tribulations are things that people generally take in stride and accept as a normal part of living. Excessive self-pity is damaging for at least three reasons. First, it turns other people off. They reach the point where even when the self-pitier has a genuine misfortune, they no longer feel sorry for him, because they have heard the story too many times before. Second, it is unfortunate because it provides a nonconstructive use of time. There are almost always better ways in which a person can spend time than in feeling sorry for himself. Third, the time spent in self-pity could be better spent correcting, or at least attempting to correct, the problem that led to it. Self-pity is like a black hole: it absorbs without giving anything back in return.

Excessive dependency. I frequently have to write letters of recommendation for job candidates. One of the things employers are most interested in knowing about is the independence of the candidate. Especially for higher-level jobs, few employers want to be stuck with someone who constantly needs assistance: they just don't have the time to deal with such people. I myself have been in the frustrating position of having employees who seem to be bottomless pits of dependency. No matter how much I give, it is never enough. You expect people who are new on a job to have some degree of dependency, but it becomes a problem when that degree does not diminish over time. Note that I am talking here about *excessive* dependency, not dependency per se. Some degree of dependency is healthy, and fear of being dependent can create at least as many problems as overdependency. Indeed, in interpersonal relationships, two of the main sources of problems are excessive dependency and fear of dependency in the first place. Few people are interested in a serious relationship with someone who is a constant clinger—who can't be left on his own for even modest amounts of time. But people also don't want a relationship with someone who is so independent that he never seems to be in need: for most people, there is as much pleasure in meeting the needs of others as in having their own needs met.

Wallowing in personal difficulties. All of us go through hard times, and it's sometimes difficult to remember that we are not unique in this respect. (Indeed, it is almost always easy to point to someone else or some other class of people who have experienced more difficulties.) Anyone who has worked with people for any length of time quickly discovers that people differ drastically in the ways in which they react to personal difficulties. Some people become utterly incapacitated. After a death in the family, a divorce, or a serious illness, they become totally unable to function constructively for long periods of time. Other people show hardly any signs of distress. It is both acceptable and understandable to show signs of distress during and after personal problems present themselves. During a marital separation, for example, a person probably will not work at peak efficiency. But employers and peers alike tend to lose respect for people who simply seem unable to get over the hump. These people go through a difficult time and then never seem to recover. We need to remember that the world would cease to function if everyone were the same way. It is important during times of personal hardship to confront the hardship and live with it, trying to control it rather than letting it control you. But there comes a time when you must move on, and part of good intelligence is knowing when this time has come.

Distractibility and lack of concentration. Did you ever try teaching someone something and find that he's not listening? Or have you ever told someone something that means a lot to you and realized that he scarcely heard anything you said? In either case, you've probably been irritated, possibly even offended. People who are highly distractible make life hard not only for themselves but, as these examples show, for others as well. They have trouble getting their work done because they are continually distracted; they have difficulty communicating with others because although they may be good talkers, they tend not to be good listeners. They seem never to be totally focused on the task at hand.

People probably have optimal distraction levels. For example, some people find that they work more effectively if they listen to a radio, whereas other people find that listening to a radio inhibits or destroys their ability to get their work done. Similarly, some people find they can best listen to others if there is at least some level of background noise present, while others find they concentrate better when there is a background of silence. Each of us needs to learn the circumstances under which we function best, and then to use these circumstances to our maximal advantage.

Spreading yourself too thin or too thick. One of the most valuable lessons I can teach my students is a lesson regarding time allocation—how to budget their time and engagement in projects so that they spread themselves neither too thick nor too thin. I find that some of the people working with me are always biting off more than they can chew. As a result, they have trouble getting things done, and the things they get done often have a shoddy quality to them. Others spread themselves too thick: they get so engrossed in a single project that they never seem to have time for anything or anyone else. The result is that they lose many good opportunities. A persistent theme in this chapter, and indeed in this book, is balance—avoiding locking yourself into one kind of extreme or another. Spreading yourself too thick or too thin represents two of the extremes; both have a debilitating effect on performance. Moreover, they can take away from your personal life and relationships. People who undertake too many work projects often find that they don't have time seriously to pursue their interpersonal relationships. Good mental self-management requires that you know how much work you can undertake— neither too much nor too little. The same, of course, applies to personal life—knowing how many interpersonal ventures you can undertake without either overcommitting yourself or losing good opportunities when they are presented.

Inability to delay gratification. One of the biggest spoilers of both work and personal life is the inability to delay gratification. In work, it often takes the form of doing the little assignments for the little rewards but thereby neglecting the big assignments with the big rewards. People who need constant little rewards in their work often preclude the opportunity to get the big rewards because they are unwilling to undertake bigger, longer-term projects that are more likely to lead to higher payoffs in the long run. Similarly, in the personal realm, an individual may lose any hope of attaining a goal by rushing toward it too hastily. In forming a close relationship, for example, few things are a bigger turnoff than the feeling of being pursued uncontrollably. Sometimes the person may feel that the pursuit has nothing to do with herself but merely satisfies needs that exist within the pursuer. It is as though almost anyone could fulfill the pursuer's needs. It makes good sense to go a bit slowly in interpersonal relationships, delaying gratification so that the foundation of the relationship can be built slowly and with care. Of course, delay of gratification can be carried out to a ridiculous extent: some people die never knowing happiness because they were always waiting for the gratification that was just around the corner. Again, balance is essential. But the big rewards in life often come to those who wait, and good mental self-managers know when to wait—and when not to.

Inability or unwillingness to see the forest for the trees.   In interviews of managers, a theme that arises again and again is that a large part of what makes a successful manager is the ability to see the forest for the trees. People differ, of course, in their intellectual styles, some being more global and some being more local. But the individual who can never see the big picture in work-related situations is one who is likely never to make it to the higher ranks. Even at the lower ranks, it helps to know why you are doing what you are doing, and where it fits into a larger picture. In science, this ability is crucial. I believe that a major distinction between greater and lesser scientists is not in the actual experiments they do but in the size of the questions they address. Better scientists address bigger questions. In interpersonal relationships as well as in work, the ability to see the big picture is crucial. Many a relationship has foundered on the shores of inconsequential problems that take on a life of their own and whose importance is magnified beyond any reasonable level. People who cannot distinguish between the little problems that are routine in virtually all relationships and the big problems that may have serious consequences are likely to be unhappy in any relationship into which they enter. Regardless of domain, then, it pays to be able to separate the big from the little, the consequential from the inconsequential—to see the forest for the trees.

Lack of balance between crucial, analytic thinking and creative, synthetic thinking.   Almost any problem we undertake to solve will require both analytic and synthetic processes for solution. Analytic processes refer to the critical thinking we do in solving a problem. When we divide a problem into its parts and relate the parts, critique possible solutions, evaluate options, and so on, we are thinking analytically. Many problems require a preponderance of analytic thinking. But there are some problems that cannot be solved by analytic thinking alone; they require synthetic, creative thinking as well. This kind of thinking applies especially when devising possible solutions and considering options that may not be obvious. An important skill in problem solving is knowing when to use analytic processes and when to use synthetic ones. There may be times when creativity does not pay off, as in the solution of trivial problems, or when it is actually punished, as in solving problems on most standardized tests. But there are other times when almost all the payoffs are associated with creativity. The scientists, businessmen, writers, artists, and others who really make a difference to the world are likely to be people who can balance synthetic and analytic thinking. They are not only competent at both; they know when to use which. Once again, balance is important to effective mental self-management.

Too little or too much self-confidence. Many people tend to have difficulty in adjusting their self-confidence to just the right level: they often seem to be either lacking in self-confidence or too self-confident. Both interfere with their work. People who lack self-confidence never believe they have done a good enough job; they are always finding fault with themselves. As a result, they may waste time trying to improve on a job that is already quite satisfactory or even superior. And even when they do a superior job, they still berate themselves. They never feel good about themselves, even when there is reason to feel good. Indeed, they often seem uncomfortable with the notion that they might actually do something well. People with too much self-confidence can be equally troublesome. They often overvalue what they do and are defensive when criticized. They may not listen to constructive suggestions or think about ways in which they could improve their performance. Moreover, they often communicate their over-self-confidence to others, and turn others off in the process. Thus, it is important to be realistic in assessing yourself and to recognize when you should and should not have confidence in yourself and your work. The same rule applies to the personal realm. People are most attracted to other people who are realistic in their self-confidence, rather than having too little or too much.

All of us have tendencies to let at least some of these obstacles block our way; the important thing is that we recognize when these blocks occur and then do something about them. The good mental self-manager is not the person who never encounters obstacles or never makes mistakes but, rather, the one who recognizes her mistakes and the obstacles along the way and does something to correct them. The correction process is a large part of what mental self-management is all about. A good mental self-manager knows how to achieve a healthy balance among adaptation to, selection of, and shaping of environments. Surmounting the obstacles described in this chapter will take you a long way in the art of mental self-management. The first step to surmounting an obstacle is to recognize that it is, indeed, a problem for you (the metacomponent of problem recognition). The second step is to set up a strategy for overcoming the obstacle (another metacomponent). For example, if you lack perseverance, work to your limit on a problem, and then force yourself to work yet more—until what at first seemed forced becomes natural for you. If you tend to perseverate—working too long on problems, past the point of diminishing returns—then set an outer time or effort limit for your work on some problems, and force yourself to stop once you have reached the limit. Again, what at first seems forced may become natural after a while, once you have reregulated the way you put effort into tasks. Finally, monitor your strategy (another metacomponent) to make sure it is working. If it is not, try another strategy. None of the obstacles presented in this chapter are insurmountable, but there is no one solution to surmounting these obstacles that works for everyone. Rather, it is a task for your intelligence to devise and implement a strategy that works for you. And this book may have helped you see that you *can* indeed set up a strategy that works for you.

Postscript

Now you have learned something about what intelligence is, how it can be tested, and how we can improve upon the intelligence we already have. But the book should not stop here. There are plenty of "smart" people walking around, making a mess of their own lives and the lives of others. The acid test is not how much intelligence you have residing comfortably in your brain but how you go about using that intelligence to make a better world for yourself and others. So take a major problem you face or a decision you need to make in your life and apply the techniques of this book to it. It's not of much use to think of intelligence as something you *have*. Think of it as something you *use*, and now go ahead and use it, making the most of your many abilities to enjoy a richer, fuller life.

Intelligence is much more than IQ. Traditional tests of intelligence, scholastic aptitude, and related constructs tell us relatively little about intelligence. And they tell us even less about a person's creativity, wisdom, and intellectual style. Even if we knew all about those things as well, we would still need to know about what may be the most important attribute of all: the ability to capitalize on strengths and to remediate or compensate for weaknesses. Practically intelligent people may excel at only one or two things, but they make the most of these excellences. And you can, too!

Appendix

Chapter 2

Answers to Verbal Analogies (see page 24)

1. c   3. d   5. d
2. c   4. a

Answers to Reading Comprehension Questions (see pages 28–30)

1. a   3. a   5. b   7. b
2. d   4. b   6. d   8. b

Answers to Vocabulary Questions (see page 31)

1. b   2. a

Answers to Learning-from-Context Problem (see page 33)

pococurante—someone showing indifference
phalacrosis—baldness   *eructation*—belch
podobromhidrosis—smelly feet

Chapter 5

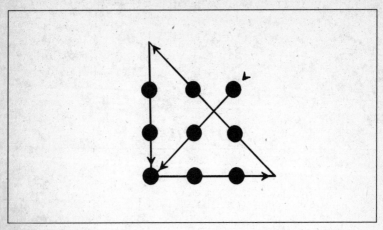

Figure 15. Solution to the nine-dot problem (see page 89).

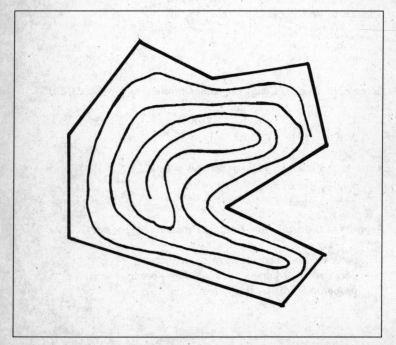

Figure 16. Solution to the searching-the-field problem (see page 95).

Solution to the Letter-Permutations Problem (see page 96)

7.	B A C D	16.	C B D A
8.	B A D C	17.	C D A B
9.	B C A D	18.	C D B A
10.	B C D A	19.	D A B C
11.	B D A C	20.	D A C B
12.	B D C A	21.	D B A C
13.	C A B D	22.	D B C A
14.	C A D B	23.	D C A B
15.	C B A D	24.	D C B A

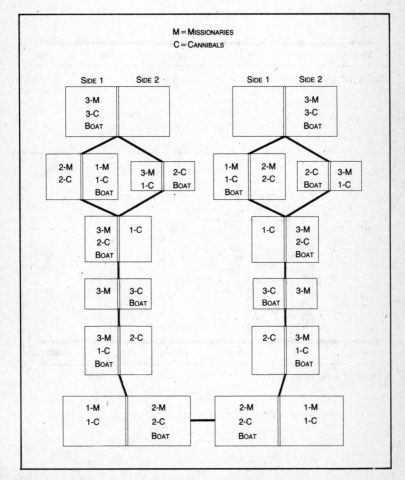

Figure 17. Solution to the missionaries-and-cannibals problem (see page 98).

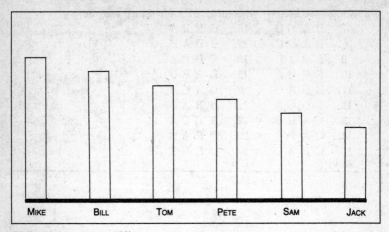

Figure 18 (see page 103).

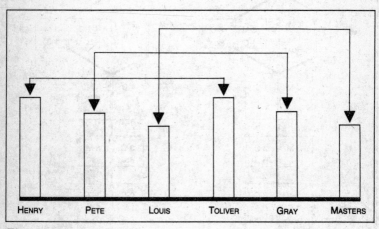

Figure 19 (see page 103).

	SAM	LOUISE	DAVE
JOAN	O	O	
PATTY			O
SANDY			

Figure 20 (see page 103). In the above figure, O's appear in the cells with the correct mother-child pairings. Joan is Louise's mother.

	LAWYER	HOUSEWIFE	PHYSICIST
GINA		X	X
BARBARA	X		X
ELAINE	X	X	

Figure 21 (see page 103).

Chapter 6

Answer Key for Inference Pairs (see page 119)

RELATIONSHIP	CLASSIFICATION
1. A sleeve is a part of a shirt.	part-whole
2. "Blue" and "threw" rhyme.	nonsemantic
3. A pencil's function is to write.	predication

4. Pliers and a wrench are both kinds of tools.	coordination
5. The natural numbers and the counting numbers are mathematically equivalent.	equality
6. "Gigantic" and "enormous" are synonymous.	similarity
7. "Reward" is "drawer" spelled backward.	nonsemantic
8. "Smooth" and "rough" are antonyms.	contrast
9. An orchard is composed of trees.	whole-part
10. All whole numbers that are not prime are nonprime.	negation
11. "Worse" is the comparative form, and "worst" the superlative form, of "bad."	word relationship
12. A chair is a kind of furniture.	subordination
13. A French horn is a musical instrument.	completion
14. A bus is a kind of vehicle.	superordination
15. A magician performs tricks.	predication

Answers to Fallacy Problems (see pages 127–30)

Here are the answers to the twenty vignettes presenting examples of everyday reasoning. Keep in mind that there are other possible classifications for the fallacies. The important thing is for you to become aware of the kinds of fallacies one can commit, and of how to stop them in your own reasoning and in the reasoning of others.

1. Invalid. Hasty generalization.
2. Valid.
3. Invalid. Irrelevant conclusion.
4. Valid.
5. Invalid. Composition.
6. Invalid. False cause.
7. Invalid. Personalization.
8. Invalid. Magnification/minimization.

9. Invalid.   Hasty generalization.
10. Valid.
11. Invalid.   Hasty generalization.
12. Invalid.   "Should" statement.
13. Invalid.   Irrelevant conclusion.
14. Valid.
15. Invalid.   Labeling.
16. Invalid.   Skill, not chance.
17. Invalid.   Invalid disjunction.
18. Invalid.   Personalization.
19. Invalid.   Division.
20. Invalid.   Emotional reasoning.

Answers to Verbal Mapping Problems (see pages 131–32)

1. An engagement indicates a probable marriage, whereas a wedding indicates a certain marriage. Thus, the two first-order relations pertain to the likelihood of marriage.

2. A French poodle and a German shepherd are both kinds of dogs. Thus, both first-order relations specify names of dogs.

3. Noon occurs at twelve o'clock, as does midnight. Thus, both first-order relations specify times of day that occur at twelve o'clock.

4. May is the month with the shortest name. September is the month with the longest name. Thus, each first-order relation specifies the length of name of a month.

5. Coffee is drunk from a mug, and wine is drunk from a goblet. Thus, the two first-order relations specify the container from which the first item is drunk.

6. "Mom" and "Dad" are both words that are palindromes (that is, they read the same both forward and backward). Similarly, 383 and 121 are both numerical palindromes. Thus, each first-order relation specifies a palindrome.

7. A seagull is part of a flock, just as a wolf is part of a pack. Thus, each first-order relation is a part-whole relation.

8. Turquoise is a shade of blue, whereas scarlet is a shade of red. Thus, each first-order relation specifies the shade one color is of another.

9. "Warts" is "straw" spelled backward. Similarly, "lived" is "devil" spelled backward. Thus, in each pair, the second word is the first word spelled backward.

10. Socks are sold in pairs. Beer is sold in six-packs. Thus, in each pair, the second element is the unit in which the first element is sold.

11. Among undergraduates, freshmen are the youngest class and seniors are the oldest class. Thus, each first-order relation relates a college class to its age.

12. Cabbage is processed into cole slaw, whereas potatoes are processed into french fries. Thus, each first-order relation relates a raw vegetable to its processed product.

13. Asia is a continent just as China is a country. Thus, each first-order relation is one of set membership (subordination).

14. "Strip" sounds the same as "trip" except for its initial "s" sound. "Slime" sounds the same as "lime" except for its initial "s." Thus, each first-order relation involves placing an "s" sound before the first term of the pair.

15. One throws a discus, whereas one wears a glove. Thus, each first-order relation specifies a predication of the second term upon the first.

Answers to Verbal Analogies (see page 135)

1. (c) A statue is frequently made of stone; a shoe is frequently made of leather.

2. (c) A father is a parent; a son is a child.

3. (b) ¼ is equal to 175%; ³⁄₂₅ is equal to 12%.

4. (c) Rodin's best-known work of art is the sculpture *The Thinker*; da Vinci's best-known work of art is the painting *Mona Lisa*.

5. (b) A cabinet is the creation of a carpenter; a novel is the creation of an author.

6. (d) A gale is a very strong breeze; a cloudburst is a very strong shower.

7. (a) Yellow is the color associated with cowardice; green is the color associated with envy.

8. (d) One who lacks the sense of touch is numb; one who lacks the sense of sight is blind.

9. (c) When eggs are stirred, they are beaten; when cream is stirred, it is whipped.

10. (c) Steam is the gaseous substance that rises from water; smoke is the gaseous substance that rises from fire.

11. (d) A compass is used to indicate direction; a watch is used to indicate time.

12. (a) A chairman presides at a meeting; a judge presides at a trial.
13. (d) "Repel" is "leper" spelled backward; "remit" is "timer" spelled backward.
14. (a) One thing made from flour is bread; one thing made from wool is a sweater.
15. (d) Silence is the absence of sound; stillness is the absence of motion.

Answer Key for Figural Analogies (see figure 8, pages 136–38)

1. d	6. a	11. a
2. b	7. b	12. c
3. b	8. d	13. b
4. d	9. b	14. a
5. c	10. c	15. c

Answer Key for Verbal Series-Completion Problems (see pages 139–40)

	ANSWER	CORRECT RESPONSE
1.	c	ADULT
2.	d	HIP
3.	a	UNLIKELY
4.	c	CUE
5.	d	TACK
6.	a	EUROPE
7.	a	BLIZZARD
8.	b	FOOD
9.	b	DAUGHTER
10.	d	22
11.	c	HUT
12.	a	NINE O'CLOCK
13.	d	CURTAIN CALL
14.	b	MURDER
15.	c	WILLOW

Answer Key for Figural Series-Completion Problems (see figure 9, pages 141–45)

1. c	6. d	11. b
2. d	7. a	12. a
3. b	8. c	13. b
4. a	9. d	14. d
5. b	10. a	15. c

Answer Key for Verbal Classification Problems (see pages 147–48)

1. (b) A MAGAZINE and a LETTER, like a BOOK, are written forms of communication.
2. (a) SCARLET and CRIMSON, like BURGUNDY, are shades of red.
3. (d) ROPE and STRING, like THREAD, are used to fasten things together.
4. (b) The ESOPHAGUS and the INTESTINES, like the STOMACH, are organs of the digestive system.
5. (c) A BRACELET and a NECKLACE, like a RING, are types of jewelry.
6. (d) TEETH and NAILS, like HAIR, are non-sensing parts of the body.
7. (a) A BABOON and a GORILLA, like a CHIMPANZEE, are monkeys.
8. (c) An ACE and a SEVEN, like a JACK, are playing cards.
9. (b) A STENCIL and a RULER, like a COMPASS, help people draw regular shapes.
10. (a) FRENCH TOAST and a WAFFLE, like a PANCAKE, are fried and eaten for breakfast.
11. (d) KETCHUP and MUSTARD, like RELISH, are condiments.
12. (c) SPAIN and ALGERIA, like TURKEY, are Mediterranean countries.
13. (a) SOIL, DIRT and EARTH are synonyms.
14. (c) CHALLENGING, HARD, and DIFFICULT are synonyms.
15. (d) A PROFESSOR and a LAWYER, like a DOCTOR, have professional positions.

Answer Key for Figural Classification Problems (see figure 11, pages 149–53)

1. b	6. c	11. b
2. c	7. d	12. d
3. a	8. d	13. c
4. b	9. a	14. a
5. d	10. b	15. c

Answers to Figural Matrix Problems (see figure 12, pages 155–59)

1. e	6. f
2. d	7. b
3. b	8. a
4. a	9. e
5. c	10. d

Answer Key for Legal Reasoning Problems (see pages 161–65)

	PRINCIPLES	FACTS	OUTCOMES
Case 1	1	4	2
Case 2	2	1	2
Case 3	1	1	1
Case 4	2	3	2
Case 5	2	1	2

Answer Key for Clinical Reasoning Problems (see pages 166–69)

	PRINCIPLES	FACTS	OUTCOMES
Subject 1	2	3	2
Subject 2	1	3	2
Subject 3	2	1	2
Subject 4	1	2	2
Subject 5	2	4	1

Chapter 7

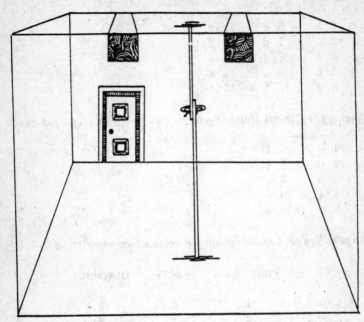

Figure 22. Solution to the hat-rack problem (see page 172).

Solutions to Selective-Encoding Problems (see pages 184–85)

1. Yes. The fourth of July is not marked as Independence Day, however.

2. The man performed the marriage ceremonies. The critical word in this problem is "married." The man married the various women, but he did not himself become married to them.

3. The man was buying house numbers. There are two numbers, one and six, to be bought, so the total cost is two dollars.

4. None. Totally deaf people cannot use the phone.

5. Two. The only males in the family are the father and his one son, who is the brother of each of his sisters.

6. Eighty minutes and one hour and twenty minutes are the same amount of time.

7. $75. Because the store manager still was not buying fifty or more toasters, she received no discount.

8. $6. The only relevant information is that the watch was marked $12.
9. Each bike is at the same distance from Gull Beach when they meet, as the bikes are immediately next to each other.
10. Roosters don't lay eggs.

Solutions to Information-Evaluation Problems (see pages 186–87)

1.	a. I	3.	a. R
	b. R		b. I
	c. R		c. R
	d. R		d. I
	e. R		

2.	a. I	4.	a. I
	b. I		b. R
	c. I		c. I
	d. R		d. I
	e. R		
	f. R		

Solutions to Mystery Problems (see pages 187–91)

1. Ms. Landry could not have known her uncle had a bullet through his left temple unless she had moved the body. Mr. Stock fell on his left side and Ramirez noticed the scar near Stock's right ear. Furthermore, the gun was found in his right hand—making it very difficult for him to have shot himself through the left temple.

2. The son's initial remark reveals that he knows something about the circumstances of his mother's death. How else does he know that the lights were off in his parents' bedroom at the time when his mother was writing the note? (The lights are on when he arrives.)

3. It is apparent that Springer is lying: since Springer has a soft voice, it is doubtful that Wilson could have heard him shouting against the wind, if they were so far apart that Springer could barely hear Wilson's louder reply, which was with the wind. The blow to the back of the head was undoubtedly caused by Springer, before Wilson fell.

4. If Mrs. Ewing had been dead for many hours, someone else must have turned off the radio that the cleaning woman heard at eight but not at eleven thirty.

Solutions to Selective-Combination Problems (see pages 193–94)

1. Three. Aside from the roses, there must be one tulip and one daisy. Aside from the tulips, there must be one rose and one daisy. Aside from the daisies, there must be one rose and one tulip. So, if there is one of each flower, the total number of flowers is three.

2. Suppose we label the slices A, B, and C. In the first round of frying, which takes three minutes, Janine can fry side 1 of slice A and side 1 of slice B. In a second round of frying, which also takes three minutes, Janine can fry side 2 of slice A and side 1 of slice C, temporarily taking slice B off the pan. In a third round of frying, which again takes three minutes, Janine can complete the job by putting slice B back on the pan and frying side 2 of that slice, and also frying side 2 of slice C. In this more efficient way, there are always two slices frying at a time, so that the job can be completed in nine minutes rather than in twelve.

3. Dale is assuming, in his calculations, that the various partitions of his time are independent and therefore additive. His additive logic would work only if none of his categories overlapped. But weekend time includes time spent eating, sleeping, doing homework, and visiting parents. As a result, the hours cannot simply be added up.

4. The correct answer is to take a checker from the box labeled "red and black checkers." Label the box with the correct label (i.e., if you pull out a red checker, label the box "red checkers," and if you pull out a black one, label the box "black checkers"). Then reverse the two labels that are left. A common mistake people make in this problem is to try taking the one checker from the box labeled "red checkers" or from the box labeled "black checkers." This procedure will not necessarily tell you what is in any of the boxes. For example, if you happen to get a red checker from the box marked "black checkers," you would not know whether the box contained only red checkers or both red and black checkers. However, because you know that every box is mislabeled, you know that both red and black checkers cannot be in the box labeled "red and black checkers." Whatever you draw from this box is what the box contains. For example, if you get a red checker, you will know that the box contains red checkers. Because all the boxes are initially mislabeled, just switch the two remaining labels and the problem is solved.

5. Your tour guide is clearly a liar. If the prime minister were a truth teller, he would have said that he was a truth teller. If he were a liar, he also would have said that he was a truth teller. Since

the tour guide has said that the prime minister admitted to being a liar, the tour guide must be a liar.

6. The last lecture will take place on October 22. The second lecture is a week after the first, the third lecture is a week after that, and the fourth lecture is a week after that. So the fourth lecture is three weeks after the first lecture.

7. In 1960. Since the population doubles every twenty years, the population was half as great twenty years before. The best way to solve this problem is to work backward from 1980 rather than forward from 1860.

8. $10. This answer meets all the conditions of the problem. If the case is worth $10, the camera is worth $90. The camera is thus worth $80 more than the case. (A common mistake people make in this problem is to assume that the camera costs $80. It does not; it costs $80 *more* than the case. To find out how much the case costs, first subtract $80 from $100. Then split the $20 in half. This gives you $10, the cost of the case.)

9. Fill the seven-cup container with flour. Pour as much of the contents as you can into the two-cup container. Now spill out the contents that you just poured into the two-cup container. You now have five cups in the seven-cup container. Again pour the contents of the seven-cup container into the two-cup container. You now have three cups of flour left in the seven-cup container.

10. $10. Sarah is now poorer by $10, so she has $50. Joe is richer by $10, so he also has $50.

Solutions to Novel Analogies (see pages 195–96)

1. SODA	6. ASIAN	11. PENDULUM
2. STRINGS	7. DESPAIR	12. PAWS
3. EYE	8. CANOPY	13. TAIL
4. WAVE	9. KEYBOARD	14. CAGE
5. AUDIBLE	10. CALF	15. CHAUFFEUR

Answers to Scientific-Insight Problems (see pages 196–98)

1. Fish feed during the day, and since the *D. galeata* remain near the surface during the day, they are much more visible and convenient prey than the *D. hyalina*, which depart to the depths during the same time.

2. Gravity pulls the bullets down; thus, unless a pilot dives, the bullets will not hit the plane.

3. Napoleon's death was caused by arsenic poisoning from the arsenic that was present in the wallpaper. Due to the dampness of the house, the wallpaper became wet and moldy. The mold's exudation containing arsenic was mixed with the air that Napoleon was breathing constantly.

4. Carotene, which is yellow and is present in carrots, oranges, and eggs, and lycopene, a red dye present in tomatoes, combined in the patient's blood to produce the orange color.

5. No, it would not cool off a room to open a refrigerator. Heat from the room would move inside it, only to be pumped back into the room.

Chapter 8

Solutions to Tacit-Knowledge Questionnaires (see pages 213–15)

Numerical ratings are not given in these solutions. Rather, answers are in the form of plus and minus signs. A plus indicates a higher rating (for example, a score of 4 or above) by individuals more advanced in the field relative to individuals less advanced in the field. A minus sign indicates a relatively lower numerical rating by individuals more advanced in the field. Keep in mind, therefore, that the pluses and minuses are *relative*. There are no correct answers per se, only trends distinguishing more experienced individuals from those who are less experienced. As you will see, in some cases, the "solutions" are counterintuitive.*

1.	a. −	3.	a. −	5.	a. −
	b. −		b. −		b. −
	c. −		c. −		c. −
	d. +		d. +		d. −
	e. −		e. −		e. −
2.	a. +	4.	a. +		
	b. −		b. +		
	c. +		c. +		
	d. −		d. −		
	e. +		e. −		

* Alternative answers can be acceptable if a compelling justification is provided.

Notes

Chapter 1. Stalking an Elusive Quarry: The Search for Intelligence

1. Wason, P. C., & Johnson-Laird P. N. (1972). *Psychology of reasoning: Structure and content.* London: B. T. Batsford.
2. Gelman, R., & Baillargeon, R. (1983). A review of some Piagetian concepts. In P. H. Mussen (series ed.) & J. Flavell & E. Markman (vol. eds.), *Handbook of child psychology: Vol. 3 Cognitive development* (4th ed.). New York: Wiley.
3. Piaget, J. (1972). *The psychology of intelligence.* Totowa, NJ: Littlefield, Adams.
4. Gardner, H. (1983). *Frames of mind: The theory of multiple intelligences.* New York: Basic Books.
5. Spearman, C. (1904). General intelligence, objectively determined and measured. *American Journal of Psychology, 15,* 201–93.
   Spearman, C. (1927). *The abilities of man.* New York: Macmillan.
6. Detterman, D. K., & Sternberg, R. J. (eds.) (1982). *How and how much can intelligence be increased?* Norwood, NJ: Ablex.
7. Bransford, J., & Stein, B. (1984). *The IDEAL problem solver.* New York: W. H. Freeman.
   Feuerstein, R. (1980). *Instrumental enrichment: An intervention program for cognitive modifiability.* Baltimore, MD: University Park Press.
   Sternberg, R. J. (1986). *Intelligence applied: Understanding and increasing your intellectual skills.* San Diego, CA: Harcourt, Brace, Jovanovich.
8. Davidson, J. E., & Sternberg, R. J. (1984). The role of insight in intellectual giftedness. *Gifted Child Quarterly, 28,* 58–64.

9. Sternberg, R. J. (1987). Most vocabulary is learned from context. In M. McKeown & M. Curtis (eds.), *The nature of vocabulary acquisition.* Hillsdale, NJ: Erlbaum.

10. Heath, S. B. (1983). *Ways with words.* New York: Cambridge University Press.

11. Scribner, S. (1984). Studying working intelligence. In B. Rogoff & J. Lave (eds.), *Everyday cognition.* Cambridge, MA: Harvard University Press.

12. Ceci, S. J., & Liker, J. (1986). Academic and nonacademic intelligence: An experimental separation. In R. J. Sternberg & R. K. Wagner (eds.), *Practical intelligence: Nature and origins of competence in the everyday world.* New York: Cambridge University Press.

13. Edgerton, R. (1967). *The cloak of competence.* Berkeley, CA: University of California Press.

14. Campione, J. C., Brown, A. L., & Ferrara, R. A. (1982). Mental retardation and intelligence. In R. J. Sternberg (ed.), *Handbook of human intelligence.* New York: Cambridge University Press.

15. Feldman, R. D. (1982). *Whatever happened to the quiz kids?* Chicago: Review Press.

Chapter 2. IQ Tests: Measuring IQ, Not Intelligence

1. Cole, M., Gay, J., Glick, J., & Sharp, D. W. (1971). *The cultural context of learning and thinking.* New York: Basic Books.

2. Sternberg, R. J., Conway, B. E., Ketron, J. L., & Bernstein, M. (1981). People's conceptions of intelligence. *Journal of Personality and Social Psychology, 41,* 37–55.

3. Baron, J. (1982) Personality and intelligence. In R. J. Sternberg (ed.), *Handbook of human intelligence.* New York: Cambridge University Press.
Kagan, J. (1966). Reflection-impulsivity of conceptual tempo. *Journal of Abnormal Psychology, 71,* 17–24.

4. Thurstone, L. L. (1924). *The nature of intelligence.* New York: Harcourt, Brace.

5. Stenhouse, D. (1973). *The evolution of intelligence: A general theory of some of its implications.* New York: Harper & Row.

6. Sternberg, R. J. (1977). *Intelligence, information processing, and analogical reasoning: The componential analysis of human abilities.* Hillsdale, NJ: Erlbaum.

7. Sternberg, R. J., & Rifkin, B. (1979). The development of analogical reasoning processes. *Journal of Experimental Child Psychology, 27,* 195–232.

8. Wagner, R. K., & Sternberg, R. J. (1987). Executive control in reading comprehension. In B. Britton & S. M. Glynn (eds.), *Executive control processes in reading.* Hillsdale, NJ: Erlbaum.

9. Sternberg, R. J., & Powell, J. S. (1983). Comprehending verbal comprehension. *American Psychologist, 38,* 878–93.

10. Sternberg, R. J., & Weil, E. M. (1980). An aptitude-strategy interaction in linear syllogistic reasoning. *Journal of Educational Psychology, 72,* 226–34.

Chapter 3. Human Intelligence:
The Model Is the Message

1. Boring, E. G. (1950). *A history of experimental psychology* (2nd ed.). New York: Appleton-Century-Crofts.

2. Spearman, C. (1927). *The abilities of man.* New York: Macmillan.

3. Thurstone, L. L. (1938). *Primary mental abilities.* Chicago: University of Chicago Press.

4. Guilford, J. P. (1967). *The nature of human intelligence.* New York: McGraw-Hill.

5. Guilford, J. P. (1982). Cognitive psychology's ambiguities: Some suggested remedies. *Psychological Review, 89,* 48–59.

6. Eysenck, H. J. (1967). Intelligence assessment: A theoretical and experimental approach. *British Journal of Educational Psychology, 37,* 81–98.

7. Horn, J. L., & Knapp, J. R. (1973). On the subjective character of the empirical base of Guilford's structure-of-intellect model. *Psychological Bulletin, 80,* 33–43.

8. Cattell, R. B. (1971). *Abilities: Their structure, growth, and action.* Boston: Houghton Mifflin.

9. Vernon, P. E. (1971). *The structure of human abilities.* London: Methuen.

10. Sternberg, R. J. (1977). *Intelligence, information processing, and analogical reasoning: The componential analysis of human abilities.* Hillsdale, NJ: Erlbaum.

11. McNemar, Q. (1964). Lost: Our intelligence? Why? *American Psychologist, 19,* 871–82.

12. Gardner, H. (1983). *Frames of mind: The theory of multiple intelligences.* New York: Basic Books.

13. Jensen, A. R. (1979). *g:* Outmoded theory or unconquered frontier? *Creative Science and Technology, 2,* 16–29.

14. Hunt, E. B. (1978). Mechanics of verbal ability. *Psychological Review, 85,* 109–30.

15. Posner, M. I., & Mitchell, R. F. (1967). Chronometric analysis of classification. *Psychological Review, 74,* 392–409.

16. Hunt, E. B., & Lansman, M. (1982). Individual differences in attention. In R. J. Sternberg (ed.), *Advances in the psychology of human intelligence* (vol. 1). Hillsdale, NJ: Erlbaum.

17. Sternberg, R. J., & Gardner, M. K. (1983). Unities in inductive reasoning. *Journal of Experimental Psychology: General, 112*, 80–116.

18. Simon, H. A. (1976). Identifying basic abilities underlying intelligent performance of complex tasks. In L. B. Resnick (ed.), *The nature of intelligence*. Hillsdale, NJ: Erlbaum.

19. Newell, A., & Simon, H. A. (1972). *Human problem solving*. Englewood Cliffs, NJ: Prentice-Hall.

20. Lesgold, A. M. (1984). Acquiring expertise. In J. R. Anderson & S. M. Kosslyn (eds.), *Tutorials in learning and memory: Essays in honor of Gordon Bower*. New York: Freeman.

Chi, M. T. H., Glaser, R., & Rees, E. (1982). Expertise in problem solving. In R. J. Sternberg (ed.), *Advances in the psychology of human intelligence* (vol. 1). Hillsdale, NJ: Erlbaum.

Larkin, J. H., McDermott, J., Simon, D. P., & Simon, H. A. (1980). Models of competence in solving physics problems. *Cognitive Science, 4*, 317–45.

21. See notes 12 and 17 above; also, Sternberg, R. J. (1985). *Beyond IQ: A triarchic theory of human intelligence*. New York: Cambridge University Press.

22. Neisser, U. (1979). The concept of intelligence. In R. J. Sternberg & D. K. Detterman (eds.), *Human intelligence: Perspectives on its theory and measurement*. Norwood, NJ: Ablex.

23. Sternberg, R. J., Conway, B. E., Ketron, J. L., & Bernstein, M. (1981). People's conceptions of intelligence. *Journal of Personality and Social Psychology, 41*, 37–55.

24. Berry, J. W. (1984). Towards a universal psychology of cognitive competence. In P. S. Fry (ed.), *Changing conceptions of intelligence and intellectual functioning*. Amsterdam: North-Holland.

25. Berry, J. W. (1974). Radical cultural relativism and the concept of intelligence. In J. W. Berry & P. R. Dasen (eds.), *Culture and cognition: Readings in cross-cultural psychology*. London: Methuen.

26. Laboratory of Comparative Human Cognition. (1982). Culture and intelligence. In R. J. Sternberg (ed.), *Handbook of human intelligence*. New York: Cambridge University Press.

27. Boas, F. (1911). *The mind of primitive man*. New York: Macmillan.

28. Charlesworth, W. R. A. (1979). An ethological approach to studying intelligence. *Human Development, 22*, 212–16.

29. Keating, D. (1984). The emperor's new clothes: The "new look" in intelligence research. In R. J. Sternberg (ed.), *Advances in the psychology of human intelligence* (vol. 2). Hillsdale, NJ: Erlbaum.

30. Jenkins, J. J. (1979). Four points to remember: A tetrahedral model of memory experiments. In L. S. Cermak & F. I. M. Craik (eds.), *Levels of processing in human memory*. Hillsdale, NJ: Erlbaum.

31. Baltes, P. B., Dittman-Kohli, F., & Dixon, R. A. (1984). New perspectives on the development of intelligence in adulthood: Toward a dual-

process conception and a model of selective optimization with compensation. In P. B. Baltes & O. G. Brim, Jr. (eds.), *Life-span development and behavior* (vol. 6). New York: Academic Press.

32. Piaget, J. (1972). *The psychology of intelligence.* Totowa, NJ: Littlefield, Adams.

33. Vygotsky, L. S. (1978). *Mind in society: The development of higher psychological processes.* Cambridge, MA: Harvard University Press.

34. Gelman, R., & Baillargeon, R. (1983). A review of some Piagetian concepts. In, P. H. Mussen (series ed.) & J. Flavell & E. Markman (vol. eds.), *Handbook of child psychology, vol. 3: Cognitive development* (4th ed.). New York: Wiley.

35. Brainerd, C. J. (1978). The stage question in cognitive-developmental theory. *Behavioral and Brain Sciences, 1,* 173–82.

Chapter 4. Understanding Mental Self-management: The Triarchic Theory of Human Intelligence

1. Jensen, A. R. (1982). The chronometry of intelligence. In R. J. Sternberg (ed.), *Advances in the psychology of human intelligence* (vol. 1). Hillsdale, NJ: Erlbaum.

2. Gardner, H. (1983). *Frames of mind: The theory of multiple intelligences.* New York: Basic Books.

3. Sternberg, R. J. (1981). Intelligence and nonentrenchment. *Journal of Educational Psychology, 73,* 1–16.

4. Sternberg, R. J. (1980a). Factor theories of intelligence are all right almost. *Educational Researcher, 9,* 6–13, 18.

5. Brown, A. L. (1974). The role of strategic behavior in retardate memory. In N. R. Ellis (ed.), *International review of research in mental retardation* (vol. 4). New York: Academic Press.
Butterfield, E. C., & Belmont, J. M. (1977). Assessing and improving executive cognitive functions of mentally retarded people. In I. Bialer & M. Sternlicht (eds.), *Psychological issues in mental retardation.* New York: Psychological Dimensions.

6. Feuerstein, R. (1980). *Instrumental enrichment: an intervention program for cognitive modifiability.* Baltimore, MD: University Park Press.
Lipman, M., Sharp, A. M., & Oscanyan, F. S. (1980). *Philosophy in the classroom* (2nd ed.). Philadelphia: Temple University Press.

7. Sternberg, R. J. (1986). *Intelligence applied: Understanding and increasing your intellectual skills.* San Diego, CA: Harcourt, Brace, Jovanovich.

8. MacLeod, C. M., Hunt, E. B., & Mathews, N. N. (1978). Individual differences in the verification of sentence-picture relationships. *Journal of Verbal Learning and Verbal Behavior, 17,* 493–507.

Paivio, A. (1971). *Imagery and verbal processes.* New York: Holt, Rinehart, and Winston.

Sternberg, R. J. (1980b). Representation and process in linear syllogistic reasoning. *Journal of Experimental Psychology: General, 109,* 119–59.

Chapter 5. Metacomponents: The "White Collar" Processes of Human Intelligence

1. Bransford, J., & Stein, B. (1984). *The IDEAL problem solver.* New York: W. H. Freeman.
   Brown, A. L. (1978). Knowing when, where, and how to remember: A problem of metacognition. In R. Glaser (ed.). *Advances in instructional psychology* (vol. 1). Hillsdale, NJ: Erlbaum.
2. Sternberg, R. J., & Rifkin, B. (1979). The development of analogical reasoning processes. *Journal of Experimental Child Psychology, 27,* 195–232.
3. Bryant, P. E., & Trabasso, T. (1971). Transitive inferences and memory in young children. *Nature, 232,* 456–58.
4. Gelman, R., & Baillargeon, R. (1983). A review of some Piagetian concepts. In P. H. Mussen (series ed.) & J. Flavell & E. Markman (vol. eds.), *Handbook of child psychology: Vol. 3 Cognitive development* (4th ed.) New York: Wiley.
5. Boring, E. G. (1923). Intelligence as the tests test it. *New Republic, 6,* June, 35–37.
   Jensen, A. R. (1969). How much can we boost IQ and scholastic achievement? *Harvard Educational Review, 39,* 1–123.
6. Bloom, B. S., & Broder, L. J. (1950). *Problem-solving processes of college students.* Chicago: University of Chicago Press.
7. Simon, H. A. (1957). *Administrative behavior* (2nd ed.). Totowa, NJ: Littlefield, Adams.
8. Hovland, C. I., & Janis, I. L. (eds.) (1959). *Personality and Persuasibility.* New Haven: Yale University Press.
9. Linville, P. (1987). Self-complexity as a cognitive buffer against stress-related illness and depression. *Journal of Personality and Social Psychology, 52,* 663–76.
10. Chase, W. G., & Simon, H. A. (1973). Perception in chess. *Cognitive Psychology, 4,* 55–81
    Lesgold, A. M. (1984). Acquiring expertise. In J. R. Anderson & S. M. Kosslyn (eds.) *Tutorials in learning and memory: Essays in honor of Gordon Bower.* New York: Freeman.
11. Chi, M. T. H. (1978). Knowledge structures and memory development. In R. S. Siegler (ed.), *Children's thinking: What develops?* Hillsdale, NJ: Erlbaum.
12. MacLeod, C. M., Hunt, E. B., & Mathews, N. N. (1978). Individual

differences in the verification of sentence-picture relationships. *Journal of Verbal Learning and Verbal Behavior, 17*, 493–507.

13. Sternberg, R. J., & Weil, E. M. (1980). An aptitude-strategy interaction in linear syllogistic reasoning. *Journal of Educational Psychology, 72*, 226–34.

14. Sternberg, R. J. (1981). Intelligence and nonentrenchment. *Journal of Educational Psychology, 73*, 1–16.

15. Hunt, E. B., & Lansman, M. (1982). Individual differences in attention. In R. J. Sternberg (ed.), *Advances in the psychology of human intelligence* (vol. 1). Hillsdale, NJ: Erlbaum. 1982.

16. Goldin, S. E., & Hayes-Roth, B. (1980, June). Individual differences in planning processes. Rand Technical Report No. N-1488-ONR.

17. Markman, E. M. (1981). Comprehension monitoring. In W. P. Dickson (ed.), *Children's oral communication skills*. New York: Academic Press.

18. Glenberg, A. M., Wilkinson, A. C., & Epstein, W. (1982). The illusion of knowing: Failure in the self-assessment of comprehension. *Memory and Cognition, 10*, 597–602.

Chapter 6. Performance Components: The "Blue Collar" Processes of Mental Self-management

1. Copi, I. M. (1978). *Introduction to logic* (5th ed.). New York: Macmillan.
2. Tversky, A., & Kahneman, D. (1974). Judgement under uncertainty: Heuristics and biases. *Science, 185*, 1124–31.
   Langer, E. (1978). Rethinking the role of thought in social interaction. In J. Harvey, W. Ickes, & R. Kidd (eds.), *New directions in attribution research*. Hillsdale, NJ: Erlbaum.
   Beck, A. T. (1976). *Cognitive therapy and the emotional disorders*. New York: International Universities Press.

Chapter 7. Knowledge-Acquisition Components: The Students of Mental Self-management

1. Davidson, J. E., & Sternberg, R. J. (1984). The role of insight in intellectual giftedness. *Gifted Child Quarterly, 28*, 58–64.
   Sternberg, R. J., & Davidson, J. E. (1983). Insight in the gifted. *Educational Psychologist, 18*, 51–57.
2. Maier, N. R. F., & Burke, R. J. (1966). Test of the concept of "availability of functions" in problem solving. *Psychological Reports, 19*, 119–25.
3. Raaheim, K. (1974). *Problem solving and intelligence*. Oslo: Universitetsforlaget.
4. Weisberg, R. W., & Alba, J. W. (1981). An examination of the alleged role of "fixation" in the solution of several "insight" problems. *Journal of Experimental Psychology, 110*, 169–92.

Chapter 8. Executive Intelligence

1. Wagner, R. K., & Sternberg, R. J. (1985). Practical intelligence in real-world pursuits: The role of tacit knowledge. *Journal of Personality and Social Psychology, 49*, 436–58.

2. Kotter, J. (1982). *The general managers.* New York: Free Press.

3. Isenberg, D. (1985). Managerial thinking: An inquiry into how senior managers think. Unpublished manuscript.

4. Streufert, S., & Swezey, R. W. (1986). *Complexity, managers, and organizations.* Orlando, FL: Academic Press.

5. Jaques, E. (1961). *Equitable payment.* England: Heinemann.

6. Klemp, G., & McClelland, D. (1986). What characterizes intelligent functioning among senior managers? In R. J. Sternberg & R. K. Wagner (eds.), *Practical intelligence: Nature and origins of competence in the everyday world.* New York: Cambridge University Press.

7. Neisser, U. (1976). General academic and artificial intelligence. In L. Resnick (ed.), *The nature of intelligence.* Hillsdale, NJ: Erlbaum.

8. Ghiselli, E. E. (1966). *The validity of occupational aptitude tests.* New York: Wiley.
   Wigdor, A. K., & Garner, W. R. (eds.) (1982). *Ability testing: Uses, consequences, and controversies.* Washington, D.C.: National Academy Press.

9. Schmidt, F. L., & Hunter, J. E. (1977). Development of a general solution to the problem of validity generalization. *Journal of Applied Psychology, 62*, 529–40.
   Schmidt, F. L., & Hunter, J. E. (1981). Employment testing: Old theories and new research findings. *American Psychologist, 36*, 1128–37.

10. McClelland, D. C. (1973). Testing for competence rather than for "intelligence." *American Psychologist, 28*, 1–14.

11. *Oxford English Dictionary.* (1933). Oxford: Clarendon Press.

12. Wagner, R. K. (1987). Tacit knowledge in everyday intelligent behavior. *Journal of Personality and Social Psychology, 52*, 1236–37.

13. Ford, M. E., & Tisak, M. S. (1983). A further search for social intelligence. *Journal of Educational Psychology, 75*, 196–206.
    Keating, D. P. (1978). A search for social intelligence. *Journal of Educational Psychology, 70*, 218–23.
    Sternberg, R. J., & Smith, C. (1985). Social intelligence and decoding skills in nonverbal communication. *Social Cognition, 2*, 168–92.
    Walker, R. E., & Foley, J. M. (1973). Social intelligence: Its history and measurement. *Psychological Reports, 33*, 839–64.

Chapter 9. Who's Intelligent?: People's Conceptions of the Nature of Intelligence

1. Neisser, U. (1979). The concept of intelligence. In R. J. Sternberg & D. K. Detterman (eds.), *Human intelligence: Perspectives on its theory and measurement*. Norwood, NJ: Ablex.
2. Intelligence and its measurement: A symposium. (1921). *Journal of Educational Psychology, 12*, 123–47, 195–216, 271–75.
3. Thorndike, E. L. (1924). The measurement of intelligence: Present status. *Psychological Review, 31*, 219–52.
4. Sternberg, R. J., Conway, B. E., Ketron, J. L., & Bernstein, M. (1981). People's conceptions of intelligence. *Journal of Personality and Social Psychology, 41*, 37–55.
5. Berg, C., & Sternberg, R. J. (1985). A triarchic theory of intellectual development during adulthood. *Developmental Review, 5*, 334–70.
6. Wober, M. (1974). Towards an understanding of the Kiganda concept of intelligence. In J. W. Berry & P. R. Dasen (eds.), *Culture and cognition: Readings in cross-cultural psychology*. London: Methuen.
7. Gardner, H. (1983). *Frames of mind: The theory of multiple intelligences*. New York: Basic Books.

Chapter 10. The Socialization of Intelligence

1. Heath, S. (1983). *Ways with words*. New York: Cambridge University Press.
2. Ochs, E., & Schiefflin, B. B. (1982). Language acquisition and socialization: Three developmental stories and their implications. *Sociolinguistic Working Paper, 105*. Austin, TX: Southwest Educational Development Laboratory.
3. McDermott, R. P. (1974). Achieving school failure: An anthropological approach to illiteracy and social stratification. In G. Spindler (ed.), *Education and the cultural process*. New York: Holt, Rinehart, and Winston.
4. Kearins, J. (1981). Visual spatial memory in Australian Aboriginal children of desert regions. *Cognitive Psychology, 13*, 434–60.
5. Super, C. M., & Harkness, S. (1980). The infants' niche in rural Kenya and metropolitan America. In L. L. Adler (ed.), *Issues in cross-cultural research*. New York: Academic Press.
6. Cole, M., Gay, J., Glick, J., & Sharp, D. W. (1971). *The cultural context of learning and thinking*. New York: Basic Books.
7. Suchmann, R. G., & Trabasso, T. (1966). Color and form preference in young children. *Journal of Experimental Child Psychology, 3*, 177–87.
8. Cole, M., & Scribner, S. (1974). *Culture and thought*. New York: Wiley.
9. Luria, A. R. (1976). *Cognitive development: Its cultural and social foundations*. Cambridge, MA: Harvard University Press.

10. See note 8 above.
11. Kahneman, D. (1973). *Attention and effort*. Englewood Cliffs, NJ: Prentice-Hall.
12. Hudson, W. (1967). The study of the problem of pictorial perception among un-acculturated groups. *International Journal of Psychology, 2*, 89–107.
13. See note 2 above.
14. Ibid., p. 24.
15. Ibid., p. 27.
16. Ibid., p. 33.
17. Brown, R., & Bellugi, U. (1964). Three processes in the child's acquisition of syntax. *Harvard Educational Review, 34*, 133–51.
    Cazden, C. (1965). Environmental assistance to the child's acquisition of grammar. Unpublished Ph.D. dissertation, Harvard University.
18. See note 2 above (p. 32).
19. Ibid., p. 41.
20. Gladwin, T. (1970). *East is a big bird*. Cambridge, MA: Belknap Press.
21. Geber, M. (1960). Problèmes posés par le développement du jeune enfant africain en fonction de son milieu social. *Travail Humain, 23*, 97–111.
22. Ainsworth, M. D. S. (1967). *Infancy in Uganda*. Baltimore, MD: Johns Hopkins University Press.
23. Sinha, D. (1983). Human assessment in the Indian context. In S. H. Irvine & J. W. Berry (eds.), *Human assessment and cultural factors*. New York: Plenum.
24. Schiefflin, B. B. (1979). Getting it together: An ethnographic approach to the study of the development of communicative competence. In E. Ochs & B. B. Schiefflin (eds.), *Developmental pragmatics*. New York: Academic Press.
25. Jensen, A. R. (1980). *Bias in mental testing*. New York: Free Press.

Chapter 11. Intellectual Styles

1. Sternberg, R. J. (in press). Mental self-government: A theory of intellectual styles. *Human Development*.
2. Myers, I. B. (1980). *Gifts differing*. Palo Alto, CA: Consulting Psychologists Press.
3. Gregorc, T. (1985). *Inside styles: Beyond the basics*. Maynard, MA: Gabriel Systems, Inc.
4. Renzulli, J. S., & Smith, L. H. (1978). *Learning styles inventory*. Mansfield Center: Creative Learning Press.
5. Holland, J. (1973). *Making vocational choices: A theory of careers*. Englewood Cliffs, NJ: Prentice-Hall.

Chapter 12. When Mental Self-management Fails

1. Amabile, T. M. (1983). *The social psychology of creativity*. New York: Springer-Verlag.
2. Thurstone, L. L. (1924). *The nature of intelligence*. New York: Harcourt, Brace.
3. Dweck, C. S., & Elliott, E. S. (1983). Achievement motivation. In P. H. Mussen (series ed.), E. M. Hetherington (vol. ed.), *Handbook of child psychology, vol. 4: Socialization, personality, and social development* (4th ed.). New York: Wiley.
4. Wagner, R. K., & Sternberg, R. J. (1986). Tacit knowledge and intelligence in the everyday world. In R. J. Sternberg & R. K. Wagner (eds.), *Practical intelligence: Nature and origins of competence in the everyday world*. New York: Cambridge University Press.

Bibliography

Ainsworth, M. D. S. (1967). *Infancy in Uganda*. Baltimore, MD: Johns Hopkins University Press.

Amabile, T. M. (1983). *The social psychology of creativity*. New York: Springer-Verlag.

Baltes, P. B., Dittman-Kohli, F., & Dixon, R. A. (1984). New perspectives on the development of intelligence in adulthood: Toward a dual-process conception and a model of selective optimization with compensation. In P. B. Baltes & O. G. Brim, Jr. (eds.), *Life-span development and behavior* (vol. 6, pp. 33–76). New York: Academic Press.

Baron, J. (1982). Personality and intelligence. In R. J. Sternberg (ed.), *Handbook of human intelligence* (pp. 308–51). New York: Cambridge University Press.

Beck, A. T. (1976). *Cognitive therapy and the emotional disorders*. New York: International Universities Press.

Berg, C. A., & Sternberg, R. J. (1985). A triarchic theory of intellectual development during adulthood. *Developmental Review, 5*, 334–70.

Berry, J. W. (1974). Radical cultural relativism and the concept of intelligence. In J. W. Berry & P. R. Dasen (eds.), *Culture and cognition: Readings in cross-cultural psychology* (pp. 225–29). London: Methuen.

Berry, J. W. (1984). Towards a universal psychology of cognitive competence. In P. S. Fry (ed.), *Changing conceptions of intelligence and intellectual functioning* (pp. 35–61). Amsterdam: North-Holland.

Bloom, B. S., & Broder, L. J. (1950). *Problem-solving processes of college students*. Chicago: University of Chicago Press.

Boas, F. (1911). *The mind of primitive man*. New York: Macmillan.

Boring, E. G. (1923). Intelligence as the tests test it. *New Republic*, *6*, June, 35–37.

Boring, E. G. (1950). *A history of experimental psychology* (2nd ed.). New York: Appleton-Century-Crofts.

Brainerd, C. J. (1978). The stage question in cognitive-developmental theory. *Behavioral and Brain Sciences*, *1*, 173–82.

Bransford, J., & Stein, B. (1984). *The IDEAL problem solver*. New York: W. H. Freeman.

Bray, D. W. (1982). The assessment center and the study of lives. *American Psychologist*, *37*, 180–89.

Brown, A. L. (1974). The role of strategic behavior in retardate memory. In N. R. Ellis (ed.), *International review of research in mental retardation* (vol. 4). New York: Academic Press.

Brown, A. L. (1978). Knowing when, where, and how to remember: A problem of metacognition. In R. Glaser (ed.), *Advances in instructional psychology* (vol. 1, pp. 77–165). Hillsdale, NJ: Erlbaum.

Brown, R., & Bellugi, U. (1964). Three processes in the child's acquisition of syntax. *Harvard Educational Review*, *34*, 133–51.

Bryant, P. E., & Trabasso, T. (1971). Transitive inferences and memory in young children. *Nature*, *232*, 456–58.

Butterfield, E. C., & Belmont, J. M. (1977). Assessing and improving the executive cognitive functions of mentally retarded people. In I. Bialer & M. Sternlicht (eds.), *Psychological issues in mental retardation*. New York: Psychological Dimensions.

Campione, J. C., Brown, A. L., & Ferrara, R. A. (1982). Mental retardation and intelligence. In R. J. Sternberg (ed.), *Handbook of human intelligence* (pp. 392–490). New York: Cambridge University Press.

Cattell, R. B. (1971). *Abilities: Their structure, growth, and action*. Boston: Houghton Mifflin.

Cazden, C. (1965). Environmental assistance to the child's acquisition of grammar. Unpublished Ph.D. dissertation, Harvard University.

Ceci, S. J., & Liker, J. (1986). Academic and nonacademic intelligence: An experimental separation. In R. J. Sternberg & R. K. Wagner (eds.), *Practical intelligence: Nature and origins of competence in the everyday world* (pp. 119–142). New York: Cambridge University Press.

Charlesworth, W. R. A. (1979). An ethological approach to studying intelligence. *Human Development*, *22*, 212–16.

Chase, W. G., & Simon, H. A. (1973). Perception in chess. *Cognitive Psychology*, *4*, 55–81.

Chi, M. T. H. (1978). Knowledge structures and memory development. In R. S. Siegler (ed.), *Children's thinking: What develops?* Hillsdale, NJ: Erlbaum.

Chi, M. T. H., Glaser, R., & Rees, E. (1982). Expertise in problem solving. In R. J. Sternberg (ed.), *Advances in the psychology of human intelligence* (vol. 1, pp. 7–75). Hillsdale, NJ: Erlbaum.

Cole, M., Gay, J., Glick, J., & Sharp, D. W. (1971). *The cultural context of learning and thinking.* New York: Basic Books.

Cole, M. & Scribner, S. (1974). *Culture and thought.* New York: Wiley.

Copi, I. M. (1978). *Introduction to logic* (5th ed.). New York: Macmillan.

Davidson, J. E., & Sternberg, R. J. (1984). The role of insight in intellectual giftedness. *Gifted Child Quarterly, 28,* 58–64.

Detterman, D. K., & Sternberg, R. J. (eds.). (1982). *How and how much can intelligence be increased.* Norwood, NJ: Ablex.

Dweck, C. S., & Elliott, E. S. (1983). Achievement motivation. In P. H. Mussen (series ed.), E. M. Hetherington (vol. ed.), *Handbook of child psychology, vol. 4: Socialization, personality, and social development* (4th ed.) (pp. 643–91). New York: Wiley.

Edgerton, R. (1967). *The cloak of competence.* Berkeley, CA: University of California Press.

Eysenck, H. J. (1967). Intelligence assessment: A theoretical and experimental approach. *British Journal of Educational Psychology, 37,* 81–98.

Feldman, R. D. (1982). *Whatever happened to the quiz kids?* Chicago: Review Press.

Feuerstein, R. (1980). *Instrumental enrichment: An intervention program for cognitive modifiability.* Baltimore, MD: University Park Press.

Ford, M. E., & Tisak, M. S. (1983). A further search for social intelligence. *Journal of Educational Psychology, 75,* 196–206.

Gardner, H. (1983). *Frames of mind: The theory of multiple intelligences.* New York: Basic Books.

Geber, M. (1960). Problèmes posés par le développement du jeune enfant africain en fonction de son milieu social. *Travail Humain, 23,* 97–111.

Gelman, R., & Baillargeon, R. (1983). A review of some Piagetian concepts. In P. H. Mussen (series ed.) & J. Flavell & E. Markman (vol. eds.), *Handbook of child psychology* (vol. 3, pp. 167–230): *Cognitive development* (4th ed.). New York: Wiley.

Gladwin, T. (1970). *East is a big bird.* Cambridge, MA: Belknap Press.

Glenberg, A. M., Wilkinson, A. C., & Epstein, W. (1982). The illusion of knowing: Failure in the self-assessment of comprehension. *Memory and Cognition, 10,* 597–602.

Goldin, S. E., & Hayes-Roth, B. (1980, June). Individual differences in planning processes. Rand Technical Report No. N-1488-ONR.

Gregorc, T. (1985). *Inside styles: Beyond the basics.* Maynard, MA: Gabriel Systems, Inc.

Guilford, J. P. (1967). *The nature of human intelligence.* New York: McGraw-Hill.

Guilford, J. P. (1982). Cognitive psychology's ambiguities: Some suggested remedies. *Psychological Review, 89,* 48–59.

Heath, S. B. (1983). *Ways with words.* New York: Cambridge University Press.

Holland, J. L. (1973). *Making vocational choices: A theory of careers*. Englewood Cliffs, NJ: Prentice-Hall.

Horn, J. L., & Knapp, J. R. (1973). On the subjective character of the empirical base of Guildford's structure-of-intellect model. *Psychological Bulletin, 80*, 33–43.

Hovland, C. I., & Janis, I. L. (eds.) (1959). *Personality and persuasibility*. New Haven: Yale University Press.

Hudson, W. (1967). The study of the problem of pictorial perception among un-acculturated groups. *International Journal of Psychology, 2*, 89–107.

Hunt, E. B. (1978). Mechanics of verbal ability. *Psychological Review, 85*, 109–30.

Hunt, E. B., & Lansman, M. (1982). Individual differences in attention. In R. J. Sternberg (ed.), *Advances in the psychology of human intelligence* (vol. 1, pp. 207–54). Hillsdale, NJ: Erlbaum.

Hunt, E. B., Lunneborg, C., & Lewis, J. (1975). What does it mean to be high verbal? *Cognitive Psychology, 7*, 194–227.

Intelligence and its measurement: A symposium (1921). *Journal of Educational Psychology, 12*, 123–47, 195–216, 271–75.

Isenberg, D. Managerial thinking: An inquiry into how senior managers think. Unpublished manuscript.

Jaques, E. (1961). *Equitable payment*. England: Heinemann.

Jenkins, J. J. (1979). Four points to remember: A tetrahedral model of memory experiments. In L. S. Cermak & F. I. M. Craik (eds.), *Levels of processing in human memory* (pp. 429–46). Hillsdale, NJ: Erlbaum.

Jensen, A. R. (1969). How much can we boost IQ and scholastic achievement? *Harvard Educational Review, 39*, 1–123.

Jensen, A. R. (1979). *g*: Outmoded theory or unconquered frontier? *Creative Science and Technology, 2*, 16–29.

Jensen, A. R. (1980). *Bias in mental testing*. New York: Basic Books.

Jensen, A. R. (1982). The chronometry of intelligence. In R. J. Sternberg (ed.), *Advances in the psychology of human intelligence* (vol. 1, pp. 255–310). Hillsdale, NJ: Erlbaum.

Kagan, J. (1966). Reflection-impulsivity of conceptual tempo. *Journal of Abnormal Psychology, 71*, 17–24.

Kahneman, D. (1973). *Attention and effort*. Englewood Cliffs, NJ: Prentice-Hall.

Kearins, J. (1981). Visual spatial memory in Australian Aboriginal children of desert regions. *Cognitive Psychology, 13*, 434–60.

Keating, D. P. (1978). A search for social intelligence. *Journal of Educational Psychology, 70*, 218–23.

Keating, D. (1984). The emperor's new clothes: The "new look" in intelligence research. In R. J. Sternberg (ed.), *Advances in the psychology of human intelligence* (vol. 2, pp. 1–46). Hillsdale, NJ: Erlbaum.

Klemp, G., & McClelland, D. (1986). What characterizes intelligent functioning among senior managers? In R. J. Sternberg & R. K. Wagner (eds.), *Practical intelligence: The nature and origins of competence in the everyday world*. New York: Cambridge University Press.

Kotter, J. (1982). *The general managers*. New York: Free Press.

Laboratory of Comparative Human Cognition (1982). Culture and intelligence. In R. J. Sternberg (ed.), *Handbook of human intelligence* (pp. 642–719). New York: Cambridge University Press.

Langer, E. (1978). Rethinking the role of thought in social interaction. In J. Harvey, W. Ickes, & R. Kidd (eds.), *New directions in attribution research*. Hillsdale, NJ: Erlbaum.

Larkin, J. H., McDermott, J., Simon, D. P., & Simon, H. A. (1980). Models of competence in solving physics problems. *Cognitive Psychology, 4*, 317–45.

Lesgold, A. M. (1984). Acquiring expertise. In J. R. Anderson & S. M. Kosslyn (eds.), *Tutorials in learning and memory: Essays in honor of Gordon Bower*. San Francisco: Freeman.

Linville, P. (1987). Self-complexity as a cognitive buffer against stress-related illness and depression. *Journal of Personality and Social Psychology, 52*, 663–76.

Lipman, M., Sharp, A. M., & Oscanyan, F. S. (1980). *Philosophy in the classroom* (2nd ed.). Philadelphia: Temple University Press.

Luria, A. R. (1976). *Cognitive development: Its cultural and social foundations*. Cambridge, MA: Harvard University Press.

McDermott, R. P. (1974). Achieving school failure: An anthropological approach to illiteracy and social stratification. In G. Spindler (ed.), *Education and the cultural process*. New York: Holt, Rinehart, and Winston.

MacLeod, C. M., Hunt, E. B., & Mathews, N. N. (1978). Individual differences in the verification of sentence-picture relationships. *Journal of Verbal Learning and Verbal Behavior, 17*, 493–507.

McNemar, Q. (1964). Lost: Our intelligence? Why? *American Psychologist, 19*, 871–82.

Maier, N. R. F., & Burke, R. J. (1966). Test of the "availability of functions" in problem solving. *Psychological Reports, 19*, 119–25.

Markman, E. M. (1981). Comprehension monitoring. In W. P. Dickson (ed.), *Children's oral communication skills*. New York: Academic Press.

Myers, I. B. (1980). *Gifts differing*. Palo Alto, CA: Consulting Psychologists Press.

Neisser, U. (1976). General academic and artificial intelligence. In L. Resnick (ed.), *The nature of intelligence*. Hillsdale, NJ: Erlbaum.

Neisser, U. (1979). The concept of intelligence. In R. J. Sternberg & D. K. Detterman (eds.), *Human intelligence: Perspectives on its theory and measurement* (pp. 179–90). Norwood, NJ: Ablex.

Newell, A., & Simon, H. A. (1972). *Human problem solving*. Englewood Cliffs, NJ: Prentice-Hall.

Ochs, E., & Schiefflin, B. B. (1982). Language acquisition and socialization: Three developmental stories and their implications. *Sociolinguistic*

Working Paper, 105. Austin, TX: Southwest Educational Development Laboratory.

Oxford English Dictionary (1933). Oxford: Clarendon Press.

Paivio, A. (1971). *Imagery and verbal processes*. New York: Holt, Rinehart, and Winston.

Piaget, J. (1972). *The psychology of intelligence*. Totowa, NJ: Littlefield, Adams.

Posner, M. I., & Mitchell, R. F. (1967). Chronometric analysis of classification. *Psychological Review, 74*, 392–409.

Raaheim, K. (1974). *Problem solving and intelligence*. Oslo: Universitetsforlaget.

Renzulli, J. S., & Smith, L. H. (1978). *Learning styles inventory*. Mansfield Center: Creative Learning Press.

Schiefflin, B. B. (1979). Getting it together: An ethnographic approach to the study of the development of communicative competence. In E. Ochs & B. B. Schiefflin (eds.), *Developmental pragmatics*. New York: Academic Press.

Schmidt, F. L. & Hunter, J. E. (1977). Development of a general solution to the problem of validity generalization. *Journal of Applied Psychology, 62*, 529–40.

Schmidt, F. L., & Hunter, J. E. (1981). Employment testing: Old theories and new research findings. *American Psychologist, 36*, 1128–37.

Scribner, S. (1984). Studying working intelligence. In B. Rogoff & J. Lave (eds.), *Everyday cognition* (pp. 9–40). Cambridge, MA: Harvard University Press.

Simon, H. A. (1957). *Administrative behavior* (2nd ed.). Totowa, NJ: Littlefield, Adams.

Simon, H. A. (1976). Identifying basic abilities underlying intelligent performance of complex tasks. In L. B. Resnick (ed.), *The nature of intelligence*. Hillsdale, NJ: Erlbaum.

Sinha, D. (1983). Human assessment in the Indian context. In S. H. Irvine & J. W. Berry (eds.), *Human assessment and cultural factors* (pp. 17–34). New York: Plenum.

Spearman, C. (1904). General intelligence, objectively determined and measured. *American Journal of Psychology, 15*, 201–93.

Spearman, C. (1927). *The abilities of man*. New York: Macmillan.

Stenhouse, D. (1973). *The evolution of intelligence: A general theory and some of its implications*. New York: Harper & Row.

Sternberg, R. J. (1977). *Intelligence, information processing, and analogical reasoning: The componential analysis of human abilities*. Hillsdale, NJ: Erlbaum.

Sternberg, R. J. (1980a). Factor theories of intelligence are all right almost. *Educational Researcher, 9*, 6–13, 18.

Sternberg, R. J. (1980b). Representation and process in linear syllogistic reasoning. *Journal of Experimental Psychology: General, 109*, 119–59.

Sternberg, R. J. (1980c). Sketch of a componential subtheory of human intelligence. *Behavioral and Brain Sciences, 3*, 573–84.

Sternberg, R. J. (1981). Intelligence and nonentrenchment. *Journal of Educational Psychology, 73*, 1–16.

Sternberg, R. J. (1985). *Beyond IQ: A triarchic theory of human intelligence.* New York: Cambridge University Press.

Sternberg, R. J. (1986). *Intelligence applied: Understanding and increasing your intellectual skills.* San Diego: CA: Harcourt, Brace, Jovanovich.

Sternberg, R. J. (1987). Most vocabulary is learned from context. In M. G. McKeown & M. E. Curtis (eds.), *The nature of vocabulary acquisition* (pp. 89–105). Hillsdale, NJ: Erlbaum.

Sternberg, R. J., Conway, B. E., Ketron, J. L., & Bernstein, M. (1981). People's conceptions of intelligence. *Journal of Personality and Social Psychology, 41*, 37–55.

Sternberg, R. J., & Davidson, J. E. (1983). Insight in the gifted. *Educational Psychologist, 18*, 51–57.

Sternberg, R. J., & Gardner, M. K. (1983). Unities of inductive reasoning. *Journal of Experimental Psychology: General, 112*, 80–116.

Sternberg, R. J., & Powell, J. S. (1983). Comprehending verbal comprehension. *American Psychologist, 38*, 878–93.

Sternberg, R. J., & Rifkin, B. (1979). The development of analogical reasoning processes. *Journal of Experimental Child Psychology, 27*, 195–232.

Sternberg, R. J., & Smith, C. (1985). Social intelligence and decoding skills in nonverbal communication. *Social Cognition, 2*, 168–92.

Sternberg, R. J., & Weil, E. M. (1980). An aptitude-strategy interaction in linear syllogistic reasoning. *Journal of Educational Psychology, 72*, 226–34.

Streufert, S., & Swezey, R. W. (1986). *Complexity, managers, and organizations.* Orlando, FL: Academic Press.

Suchmann, R. G., & Trabasso, T. (1966). Color and form preference in young children. *Journal of Experimental Child Psychology, 3*, 177–87.

Super, C. M., & Harkness, S. (1980). The infants' niche in rural Kenya and metropolitan America. In L. L. Adler (ed.), *Issues in cross-cultural research.* New York: Academic Press.

Thorndike, E. L. (1924). The measurement of intelligence: Present status. *Psychological Review, 31*, 219–32.

Thurstone, L. L. (1924). *The nature of intelligence.* New York: Harcourt, Brace.

Thurstone, L. L. (1938). *Primary mental abilities.* Chicago: University of Chicago Press.

Tversky, A., & Kahneman, D. (1974). Judgment under uncertainty: Heuristics and biases. *Science, 185*, 1124–31.

Vernon, P. E. (1971). *The structure of human abilities*. London: Methuen.

Vygotsky, L. S. (1978). *Mind in society: The development of higher psychological processes*. Cambridge, MA: Harvard University Press.

Wagner, R. K. (1987). Tacit knowledge in everyday intelligent behavior. *Journal of Personality and Social Psychology, 52*, 1236–47.

Wagner, R. K., & Sternberg, R. J. (1985). Practical intelligence in real-world pursuits: The role of tacit knowledge. *Journal of Personality and Social Psychology, 49*, 436–58.

Wagner, R. K., & Sternberg, R. J. (1986). Tacit knowledge and intelligence in the everyday world. In R. J. Sternberg & R. K. Wagner (eds.), *Practical intelligence: Nature and origins of competence in the everyday world* (pp. 51–83). New York: Cambridge University Press.

Wagner, R. K., & Sternberg, R. J. (1987). Executive control in reading comprehension. In B. Britton & S. M. Glynn (eds.), *Executive control processes in reading* (pp. 1–22). Hillsdale, NJ: Erlbaum.

Walker, R. E., & Foley, J. M. (1973). Social intelligence: Its history and measurement. *Psychological Reports, 33*, 839–64.

Wason, P. C., & Johnson-Laird, P. N. (1972). *Psychology of reasoning: Structure and content*. London: B. T. Batsford.

Weisberg, R. W., & Alba, J. W. (1981). An examination of the alleged role of "fixation" in the solution of several "insight" problems. *Journal of Experimental Psychology, 110*, 169–92.

Wober, M. (1974). Towards an understanding of the Kiganda concept of intelligence. In J. W. Berry & P. R. Dasen (eds.), *Culture and cognition: Readings in cross-cultural psychology*. London: Methuen.

Index

Scientific American, 171
scientific-insight problems, 196–98
Scribner, Sylvia, 12, 257, 259
searching-the-field problem, 95–96
selection, environmental, 14–16, 65, 66–
67, 70, 269, 293
selective comparison, 171, 179–81, 194–
196, 202–204, 257–58
selective encoding, 26, 171, 177–78, 180,
181–92, 200–201, 210, 257
self-confidence, 306–307
self-pity, 302
sentence-picture comparison task,
100–101
series-completion problems, 39, 40, 43, 69,
135–45, 174
exercises on, 139–40, 141–45
"Sesame Street," 256
set breakers, 25–26
Shaffer, Peter, 241
shaping, environmental, 16–17, 65, 66–67,
70, 266–69, 292, 293
"should" statements, fallacy of, 124
Simon, Herbert, 42, 44, 92
Simon, Theophile, 4
Sinha, Durganand, 266
skill not chance, fallacy of, 122
Smith, Linda, 293
social intelligence, 228, 233, 234, 239, 246–
247
socialization, xiv, 6, 7, 11, 37, 46, 47–48,
72, 75, 234, 235–36, 239, 250–71
adaptation to environments in, 262–66,
270
attitudes toward children and, 262–63
automatization in, 261–62
class differences in, 250, 251–53, 254–
256, 258–64, 267–69, 270
communication modes in, 258
contextual subtheory and, 262–69
creativity and, 258, 259–61, 262, 263,
267, 268
cultural differences in, 250, 251, 253–54,
257–58, 261–62, 264–67, 269, 270
experiential subtheory in, 259–62
intellectual styles and, 263, 293–94, 295
intelligence testing and, 7, 19–20, 63–
64, 69, 75, 253–54, 266, 270–71
knowledge-acquisition components in,
257–59
language acquisition in, 251, 258–59,
264–66, 268
metacomponents in, 251–55
naming in, 251–52
novelty in, 253, 259–61, 270
performance components in, 255–57
reading and, 256
resource allocation in, 254–55
response to requests and, 252

school performance and, 251–53, 256–
257, 258, 260–61, 262–64, 267–69, 271
selection of environments in, 269
shaping of environments in, 266–69
spatial abilities and, 253–54, 266
triarchic theory and, 251–69, 270–71
values in, 263–64, 267–68
sociological models, 50–51
socks problem, 178, 183
Solomon, King, 240
solution monitoring, 78–79, 109–14, 217–
218, 307
Solve It (Fixx), 171
sorting tests, 19–20
space allocation, 254–55
spatial abailities, 34, 37, 39, 41, 253–54,
266, 299
Spearman, Charles, 8, 38–39, 40, 69, 228
Stanford-Binet Intelligence Test, xii, 20,
70, 199
Stein, Gertrude, 37
Stenhouse, David, 23
Sternberg, Robert, 42, 43–44, 46, 224
Sternberg Multidimensional Abilities Test,
70
storytelling, 258, 259, 260–61, 262, 267,
268
strategy selection, 81–83, 93–98, 113, 217,
252–54, 306–307
Streufert, Siegfried, 210
Strong-Campbell Interest Inventory, 293
structure-of-intellect model, 39–40
Swezey, Robert, 210
syllogisms, 34, 43, 101, 103–104, 174, 262

tables, representational, 104
tacit knowledge, 211, 213–29
actualities vs. ideals in, 222–23, 224, 228
categories of, 220–22, 225, 227, 228
exercise on, 213–15
experts vs. novices and, 44, 99–100,
212–13, 220–21, 223–25, 226–27, 228
formal instruction in, 212–13
general vs. specific nature of, 228
intelligence testing and, 220, 227–28
job performance and, 219–20, 225, 226–
227, 228
measurement of, 220–26
orientations of, 220–22, 225, 228
prototype of, 223–24
rules of thumb in, 215–20, 225–26
talents, 42, 43, 73, 241
Temne tribe, 266
Terman, Lewis M., 231
Thorndike, Edward L., 231
3M Corporation, 216–17
Thucydides, 231
Thurstone, Louis, 23, 38, 39, 40, 69, 74,
297